Krzysztof Sonek
Truth, Beauty, and Goodness in Biblical Narratives

Beihefte zur Zeitschrift für die alttestamentliche Wissenschaft

Herausgegeben von
John Barton · Reinhard G. Kratz
Choon-Leong Seow · Markus Witte

Band 395

Walter de Gruyter · Berlin · New York

Krzysztof Sonek

Truth, Beauty, and Goodness in Biblical Narratives

A Hermeneutical Study of Genesis 21:1−21

Walter de Gruyter · Berlin · New York

∞ Printed on acid-free paper which falls within the guidelines of the ANSI to ensure permanence and durability.

ISBN 978-3-11-020974-7
ISSN 0934-2575

Library of Congress Cataloging-in-Publication Data

A CIP catalogue record for this book is available from the Library of Congress.

Bibliographic information published by the Deutsche Nationalbibliothek

The Deutsche Nationalbibliothek lists this publication in the Deutsche Nationalbibliografie; detailed bibliographic data are available in the Internet at http://dnb.d-nb.de.

© Copyright 2009 by Walter de Gruyter GmbH & Co. KG, 10785 Berlin
All rights reserved, including those of translation into foreign languages. No part of this book may be reproduced or transmitted in any form or by any means, electronic or mechanical, including photocopy, recording, or any information storage and retrieval system, without permission in writing from the publisher.

Printed in Germany

Cover design: Christopher Schneider, Laufen

For my mother

Acknowledgements

This volume represents a slightly improved version of my doctoral thesis, which I submitted to the Oxford University Examination Schools in July 2007, and successfully defended during my *viva voce examination* in October 2007. Many scholars whom I have met over the last few years told me that the most important virtues which an able doctoral student must possess in order to complete a thesis are patience and perseverance. Since writing a thesis can be likened to a long distance run, much depends on the student's determination and endurance. I am now convinced that their words were true, but I have also learnt that this "doctoral long distance run" is never a solitary activity. At each consecutive stage of my work, I have met many friends always willing to help and give advice. Certainly, I am not able to mention here everybody to whom I owe a debt of thanks, but I would like to tell them all that I will always be grateful for their kindness and friendship.

First and foremost, I am indebted to my supervisor, Prof John Barton, Oriel and Laing Professor of the Interpretation of Holy Scripture, for his constant and professional assistance, which I experienced even before I came to Oxford. Had I not become acquainted with his books while studying in Jerusalem, I would not have become interested in biblical interpretation. Then I have benefited in so many different ways from discussions and help offered by Mrs Anna Baidoun, Dr Vivian Boland, Dr Valerie Dodd, Mrs Gillian Harrison, Ms Marta Herschkopf, Dr Fergus Kerr, Dr Emily Lygo, Dr Aidan Nichols, Mr Stephen Priest, Fr David Sanders, and Dom Henry Wansbrough. To all of them I offer my deep appreciation. I also owe a special acknowledgement to the professors and the community of the Ecole Biblique in Jerusalem, especially to Prof Krzysztof Modras, Prof Jerome Murphy-O'Connor, Prof Jean-Michel Poffet, Prof Marcel Sigrist, and Prof Justin Taylor, as well as to Prof Wojciech Giertych, now the Theologian of the Pontifical Household, who supervised me when I was doing my first degree, and has always encouraged me to pursue my interests and studies.

There are many more people to whom I am indebted. I am grateful to my examiners, Prof Paul S. Fiddes and Dr Katharine Dell, for their close reading and valuable critique of my thesis, which inspired me to rethink further some parts of the argument. My everyday life at Blackfriars Priory and Hall in Oxford in the years 2003-2007 obliges me to extend my special thanks to the community and staff who live and work there, especially to Dr Denis Minns, then Prior of Blackfriars, and Dr Richard Finn, Regent of Blackfriars Hall. I would also like to mention here the friendly staff of various Oxford libraries, in particular of the Theology Faculty Library and the Blackfriars Hall Library, where Ms Kate Alderson-Smith, Miss Ruth Harris, Mrs Elizabeth Birchall, and Ms Irim Sarwar were always ready to help. Moreover, this publication would not be possible without the green light given by the editors of the BZAW series, as well as without professional assistance offered by Dr Albrecht Döhnert, Dr Sabine Krämer, and Ms Sabina Dabrowski. Last but not least, I would like to thank the Arts and Humanities Research Council in the United Kingdom for offering a generous grant which greatly helped to complete my project.

Contents

Abbreviations xi

Introduction 1

1. General or Special Hermeneutics? 5
   1.1. The Bible and Literature 5
   1.2. Features of Hebrew Narratives 13
   1.3. Critical Concepts Introduced 20

2. The Illustrative Pericope Gen 21:1-21 33
   2.1. The Original Text and a Modern Translation 35
   2.2. The Narrative Delimitation of the Pericope 56
   2.3. The Literary Sources of the Pericope 63
   2.4. Synchronic versus Diachronic Approaches 69

3. A General Hermeneutical Model 73
   3.1. The Threefold Interests of the Reader in the Text 73
   3.2. The Three Dimensions of Biblical Narratives 80
   3.3. Meaning and Significance 85
   3.4. Ricoeurian Hermeneutics 96
   3.5. The Three Types of the Reader's Knowledge 103
   3.6. A Philosophical Basis for the Hermeneutical Model ... 109

4. Immanent Knowledge 125

5. Narrative Knowledge 137
   5.1. The Cognitive Dimension of Gen 21:1-21 137
      5.1.1. The Cognitive Significance of the Pericope 138
         5.1.1.1. Narratological Concepts at Work 139
         5.1.1.2. Rhetorical Criticism: The Use of Irony 148
      5.1.2. The Cognitive Meaning of the Pericope 154
      5.1.3. The Refinement of Truth 163

5.2. The Aesthetic Dimension of Gen 21:1-21 166
     5.2.1. Literary Aesthetics 167
     5.2.2. Theological Aesthetics 183
     5.2.3. Beauty in Scripture 196
  5.3. The Practical Dimension of Gen 21:1-21 200
     5.3.1. An Analysis of the Plot 202
     5.3.2. The Concept of Gaps 212
     5.3.3. Goodness in the Bible 224

6. Transcendental Knowledge 229
  6.1. The Platonic Triad and Its Divine Source 230
  6.2. Time and Eternity in Narrative 236

7. The General Hermeneutical Model: Corollaries 253
  7.1. The Horizon of the Reader's Knowledge 253
  7.2. The Diversity and Unity of Critical Approaches 256

Conclusion 265

Bibliography 271
Index of Authors 285
Index of Subjects 289

Abbreviations

AB	Anchor Bible
ABD	*The Anchor Bible Dictionary*. 6 vols. Edited by D. N. Freedman. New York: Doubleday, 1992.
ACCSOT	Ancient Christian Commentary on Scripture Old Testament
AnBib	Analecta Biblica
ANET	*Ancient Near Eastern Texts Relating to the Old Testament*. Edited by J. B. Pritchard. 3rd ed. Princeton: Princeton University Press, 1969.
ANH	*Aramäisch-Neuhebräisches Handwörterbuch*. Gustaf Dalman. Götingen: Eduard Pfeiffer, 1938.
ASem	Advances in Semiotics
BABOM	The Bible in Aramaic Based on Old Manuscripts and Printed Texts
BDB	*The Brown-Driver-Briggs Hebrew and English Lexicon: With an Appendix Containing the Biblical Aramaic*. Peabody: Hendrickson, 2005.
BHS	*Biblia Hebraica Stuttgartensia*. Edited by Karl Elliger, Wilhelm Rudolph, Hans P. Rüger, and Adrian Schenker. Editio quinta emendata. Stuttgart: Deutsche Bibelgesellschaft, 1997.
BIRS	Bibliographies and Indexes in Religious Studies
BJRL	*Bulletin of the John Rylands University Library of Manchester*
BLS	Bible and Literature Series
BOS	Berit Olam Studies in Hebrew Narrative and Poetry
BS	Bollingen Series
BSIVV	Biblia Sacra Iuxta Vulgatam Versionem
CCA	*The Cambridge Companion to Aristotle*. Edited by Jonathan Barnes. Cambridge: Cambridge University Press, 1995.
CDP	*The Cambridge Dictionary of Philosophy*. Edited by R. Audi. Cambridge: Cambridge University Press, 1995.
CENL	Charles Eliot Norton Lectures

CEWIK	The Cambridge Edition of the Works of Immanuel Kant
CFTLN	Clark's Foreign Theological Library New Series
CREP	*Concise Routledge Encyclopedia of Philosophy*. Edited by E. Craig. London: Softback Preview, 2000.
CSP	Cambridge Studies in Philosophy
CTC	Critics of the Twentieth Century
CWA	*The Complete Works of Aristotle: The Revised Oxford Translation*. 2 vols. Edited by J. Barnes. BS 71, 2. Princeton: Princeton University Press, 1984.
EJ	*Encyclopaedia Judaica*. 16 vols. Edited by C. Roth and G. Wigoder. Jerusalem: Encyclopaedia Judaica / Macmillan, 1972.
EL	Everyman's Library
FOTL	The Forms of the Old Testament Literature
GBH	*A Grammar of Biblical Hebrew*. Paul Joüon and T. Muraoka. SubBi 14/1-2. Roma: Pontificio Istituto Biblico, 1991.
GBSNTS	Guides to Biblical Scholarship New Testament Series
GHAT	Göttinger Handkommentar zum Alten Testament
GKC	*Gesenius' Hebrew Grammar*. Edited by E. Kautzsch. Translated by A. E. Cowley. 2nd ed. Oxford: Clarendon Press, 1910.
HALOT	*The Hebrew and Aramaic Lexicon of the Old Testament*. 5 vols. L. Köhler, W. Baumgartner, and J. J. Stamm. Translated and edited by M. E. J. Richardson. Leiden: Brill, 1994-2000.
HC	Hackett Classics
IBC	Interpretation: A Bible Commentary for Teaching and Preaching
ICC	International Critical Commentary
IHUB	Introduction to Hans Urs von Balthasar
ISBL	Indiana Studies in Biblical Literature
JAAR	*Journal of the American Academy of Religion*
JLT	*Journal of Literature and Theology*
JPSTC	JPS Torah Commentary
JSOT	*Journal for the Study of the Old Testament*
JSOTSup	Journal for the Study of the Old Testament Supplement Series
LCL	Loeb Classical Library
LWL	Landmarks of World Literature

LXX	Septuagint: *Vetus Testamentum Graecum. Auctoritate Academiae Scientiarum Gottingensis editum*. Göttingen: Vandenhoeck & Ruprecht, 1931-.
MLBS	Mercer Library of Biblical Studies
Mm	Masorah magna
Mp	Masorah parva
MT	Masoretic Text
MTh	*Modern Theology*
NICOT	New International Commentary on the Old Testament
NJBC	*The New Jerome Biblical Commentary*. Edited by R. E. Brown, J. A. Fitzmyer, and R. E. Murphy. Englewood Cliffs: Prentice Hall, 1990.
NLH	*New Literary History*
NRSV	*New Revised Standard Version: Catholic Edition*. London: DLT, 2005.
OBC	*The Oxford Bible Commentary*. Edited by J. Barton and J. Muddiman. Oxford: Oxford University Press, 2001.
OCTh	Outstanding Christian Thinkers
OHBS	*The Oxford Handbook of Biblical Studies*. Edited by J. W. Rogerson and J. M. Lieu. Oxford: Oxford University Press, 2006.
OTL	Old Testament Library
PBEV	*The Penguin Book of English Verse*. Edited by J. Hayward. Harmondsworth: Penguin Books, 1956.
PL	*Patrologia Latina*. Edited by Jacques-Paul Migne. Paris, 1844-1855, 1862-1865.
PM	Past Masters
PMC	Penguin Modern Classics
Proof	*Prooftexts*
PT	*Poetics Today*
PTr	Philosophical Traditions
RSV	*The Holy Bible: Revised Standard Version Containing the Old and New Testaments with the Apocrypha/ Deuterocanonical Books*. Expanded ed. New York: Collins, 1973.
SBLSS	Society of Biblical Literature Semeia Studies
SBT	Studies in Biblical Theology
SCMC	SCM Classics
SEL	*Studies in English Literature, 1500-1900*
SHCT	Studies in the History of Christian Thought

SP	Samaritan Pentateuch: *Der Hebräische Pentateuch der Samaritaner*. 5 vols. Edited by August Freiherrn von Gall. Giessen: Verlag von Alfred Töpelmann, 1914.
SPEP	Studies in Phenomenology and Existential Philosophy
SR	*Social Research*
SSJ	Suny Series in Judaica
SubBi	Subsidia Biblica
SVTG	Septuaginta Vetus Testamentum Graecum
TDOT	*The Theological Dictionary of the Old Testament*. 15 vols. Edited by G. Johannes Botterweck and Helmer Ringgren. Grand Rapids: Eerdmans, 1977-2006.
TO	Targum Onkelos: *The Pentateuch According to Targum Onkelos*. Edited by Alexander Sperber. BABOM 1. Leiden: Brill, 1959.
Vg	Vulgate: *Genesis – Psalmi*. Edited by R. Weber. BSIVV 1. Stuttgart: Württembergische Bibelanstalt, 1969.
VT	*Vetus Testamentum*
WBC	Word Biblical Commentary
WC	Westminster Commentaries
WSPL	Warwick Studies in Philosophy and Literature

Introduction

It has long been recognized that every narrative is a "mode of cultural self-expression."[1] This basic fact stems from the very nature of human reality. As Wayne C. Booth reminds us, we live our lives "*in* stories,"[2] and it is impossible to escape the narrative character of both fundamental and ephemeral events which constitute our existence. People have been telling stories since time immemorial, and many of them have been preserved for future generations by becoming part of the literary canon.[3] Biblical narratives, a mode of the self-expression of early Judaism and Christianity, have also found their way to the literary canon, and since then they have deeply influenced the culture of various peoples, reaching far beyond the Mediterranean milieu of their origin. Indeed, one should marvel at the extent to which biblical narratives have become international, transhistorical, and transcultural.[4] The relatively tight cultural borders of Judaism, reinforced by the strong conviction of exclusivity, were amazingly transcended in the course of historical development. As a consequence, the rich religious traditions belonging to Israelite tribes, and later, to all Jews, as well as the testimony of the early Christian Church, became a part of European and world cultural heritage, shaping people's minds and practical life attitudes for many centuries.

It is a commonplace to say that an acquaintance with biblical narratives is indispensable for understanding many aspects of both past and contemporary culture. In many respects, they provide us with a code needed to unlock and decipher various cultural phenomena. What is more, it is true, as Stephen Prickett observes, that the "Bible has always been found in need of interpretation,"[5] and readers belonging

---

1 Bal, *Narratology*, xi. I shall introduce a distinction between *narrative* and *story* in chapter 5. In this book, I generally follow this distinction.
2 Booth, *The Company*, 14.
3 Roland Barthes emphasizes the universality of narrative in a few apt words: "All classes, all human groups, have their narratives, enjoyment of which is very often shared by men with different, even opposing, cultural backgrounds" (*Image*, 79).
4 Cf. Barthes, *Image*, 79.
5 Prickett, *Reading the Text*, 1.

to diverse reading communities constantly raise a number of interpretive questions. These questions are as many as there are readers and cultural environments in which biblical texts are perused. Apart from that, even those whose cultural horizon hardly encompasses biblical narratives can potentially discover their value. If biblical narratives were of intellectual and existential value to so many generations, one can reasonably assume that their dormant influence spreads to our own times.

In this book, I would like to focus on the last two features mentioned above. Hence, first, I intend to discuss and answer certain hermeneutical questions which arise when modern readers interpret biblical narratives. Secondly, I aim to show the lasting value of biblical narratives, and their enduring power to influence and transform modern culture. In other words, I hope to offer interpretive help to those who read biblical narratives, and to suggest possible ways of reading to those who wish to encounter biblical narratives in their lives. Since modern literary criticism and hermeneutics comprise a large number of approaches, I shall evaluate some of them, and show their applicability to biblical interpretation. This is why my way of proceeding will be, in principle, pluralistic. In this respect, I share R. Crane's conviction: "The best hope for criticism in the future, indeed, lies in the perpetuation of this multiplicity [of critical languages]. ... For the great obstacle to advance in criticism is not the existence of independent groups of critics each pursuing separate interests, but the spirit of exclusive dogmatism which keeps them from learning what they might from one another."[6]

To show the validity of the pluralistic approach to biblical narratives, I shall propose a general hermeneutical model which will be organized around three main ideas. First, I will look for possible dimensions of biblical narratives resulting from readers' various literary interests. Secondly, I shall make a distinction between the viewpoint of the original ancient reader and that of the modern reader. Thirdly, I will examine the ability of biblical narratives to transcend the world of the reader, and to lead him or her towards a transcendent world projected by the narrative text.[7] Even though *narrative* is the fundamental concept present in this book, in order to explain the transcendental feature of biblical narratives, as well as their various dimensions, I will

---

6   Crane, *The Languages of Criticism*, 193.
7   In the first three chapters of the book, I shall use the term *transcendent world* or its close equivalents. From chapter 3 onwards, where I will explain the ontological status of that term, I will speak of the *divine sphere* and the *transcendent world* interchangeably.

need to use not only narrative analysis, but many other approaches such as the New Criticism, rhetorical criticism, reader-response criticism, the historical-critical method, and deconstruction.[8] This, in turn, will provide me with an excellent opportunity to assess the applicability of these critical approaches to biblical interpretation.

I have decided to impose a double limitation on my project in order to avoid pointless generalizations. This is why in the following discussion, I shall pay close attention to Hebrew Bible narratives only, even though I hope that many parts of my argument will also be applicable to the New Testament. In addition, I have chosen one particular pericope, Gen 21:1-21, which will serve as my model text and a touchstone for the hermeneutical model which will be put forward here. Hence, in chapter 1, I will begin by placing the Bible on the map of general literature, and discussing the type of hermeneutics which is needed in the interpretation of biblical narratives, and Hebrew narratives in particular. Then, in chapter 2, I shall establish the text of the model narrative Gen 21:1-21, and I will examine its delimitation. The main objective of chapter 3 will be to introduce the general hermeneutical model upon which my whole argument is based. As will soon be obvious, in this hermeneutical model, I postulate the existence of three spheres of the reader's knowledge: immanent, narrative, and transcendental. Therefore, in chapter 4, I shall briefly look at some chosen aspects of immanent knowledge, whereas chapter 5, which occupies almost half of the book, will be the place where I will put my model into exegetical practice. The logic of my argument demands that I should discuss transcendental knowledge in chapter 6. Finally, in chapter 7, I will present the corollaries of my general hermeneutical model for biblical interpretation, and I will round off the argument with a set of conclusions.

---

8   Some scholars distinguish between exegetical *methods* and *approaches* (see e.g. Fitzmyer, *The Biblical Commission's Document*, 24). I shall use both terms interchangeably.

1. General or Special Hermeneutics?

"Some books are to be tasted, others to be swallowed, and some few to be chewed and digested; that is, some books are to be read only in parts; others to be read, but not curiously; and some few to be read wholly, and with diligence and attention," argues Francis Bacon in his essay "Of Studies."[1] Can we gainsay the fact that a prominent place among those books which are to be read "with diligence and attention" belongs to the Bible? The Bible was born in the Jewish milieu. It was accepted by early Christian communities in its Greek translation as the Septuagint, supplemented by the Gospels and the apostolic writings, and then it embarked upon a long journey through history to reach our own generation. It has not travelled in solitude, but has enjoyed the company of a growing corpus of literary works. *In statu nascendi*, it was under the influence of great ancient Near East literature, but subsequently it has shaped the literature of all historical periods which it encountered on its long way. It was "chewed and digested," yet has remained unchanged. Instead, it has generated innumerable books on its interpretation. Some of us read it for pious reasons, and do not ask too many questions. Some, however, are more inquisitive, and want to satisfy their curiosity. Can the Bible be called literature? What is its relation to the vast corpus of literary works? Does the Bible have distinguishing features? What are the most appropriate critical tools for its interpretation? The goal of this introductory chapter is to put forward tentative answers to these questions.

1.1. The Bible and Literature

Can we call the Bible *literature* in the proper sense of the word, or only metaphorically? Should we reserve for Scripture a special category within belles-lettres, or, owing to its sacrosanct character, should it be regarded as different from the corpus of literary works? The answer to these questions has never been obvious. Even the debate over the can-

---

1   Bacon, *The Philosophical Works*, 797.

onical status of some biblical books shows that the prevalent view was to treat Scripture as distinct from general literature. To define the scriptural canon meant, for Jews, to determine which books "soiled the hands," and, in consequence, should be considered sacred,[2] or, for Christians, which books are "apostolic, catholic, orthodox, and in traditional use."[3] Although the Christian and Jewish approach to the problem of canonicity emphasizes that we deal with "books," and thus with a kind of literature, the point is always to draw a distinct line between those books which are sacred and those which are profane. The controversy surrounding the canonical status of the book of Esther,[4] or, to give a more recent example, a custom observed in many traditional Presbyterian houses in Scotland that only the Bible can be read on Sundays, prove that the effort to define the boundaries of Scripture, and to attribute a special status to the Holy Book, as opposed to "ordinary" and "secular" books, has been dominant throughout the centuries. As a result, both the intellectual debates over the Bible and its everyday use show that it has been approached with deep respect as well as clearly distinguished from other literary works.

Certainly, much depends on what we understand by *literature*. Moreover, to define what literature is, we should also put forward a definition of *text*. Hans-Georg Gadamer defines text as "a series of signs that fixates the unified sense of something spoken,"[5] and then he qualifies this definition by saying that the text is "the authoritative datum to which understanding and interpretation have to measure up."[6] This brief statement provides Gadamer with the springboard for a definition of literature. A text becomes literature, belles-lettres, or, in Gadamer's manner of speaking, an "eminent text," when "it is part of a unique, enduring existence which embraces everything that matters."[7] He then adds: "This clearly involves the notion that such a text claims a validity which in the end is independent of its content. It does not only satisfy a contemporary need for information."[8] Hence we might say that, first, a literary text through the act of re-reading provides its present readers with "much more" than its content only. It becomes significant for its

---

2   Sanders, "Canon: Hebrew Bible," *ABD* 1:839.
3   Gamble, "Canon: New Testament," *ABD* 1:857.
4   See Moore, "Esther," *ABD* 2:635-39.
5   Gadamer, "The Eminent Text," 339.
6   Gadamer, "The Eminent Text," 341. By comparison, Paul Ricoeur defines text as "any discourse fixed by writing" (*Hermeneutics*, 145).
7   Gadamer, "The Eminent Text," 340.
8   Gadamer, "The Eminent Text," 340.

readers on many new levels, which were not yet present or imaginable when the text was created. Secondly, a literary text does not communicate only some kind of information: it contains other dimensions such as aesthetic, to give an example. Aristotle's remark about the three aims of music, which can be broadened to include literature, comes to mind in this context.[9] The three aims are *education, catharsis,* and *entertainment*: "Music should be studied, not for the sake of one, but of many benefits, that is to say, with a view to education, or purgation; … music may also serve for intellectual enjoyment, for relaxation and for recreation after exertion."[10] Moreover, Gadamer emphasizes, "the eminent text is a construct that wants to be read anew, again and again, even when it has already been understood."[11] Thus, thirdly, a literary text demands from its audience to be continually revisited and reinterpreted. Robert Scholes puts this third characteristic of literature in the following way: "literature is writing that endures, writing that the world, in Milton's durable phraseology, 'will not willingly let die.'"[12]

It seems that the above properties of literature can be successfully put within a broader conceptual framework proposed by John Barton in his dialectic article "Reading the Bible as Literature." He suggests that we should take into consideration two factors whose interplay results in the phenomenon called *literature*. The first factor is "a particular use of language, which … ceases to be merely a tool for the expression of thoughts … and becomes instead an object of interest in its own right."[13] In other words, a literary work should exhibit, to a greater or lesser extent, various artistic qualities: elevated style, literary devices, and original ideas. As J. A. Cuddon puts it: "There are many works which cannot be classified in the main literary genres which nevertheless may be regarded as literature by virtue of the excellence of their writing, their originality and their general aesthetic and artistic merits."[14] The second factor is the fictionality of literature, and to explain this idea, Barton quotes J. A. Burrow: "Literature is distinguished from history or philosophy or science as a fictional, or non-affirmative,

---

9 This interpretation of the aims of literature, which are identical with the aims of music, is supported in the light of Aristotle's remarks in *The Politics, The Poetics,* and according to different commentators (see e.g. Aristotle, *Pol.* 1339a 13 – 1340b 19 (*CWA* 2:2124-26); Aristotle, *Poetics I, with the Tractatus Coislinianus,* 5).
10 Aristotle, *Pol.* 1341b 36 – 1342a 1 (*CWA* 2:2128).
11 Gadamer, "The Eminent Text," 341.
12 Scholes, "Stillborn Literature," 53.
13 Barton, "Reading the Bible as Literature," 148.
14 Cuddon, *The Penguin Dictionary of Literary Terms,* 472.

or non-pragmatic, or non-hypothetical mode of discourse. It is not committed, in any ordinary, straightforward fashion, to the truth of the events which it reports or the ideas which it propounds."[15] However, not all literary works exhibit the two above factors, and, in consequence, we often have to narrow our definition of literature to the first factor only in order to encompass a greater number of works. "There is a great deal of medieval writing," remarks Barton, and this observation applies also to ancient Hebrew writings, "that occupies a sort of middle ground; which we certainly want to claim for 'literature,' yet which has as its aim a *direct*, rather than an oblique, relation to truth, especially theological or moral truth."[16] Cuddon takes a similar stand, when he tells us that the aesthetic factor is usually sufficient to classify a particular work as literature. If we had always insisted on the fictionality of a literary work, we would have had to exclude from the literary corpus such oeuvres as Augustine's *De Civitate Dei*, or Aristotle's *Poetics*.[17] At the same time, we would have had to agree that the book of Jonah, owing to its fictionality, is literature, whereas the books of Chronicles are not. In consequence, it seems reasonable to adopt a broader definition of literature, and to stress the crucial importance of the aesthetic factor in determining the literary character of a given work.[18]

As a result, I have arrived at the definition of literature which explains *literariness* as a quadruple phenomenon. A *text* becomes *literature* when it is significant to its readers in a way not restricted only by its content. It usually communicates information, but, more importantly, it effectuates *catharsis*, and provides entertainment. It invites its readers to make an interpretive effort, and the urgency with which it does this is one of the foundations of its enduring relevance. It is characterized by aesthetic and artistic merits. In view of that, whether a work does or does not belong to the literary corpus results from both internal and external factors. To classify a text as literature, it should have an appropriate make-up and certain intrinsic characteristics. It must, however,

---

15 Barton, "Reading the Bible as Literature," 149.
16 Barton, "Reading the Bible as Literature," 149.
17 See Cuddon, *The Penguin Dictionary of Literary Terms*, 472.
18 In chapter 3, I will discuss further the notion of fictionality in literature, and I will show that, in fact, the concept of *fiction* is not opposed to *reality* and *fact* but to *non-fiction*. As a result, we may regard a great deal of Hebrew Bible texts as fiction as long as we remember that the fictionality of a given work does not exclude links between the work and historical reality.

also be recognized as such by its readers. Hence every work to be properly called literature must be literature both *per se* and *for* its readers.

Now, there is no doubt that the above four factors apply, to a great extent, to the Bible. Readers of all historical periods have been discovering new levels of meaning in the Bible, and have been applying its teachings to their existential situation.[19] Bernard of Clairvaux's *Sermons on the Song of Songs*, as well as many other examples of ancient and mediaeval allegorical interpretation, are proof that readers were often looking for more than the original meaning of the book. The same can be said about the modern practice of reading and preaching on Scripture in various communities of faith. Although Scripture forms a basis for doctrinal teaching in those communities, their most exemplary members have seldom limited the importance of Scripture to its dogmatic role. St Augustine, who is known for his dogmatic treatises based on Scripture, confessed that one day he came across the passage from Rom 13:13-14, and "with the last words of this sentence, it was as if a light of relief from all anxiety flooded into my heart."[20] By saying this, he acknowledged the existential role of the Bible in human transformation.[21] Moreover, the need for constant biblical reinterpretation is obvious when we remember that "in every age interpreters ask different questions, and so different aspects of the text's meaning emerge. The task of interpretation, unlike that of research, is never finished even in principle."[22] Thus, because Scripture is constantly revisited by its interpreters, it becomes a literary corpus which "the world will not willingly let die." Finally, there is no doubt that a majority of biblical texts exhibit complex aesthetic features. The scholarly literature investigating the complexity of biblical poetics is vast and still growing.[23]

Nevertheless, it appears that most Christian readers would strongly object to the suggestion that the book of the Apocalypse belongs to the same category as Dante's *Divine Comedy*, whilst for pious Jewish read-

---

19   In this context, I use the term *meaning* in a general sense. In chapter 3, I will define *meaning* as different from *significance*.
20   Augustine, *Conf.* VIII. xii (29) (transl. Chadwick, 153).
21   Augustine's experience bears all the signs of the cathartic experience mentioned by Aristotle.
22   Barton, "Introduction," *The Cambridge Companion*, 1.
23   Among the best-known studies of biblical poetics are: Sternberg, Meir. *The Poetics of Biblical Narrative: Ideological Literature and the Drama of Reading*. ISBL. Bloomington: Indiana University Press, 1987; Alter, Robert. *The Art of Biblical Narrative*. London: George Allen & Unwin, 1981; Bar-Efrat, Shimon. *Narrative Art in the Bible*. JSOTSup 70. Sheffield: Almond Press, 1989; Berlin, Adele. *Poetics and Interpretation of Biblical Narrative*. BLS 9. Sheffield: Almond Press, 1983.

ers, equating the book of Chronicles with Herodotus's *Histories* would smack of exaggeration if not heresy. In fact, even in the world of academia, there has recently been a vivid debate about the issue. The line of reasoning of those scholars who argue against calling the Bible literature can be summarized under four headings. First, they say that Scripture contains material that is too diverse to be properly called literature. By way of illustration, James Kugel enumerates legal, historical, sermonic, wisdom, and oracular material, and asks whether we would also categorize a similar conglomerate of "secular" genres as literature.[24] Although his argument has a certain rhetorical power, the answer to his question is positive. Certainly, some parts of the Bible have a "less literary" character than others (e.g. its legal codices versus the Song of Songs), yet the majority of scriptural texts fit well the definition of literature, regardless of their diversity. Adele Berlin rightly notices that we can draw literary parallels between many biblical texts and "Lincoln's Gettysburg Address, the fables of La Fontaine, the essays of Ahad Ha'Am, the Icelandic Sagas,"[25] and these can hardly be considered anything else than literature. If we doubt the overall literary unity of the Bible, it still remains a collection of literary works, and bears the stamp of literature on its pages. If, however, we agree with Gabriel Josipovici that the Christian Bible is a literary and theological whole,[26] and is similar to a Gothic cathedral, which was "built over a long period, ... by different master masons, with different bands of workmen," yet whose builders remained "true to the spirit of the whole,"[27] then Kugel's reasoning is even less convincing.

Secondly, Kugel claims that since the Bible does not contain any apparent claims to be literature, it should not be regarded as such.[28] This argument can also be dismissed easily. As Berlin puts it: "Few works, after all, claim to be literature; great novels do not advertise themselves as fictional – on the contrary, it is precisely their 'realness' (verisimilitude) that makes them great."[29] Thirdly, Berlin's remark about verisimilitude provides a counterargument against another view which rejects the literariness of Scripture on the grounds that the Bible is "about real not invented people."[30] As I will show in chapter 3, we can

---

24   See Kugel, "On the Bible," 218-19.
25   Berlin, "On the Bible," 323.
26   See Josipovici, *The Book of God*, 42.
27   Josipovici, *The Book of God*, 302.
28   See Kugel, "On the Bible," 219.
29   Berlin, "On the Bible," 324.
30   Josipovici, *The Book of God*, 298. Josipovici ascribes this opinion to J. Barr.

give many examples of fictional works referring to real, historical characters. What is more, such biblical characters as Abraham, Isaac, or Jacob are *real* not because we can prove historically their existence, but because they are verisimilar, and their verisimilitude contributes to the literariness of the patriarchal narratives.

Finally, T. S. Eliot criticizes those who call Scripture a "monument of English prose," because this way of speaking means "admiring it [the Bible] as a monument over the grave of Christianity."[31] Eliot explains his point of view: "The Bible has had a *literary* influence upon English literature *not* because it has been considered as literature, but because it has been considered as the report of the Word of God. And the fact that men of letters now discuss it as 'literature' probably indicates the *end* of its 'literary' influence."[32] There is no doubt that Eliot's deep concern was to preserve the divine authority of the Bible as well as its influence on general literature. What is more, Eliot is right in saying that relegating Scripture to a category within general literature may, at least for some readers, decrease its influence. "Why should I bother about Scripture if it is of no more value than Greek or Roman myths?," one might ask. However, can we prove with the same degree of certainty that keeping a privileged place for Scripture really strengthens its influence? If the Bible is an antique and untouchable set of divine oracles and precepts, why not leave it to theologians and preachers, and deal with more accessible books instead? Detweiler and Robbins are then right when they observe that Eliot "failed to see that the Bible's stature as a culture's sacred text, if it could be saved at all in the secular age, would be saved by a thoroughgoing literary investigation that would disclose the Bible's awesome resourcefulness as model and structure of Western thought."[33]

To conclude, I believe that from a theological point of view, Scripture is both the word of God and the word of man transmitted in written form. From a secular point of view, and this position cannot be ignored or passed over in silence, the Bible is only the word of man conveyed in exquisite literary form. Non-believing literary critics would say that the theological standpoint contains presuppositions

---

31 Eliot, "Religion and Literature," 390.
32 Eliot, "Religion and Literature," 390.
33 Detweiler and Robbins, "From New Criticism to Poststructuralism," 234. On the other hand, Eliot's critique of the literariness of Scripture becomes less severe if we agree with Barr's remark that Eliot disagreed that Scripture "could be rightly read if it was read *solely* as literature, without any concern at all for the objects which concerned the writers" (Barr, "Reading the Bible as Literature," 15).

which they cannot accept. Theologians would claim that the secular view, albeit not false, is reductionist. Both views, however, are openly expressed in academia, so a compromise must be reached in order to continue scholarly debate. Secular critics should allow a theoretical possibility of divine inspiration, whilst theologians ought to understand the reasons for their secular colleagues' intellectual position. All of them, however, contribute in different ways to biblical exegesis, and their intellectual presuppositions must be treated with respect.[34]

Hence the Bible *is* literature, even if it is *much more* than literature. C. S. Lewis, whose deep faith and theological sensitivity cannot be disputed, states that it is nonsensical to read Scripture without paying attention to its main theological ideas. In this respect, he is supported by Barr who insists that "the Bible must be read in a theological mode ... as a source of true knowledge about the objects described in the Bible – about God, about the creation of the world, about his redemption of mankind."[35] Nonetheless, Lewis further qualifies his views: "But there is a saner sense in which the Bible, *since it is after all literature* [my emphasis], cannot properly be read except as literature; and the different parts of it as the different sorts of literature they are. Most emphatically the Psalms must be read as poems ... if they are to be understood."[36] Ignorance of the literary form of the Bible results in misunderstanding of what it says. After all, even those who refuse to call it literature use various methods of literary analysis, and thereby silently admit that *it is* literature. "If we cannot read the Bible as literature," observes Berlin, "we cannot read it at all."[37]

However, a feeling of unease remains. The Bible can be called literature, but, at the same time, it appears to be literature of a very specific kind. Is this *specificity* of the Bible something which we readers attribute to it, or is it one of its intrinsic features? To answer this question, I would now like to take a closer look at the corpus of Hebrew Bible narratives.

---

34 Prickett and Barnes add an interesting remark: "This is partly an aspect of the secularization of western societies: as most members of those societies have gradually lost their interest in the Bible as a 'sacred' book (and indeed have very largely lost interest in it altogether), it has at last become possible to consider it as a work of literature" (*The Bible*, 101).
35 Barr, "Reading the Bible as Literature," 13.
36 Lewis, *Reflections on the Psalms*, 10.
37 Berlin, "On the Bible," 324. Alter and Kermode make a similar point, and also warn us that the ability "to read it [the Bible] well" is the only way to avoid the mistakes already made in the history of Western culture (*The Literary Guide to the Bible*, 2).

1.2. Features of Hebrew Narratives

Trying to establish what constitutes a sacred text, Detweiler emphasizes "the importance of power and authority in formally designating certain texts as sacred."[38] At the same time, however, he distinguishes a number of features which are characteristic of all sacred texts. Detweiler tries to differentiate between those features which are superimposed onto a sacred text by its readers and those which are inherent in it. Answering the question "what are the traits of a sacred text as its readers who are believers understand them?,"[39] he lists the following: claiming or generating claims of divine inspiration; revelatory of divinity; somehow encoded or "hidden"; requiring a privileged interpreter; effecting the transformation of lives; being the necessary foundation of religious ritual; and evocative of divine presence.[40] I believe that at least four of these traits should be considered secondary for our discussion. A text requires a privileged interpreter because it is divinely inspired and encoded. The idea of existential transformation is often present in a sacred text, but may be ignored by its readers, and, in consequence, does not affect their lives. The same can be said about a sacred text's cultic and evocative role. This is why I think that only the first three features are fundamental to and inherent in a sacred text.[41]

To apply Detweiler's scheme to Hebrew narratives, we should, first, mention their claims of divine inspiration. They are present in the numerous passages where God declares something, or where his divine or human messengers reveal his will.[42] We learn from the first chapter of Genesis that God is the creator of everything that exists as well as the supreme Lord of human history. Hence every subsequent statement in the Bible that God proclaims something directly or through a messenger confirms that the biblical text is inspired. Of course, in this case, we cannot claim the *objective* inspiration of the text.

---

38   Detweiler, "What Is a Sacred Text?," 213.
39   Detweiler, "What Is a Sacred Text?," 214.
40   Detweiler, "What Is a Sacred Text?," 223.
41   Ricoeur objects to the term *sacred*, which he regards as something *antihistorical* and *immutable*. In this sense, the *sacred text* cannot be reconciled with the process of revelation which is a "permanent process of opening something that is closed" ("The 'Sacred' Text," 72). Instead, Ricoeur suggests the term *authoritative* as a better alternative ("The 'Sacred' Text," 69).
42   In the biblical context, this and the next feature of the sacred text are rooted in the basic fact observed by Ricoeur: "One of the traits that makes for the specificity of the biblical discourse … is the central place of God-reference in it" ("Philosophy and Religious Language," 45).

As Detweiler points out, the numerous passages in the Bible where God communicates something offer "textual evidence of divine inspiration."[43]

As a result, and secondly, we learn the content of God's message, and have a share in divine revelation. When God asks David through the prophet Nathan: "Would you build me a house to dwell in?" (2 Sam 7:5),[44] we become aware not only of the immediate events, but also of God's plan that the Davidic royal line will be established forever. We become initiated into the world of divine purposes. To put it another way, the language of the Bible continuously and strongly points to a transcendent reality. Interestingly, this trait of Hebrew narratives, and all biblical texts in general, has drawn the attention of many a scholar because it belongs to the very nature of Scripture. The Biblical Commission's document *The Interpretation of the Bible in the Church* expresses this phenomenon using a famous Ricoeurian phrase: "The religious language of the Bible is a symbolic language which 'gives rise to thought' (*'donne à penser'*), a language the full richness of which one never ceases to discover, a language which points to a transcendent reality and which, at the same time, awakens human beings to the deepest dimensions of personal existence."[45] Hence biblical narratives may be viewed as a bridge which connects the world of the reader with the transcendent world to which those narratives bear witness.[46]

By way of illustration, the narrative in Gen 15 tells us about God's covenant with Abram, and communicates the content of God's promise made to the patriarch. At the same time, however, it provides a link between modern readers[47] and the transcendent sphere in which God dwells. The God of Abram is also the God of readers. The promise given to Abram is also to be shared by readers. Additionally, the natural phenomena present in the narrative reinforce a sense of mystery: the starry sky (v. 5), the birds of prey (v. 11), the sunset, deep and terrifying darkness (v. 12), a smoking fire-pot, and a flaming torch (v. 17). If the theophany in Gen 15 is accompanied by so many awe-inspiring

---

43 Detweiler, "What Is a Sacred Text?," 219.
44 Unless stated otherwise, all biblical quotations in English except Gen 21:1-21, which is my own translation, are from the RSV (the Revised Standard Version, see *The Holy Bible*).
45 Fitzmyer, *The Biblical Commission's Document*, 113.
46 The question which arises in this context is: What is the relationship between the sacred text and the revelation which that text communicates? I shall deal with this problem in chapter 3.
47 I shall explain the term *modern reader* in the next section of this chapter.

phenomena, readers rightly expect that God, the originator of the theophany, is even more mysterious and awe-inspiring. Moreover, they learn about God's plans concerning Abram and his progeny. The knowledge that readers acquire is, however, only fragmentary. God does not put his cards on the table, and does not reveal all mysteries at once. This is why readers must keep reading and looking for other narratives that will help them to have another glance at God's transcendent reality. What is important, the whole process of mediating between readers and the transcendent sphere happens irrespective of whether they believe in the real existence of that sphere or not. They may be deeply convinced that the transcendent sphere is a purely textual construct, or that it is the ultimate ontological foundation of all beings. In both cases, however, the biblical text points to a reality which is different from the real world which readers inhabit.

To develop these observations, we may say, after Robert Alter, that Scripture seems to be

> a literature that speaks to us urgently, with the power to "draw us out" of ourselves. It is able to do this in part because it scrutinizes the human condition with such a probing, unblinking gaze that is conveyed in the most subtle narrative vehicle, ... But it is also able to do this by the boldness with which it represents human figures confronted, challenged, confounded by a reality beyond human ken.[48]

In other words, readers of ancient Hebrew narratives recognize in them truth about their own condition. Because of the mimetic force of biblical narratives, they empathize with the characters, and find themselves equally confronted by a transcendent reality to which the narratives consistently refer. It seems that this trait of biblical narratives is strengthened by what Eric Auerbach calls "the claim to absolute authority," and the ability "to overcome our reality."[49] Even though some of his remarks can now be challenged in the light of what we know about the history of formation and the nature of biblical narratives, he remains an unquestionable master of close literary analysis.[50] Starting

---

48 Alter, *The World of Biblical Literature*, 23.
49 Auerbach, *Mimesis*, 15.
50 When Auerbach states that "the Biblical narrator, the Elohist, had to believe in the objective truth of the story of Abraham's sacrifice" (*Mimesis*, 14), he is down the slippery slope of believing that we can easily establish the intention of the original author, or that the story had, in fact, an author in the modern sense of the word. Josipovici downplays certain aspects of Auerbach's analysis, and says that "it is difficult to tell how far Auerbach is merely trying to express what is unique to this text, and how far he is trying to find words to make us grasp that we simply cannot treat the Bible as a 'text,' even a unique one" (Josipovici, *The Book of God*, 300).

with a literary comparison between book 19 of the *Odyssey* and chapter 22 of Genesis, he subsequently arrives at some general remarks about the difference between the style of Homeric epics and of Hebrew Bible narratives. Hence, when he observes that, reading the biblical narrative, "we are to fit our own life into its world, feel ourselves to be elements in its structure of universal history,"[51] he stresses that the biblical text, owing to its internal literary characteristics, exerts on its readers considerable influence, and invites them to discover a world which is beyond their own.

Shall we say that all Hebrew narratives exhibit this trait to the same extent? Not at all. They undoubtedly point to a transcendent reality when considered as a whole. Moreover, the transcendental character of those narratives which deal directly with theological themes is also beyond question. Even if a particular narrative may not refer to God or mention theological themes, its context usually provides a "transcendental framework." By way of illustration, 2 Sam 11 recounts David's sin and his subsequent plan to kill Uriah. Apart from v. 11, which mentions the Ark of the Covenant, the chapter does not contain either the divine name or theological themes. There is no doubt, however, that when we read 2 Sam 11 in the context of the whole David cycle, its theological importance is unquestionable. David's sin triggers God's reaction. The prophet Nathan foretells the future of David's house. As a result, David's and Bathsheba's child dies, yet, afterwards, it is Bathsheba who gives David his successor Solomon. We can easily imagine 2 Sam 11 being part of an ancient secular royal chronicle. Yet, in the Bible, this seemingly non-theological narrative becomes an element of a bigger whole: a salvation story telling of God's plan for his people.[52]

An interesting case is that of the book of Esther, which is often given as a paramount example of biblical "secular" literature, and which, in its Hebrew original, is characterized by "the total absence of references to God or to the primary religious institutions of Israel."[53] Never-

---

51 Auerbach, *Mimesis*, 15.
52 Von Rad makes a number of interesting remarks on the whole narrative of the succession to the throne of David, which he regards as "the oldest specimen of ancient Israelite historical writing" ("The Beginnings of Historical Writing," 176). In the narrative, and indeed in many other Hebrew narratives, God operates "as a much more constant, much more widely embracing factor concealed in the whole breadth of secular affairs, and pervading every single sphere of human life" ("The Beginnings of Historical Writing," 204).
53 Dumm, "Esther," *NJBC*, 576.

theless, even this book, interpreted through the prism of Jewish tradition, contains a few verses which allude to the transcendent sphere in a veiled way. In 3:1, we read: "After these things King Ahasuerus promoted Haman the Agagite, the son of Hammedatha, and advanced him and set his seat above all the princes who were with him." Rashi comments on this verse: "This remedy was created to be a salvation for Israel. For the Holy One, blessed be He, creates a remedy for Israel's blow before He brings the blow upon them."[54] Then, in 4:14, we have: "For if you keep silence at such a time as this, relief and deliverance will rise for the Jews from another quarter (ממקום אחר), but you and your father's house will perish. And who knows whether you have not come to the kingdom for such a time as this (לעת כזאת)?" The traditional understanding of this verse is summarized by Dumm who interprets "another quarter" (or, better, "another place") as a sign of possible divine intervention, and Esther's career "for such a time as this" as a token of divine providence.[55] Furthermore, the king's insomnia in 6:1 is explained by Rashi as a miracle,[56] whereas Haman's behaviour in 7:8 ("Haman was falling on the couch where Esther was") is the result of an angel's intervention.[57] Certainly, we may accuse Rashi of reading into the text ideas which are not present there. However, no text is independent of its context, and, in the case of Esther, the context is provided by the remaining part of Scripture as well as by rabbinical tradition. Long before Esther became part of the Hebrew canon, the Greek translator of the book had extended its text, and, in consequence, changed its focus from secular to more religious.[58] Since almost all of Scripture has a strong religious emphasis, why should Esther be devoid of it?[59]

---

54 Rosenberg, "The Judaica Press Complete Tanach with Rashi," n.p (to my knowledge, this is the only existing English translation of Rashi's commentary on Esther). Rashi's commentary follows closely the tradition of the Babylonian Talmud (*Meg.* 13b).
55 See Dumm, "Esther," *NJBC*, 578.
56 The Talmud alludes here to God, the King of the Universe (*Meg.* 15b).
57 See Rosenberg, "The Judaica Press Complete Tanach with Rashi," n.p.
58 See Dumm, "Esther," *NJBC*, 576.
59 Barry D. Walfish gives a useful résumé of how Jewish mediaeval exegetes dealt with the lack of the divine name in the book. Their argumentation was twofold: "Some addressed the problem directly, seeking to explain why God's name was omitted from the book, while others sought to show that, whether or not God's name appears in the book, his presence behind the scenes and his orchestration of events in the story are easily demonstrable" (*Esther in Medieval Garb*, 76).

The third important trait mentioned by Detweiler is that a sacred text is often encoded or "hidden." That trait applies to prophetic and apocalyptic texts more than to narratives, but a close analysis of Hebrew narratives proves that they also are characterized by a certain kind of obscurity. Auerbach's remarks help to bring this feature to our notice:

> The externalization of only so much of the phenomena as is necessary for the purpose of the narrative, all else left in obscurity; the decisive points of the narrative alone are emphasized, what lies between is nonexistent; ... the whole, permeated with the most unrelieved suspense and directed toward a single goal (and to that extent far more of a unity), remains mysterious and "fraught with background."[60]

Thus, even apart from the narratives which are evidently difficult to interpret, such as "Jacob Wrestling at Peniel" in Gen 32:22-32, most seemingly uncomplicated stories are written in a literary style which is "mysterious and 'fraught with background,'" and which, in consequence, demands a constant reinterpretation of those stories. It is worth noting that this feature does not simply result from the ancient character of Hebrew texts. Both the Homeric epics and many ancient Near East folk stories lack mysteriousness, and, by contrast, are "of the foreground."[61]

To summarize the discussion, a number of observations must be made. First, the application of Detweiler's analysis to Hebrew narratives shows that those narratives exhibit three intrinsic features: they claim divine inspiration; they point to a transcendent reality; and they remain, to a certain extent, encoded and "fraught with background." The second feature is of paramount importance, and presupposes the first one: a text which is revelatory of the transcendent world posits, at least "textual," divine inspiration. In turn, the third feature emphasizes the second: since the text is encoded, the ultimate subject possessing the knowledge needed for its clarification is God alone. Thus the transcendental character of Hebrew narratives is their foremost trait. Secondly, as Auerbach's and Josipovici's in-depth analyses clearly

---

60 Auerbach, *Mimesis*, 11-12.
61 Auerbach, *Mimesis*, 12. Auerbach states that the "destiny [of the Homeric heroes] is clearly defined," they "wake every morning as if it were the first day of their lives: their emotions, though strong, are simple and find expression instantly" (*Mimesis*, 12). An example of a Near East folk story which lacks the depth characteristic of Hebrew narratives is "The Epic of Gilgamesh". When Gilgamesh laments the loss of the plant of life, he is so different in portrayal from the man and his wife in Gen 3 (see "The Epic of Gilgamesh," transl. E. A. Speiser, *ANET*, 96-97).

show, a full list of narrative features is much longer. To enumerate at least some of them, Auerbach should again be given the floor: "certain parts brought into high relief, others left obscure, abruptness, suggestive influence of the unexpressed, 'background' quality, multiplicity of meanings and the need for interpretation, universal-historical claims, development of the concept of the historically becoming, and preoccupation with the problematic."[62] Thirdly, and most importantly, none of the above traits is, in any way, reserved for Scripture. The Koran and the Bhagavad-Gita claim divine inspiration. George Herbert's "Love" points to a transcendent reality, is "fraught with background," and certainly demands interpretation. Shakespearean *Macbeth* is preoccupied with the problematic. As a result, all the features which the Bible undoubtedly has can also be recognized in other literary works.[63] However, if we had written a new book characterized by exactly the same literary traits as the Bible, would we have been able to call it Scripture? The answer is negative. The Bible is inimitable by virtue of the unique configuration of both its contents and features.[64] This approach to the problem of biblical hermeneutics is further confirmed by Paul Ricoeur, who is convinced that biblical hermeneutics is, on the one hand, a type of the general hermeneutics of literary texts because of the literariness of its subject, but, on the other, it is a special hermeneutics because "all its [biblical] partial forms of discourse are referred to that Name which is the point of intersection and the vanishing point of all our discourse about God, the name of the unnameable."[65] Ricoeur is convinced that what makes biblical hermeneutics unique is that it must account for the revelatory character of Scripture, which is exceptional because of the inimitable configuration of the biblical forms of discourse and the transcendent reality to which those forms of discourse refer the reader.

Finally, we may say that the Bible is like a person: similar to other books, sharing with them the same literary nature, yet only one of its kind. According to Josipovici, the Bible is surrounded by an aura, by which he understands

---

62 Auerbach, *Mimesis*, 23.
63 Paul Fiddes in *Freedom and Limit* discusses different ways in which imaginative literature transcends itself towards a mystery (see esp. pp. 3-64).
64 Prickett and Barnes call the Bible a "landmark of world literature" because it laid the foundations for the development of Western literature and literary criticism. The Bible is characterized by its narrativity which brings meaning to human existence, by its notion of unity with diversity, its interpretive value, and intertextuality (see *The Bible*, 2-5).
65 Ricoeur, *Essays*, 104.

that distinct quality of uniqueness which, though indefinable, is felt by all of us when we encounter a particular person or natural object. Looked at in this way, the Bible can be seen to be unique not because it is uniquely authoritative but because it is itself and not something else. Jubilees and Ecclesiasticus may be its brothers, the Koran, *Paradise Lost* and *Joseph and His Brothers* its cousins, once or twice removed, and so may the works of Homer and Sophocles, Kafka, Celan and Proust. They all share certain gestures and expressions, but no one who had once got to know them would ever mistake one for the other.[66]

Since, in this book, I intend to catch a glimpse of the biblical aura, it is now high time to prepare the critical tools which will help me to perform this task as well as possible. I shall now turn to enumerating and defining fundamental critical concepts upon which my hermeneutical enterprise is based.

1.3. Critical Concepts Introduced

To begin with, I shall briefly summarize my views on the relationship between the Bible and the rest of the literary corpus, as well as on the features of ancient Hebrew narratives, which I have introduced in the previous two subchapters. I have shown that, provided that we define *literature* in a broad sense, and stress the importance of the aesthetic factor in deciding whether a text belongs to the literary corpus, we can call the Bible literature. The most crucial corollary of this fact is that, in our critical proceedings, we are allowed to use the same approaches as we employ in the interpretation of general, "secular" literature. Since the biblical literature has numerous genres, we should use a wide variety of critical approaches which take into account the literary modes characteristic of each genre. Having said this, we must remember that, in the case of Scripture, we are dealing with an ancient literary work, or, properly speaking, a library of works, which exhibit a set of uniquely configured features. This is why a particular kind of general hermeneutics which we use in interpretation should facilitate foregrounding and analysing those features in the context of a given passage or book. Biblical narratives' most important feature is their ability to mediate between the reader and the transcendent world.[67] Other fea-

---

66 Josipovici, *The Book of God*, 307.
67 Barr states: "We may perfectly well admit that a theological use of the Bible needs to go *beyond* what the literary reading of it can provide. But I think that I have shown that there is no real *contradiction* between a literary reading of the Bible and the per-

tures, which result from the definition of literature adopted at the beginning of this chapter, comprise the biblical text's significance, which is not restricted by its content, its informative, cathartic, and aesthetic dimension, and its need for constant reinterpretation.

There are still a number of preliminary issues that I must discuss here. What is the nature of literary criticism? Who is the critic and what is his or her role in interpretation? Interestingly, T. S. Eliot's views expounded in his critical essays throw an interesting light on these questions.[68] Eliot, as both a poet and a critic, is unanimously numbered among the theoreticians and practitioners of the New Criticism, a school of Anglo-American criticism which reigned supreme during the interwar period of the last century.[69] Even though most contemporary critics agree that the New Criticism already belongs to the critical past, many of the movement's ideas and presuppositions have survived in different trends within modern criticism. This is why I would now like to introduce and analyse Eliot's stance on literary criticism, as well as to show some implications that his views have for biblical criticism and exegesis.[70] I must emphasize that I do not think that *all* of Eliot's critical ideas are of equal value for biblical criticism. Neither do I want to suggest that the interpretive model presented in this book uses Eliot's approach to literature as its basis. What I intend to do is to show that certain critical concepts and ways of approaching crucial issues in literary studies practised by Eliot offer valuable and practical guidelines for biblical interpretation. Moreover, as I will show at the end of this chapter, some of Eliot's views are less typical of the New Criticism than we would expect.

---

spectives which will be perceived and made use of in the religious life" ("Reading the Bible as Literature," 18).

68   I shall focus on six of Eliot's essays on literary criticism, which, I believe, are a representative sample of his critical views. I have chosen: "Hamlet" (1919), "The Metaphysical Poets" (1921), "The Function of Criticism" (1923), "Religion and Literature" (1935), "What Dante Means to Me" (1950), and "To Criticize the Critic" (1961). I will also look at Eliot's lectures on the Metaphysical Poets delivered at Cambridge and the Johns Hopkins University in 1926 and 1933 respectively, and published as *The Varieties of Metaphysical Poetry*.

69   J. A. Cuddon summarizes the most salient features of the New Criticism: "The New Critics advocated 'close reading' and detailed textual analysis of poetry rather than an interest in the mind and personality of the poet, sources, the history of ideas and political and social implications" (*The Penguin Dictionary of Literary Terms*, 544).

70   There are scholars who value Eliot more as a critic than as a poet. F. W. Bateson writes: "I regard him [Eliot] as an interesting, even good minor poet (more American than English) who was a major literary critic (an *English* critic and of the stature of Johnson, Coleridge and Arnold)" ("Criticism's Lost Leader," 11).

Eliot speaks in "The Function of Criticism" in a straightforward manner: "When I say criticism, I mean of course in this place the commentation and exposition of works of art by means of written words."[71] Thus, for Eliot, literary criticism comprises two tasks: it expresses opinions about a literary work of art; secondly, it explains the meaning of the work. Moreover, literary criticism is practised "by means of written words"; hence it is a kind of literature, and a separate literary genre. Just as there are two interconnected tasks within literary criticism, so the critical activity has also two ends: "the elucidation of works of art and the correction of taste."[72] Eliot emphasizes that literary criticism is by no means an autotelic enterprise. It is its subject, art, which is basically autotelic: "I do not deny that art may be affirmed to serve ends beyond itself; but art is not required to be aware of these ends, and indeed performs its function, whatever that may be, according to various theories of value, much better by indifference to them."[73]

Speaking about literary criticism in "To Criticize the Critic," he further qualifies his beliefs: "Literary criticism … is an instinctive activity of the civilized mind."[74] Eliot finds a link between literary criticism and metaphysics, and in a jocular manner applies F. H. Bradley's description of metaphysics to criticism: "the finding of bad reasons for what we believe upon instinct, but to find these reasons is no less an instinct."[75] As a result, Eliot's critical practice is far removed from those schools of literary criticism which demand that criticism should be performed in a manner similar to science (such as structuralism, to give an example). If anything is "scientific" in Eliot's literary realm, it is the mind of the reader. It ought to be "civilized," acute, erudite, and critical. However, when that critical mind analyses literature, the outcome of its activity becomes less cut-and-dried because literature is, by its nature, less exact and scientific. In *The Varieties of Metaphysical Poetry*, Eliot states:

> One must always be as exact and clear as one can – as clear as one's subject matter permits. And when one's subject matter is literature, clarity beyond a certain point becomes falsification. This is a very important restriction on the activity of literary criticism. When a subject matter is in its nature vague, clarity should consist, not in making it so clear as to be unrecognisable, but in recognising the vagueness, where it begins and ends and the

---

71 Eliot, "The Function of Criticism," 24.
72 Eliot, "The Function of Criticism," 24.
73 Eliot, "The Function of Criticism," 24.
74 Eliot, "To Criticize the Critic," 19.
75 Eliot, "To Criticize the Critic," 11.

causes of its necessity, and in checking analysis and division at the prudent point.[76]

According to Eliot, we must remember that a good analysis cannot consist in a mechanical application of any system or classification, but in a thorough and sensitive search of the most significant literary dimensions and features of a work. Thus the instinctive, or intuitive, approach to literary work is not subjective, informal, or imperfect; on the contrary, it is fully legitimate and highly commendable. In other words, as far as criticism is concerned, insisting on ideal accuracy may lead to reprehensible fallacy.

Eliot's emphasis on the intuitive approach to criticism applies to biblical exegesis. By way of example, a historical-critical exegesis that puts too much stress on historical issues may easily forget about its primary exegetical task, which is the exposition of the text. Similarly, modern literary methods of analysis based upon structuralism may get bogged down in endless deliberations concerning the definitions of literary terms. It sometimes happens that when everything is clearly defined and precise, the text does not conform to neat literary categories, and shows its own surprising dynamics. This is why Eliot's cautious approach, which allows a margin of imprecision, appears to be highly commendable in the case of biblical interpretation.

Furthermore, Eliot states that "it is impossible to fence off *literary* criticism from criticism on other grounds, and that moral, religious or social judgments cannot be wholly excluded."[77] By saying this, Eliot takes quite a conservative stand on the matter. Most modern critics would rather say that art should be liberated from moral and religious constraints. To take a typical case, whether art offends the religious sensitivity of the viewer or, on the contrary, is conducive to the viewer's deep religious experience, is irrelevant to the task of the evaluation of art. Art may be offensive and yet exceptional, immoral but outstanding. This view is, however, worlds apart from Eliot's beliefs. For Eliot, the category of beauty, which is central to the evaluation of art, is inseparable from the categories of goodness and truth.

We find what is probably the most fervent defence of the moral duty incumbent upon the practitioners of literary criticism in Eliot's essay "Religion and Literature," published eight years after Eliot's bap-

---

76 Eliot, *The Varieties of Metaphysical Poetry*, 59-60. In *The Varieties of Metaphysical Poetry*, Eliot concentrates on the poetry of the Metaphysicals, and draws daring comparisons between them and the poetry of Dante, as well as the poetry of some nineteenth century French writers.
77 Eliot, "To Criticize the Critic," 25.

tism and reception into the Church of England. "Religion and Literature" fully deserves our attention, even if it slightly smacks of the author's neophytic attitude. We must remember that Eliot's faith was the mature choice of a poet and philosopher. He was neither bigoted nor hidebound. As Peter Ackroyd notes: "In a discussion with Hugh Sykes Davies about Marxists, he [Eliot] said, 'They seem so certain of what they believe. My own beliefs are held with a scepticism which I never even hope to be rid of.'"[78] Eliot begins "Religion and Literature" with an examination of the condition of modern literature. He claims that contemporary literature is seriously ill, and needs specialist treatment, which can only be given by Christian readers and critics. What is the central problem affecting literature? Eliot's response is unambiguous: it is secularism. "What I do wish to affirm is that the whole of modern literature," states Eliot, "is corrupted by what I call Secularism, that it is simply unaware of, simply cannot understand the meaning of, the primacy of the supernatural over the natural life: of something which I assume to be our primary concern."[79] Eliot deplores the fact that modern literature creates the impression that the religious sphere should not be regarded as something crucial and central to our lives. As a result, "while individual modern writers of eminence can be improving, contemporary literature as a whole tends to be degrading."[80] Thus, it is the readers who pay the price for the bad condition of modern literature. They are affected, and they suffer unnecessarily. This state of affairs is even worse because readers are flooded and choked with a "mass movement of writers who, each of them, think that they have something individually to offer, but are really all working together in the same direction."[81] Because of this, modern readers become unaware of the great tradition of past masters; their literary world is "so parochial, so shut off from the past."[82]

What is the remedy that Eliot suggests to overcome the ills of modern literature? The answer is as clear as was the diagnosis: "Literary criticism should be completed by criticism from a definite ethical and theological standpoint. ... The 'greatness' of literature cannot be determined solely by literary standards; though we must remember that whether it is literature or not can be determined only by literary stand-

---

78 Ackroyd, *T. S. Eliot*, 163.
79 Eliot, "Religion and Literature," 398.
80 Eliot, "Religion and Literature," 396.
81 Eliot, "Religion and Literature," 398.
82 Eliot, "Religion and Literature," 398.

ards."[83] To help us achieve the satisfactory mode of literary criticism, Eliot distinguishes between two things which are important for literary criticism: we should be aware of "what we like," as well as of "what we *ought* to like."[84] A mature reader does not read books only to get emotional, aesthetic, and intellectual satisfaction. Such a reader is interested in the refinement of his or her literary taste and sensitivity. For Eliot, Christians, owing to the ethical standards they profess, are obliged to help others discover what they *ought* to like: "What I believe to be incumbent upon all Christians is the duty of maintaining consciously certain standards and criteria of criticism over and above those applied by the rest of the world; and that by these criteria and standards everything that we read must be tested."[85] Samuel Hynes comments: "It was simply a kind of criticism that would be integrated by the critic's beliefs, and the religious tradition to which he belonged, ... and which would urge the relevance of a religious view of life both to the making and to the experiencing of literature."[86]

I agree with Eliot's remarks concerning the process of secularization affecting modern literature. Even though we may find exceptions to this fact, Eliot is, by and large, right. There is a startling contrast between the extent to which religion is significant to ordinary people of our generation and the lack of religious motifs in literary works. Yet, at the same time, many a modern reader would welcome the presence of such motifs only with reservations, and would suspect that the author is trying to sell religious propaganda. It should be observed that such a reaction would have been unusual in the Middle Ages or in the Renaissance. It is then no surprise that modern literature, which, on the one hand, does not represent reality as it is, and, on the other, severs links to the tradition of the past, may have and often has a degrading influence on readers. A fear of religion and religious topics, instead of bringing promised liberation and neutrality, results in a very blinkered view of human life and its final destination.[87]

---

83 Eliot, "Religion and Literature," 388.
84 Eliot, "Religion and Literature," 399.
85 Eliot, "Religion and Literature," 399.
86 Hynes, "The Trials of a Christian Critic," 78.
87 It appears that Eliot's success as a Christian critic was incomplete. Hynes is right in saying: "One must conclude that Eliot failed because he misunderstood what success would have been. Auden (who was wiser in these matters) once remarked that there can no more be a Christian art than a Christian science or a Christian diet. There are only Christians who are artists or scientists or cooks; and the same is surely true of criticism. ... Eliot would have succeeded as a Christian critic if he had made his Christianity invisible" ("The Trials of a Christian Critic," 87).

It seems to me that in the context of Eliot's views on religion and literature, Scripture plays a twofold role. First, the Bible itself is an object of literary criticism. It is then true that a mature kind of biblical criticism is not restricted only to purely literary issues, but it ought to take into consideration a "definite ethical and theological standpoint."[88] Secondly, biblical studies may help to establish standards and criteria for literary judgment. In many of his essays, Eliot suggests implicitly that there exists a corpus of *foundational literature* [my term], which serves as a basis for critical considerations, a touchstone for literary quality, and a point of reference in the dense woods of literature. In "What Dante Means to Me," Eliot states: "One test of the great masters, of whom Shakespeare is one, is that the appreciation of their poetry is a lifetime's task, because at every stage of maturing – and that should be one's whole life – you are able to understand them better. Among these are Shakespeare, Dante, Homer and Virgil."[89] I believe that Eliot would have added biblical authors to this list, if only he had agreed that the Bible is literature. We need "great masters" to discover not only "what we like," but, first and foremost, "what we *ought* to like." By analogy, we need the Bible in order to stand on the ethical, aesthetic, and cognitive high ground. Comprehensive biblical exegesis may teach us "these criteria and standards" by which "everything that we read must be tested."[90]

Turning now to Eliot's views on the role which the critic plays in the process of evaluating literature, Eliot's principal postulate concerning objectivity is stated in the following words: "The critic, one would suppose, if he is to justify his existence, should endeavour to discipline his personal prejudices and cranks – tares to which we are all subject – and compose his differences with as many of his fellows as possible, in the common pursuit of true judgment."[91] The critic is then invited to make a double effort: first, he or she should ensure that the process of critical evaluation is carried out according to the highest possible standards of objectivity; secondly, criticism is not to be practised in isolation, because the presence and work of other critics create an adequate environment for the exchange of ideas and searching for truth. Eliot warns us that the critic's principal task should be "to study a work of art,"[92] and this task ought not to be confused with personal cre-

---

88   Eliot, "Religion and Literature," 388.
89   Eliot, "What Dante Means to Me," 127.
90   Eliot, "Religion and Literature," 399.
91   Eliot, "The Function of Criticism," 25.
92   Eliot, "Hamlet," 141.

ativity. The worst possible fault of the critic is to have a "mind which is naturally of the creative order, but which through some weakness in creative power exercises itself in criticism instead."[93] In this case, the critic, in place of mature judgments, produces highly subjective opinions concerning a work of art.

"Comparison and analysis," says Eliot with emphasis, "are the chief tools of the critic. ... They are not used with conspicuous success by many contemporary writers. You must know what to compare and what to analyse."[94] This remark sounds rather general, but if we have a close look at how Eliot makes use of these two tools in his critical practice, we may arrive at a number of interesting observations. First, in "The Metaphysical Poets," Eliot compares particular metaphysical poets to each other in order to find the characteristics of the style of each of them. By way of illustration, we learn by comparison that "Donne, and often Cowley, employ a device which is sometimes considered characteristically 'metaphysical'; the elaboration (contrasted with the condensation) of a figure of speech to the furthest stage to which ingenuity can carry it."[95] Secondly, he also compares the Metaphysicals to their successors in the eighteenth and nineteenth centuries, and shows how the "dissociation of sensibility" set in and has developed until modern times. In turn, using the tool of analysis, Eliot explains the meaning and formal features of chosen poems, and proves his chief thesis concerning the balance of thought and feeling within the poetic tradition of the Metaphysicals.

At this point of the discussion, it seems reasonable to digress a little, and define the term *modern reader*, which I constantly use in this book. By and large, my understanding of the term *modern reader* is similar to what Robert M. Fowler calls the *reader*. For Fowler, the term *reader* contains three elements: a *critical reader*, an *ideal reader*, who is the "abstracted total experience of my critical community," and an *implied reader* present in text.[96] Fowler further explains: "To be a critical reader means for me: (1) to affirm the enduring power of the Bible in my culture and in my own life; (2) and yet to remain open enough to ask any question and to risk any judgment, even if it should mean repudiating (1)."[97] Eliot's exemplary critic described above, who strives hard to be

---

93 Eliot, "Hamlet," 141.
94 Eliot, "The Function of Criticism," 32-33.
95 Eliot, "The Metaphysical Poets," 282.
96 Fowler, "Who Is the 'Reader,'" 21.
97 Fowler, "Who Is the 'Reader,'" 10. Fowler's discussion is based upon George Steiner's article "'Critic'/'Reader,'" in which Steiner writes: "The dualities [concerning

objective, who does not work in isolation, but subjects his or her work to other critics' assessment, and who uses comparison and analysis as the basic tools of criticism, corresponds, in Fowler's system, to the critical reader (the emphasis on the reader's ego) and the ideal reader (the emphasis on the reader's critical community). Fowler, however, in order to explain fully the complexity of the term *reader*, adds the category of *implied reader*, which appeared in literary theory only in the post-New-Critical period. In view of that, my *modern reader* should make an effort to become the implied reader, which I define as a role which the real reader has to play in order to penetrate fruitfully the world of narrative.[98] Then, the modern reader ought to be aware of the critical presuppositions of the reading community to which he or she belongs. Finally, the modern reader is invited to recognize, at least to some extent, the significance of Scripture for modern culture, but this recognition must not be blind, but critical and open to doubt.

Now, when we go back to Eliot, and reflect on his views regarding the role of the critic in the context of biblical criticism, we see that he provides us with useful tools against the excesses of postmodernism and deconstruction.[99] Deconstruction, even if it seemingly places emphasis on the text itself, encourages the reader to exercise all his creative powers in order to explore all possible inconsistencies and contradictions present in the text. As a result, the critic plays the role of the master, whereas the text is simply the slave. The idea of the "bespoke tailor,"[100] who, on the free market of ideas, sells biblical interpretations, which suit the needs of different interpretative communities, irrespective of whether these interpretations are "true" or not, is an extreme example of postmodern subjectivism. Eliot, on the contrary, suggests that the critical process should begin with an objective judgment of the critic, and then it should be verified in the light of the work of other critics, who are no less objective in their work, and this process would thus ensure a further degree of verification. Furthermore, certain examples of practising deconstruction immediately spring to mind when Eliot speaks about a "mind which is naturally of the creative order, but which through some weakness in creative power exercises itself in criti-

---

the critic and the reader] which I have cited, and many other implicit in the argument, can best be subsumed under one fundamental antithesis. ... The critic is judge and master of the text. The reader is servant to the text" (p. 449).
98   Cf. Ska, *Our Fathers Have Told Us*, 43.
99   I discuss postmodernism and deconstruction in chapter 4.
100 Exum and Clines, *The New Literary Criticism*, 87.

cism instead."[101] Their often academically serious attempts to discover the biblical text's significance for contemporary culture get bogged down in a stream of the critic's consciousness and loose associations.

By analogy, Eliot's remarks about comparison and analysis, which he regards as the chief tools of the critic, also have their counterpart in biblical criticism. While Eliot deals with the corpus of English and European poetry, we discuss the corpus of biblical writings, which was produced by different authors and redactors living in different historical periods. First, with regard to analysis, we are interested in the meaning of the biblical text, and its formal features. By and large, the historical-critical method provides us with tools suitable for establishing meaning. Narrative analysis, is, in turn, interested in the formal features of the text. Secondly, as regards comparison, it appears that at least some aspects of the critical proceedings based upon the comparison of authors writing within the same period or the same tradition are characteristic of canonical criticism. Canonical criticism, albeit not devoid of some theoretical deficiencies,[102] offers interesting insights into the theological dimension of Scripture.[103]

Finally, a careful study of Eliot's critical stance shows that he is not as stern a New Critic as some would like him to be, by which I mean that his critical theory does not remain solely within the text-centred type of approaches, but borrows certain elements typical of author-centred approaches. By way of illustration, Eliot introduces the concept of the "sense of fact," and gives its ostensive definition in "The Function of Criticism." He tells us about the *sine qua non* of every mature critic, which he regards as the "most important qualification which I have been able to find, which accounts for the peculiar importance of the criticism of practitioners," and whose "complete development means perhaps the very pinnacle of civilisation."[104] First, Eliot states

---

101 Eliot, "Hamlet," 141.
102 See e.g. Barr, *Holy Scripture*; Barr, "Childs' Introduction"; Barton, *Reading the Old Testament*, 77-103, 140-57.
103 Brevard S. Childs suggests what kind of insights canonical criticism may offer when he speaks in *Introduction to the Old Testament as Scripture*: "Because of the predominantly historical interest, the critical Introduction fails to understand the peculiar dynamics of Israel's religious literature, which has been greatly influenced by the process of establishing the scope of the literature, forming its particular shape, and structuring its inner relationships. The whole dimension of resonance within the Bible which issues from a collection with fixed parameters and which affects both the language and its imagery is lost by disregarding the peculiar function of canonical literature" (p. 40).
104 Eliot, "The Function of Criticism," 31.

that everybody "who is skilled in fact" can easily grasp the veracity of an interpretation which is, to some extent, intuitive and difficult to confirm by external evidence.[105] To put it another way, Eliot refers to his well-known idea of criticism as an intuitive discipline, and points to the necessary qualities that a good critic ought to have in order to practise the discipline in a responsible way. Secondly, and surprisingly, he states that the "sense of fact" involves the knowledge of the conditions, the settings, and the genesis of a literary work.[106] He thereby recommends all those aspects of a literary work in which traditional Romantic critics were seriously interested. He adds with conviction: "But *fact* cannot corrupt taste; it can at worst gratify one taste – a taste for history, let us say, or antiquities, or biography – under the illusion that it is assisting another. The real corrupters are those who supply opinion or fancy."[107]

The argument that when Eliot wrote these words in 1923, his critical views were still *in statu nascendi*, can be easily overturned. In "To Criticize the Critic" (1961), we read that

> no literary criticism can for a future generation excite more than curiosity, unless it continues to be of use in itself to future generations, to have intrinsic value out of its historical context. But if any part of it does have this timeless value, then we shall appreciate that value *all the more precisely* if we also attempt to put ourselves *at the point of view of the writer and his first readers* [my emphasis].[108]

As a result, we see that Eliot gives precedence to the works of literature which have timeless value, and that intrinsic value is discovered in their historical context. Yet, at the same time, he takes a bow towards that part of his audience which is attached to more traditional forms of criticism. Works of timeless value can be even better appreciated in the light of their historical origin. After all, what Eliot seeks is truth, and his critical theory is goal-oriented: "For the kinds of critical work which we have admitted, there is the possibility of cooperative activity, with the further possibility of arriving at something outside of ourselves, which may provisionally be called truth."[109]

The purpose of this book can also be called a quest for truth about biblical narratives and about the world to which they refer us. Certainly, the knowledge of truth comes with time and experience, and

---

105 See Eliot, "The Function of Criticism," 32.
106 See Eliot, "The Function of Criticism," 32.
107 See Eliot, "The Function of Criticism," 33.
108 Eliot, "To Criticize the Critic," 17.
109 Eliot, "The Function of Criticism," 34.

cannot be limited to a singular enterprise. Keeping this in mind, I would now like to make another step on that quest, and to establish the biblical text which will be analysed, but which will also serve as a window offering a "possibility of arriving at something outside of ourselves."

2. The Illustrative Pericope Gen 21:1-21

Arthur Conan Doyle is correct when he writes in *The Adventures of Sherlock Holmes*: "It is a capital mistake to theorise before one has data. Insensibly one begins to twist facts to suit theories, instead of theories to suit facts."[1] Since the temptation to theorize without applying the theory to the text is not uncommon among literary theoreticians, the purpose of this chapter will be to provide data for my hermeneutical theory.[2] The data will comprise the original text of Gen 21:1-21 and its translation, and both will be established with the tools of textual criticism.[3] The next step will be to discover the external and internal limits of the narrative under discussion. Interestingly, this question can be approached from two different angles. Most modern readers, who do not know the original biblical languages, and have no or very little knowledge of biblical historical criticism, tend to look at the text synchronically, and they read it in a way similar to the way they read novels. On the contrary, a majority of those who belong to the highly specialized biblical guild are usually more interested in diachronic problems concerning the text.

It is my strong conviction, however, that if we want to practise a style of biblical exegesis which is open to both *historical* and *literary* approaches,[4] and which is accessible to general readers, we should always

---

1   Doyle, *The Adventures of Sherlock Holmes*, 23.
2   Even the greatest hermeneutists, like Paul Ricoeur, do not always provide sufficient material to exemplify their statements. *Essays on Biblical Interpretation* are a typical case.
3   I am aware that Gen 21:1-21 as my model text is interpreted in a certain isolation from its context. An attempt to apply the hermeneutical model which will be introduced in the next chapter to the text, and, at the same time, to take into consideration its context would exceed the limits of this book. However, when I discuss Gen 21:1-21 in the light of the historical-critical method, I pay attention to the pericope's broader context.
4   When I use the distinction between the *historical* and *literary* methods of biblical interpretation, I mean the approaches which concentrate on the author, in the first case, or on the text or the reader, in the second. This distinction parallels, to some extent, the distinction between the *diachronic* and *synchronic* modes of interpretation. I am well aware that *historical* approaches are also *literary* in the general sense of the

proceed from a synchronic to a diachronic perspective rather than the other way round. This direction seems more natural for those readers who would like to be initiated into the mysteries of modern exegesis, but who are sometimes put off by its technical jargon. Moreover, if we begin with a synchronic approach to the text, we can more easily find a rationale for asking historical questions because of the text's discrepancies. As Barton aptly observes, the starting point for the founders of the historical method was a synchronic reading of the biblical text. As the historical method has developed, many of its devotees have forgotten about its roots, yet they can and should be kept in mind.[5] Perhaps the partial inability of biblical scholarship to influence modern culture stems from regarding synchronic approaches as the remote goal of our proceedings rather than their starting point. Jacques Berlinerblau asks rhetorically: "God bless the microspecialist who scrutinizes eastern Aramaisms in The Wisdom of Ben Sira. But should the entire field be cast in his or her image? Can philology and archaeology alone illuminate a document whose trajectory runs across the entire breadth of Occidental civilization?"[6] I believe that neither synchronic nor diachronic approaches alone are able to illuminate fully the richness of Scripture. Both are needed if our interpretive efforts are to be successful.[7] Yet, given the somewhat peripheral place of biblical scholarship on the map of general scholarship, it appears sensible to invite modern readers to become part of the guild by talking to them in a language which is accessible, and such is, to a great extent, the language of synchronic analysis. Apart from the reasons presented above, the "synchronic to diachronic" mode of proceeding is characteristic of this book. In chapter 3,

---

word because they deal with literary texts, and use literary concepts. Similarly, *literary* approaches may sometimes, although incidentally, raise questions of a purely *historical* nature.

5   See Barton, *Reading the Old Testament*, 20-26.
6   Berlinerblau, "What's Wrong," n.p.
7   The following remark by Alter is worth quoting: "I do not mean to suggest that the historical-philological and the literary approaches to the Bible are mutually contradictory undertakings. On the contrary, the exacting deployment of broad learning in the JPS commentaries demonstrates how much literary students of the Bible can refine their own analysis by attending to what the cumulative enterprise of scholarship has discovered about … the possibilities of sedimentation and sutures in the text. Many of the historical scholars, for their part, still need to understand better that a literary text … is more than the broken pieces of a potsherd in an archaeological find to be fitted together like a jigsaw puzzle" (*The World of Biblical Literature*, 152).

I ask questions about the text's ability to communicate the aspects of truth, beauty, and goodness, and only then do I proceed to various synchronic and diachronic approaches in order to show that all of them contribute to the elucidation of the text. In view of that, in the present chapter, I shall first discuss the narrative delimitation of Gen 21:1-21 (from a synchronic perspective), and then I shall deal with the historical literary sources of the pericope (from a diachronic perspective). Finally, since many interesting problems arise when both perspectives are introduced, I will examine the interrelationship between the narrative and source-critical approaches.

2.1. The Original Text and a Modern Translation

In order to provide a modern translation of Gen 21:1-21, I should establish the original text of the pericope, and compare it to some of its ancient versions and translations. In doing this, I will try to bridge the historical, cultural, and linguistic gap existing between the ancient Hebrew world, in which the original pericope Gen 21:1-21 is rooted, and our modern world with the English language as one of its important modes of linguistic expression.[8] When I speak of the *original* text, I mean, of course, a version of the text which is as close as possible to the manuscript written by an author or composed by a redactor. However, I am aware of the elusive nature of such an enterprise. As Gerard Norton sums up: "When we deal with the biblical text, we must recognise that we do not yet have the original text of the biblical author and in many cases we do not know how this relates to the earliest attainable text in the original languages."[9]

Following the general opinion of specialists on Hebrew Bible textcritical problems, such as J. Weingreen among others, I shall adopt as the basis for my translation the Masoretic Text (MT), established in the ninth and early tenth century A.D. by the Ben Asher family from Galilee, and preserved in the Leningrad Codex B 19A, which is dated to the beginning of the eleventh century.[10] A modern critical edition of the

---

8   Inevitably, before I can debate the limits of the narrative under discussion, I must tentatively assume that the narrative begins in v. 1 and ends in v. 21. Schleiermacher's idea of the hermeneutical circle applies here (see e.g. Thiselton, *New Horizons*, 221).
9   Norton, "The Old Testament Words of God," 29; see also Barton, "Introduction to the Old Testament," *OBC*, 7.
10 See Brown, Johnson, and O'Connell, "Texts and Versions," *NJBC*, 1090. Weingreen

Leningrad Codex has been published as the *Biblia Hebraica Stuttgartensia* (*BHS*), and has become the "best available source for a dependable text combined with an indication of the variants suggested by textual criticism."[11] The adoption of the MT as a basis for translation seems to be justified in the light of the following scholarly opinion:

> [There are] two fundamental characteristics of the MT. First, it preserves one of several recensions that emerged in the post-exilic era. Second, it is a composite text consisting of (a) an original consonantal text, often originally written without *matres lectiones* [sic], (b) the vowel letters, (c) the Masoretic additions of the vowel points, and (d) the accentual or cantillation marks. ... A complex body of evidence indicates that the MT could not, in any serious or systematic way, represent a reconstruction or faking of the data. ... Our stance toward the MT is based on cautious confidence.[12]

Therefore, in this subchapter, I will present the MT of Gen 21:1-21, together with the linguistic observations provided by its *Masora parva* (Mp) and *Masora magna* (Mm), as well as by the critical apparatus of the *BHS*. In order to translate the Aramaic remarks of the Mp, I shall use the textbooks by R. Wonnenberger and P. H. Kelley. The listings of the Mm will be quoted after the edition prepared by G. E. Weil. As regards the ancient versions of Gen 21:1-21, I shall use the text of the Samaritan Pentateuch (A. F. von Gall's edition), the *Targum Onkelos* (A. Sperber's edition), the Septuagint (J. W. Wevers's edition), as well as the Vulgate (R. Weber's edition). I shall not, however, discuss the critical apparatus of those editions because that would make the discussion too long and complicated. Moreover, I will examine the text of those ancient versions only in the case when they differ significantly from the MT, or when they are directly relevant to the translation.

In producing my own translation, I would like to find a balance between fidelity to the text and accessibility of the translation to modern readers. Hence what the NRSV translators say about their own work reflects also the goal of my translatorial efforts: "The Committee has followed the maxim, 'As literal as possible, as free as necessary.' As a consequence, the NRSV remains essentially a literal translation. Paraphrastic renderings have been adopted only sparingly, and then chiefly to compensate for a deficiency in the English language."[13] Furthermore,

---

defines the role of the textual critic: to establish "the actual wording of the text of the Hebrew Bible, as it has come down to us in the authorized Jewish recension known as the Masoretic" (*Introduction to the Critical Study*, 1).
11 Brown, Johnson, and O'Connell, "Texts and Versions," *NJBC*, 1091.
12 Waltke and O'Connor, *Introduction*, 3, 22-28.
13 NRSV, xvii.

even though the Hebrew text is indispensable for any good exegetical analysis, the importance of a modern translation should not be underestimated. After all, a modern translation is the type of the biblical text most often encountered by both contemporary readers of and listeners to the Bible. Northrop Frye observes:

> In contrast, while Christian scholarship is naturally no less aware of the importance of the language, Christianity as a religion has been from the beginning dependent on translation. The New Testament was written in a *koine* Greek unlikely to have been the native language of its authors, and, whatever the degree of familiarity of those authors with Hebrew, they tended to make more use of the Septuagint Greek translation in referring to the Old Testament.[14]

The discussion of each verse of Gen 21:1-21 is presented according to the following pattern:

    a. the Masoretic Text (MT)
    b. the Samaritan Pentateuch (SP)
    c. the *Targum Onkelos* (TO)
    d. the Septuagint (LXX)
    e. the Vulgate (Vg)
    f. remarks of the *Masorah parva* (Mp), *Masorah magna* (Mm), and the critical apparatus of the *BHS*
    g. my English translation of the pericope (in bold print)
    h. remarks concerning the translation, and the discussion of exegetical cruces, where appropriate[15]

21:1 וַיהוָה פָּקַד אֶת־שָׂרָה כַּאֲשֶׁר אָמָר וַיַּעַשׂ יְהוָה לְשָׂרָה כַּאֲשֶׁר דִּבֵּר׃

21:1 ויהוה פקד את שרה כאשר אמר ויעש יהוה לשרה כאשר דבר׃

21:1 ויוי דכיר ית שרה כמא דאמר ועבד יוי לשרה כמא דמליל׃

21:1 καὶ κύριος ἐπεσκέψατο τὴν Σαρραν καθὰ εἶπεν καὶ ἐποίησεν κύριος τῇ Σαρρα καθὰ ἐλάλησεν

21:1 visitavit autem Dominus Sarram sicut promiserat et implevit quae locutus est

The Mp notes that the form וַיהוָה is found 22 times in the Pentateuch, whilst the verb אָמָר (with *qamets* in both syllables) is found 3 times in

---

14 Frye, *The Great Code*, 3.
15 There are a number of minor textual and interpretive difficulties in the narrative which I will not discuss because they are not relevant to the main subject of this book. Some of them, however, will be mentioned in chapter 2 ("The Literary Sources of the Pericope").

the Hebrew Bible. The Mm lists these places: Gen 18:17, 21:1, and Exod 18:24.

21:1 The Lord visited Sarah according to what he had said, and he did to Sarah as he had promised.

The conjunction ו in ויהוה plays a disjunctive role and indicates the beginning of a new episode.[16] The verb פקד may have many possible meanings. Apart from its basic idea of "visiting," there are such meanings as "paying attention to," "attending," "seeking," and "visiting graciously."[17] The translation of the TO (דכיר) adds, in turn, such meanings as "eingedenk sein" ("to be mindful of"), and "erwähnen" ("to mention").[18]

The lexicon by Köhler and Baumgartner lists a whole range of possible denotations of the adverb כאשר. They are: "as," "according as," "the more ... the more ...," "because," "as though," "when," and "after."[19] When we take into account the context, the best rendition is "according as" or "according to." As regards the Piel verb דבר, I have decided to translate it as "he promised," following Köhler and Baumgartner,[20] as well as the context of the verse.

21:2 וַתַּהַר וַתֵּלֶד שָׂרָה לְאַבְרָהָם בֵּן לִזְקֻנָיו לַמּוֹעֵד אֲשֶׁר־דִּבֶּר אֹתוֹ אֱלֹהִים׃

21:2 ותהר ותלד שרה לאברהם בן לזקניו למועד אשר דבר אתו אלהים׃

21:2 ועדיאת וילידת שרה לאברהם בר לסיבתוהי לזמנא דמליל יתיה יוי׃

21:2 καὶ συλλαβοῦσα ἔτεκεν Σαρρα τῷ Αβρααμ υἱὸν εἰς τὸ γῆρας εἰς τὸν καιρόν καθὰ ἐλάλησεν αὐτῷ κύριος

21:2 concepitque et peperit filium in senectute sua tempore quo praedixerat ei Deus

The Mp comments that the form לִזְקֻנָיו appears twice and is defective (without ו). As regards the ה in the particle אֹתוֹ, the Mp notes: "There

---

16 See Waltke and O'Connor, *Introduction*, 650-52.
17 BDB, 823.
18 ANH, 98.
19 HALOT 2:455.
20 HALOT 1:210.

are 9 places [where ת] has *rafé*, and all occurrences in Ezekiel are written like this." The Mm lists those 9 places: Gen 21:2, Num 26:3, 1 Kgs 22:24, 2 Chr 18:23, Jer 1:16, 4:12, 5:5, 12:1, 35:2. Joüon and Muraoka explain: "In order to indicate the fricative sound, a horizontal stroke called *rafé* is written over the letter concerned; that, at any rate, is how it is marked in the manuscripts. But in the printed editions of the Bible, the absence of *dagesh* is a sufficient indication that the consonant is *rafé*."[21] The critical apparatus states that two Hebrew manuscripts as well as the LXX read כאשר־דבר instead of אשר־דבר.

21:2 Sarah conceived and bore Abraham a son in her husband's old age. This happened at the appointed time promised to Abraham by God.

I have translated the form לזקניו (literally, "to his old age") as "her husband's old age" in order to avoid equivocation caused by "his" (may be related to "a son"). I have also decided to render v. 2 as two independent clauses, which emphasizes two main ideas contained in the verse: birth and the fulfilment of promises. Like in v. 1, I rendered the verb דבר as "he promised." The problem resulting from reading כאשר־דבר instead of אשר־דבר is solved by translating the phrase as "at the appointed time promised."

21:3 וַיִּקְרָא אַבְרָהָם אֶת־שֶׁם־בְּנוֹ הַנּוֹלַד־לוֹ אֲשֶׁר־יָלְדָה־לּוֹ שָׂרָה יִצְחָק׃
21:3 ויקרא אברהם את שם בנו הנולד לו אשר ילדה לו שרה יצחק׃
21:3 וקרא אברהם ית שם בריה דאתיליד ליה דילידת ליה שרה יצחק׃
21:3 καὶ ἐκάλεσεν Ἀβρααμ τὸ ὄνομα τοῦ υἱοῦ αὐτοῦ τοῦ γενομένου αὐτῷ ὃν ἔτεκεν αὐτῷ Σαρρα Ισαακ
21:3 vocavitque Abraham nomen filii sui quem genuit ei Sarra Isaac

We have only one remark of the Mp concerning this verse: the noun שֶׁם (vocalized with *segol*) occurs 6 times. The Mm lists the occurrences: Gen 16:15, 21:3, 1 Sam 8:2, 1 Kgs 16:24, Ezek 39:16, Prov 30:4.

21:3 Abraham gave the name Isaac to his newborn son, whom Sarah bore him.

---

21 *GBH*, 30.

I have decided to render the double syntactical structure of the verse as "newborn ... whom Sarah bore him" in order to emphasize the idea of "giving birth." It is worth noting that the Vg simplifies the syntactical structure of the verse.

21:4 וַיָּ֤מָל אַבְרָהָם֙ אֶת־יִצְחָ֣ק בְּנ֔וֹ בֶּן־שְׁמֹנַ֖ת יָמִ֑ים כַּאֲשֶׁ֛ר צִוָּ֥ה אֹת֖וֹ אֱלֹהִֽים׃
21:4 וימל אברהם את יצחק בנו בן שמנת ימים כאשר צוה אתו אלהים:
21:4 וגזר אברהם ית יצחק בריה בר תמניה יומין כמא דפקיד יתיה יוי:
21:4 περιέτεμεν δὲ Αβρααμ τὸν Ισαακ τῇ ὀγδόῃ ἡμέρᾳ καθὰ ἐνετείλατο αὐτῷ ὁ θεός
21:4 et circumcidit eum octavo die sicut praeceperat ei Deus

There are two remarks of the Mp concerning v. 4. Firstly, all but one occurrences of the cardinal number שְׁמֹנַת are defective (without ו). The only exception is 1 Chr 29:7. Secondly, according to the Mm the phrase צִוָּה אֹתוֹ אֱלֹהִים occurs 3 times: Gen 6:22, 7:16, 21:4. Interestingly, the Vg omits the proper names.

21:4 Abraham circumcised his son Isaac when the child was eight days old, as God ordered him to do.

I have added "to do" at the end of the verse to achieve a balance between the two halves of the verse, and to improve its rhythm. Like in v. 2, reading "the child" instead of "he" helps to avoid ambiguity.

21:5 וְאַבְרָהָ֖ם בֶּן־מְאַ֣ת שָׁנָ֑ה בְּהִוָּ֣לֶד ל֔וֹ אֵ֖ת יִצְחָ֥ק בְּנֽוֹ׃
21:5 ואברהם בן מאת שנה בהולד לו את יצחק בנו:
21:5 ואברהם בר מאה שנין כד איתיליד ליה ית יצחק בריה:
21:5 Αβρααμ δὲ ἦν ἐτῶν ἑκατὸν ἡνίκα ἐγένετο αὐτῷ Ισαακ ὁ υἱὸς αὐτοῦ
21:5 cum centum esset annorum hac quippe aetate patris natus est Isaac

21:5 Abraham was a hundred years old when his son Isaac was born to him.

21:6 וַתֹּ֣אמֶר שָׂרָ֔ה צְחֹ֕ק עָ֥שָׂה לִ֖י אֱלֹהִ֑ים כָּל־הַשֹּׁמֵ֖עַ יִֽצְחַק־לִֽי׃
21:6 ותאמר שרה צחק עשה לי אלהים כל השמע יצחק לי:
21:6 ואמרת שרה חדוא עבד לי יוי כל דשמע יחדי לי:

21:6 εἶπεν δὲ Σαρρα γέλωτά μοι ἐποίησεν κύριος ὃς γὰρ ἂν ἀκούσῃ συγχαρεῖταί μοι
21:6 dixitque Sarra risum fecit mihi Deus quicumque audierit conridebit mihi

According to the Mp, the noun צְחֹק is a *hapax legomenon*, and is defective, i.e. without an expected ו. The phrase לִי אֱלֹהִים occurs 11 times and is listed in the Mm: Gen 4:25, 21:6, 48:9, Judg 1:7, 1 Sam 22:3, 2 Sam 3:35, 19:14, 1 Kgs 2:23, 20:10, 2 Kgs 6:31, Ps 51:12. The verb יִצְחַק is also a *hapax legomenon* (vocalized in this way).

21:6 Sarah said: "God made me laugh, and everybody who hears about it will rejoice with me."

I have decided to render the Semitic phrase "God made laughter for me" as "God made me laugh." Although the second half of v. 6 should be translated literally "will laugh concerning me,"[22] the context of the verse and the LXX allow us to translate "will rejoice with me" without a violation of the sense, and to avoid the translation "will laugh at me," which would be against the context.

21:7 וַתֹּאמֶר מִי מִלֵּל לְאַבְרָהָם הֵינִיקָה בָנִים שָׂרָה כִּי־יָלַדְתִּי בֵן לִזְקֻנָיו׃
21:7 ותאמר מי מלל לאברהם היניקה בנים שרה כי ילדתי לו בן לזקניו:
21:7 ואמרת מהימן דאמר לאברהם וקיים דתוניק בנין שרה ארי ילידית בר לסיבתוהי:
21:7 καὶ εἶπεν τίς ἀναγγελεῖ τῷ Αβρααμ ὅτι θηλάζει παιδίον Σαρρα ὅτι ἔτεκον υἱὸν ἐν τῷ γήρει μου
21:7 rursumque ait quis auditurum crederet Abraham quod Sarra lactaret filium quem peperit ei iam seni

The Mp comments that the verb מִלֵּל has two occurrences: once it is written *plene* and once it is defective. The form לִזְקֻנָיו also occurs twice, and both occurrences are defective. The critical apparatus informs us that the SP as well as the *Targum Pseudo-Jonathan* add the preposition לו after כי־ילדתי.

---

22 BDB, 850.

21:7 "Who would have said to Abraham that Sarah would nurse children? Nevertheless, I have borne a son in Abraham's old age."

I have rendered the phrase מִי מִלֵּל as "who would have said," following the observation of grammarians that the verb מלל is "qatal in surprised question."[23] In my translation, I follow the MT, and I do not add the preposition לוֹ after כִּי־יָלַדְתִּי. The TO does not make this emendation either and says simply: ארי ילידית בר. The context of the first half of v. 7 suggests that the subordinating conjunction כִּי may be translated as "nevertheless," "yet," or "still." It should be also noted that the LXX changes the subject of "old age" and reads ἐν τῷ γήρει μου.

21:8 וַיִּגְדַּל הַיֶּלֶד וַיִּגָּמַל וַיַּעַשׂ אַבְרָהָם מִשְׁתֶּה גָדוֹל בְּיוֹם הִגָּמֵל אֶת־יִצְחָק׃

21:8 ויגדל הילד ויגמל ויעש אברהם משתה גדול ביום הגמל את יצחק בנו:

21:8 ורבא רביא ואתחסיל ועבד אברהם משתיא רבא ביומא דאתחסיל יצחק:

21:8 καὶ ηὐξήθη τὸ παιδίον καὶ ἀπεγαλακτίσθη καὶ ἐποίησεν Αβρααμ δοχὴν μεγάλην ᾗ ἡμέρᾳ ἀπεγαλακτίσθη Ισαακ ὁ υἱὸς αὐτοῦ

21:8 crevit igitur puer et ablactatus est fecitque Abraham grande convivium in die ablactationis eius

The Mp notes that the verb וַיִּגָּמַל is a *hapax legomenon*, whereas the phrase מִשְׁתֶּה גָדוֹל occurs twice: Gen 21:8 and Esth 2:18.

21:8 The child grew up and was weaned, and Abraham gave a grand banquet on the day when Isaac was weaned.

21:9 וַתֵּרֶא שָׂרָה אֶת־בֶּן־הָגָר הַמִּצְרִית אֲשֶׁר־יָלְדָה לְאַבְרָהָם מְצַחֵק׃

21:9 ותרא שרה את בן הגר המצרית אשר ילדה לאברהם מצחק:

21:9 וחזת שרה ית בר הגר מצריתא דילידת לאברהם מחאיך:

21:9 ἰδοῦσα δὲ Σαρρα τὸν υἱὸν Αγαρ τῆς Αἰγυπτίας ὃς ἐγένετο τῷ Αβρααμ παίζοντα μετὰ Ισαακ τοῦ υἱοῦ αὐτῆς

21:9 cumque vidisset Sarra filium Agar Aegyptiae ludentem dixit ad Abraham

---

23   *GBH*, 364; *GKC*, 313, 476.

The critical apparatus reminds us that the LXX adds the phrase μετὰ Ισαακ τοῦ υἱοῦ αὐτῆς at the end of the verse.

21:9 Sarah noticed that the son of Hagar the Egyptian, whom she bore to Abraham, was playing with her son Isaac.

The main bone of contention in Gen 21:1-21 is the meaning of v. 9, or, strictly speaking, the last word in the verse, which is, from a grammatical point of view, the participle active Piel of the verb צחק. In other words, the question is whether Ishmael, as portrayed in v. 9, is an innocent victim playing with his younger brother, or a vile brat humiliating Isaac.[24]

Westermann and Driver provide us with two opposite ways of translating v. 9. Westermann reads: "But when Sarah saw the son of Hagar the Egyptian, whom she had borne to Abraham, playing with her son Isaac," and notes that he adds the phrase "with her son Isaac" after the LXX, the Vg, and the majority of exegetes, "as both the sense and the rhythm require."[25] Driver, on the contrary, translates: "And Sarah saw the son of Hagar the Egyptian, which she had borne unto Abraham, mocking."[26] The former rendering suggests either neutral or positive moral behaviour of Isaac, and makes Sarah's reaction less justified. In the latter case, it is Ishmael whose vile conduct provokes Sarah's anger.[27] Von Rad, Speiser, and Westermann are in favour of rendering מצחק as "playing." Von Rad admits that "whether the verb (ṣāḥaq, again an allusion to the name Isaac) here means simply 'playing' or 'behaving wantonly with someone' can no longer be decided."[28] Yet he prefers to translate the participle as "playing" because "the picture of the two boys playing with each other on an equal footing is quite sufficient to bring the jealous mother to a firm conclusion: Ishmael must go!"[29] Speiser argues that "'mocking' would require the preposition b- to designate the object," and that "there is nothing in the

---

[24] Ishmael is not mentioned by name in Gen 21:1-21. However, I use his name here to avoid ambiguity.
[25] Westermann, *Genesis 12-36*, 336-37, 39.
[26] Driver, *The Book of Genesis*, 210-11.
[27] Driver's interpretation is supported by some ancient commentaries. Ephrem the Syrian (*Commentary on Genesis* 18.1) suggests that Ishmael mocked Isaac. An anonymous contributor to *Catena on Genesis* 3.1206 says that Ishmael actually struck his brother. Chrysostom in *Homilies on Genesis* 46.2 criticizes Ishmael's brashness (quoted after Sheridan, *Genesis 12-50*, 94-95).
[28] Von Rad, *Genesis*, 227.
[29] Von Rad, *Genesis*, 227.

text to suggest that he [Ishmael] was abusing him [Isaac], a motive deduced by many troubled readers in their effort to account for Sarah's anger."³⁰ Speiser's remark means that rendering מצחק as "mocking" is reading our own ideas into the text. The reader assumes that Sarah is a paragon of virtue, and, as a result, evil intentions must be ascribed to Ishmael.

In Westermann's commentary, we are given a very strong argument in favour of "playing." He states that there is no need to seek for a special justification of Sarah's reaction because her response is in accordance with the rules of ancient patriarchal society. Westermann writes convincingly:

> Hagar's son, "whom she had borne to Abraham," threatens both her son's and her own future, even though he is also Abraham's son. And so he must go. ... To censure Sarah's demand from the point of view of individual ethic or our own religious attitude is to fail to see that Sarah is engaged in a struggle for her own very existence; in later forms of society such struggles are transferred to the social or political sphere, while here they take place within the family circle.³¹

However, Westermann mentions that the Letter to the Galatians interprets Gen 21:9 negatively, and this remains as a strong argument against translating מצחק as "playing."³² Galatians 4:29 reads: "But as at that time he who was born according to the flesh persecuted him who was born according to the Spirit, so it is now." However, we do not know whether St Paul's allegorical interpretation of Gen 21:9 was common among his contemporaries, or whether he invented this explanation to present his teaching on the Law in a lucid and convincing manner. Driver suggests that St Paul may have been influenced by some contemporary Jewish Haggadahs, which portrayed Ishmael in an unfavourable light.³³ In any case, Brueggemann is right in saying in his commentary: "It is clear that both pairs, Hagar-Ishmael and Sarah-Isaac have now become theological types. Powerful theological meanings are assigned to them that run well beyond the claims of this text."³⁴

---

30 Speiser, *Genesis*, 155.
31 Westermann, *Genesis 12-36*, 339.
32 See Westermann, *Genesis 12-36*, 339.
33 Driver, *The Book of Genesis*, 210 n. 1.
34 Brueggemann, *Genesis*, 184. According to Origen (*Homilies on Genesis* 7.2, 3), St Paul used this passage to present his theological ideas. The two children simply *played* with each other, yet the passage can also be understood spiritually as depicting the opposition between the spirit represented by Isaac and the flesh symbolized by Ishmael (after Sheridan, *Genesis 12-50*, 92-94).

Gunkel takes the same stand on the matter, and translates: "Nun sah Sarah, wie der Sohn der Ägypterin Hagar, den sie Abraham geboren hatte, 'mit ihrem Sohn Isaaq' spielte."[35] In turn, Skinner remarks: "It is the spectacle of the two young children playing together, innocent of social distinctions, that excites Sarah's maternal jealousy and prompts her cruel demand."[36] De Vaux, Vawter, and Sarna translate respectively: "qui jouait avec son fils Isaac,"[37] "playing with her son Isaac,"[38] and "playing"[39] (without supplementing the participle with an object); but Sarna reminds us of the fact that rabbinic interpretations were seldom in favour of Ishmael. "One rabbinic interpretation of Hebrew metsaḥek," writes Sarna, "has Ishmael ridiculing the fuss made of Isaac and asserting his own claim to first-born status with its right to a double share of the paternal estate."[40]

On the other hand, Coats proposes a certain shift in meaning when he translates the participle as "laughing" (without an object), and states: "Now the wordplay, so crucial for the whole story, sets out the weight of the conflict. It does not imply that Ishmael has done something amiss with Isaac. It suggests, to the contrary, that Sarah saw Ishmael məṣaḥēq, playing the role of Isaac. Indeed, the act implies some disdain on Ishmael's part, perhaps an equivalent to the curse of Hagar in 16:4."[41] Hamilton suggests another way of understanding the difficult phrase. He assumes that the action described in v. 9 happened in the context of Isaac's weaning. "Sarah was riled," argues Hamilton, "by Ishmael enjoying himself and playing happily on an occasion when the spotlight should be exclusively on her son."[42] Finally, among those who argue for Ishmael's guilt, we have Alter, who translates the participle as "laughing," and enumerates three ways of understanding Ishmael's behaviour: sexual dalliance, mocking laughter, or playing the role of Isaac (in other words, "Isaac-ing-it").[43] Moving on now to those who render מצחק as "mocking," we must again mention Driver, who translates the contentious participle in this way, yet admits that such a translation is doubtful.[44] Apart from Driver, we have Wenham, who invokes

---

35 Gunkel, *Genesis: übersetzt und erklärt*, 228.
36 Skinner, *A Critical and Exegetical Commentary*, 322.
37 De Vaux, *La Genèse*, 103.
38 Vawter, *On Genesis*, 247.
39 Sarna, *Genesis*, 146.
40 Sarna, *Genesis*, 146.
41 Coats, *Genesis*, 153.
42 Hamilton, *The Book of Genesis*, 79.
43 Alter, *Genesis*, 98.
44 See Driver, *The Book of Genesis*, 210-11.

the well-established tradition of the negative interpretation of Ishmael's behaviour by Jewish exegetes, Calvin, and Jacob.[45] According to Wenham, among different possible ways of explaining Ishmael's behaviour, "more likely is the view that Ishmael was making fun of Isaac's status or the circumstances of his birth, which were a source of joyous laughter to Sarah."[46]

I believe that the attempt to explain Sarah's anger through recourse to negative ways of understanding the participle מְצַחֵק is not sufficiently justified. The fundamental procedure applied by historical-critical exegetes should be an analysis of the historical reality to which the text refers. Westermann does such an analysis, and he proves that Sarah's reaction should be regarded as normal, given the circumstances of ancient patriarchal culture. Thus, if this basic explanation suffices to solve the problem, why should we seek other more complicated and less probable theories? Moreover, a comparison between the MT of Gen 21:9 and other ancient versions and translations hardly supports the arguments of those who opt for evil intentions of Ishmael. The TO is in favour of the "positive" translation. Dalman proposes the meanings "lachen" and "scherzen" for the root חוך (the participle is מְחָאִיךְ).[47] Both meanings can hardly signify a contemptuous action. As far as the LXX and the Vg are concerned, both participles (παίζοντα and *ludentem*) may be, as in Hebrew, translated in two ways: positive and negative. To sum up, the incident told in v. 9 was, in all probability, a normal play between two children, which may have contained banter, but was a positive or neutral action. Ishmael was not a spoilt brat. Sarah was not a cruel villain either.

Although the MT does not read "with her son Isaac," I have added this phrase to my translation, after the LXX, and because of the context. Without this addition the translation would sound awkward and partially incomprehensible.

21:10 וַתֹּאמֶר לְאַבְרָהָם גָּרֵשׁ הָאָמָה הַזֹּאת וְאֶת־בְּנָהּ כִּי לֹא יִירַשׁ בֶּן־הָאָמָה הַזֹּאת עִם־בְּנִי עִם־יִצְחָק׃
21:10 ותאמר לאברהם גרש את האמה הזאת ואת בנה כי לא יירש בן האמה הזאת עם בני עם יצחק׃

---

45   See Wenham, *Genesis 16-50*, 82.
46   Wenham, *Genesis 16-50*, 82.
47   *ANH*, 139.

21:10 ואמרת לאברהם תריך אמתא הדא וית ברה ארי לא יירת בר אמתא הדא עם ברי עם יצחק:
21:10 καὶ εἶπεν τῷ Αβρααμ ἔκβαλε τὴν παιδίσκην ταύτην καὶ τὸν υἱὸν αὐτῆς οὐ γὰρ κληρονομήσει ὁ υἱὸς τῆς παιδίσκης ταύτης μετὰ τοῦ υἱοῦ μου Ισαακ
21:10 eice ancillam hanc et filium eius non enim erit heres filius ancillae cum filio meo Isaac

There are 3 occurrences of the imperative גָּרֵשׁ: Gen 21:10, Exod 11:1, Prov 22:10. The phrase וְאֶת־בְּנָהּ occurs twice: Gen 21:10 and 1 Kgs 3:20. According to the critical apparatus, both the SP and the Targum Pseudo-Jonathan add את before האמה in the first half of the verse.

21:10 So she said to Abraham: "Expel this slave woman and her son because the son of this slave woman shall not share inheritance with my son Isaac."

The English construction "shall not share" underlines the determination of the speaker.

21:11 וַיֵּרַע הַדָּבָר מְאֹד בְּעֵינֵי אַבְרָהָם עַל אוֹדֹת בְּנוֹ:
21:11 וירע הדבר מאד בעיני אברהם על אודת בנו:
21:11 ובאיש פתגמא לחדא בעיני אברהם על עיסק בריה:
21:11 σκληρὸν δὲ ἐφάνη τὸ ῥῆμα σφόδρα ἐναντίον Αβρααμ περὶ τοῦ υἱοῦ αὐτοῦ
21:11 dure accepit hoc Abraham pro filio suo

The Mp comments that the form בְּעֵינֵי occurs 33 times in the Pentateuch, while the plural noun אוֹדֹת has 3 occurrences and all of them are defective, i.e. without an expected ו.

21:11 Abraham found these words evil on account of his son.

21:12 וַיֹּאמֶר אֱלֹהִים אֶל־אַבְרָהָם אַל־יֵרַע בְּעֵינֶיךָ עַל־הַנַּעַר וְעַל־אֲמָתֶךָ כֹּל אֲשֶׁר תֹּאמַר אֵלֶיךָ שָׂרָה שְׁמַע בְּקֹלָהּ כִּי בְיִצְחָק יִקָּרֵא לְךָ זָרַע:
21:12 ויאמר אלהים אל אברהם אל ירע בעיניך על הנער ועל אמתך כל אשר תאמר אליך שרה שמע בקולה כי ביצחק יקרא לך זרע:
21:12 ואמר יוי לאברהם לא יבאש בעינך על עולימא ועל אמתך כל דתימר לך שרה קביל מינה ארי ביצחק יתקרון לך בנין:

21:12 εἶπεν δὲ ὁ θεὸς τῷ Αβρααμ μὴ σκληρὸν ἔστω τὸ ῥῆμα ἐναντίον σου περὶ τοῦ παιδίου καὶ περὶ τῆς παιδίσκης πάντα ὅσα ἐὰν εἴπῃ σοι Σαρρα ἄκουε τῆς φωνῆς αὐτῆς ὅτι ἐν Ισαακ κληθήσεταί σοι σπέρμα
21:12 cui dixit Deus non tibi videatur asperum super puero et super ancilla tua omnia quae dixerit tibi Sarra audi vocem eius quia in Isaac vocabitur tibi semen

The Mp makes 5 remarks on Gen 21:12. First, the phrase וַיֹּאמֶר אֱלֹהִים occurs 25 times in the Hebrew Bible: Gen 1:3, 1:6, 1:9, 1:11, 1:14, 1:20, 1:24, 1:26, 1:29, 6:13, 9:8, 9:12, 9:17, 17:9, 17:15, 17:19, 21:12, 35:1, 46:2, Exod 3:14, Num 22:12, 1 Kgs 3:5, 3:11, Jonah 4:9, 2 Chr 1:11. Secondly, the form בְּעֵינֶיךָ occurs 66 times. Thirdly, the phrase עַל־הַנַּעַר is a *hapax legomenon*. Fourthly, the form בְּקֹלָה is a defective *hapax legomenon* (without ו). Finally, the verb יִקָּרֵא occurs 21 times: Gen 2:23, 17:5, 21:12, 35:10, Num 23:3, Deut 3:13, 22:6, 1 Sam 9:9, Isa 1:26, 4:1, 14:20, 31:4, 32:5, 35:8, 54:5, 56:7, 62:4, 62:12, Jer 19:6, Prov 16:21, Esth 4:11.

21:12 But God said to Abraham: "Do not regard as evil the matter concerning the boy and your slave woman. Grant Sarah whatever she asks you, since it is through Isaac that your descendants will be named."

In v. 12, God challenges Abraham's opinion concerning Sarah's reaction, so the co-ordinating conjunction ו may be rendered as "but."

21:13 וְגַם אֶת־בֶּן־הָאָמָה לְגוֹי אֲשִׂימֶנּוּ כִּי זַרְעֲךָ הוּא׃
21:13 וגם את בן האמה הזאת לגוי גדול אשימנו כי זרעך הוא׃
21:13 ואף ית בר אמתא לעמא אשויניה ארי ברך הוא׃
21:13 καὶ τὸν υἱὸν δὲ τῆς παιδίσκης εἰς ἔθνος μέγα ποιήσω αὐτόν ὅτι σπέρμα σόν ἐστιν
21:13 sed et filium ancillae faciam in gentem magnam quia semen tuum est

The Mp notes that the phrase וְגַם occurs 13 times at the beginning of the verse in the Pentateuch. The next note of the Mp appears to be imprecise. It says that the phrase וְגַם אֶת occurs 9 times in the Hebrew Bible. In fact, it occurs many more times, but it does occur 9 times in the Pentateuch only. The critical apparatus informs us that the SP, the LXX, the Peshitta, and the Vg insert the adjective גדול between לגוי and אשימנו.

21:13 "I will also make the son of the slave woman a nation because he is your offspring."

Although the SP, the LXX, the Peshitta, and the Vg read "great nation" instead of "nation," I have decided to follow here the MT. The phrase "great nation" will appear in v. 18.

21:14 וַיַּשְׁכֵּם אַבְרָהָם בַּבֹּקֶר וַיִּקַּח־לֶחֶם וְחֵמַת מַיִם וַיִּתֵּן אֶל־הָגָר שָׂם עַל־שִׁכְמָהּ וְאֶת־הַיֶּלֶד וַיְשַׁלְּחֶהָ וַתֵּלֶךְ וַתֵּתַע בְּמִדְבַּר בְּאֵר שָׁבַע:

21:14 וישכם אברהם בבקר ויקח לחם וחמת מים ויתן אל הגר שם על שכמה ואת הילד וישלחה ותלך ותתע במדבר באר שבע:

21:14 ואקדים אברהם בצפרא ונסיב לחמא ורוקבא דמיא ויהב להגר שוי על כתפה וית רביא ושלחה ואזלת וטעת במדבר באר שבע:

21:14 ἀνέστη δὲ Αβρααμ τὸ πρωὶ καὶ ἔλαβεν ἄρτους καὶ ἀσκὸν ὕδατος καὶ ἔδωκεν Αγαρ καὶ ἐπέθηκεν ἐπὶ τὸν ὦμον καὶ τὸ παιδίον καὶ ἀπέστειλεν αὐτήν ἀπελθοῦσα δὲ ἐπλανᾶτο τὴν ἔρημον κατὰ τὸ φρέαρ τοῦ ὅρκου

21:14 surrexit itaque Abraham mane et tollens panem et utrem aquae inposuit scapulae eius tradiditque puerum et dimisit eam quae cum abisset errabat in solitudine Bersabee

According to the Mp, the phrase וְאֶת־הַיֶּלֶד is a *hapax legomenon*, the form וַיְשַׁלְּחֶהָ occurs twice, and the verb וַתֵּתַע is again a *hapax legomenon*. However, we encounter the form תֵּתַע (without ו) in Prov 7:25. The critical apparatus suggests that the phrase ואת־הילד may be transposed and inserted after אל־הגר. The rationale for such an emendation may be found in some minuscule codices of the LXX (numbered 19 and 314) as well as in the Peshitta.

21:14 Early in the morning Abraham took bread and a skin of water, and gave them to Hagar, putting them and the child on her shoulders, and sent her away. She left and wandered in the wilderness of Beersheba.

The phrase וישכם ... בבקר ויקח is translated "early in the morning he took" because וישכם may be considered an auxiliary verb.[48] Moreover, for the reason of clarity, I have adopted the suggestion of the critical

---

48   HALOT 4:1493.

apparatus concerning the transposition of the phrase וְאֶת־הַיֶּלֶד. This emendation is supported by the grammar of Gesenius-Kautzsch.⁴⁹

21:15 וַיִּכְלוּ הַמַּיִם מִן־הַחֵמֶת וַתַּשְׁלֵךְ אֶת־הַיֶּלֶד תַּחַת אַחַד הַשִּׂיחִם:
21:15 ויכלו המים מן החמת ותשלך את הילד תחת אחד השחים:
21:15 ושלימו מיא מן רוקבא ורמת ית רביא תחות חד מן אילניא:
21:15 ἐξέλιπεν δὲ τὸ ὕδωρ ἐκ τοῦ ἀσκοῦ καὶ ἔρριψεν τὸ παιδίον ὑποκάτω μιᾶς ἐλάτης
21:15 cumque consumpta esset aqua in utre abiecit puerum subter unam arborum quae ibi erant

The verb וַיִּכְלוּ occurs 3 times, and, similarly, there are 3 occurrences of the verb וַתַּשְׁלֵךְ listed in the Mm: Gen 21:15, Judg 9:53, Ps 50:17. Furthermore, the numeral אַחַד occurs 25 times: Gen 21:15, 22:2, 26:10, 32:23, 37:9, 48:22, Lev 13:2, Num 16:15, Deut 1:2, 25:5, Judg 17:5, 1 Sam 9:3, 26:15, 2 Sam 6:20, 7:7, 1 Chr 17:6, 2 Sam 17:22, 1 Kgs 19:2, 22:13, 2 Kgs 6:12, 18:24, Isa 36:9, Ezek 33:30, 45:7, Dan 10:13. In contrast, the plural noun הַשִּׂיחִם is a *hapax legomenon*.

21:15 When the water in the skin had run out, she threw the child under a bush.

I believe that the numeral אחד indicates indeterminacy of the following noun, so I have translated: "a bush."⁵⁰

21:16 וַתֵּלֶךְ וַתֵּשֶׁב לָהּ מִנֶּגֶד הַרְחֵק כִּמְטַחֲוֵי קֶשֶׁת כִּי אָמְרָה אַל־אֶרְאֶה בְּמוֹת הַיָּלֶד וַתֵּשֶׁב מִנֶּגֶד וַתִּשָּׂא אֶת־קֹלָהּ וַתֵּבְךְּ:
21:16 ותלך ותשב לה מנגד הרחק כמטחוי קשת כי אמרה אל אראה במות הילד ותשב מנגד ותשא את קולה ותבך:
21:16 ואזלת ויתיבת לה מקבל ארחיקת כמגד בקשתא ארי אמרת לא אחזי במותיה דרביא ויתיבת מקבל וארימת ית קלה ובכת:
21:16 ἀπελθοῦσα δὲ ἐκάθητο ἀπέναντι αὐτοῦ μακρόθεν ὡσεὶ τόξου βολήν εἶπεν γὰρ οὐ μὴ ἴδω τὸν θάνατον τοῦ παιδίου μου καὶ ἐκάθισεν ἀπέναντι αὐτοῦ ἀναβοῆσαν δὲ τὸ παιδίον ἔκλαυσεν

---

49 *GKC*, 490.
50 See *GBH*, 513; see also Waltke and O'Connor, *Introduction*, 251.

21:16 et abiit seditque e regione procul quantum potest arcus iacere dixit enim non videbo morientem puerum et sedens contra levavit vocem suam et flevit

The Mp comments that the form וַתֵּשֶׁב occurs 12 times in the Bible: Gen 21:16 (twice), 31:34, 38:11, 38:14, 49:24, Josh 6:25, 1 Sam 1:23, 2 Sam 13:20, 1 Kgs 2:19, Ruth 2:14, 2:23. The critical apparatus suggests that instead of ותשא את־קלה ותבך we should probably read וַיִּשָּׂא אֶת־קֹלֹה וַיֵּבְךְ, after the LXX.

21:16 Then she sat down opposite, at the distance of a bowshot, since she said: "I do not wish to look at the death of the child." So she sat down opposite and burst out crying.

The form ותשב לה means simply "and she sat down"; the preposition ל does not need to be translated, since it is an example of an "indirect reflexive nuance."[51] The phrase אל־אראה is a volitional form, that is why, taking into account the emotional mood permeating the scene, I have decided to translate it "I do not wish to."[52]

I do not follow the suggestion of the critical apparatus concerning the change of person ("and he [the child] burst out crying"). Westermann, however, does and translates: "but the child raised his voice and cried." He justifies his choice in the light of v. 17: "God heard the voice of the boy."[53] I must admit that Westermann's argument is strong, but having to choose between the MT and the LXX, I opt for the former.

21:17 וַיִּשְׁמַע אֱלֹהִים אֶת־קוֹל הַנַּעַר וַיִּקְרָא מַלְאַךְ אֱלֹהִים אֶל־הָגָר מִן־הַשָּׁמַיִם וַיֹּאמֶר לָהּ מַה־לָּךְ הָגָר אַל־תִּירְאִי כִּי־שָׁמַע אֱלֹהִים אֶל־קוֹל הַנַּעַר בַּאֲשֶׁר הוּא־שָׁם:

21:17 וישמע אלהים את קול הנער ויקרא מלאך אלהים אל הגר מן השמים ויאמר לה מה לך הגר אל תיראי כי שמע אלהים את קול הנער באשר הוא שם:

21:17 ושמיע קדם יוי ית קליה דרביא וקרא מלאכא דיוי להגר מן שמיא ואמר לה מא ליך הגר לא תדחלין ארי שמיע קדם יוי קליה דרביא באתר דהוא תמן:

---

51 GBH, 488; see also GKC, 381.
52 Cf. Waltke and O'Connor, *Introduction*, 573ff.; GKC, 319.
53 Westermann, *Genesis 12-36*, 341.

21:17 εἰσήκουσεν δὲ ὁ θεὸς τῆς φωνῆς τοῦ παιδίου ἐκ τοῦ τόπου οὗ ἦν καὶ ἐκάλεσεν ἄγγελος τοῦ θεοῦ τὴν Αγαρ ἐκ τοῦ οὐρανοῦ καὶ εἶπεν αὐτῇ τί ἐστιν Αγαρ μὴ φοβοῦ ἐπακήκοεν γὰρ ὁ θεὸς τῆς φωνῆς τοῦ παιδίου σου ἐκ τοῦ τόπου οὗ ἐστιν

21:17 exaudivit autem Deus vocem pueri vocavitque angelus Domini Agar de caelo dicens quid agis Agar noli timere exaudivit enim Deus vocem pueri de loco in quo est

The phrase שָׁמַע אֱלֹהִים occurs 3 times in the Bible: Gen 21:17, Ps 66:19, 78:59. The form בַּאֲשֶׁר, in turn, occurs 15 times: Gen 21:17, 39:9, 39:23, Judg 5:27, 17:8, 17:9, 1 Sam 23:13, 2 Kgs 8:1, Isa 47:12, 56:4, Jonah 1:8, Ruth 1:17, Qoh 3:9, 7:2, 8:4. According to the critical apparatus, many (i.e. 21-60) Hebrew manuscripts, the SP, and the Targum Pseudo-Jonathan read אֶת־קוֹל instead of אֶל־קוֹל in v. 17b.

21:17 God heard the voice of the boy, and the angel of God called to Hagar from heaven saying to her: "What worries you, Hagar? Fear not, since God has heard the voice of the boy where he is."

The suggestion of the critical apparatus concerning reading אֶת־קוֹל instead of אֶל־קוֹל in the second half of v. 17 should be accepted because it is based upon a number of important witnesses. The phrase מַה־לָּךְ is an example of the usage of מַה with the *lamed of interest* in an interrogative phrase. Waltke and O'Connor explain: "the question concerns the object of *l* in a loosely or elliptically defined way."[54]

Another important problem here is the figure of the angel of God. Is he identical with the Lord (v. 1) and God (vv. 2, 4, 6, 12, 17, 19, 20)? The striking feature of the angel's message is that in v. 17 he speaks as if he were distinct from God, whereas in v. 18 he says: "I will make him a great nation," and practically the same words are spoken by God in v. 13: "I will also make the son of the slave woman a nation." I agree with the opinion of Carol A. Newsom, who writes:

> Numerous suggestions have been put forward to account for this peculiar feature. ... But the explanation that seems most likely is that the interchange between Yahweh and *mal'ak yhwh* in various texts is the expression of a tension or paradox: Yahweh's authority and presence in these encoun-

---

54 Waltke and O'Connor, *Introduction*, 323.

ters is to be affirmed, but yet it is not possible for human beings to have an unmediated encounter with God.[55]

In Genesis, we have three other passages where the angel of God (or the angel of the Lord) must be regarded as identical with God to make sense of the text. In Gen 16:7-13, it is the angel of the Lord who speaks to Hagar, who promises to multiply her progeny, and yet we learn from v. 13 that it was "the Lord who spoke to her." In Gen 22:11-18, Abraham listens to the angel of the Lord, who does not appear to be different from the Lord either. In Gen 31:10-13, Jacob tells his wives about a dream he had. In the dream, the angel of God reveals his identity, and calls himself "the God of Bethel." In view of that, I will regard God and the angel of God in Gen 21:17 as one character; otherwise, the long sentence in vv. 17b-18 would be incomprehensible. From a literary perspective, the angel of God is a stylistic feature of the text helping to emphasize God's sovereignty and infinite majesty rather than a separate being which should be considered an additional character present in the episode. It ought to be stressed, however, that the decision of labelling the angel of God as God himself must be undertaken in each separate case on the grounds of close literary and theological analysis of a passage.[56]

21:18 קוּמִי שְׂאִי אֶת־הַנַּעַר וְהַחֲזִיקִי אֶת־יָדֵךְ בּוֹ כִּי־לְגוֹי גָּדוֹל אֲשִׂימֶנּוּ׃
21:18 קומי שאי את הנער והחזיקי את ידך בו כי לגוי גדול אשימנו׃
21:18 קומי טולי ית רביא ואתקיפי ית ידיך ביה ארי לעם סגי אשויניה׃
21:18 ἀνάστηθι λαβὲ τὸ παιδίον καὶ κράτησον τῇ χειρί σου αὐτό εἰς γὰρ ἔθνος μέγα ποιήσω αὐτόν
21:18 surge tolle puerum et tene manum illius quia in gentem magnam faciam eum

The Mp notes that the imperative קוּמִי occurs 4 times at the beginning of the verse, and the references given by the Mm are: Gen 21:18, Isa 60:1, Mic 4:13, Lam 2:19. The imperative שְׂאִי occurs 8 times, whilst another imperative וְהַחֲזִיקִי is a *hapax legomenon*. Interestingly, the Vg has

---

55 Newsom, "Angels," *ABD* 1:250.
56 Freedman and Willoughby remind us that "in some passages it is no longer possible to distinguish God from his mal'āk in interactions with human beings. Gerhard von Rad has disclosed a system in this apparently inconsistent usage: 'When the reference is to God apart from man, Yahweh is used; when God enters the apperception of man, the [mal'āk YHWH] is introduced'" (*TDOT* 8:319). Thus, in our case, the angel of God is God himself as perceived by Hagar.

"manum illius," and, in this respect, is different from other versions and translations.

21:18 "Arise, lift up the boy, and seize him with your hand because I will make him a great nation."

21:19 וַיִּפְקַח אֱלֹהִים אֶת־עֵינֶיהָ וַתֵּרֶא בְּאֵר מָיִם וַתֵּלֶךְ וַתְּמַלֵּא אֶת־הַחֵמֶת מַיִם וַתַּשְׁקְ אֶת־הַנָּעַר:
21:19 ויפקח אלהים את עיניה ותרא באר מים ותלך ותמלא את החמת מים ותשק את הנער:
21:19 וגלא יוי ית עינהא וחזת בירא דמיא ואזלת ומלת ית רוקבא מיא ואשקיאת ית רביא:
21:19 καὶ ἀνέῳξεν ὁ θεὸς τοὺς ὀφθαλμοὺς αὐτῆς καὶ εἶδεν φρέαρ ὕδατος ζῶντος καὶ ἐπορεύθη καὶ ἔπλησεν τὸν ἀσκὸν ὕδατος καὶ ἐπότισεν τὸ παιδίον
21:19 aperuitque oculos eius Deus quae videns puteum aquae abiit et implevit utrem deditque puero bibere

21:19 God opened her eyes, and she noticed a well of water. She filled the skin with water and gave the boy water to drink.

In the phrase ותלך ותמלא the first verb only illustrates and emphasizes the second, therefore it may be omitted in translation. The emphasis means "she immediately / promptly filled."

21:20 וַיְהִי אֱלֹהִים אֶת־הַנַּעַר וַיִּגְדָּל וַיֵּשֶׁב בַּמִּדְבָּר וַיְהִי רֹבֶה קַשָּׁת:
21:20 ויהי אלהים את הנער ויגדל וישב במדבר ויהי רבי קשת:
21:20 והוה מימרא דיוי בסעדיה דרביא ורבא ויתיב במדברא והוה רביא קשתא:
21:20 καὶ ἦν ὁ θεὸς μετὰ τοῦ παιδίου καὶ ηὐξήθη καὶ κατῴκησεν ἐν τῇ ἐρήμῳ ἐγένετο δὲ τοξότης
21:20 et fuit cum eo qui crevit et moratus est in solitudine et factus est iuvenis sagittarius

According to the Mp, both the participle רֹבֶה and the noun קַשָּׁת are *hapax legomena*. The critical apparatus suggests with a degree of uncertainty that we may read רֹבֶה קַשָּׁת instead of רֹבֶה קַשָּׁת at the end of v. 20. This emendation is suggested by the SP, the LXX, the Peshitta, the *Targum Pseudo-Jonathan*, and the Vg.

21:20 God was with the boy, and he became an adult. He dwelt in the wilderness and became an archer.
The emendation suggested by the critical apparatus seems helpful here and is confirmed by a number of important versions, so I have accepted it in my translation.

21:21 וַיֵּשֶׁב בְּמִדְבַּר פָּארָן וַתִּקַּח־לוֹ אִמּוֹ אִשָּׁה מֵאֶרֶץ מִצְרָיִם:
21:21 וישב במדבר פראן ותקח לו אמו אשה מארץ מצרים:
21:21 ויתיב במדברא דפארן ונסיבת ליה אימיה איתתא מארעא דמצרים:

21:21 καὶ κατῴκησεν ἐν τῇ ἐρήμῳ τῇ Φαραν καὶ ἔλαβεν αὐτῷ ἡ μήτηρ γυναῖκα ἐκ γῆς Αἰγύπτου

21:21 habitavitque in deserto Pharan et accepit illi mater sua uxorem de terra Aegypti

21:21 He dwelt in the wilderness of Paran, and his mother took a wife for him from the land of Egypt.

The translation of the whole pericope Gen 21:1-21 is as follows:

1 The Lord visited Sarah according to what he had said, and he did to Sarah as he had promised.
2 Sarah conceived and bore Abraham a son in her husband's old age. This happened at the appointed time promised to Abraham by God.
3 Abraham gave the name Isaac to his newborn son, whom Sarah bore him.
4 Abraham circumcised his son Isaac when the child was eight days old, as God ordered him to do.
5 Abraham was a hundred years old when his son Isaac was born to him.
6 Sarah said: "God made me laugh, and everybody who hears about it will rejoice with me.
7 Who would have said to Abraham that Sarah would nurse children? Nevertheless, I have borne a son in Abraham's old age."
8 The child grew up and was weaned, and Abraham gave a grand banquet on the day when Isaac was weaned.
9 Sarah noticed that the son of Hagar the Egyptian, whom she bore to Abraham, was playing with her son Isaac.
10 So she said to Abraham: "Expel this slave woman and her son because the son of this slave woman shall not share inheritance with my son Isaac."

11 Abraham found these words evil on account of his son.
12 But God said to Abraham: "Do not regard as evil the matter concerning the boy and your slave woman. Grant Sarah whatever she asks you, since it is through Isaac that your descendants will be named.
13 I will also make the son of the slave woman a nation because he is your offspring."
14 Early in the morning Abraham took bread and a skin of water, and gave them to Hagar, putting them and the child on her shoulders, and sent her away. She left and wandered in the wilderness of Beersheba.
15 When the water in the skin had run out, she threw the child under a bush.
16 Then she sat down opposite, at the distance of a bowshot, since she said: "I do not wish to look at the death of the child." So she sat down opposite and burst out crying.
17 God heard the voice of the boy, and the angel of God called to Hagar from heaven saying to her: "What worries you, Hagar? Fear not, since God has heard the voice of the boy where he is.
18 Arise, lift up the boy, and seize him with your hand because I will make him a great nation."
19 God opened her eyes, and she noticed a well of water. She filled the skin with water and gave the boy water to drink.
20 God was with the boy, and he became an adult. He dwelt in the wilderness and became an archer.
21 He dwelt in the wilderness of Paran, and his mother took a wife for him from the land of Egypt.

2.2. The Narrative Delimitation of the Pericope

What are the criteria for the narrative delimitation of Gen 21:1-21? Jean Louis Ska, who is an expert on both diachronic and synchronic approaches, emphasizes the role of the plot, or, in other words, the dramatic action, in determining the narrative limits: "The main divisions (and subdivisions) of a narrative are divisions of this dramatic action. The signals of change of action are normally shifts or breaks in the temporal succession of events. Change of time, change of place, change of characters can be signals of passage from one unit to the other if they indicate a shift or a progress in the dramatic action."[57] In view of that,

---

57 Ska, *Our Fathers Have Told Us*, 3.

an analysis of the dramatic action of Gen 21:1-21 should be the first step I will take.

There are many different models of the narrative plot, and here I would like to adopt a model introduced by Ska.[58] Hence in Gen 21:1-21 we can distinguish the following moments of the plot:

a. exposition (vv. 1-8) – the exposition is long; it introduces all the main characters except Ishmael and gives information about spatial, temporal, and social settings of the story; in brief, it is a "presentation of *indispensable* pieces of information about the state of affairs that *precedes* the beginning of the action itself"[59]

b. inciting moment (v. 9) – Sarah notices Abraham's two children playing together; this is the moment when the reader's interest is initiated; it must be underlined that before v. 9 we do not have an event which could be called the inciting moment in the proper sense; in none of vv. 1-8 can we observe "the moment in which the conflict or the problem appears for the first time and arouses the interest of the reader";[60] vv. 1-8 serve rather as a link to the preceding chapters, and preparation for subsequent action

c. complication (vv. 10-14) – as Ska notices aptly,[61] the complication often has a climactic structure; the tension in the narrative under discussion is built up in three clear steps: Sarah intervenes on behalf of her son (v. 10); God gives his message to Abraham (vv. 12-13); Abraham sends away Hagar and Ishmael (v. 14)

d. climax (vv. 15-16) – the narrative achieves the moment of the highest tension in the description of Hagar's desperate behaviour in the face of forthcoming death

e. turning point (vv. 17-18) – God's action brings rescue to Hagar and her son; it is, as Cuddon says, "the observable moment when ... there is a definite change in direction and one becomes aware that it is now about to move towards its end"[62]

---

58 Ska, *Our Fathers Have Told Us*, 20-30. The model introduced by Ska is the most widely used and is Aristotelian in origin. Among other models are: Labov's model (abstract, orientation, complicating action, evaluation, result or resolution, and coda), and the semiotic model (manipulation, competence, performance, and sanction) (Ska, *Our Fathers Have Told Us*, 30-33).
59 Ska, *Our Fathers Have Told Us*, 21.
60 Ska, *Our Fathers Have Told Us*, 25.
61 See Ska, *Our Fathers Have Told Us*, 26.
62 Cuddon, *The Penguin Dictionary of Literary Terms*, 950.

f. resolution (v. 19) – Hagar acts according to God's advice; the whole suspense of the story ends here, and the reader's emotional tension is resolved

g. dénouement (vv. 20-21) – the reader learns about further events of Hagar's and Ishmael's life

Ska warns us that establishing the moments of the plot does not equate to the delimitation of the narrative; the moments "are rather the principal articulations of the dramatic action."[63] As a result, a further discussion of time, place, and characters in the narrative is needed. Now, we see that no significant change of *time* takes place when we analyse the sensitive points of the text, namely the transitions between v. 7 and v. 8, as well as between v. 8 and v. 9. In terms of time, v. 8 appears to be a continuation of v. 4 and vv. 5-7 respectively: Abraham circumcised his newborn son (v. 4), the child grew, and was finally weaned (v. 8). Vv. 5-7, for their part, create the effect of pause – the time in the story is suspended. Similarly, we can conjecture that no significant time passed between v. 8 and v. 9. The weaned Isaac (v. 8) must have been three years old,[64] and this age seems to be enough for him to play with the son of Hagar (v. 9). We also see that the next part of the story, vv. 10-19, is set within the same temporal unit. Sarah intervenes immediately (v. 10) upon seeing the two children playing together (v. 9), and the subsequent events develop rapidly. Only in vv. 20-21 (the dénouement of the story) has the temporal dimension become more indefinite. In consequence, the whole passage is unified in terms of time. In respect of *place*, vv. 1-14a are set in one locale, namely Abraham's house. From v. 14b we accompany Hagar and her son in their ordeal in the wilderness. Similarly, the dénouement in vv. 20-21 is set in the wilderness. However, a much more significant change concerns the *characters*, and occurs between v. 8 and v. 9. In v. 9, two new characters appear on the stage of the narrative: Abraham's Egyptian concubine Hagar and her son Ishmael (the latter is unnamed through the story).[65]

Therefore, there is a change of characters between v. 8 and v. 9, as well as a change of place in v. 14. When we keep in mind that vv. 1-8 are the exposition of the story, and only in v. 9 do we have the inciting moment, it follows that we can distinguish three units in the passage. Ska tells us that we can "call the first subdivision of a larger narrative

---

63 Ska, *Our Fathers Have Told Us*, 21.
64 See Westermann, *Genesis 12-36*, 338.
65 In Mlakuzhyil's words: "There is a change of scene if one of the main characters or the place or time is changed" (*The Christocentric Literary Structure*, 112 n. 60).

an 'episode' and the subdivisions of an episode 'scenes.'"[66] Therefore, we should regard Gen 21:1-21 as one episode,[67] which is divided into three scenes: vv. 1-8, vv. 9-13, and vv. 14-21. It does not seem necessary to regard the beginning of the third scene as v. 14b. The whole v. 14 is a logical unit: Abraham's action results in expelling Hagar and her son into the wilderness. Moreover, v. 13 marks the end of God's speech, so, taking into account the shape of the narrative, we can consider v. 14 to be the beginning of the third scene.

Such a way of dividing the episode Gen 21:1-21 into three scenes is further confirmed in the light of the structural criteria given by George Mlakuzhyil in his sophisticated analysis of the Fourth Gospel.[68] First, Mlakuzhyil reminds us of "the law of stage duality," which is an "ancient maxim that no more than two active characters shall normally appear on stage on one time."[69] The law of stage duality confirms the division between v. 13 and v. 14. In vv. 1-13, the two active human characters are Sarah and Abraham. Although God occupies a supreme place in the narrative, he acts directly only in v. 1 and vv. 12-13. Similarly, Isaac's and Ishmael's role in the story is secondary. In contrast, in vv. 14-21, God becomes more active, and forms a duo with Hagar. Mlakuzhyil points out that the law of stage duality is sometimes combined with "'the law of vanishing characters' according to which an active character of the previous scene is instrumental in introducing the next scene and then practically disappears or vanishes from the stage."[70] In our case, the vanishing character is Abraham, who, in v. 14, sends away Hagar and Ishmael, and then leaves the dramatic stage.

Secondly, an episode can be split into a number of scenes on the basis of different literary genres, or, strictly speaking, "micro-genres" present therein.[71] Hence we can call scene 1 a "pastoral idyll," scene 2 a "conflict story," and scene 3 a "rescue story." It appears that v. 8 belongs to the pastoral idyll to much a greater extent than to the conflict story. V. 8 has peaceful and joyful overtones, which harmonize with vv. 1-7 rather than with vv. 9-13. Finally, I should add that the exegesis of the model pericope given in chapter 5 is based upon the above divi-

---

66 Ska, *Our Fathers Have Told Us*, 33.
67 Cf. Ska, *Our Fathers Have Told Us*, 33-36.
68 Mlakuzhyil divides the criteria into three groups: twelve literary criteria, twelve dramatic techniques, and four structural patterns (*The Christocentric Literary Structure*, 87-135).
69 J. L. Martyn quoted in Mlakuzhyil, *The Christocentric Literary Structure*, 115.
70 Mlakuzhyil, *The Christocentric Literary Structure*, 116.
71 See Mlakuzhyil, *The Christocentric Literary Structure*, 111-12.

sion into three scenes. I will then show in chapter 5 that this particular division serves well the purpose of explaining the pericope's cognitive, aesthetic, and practical dimensions.[72]

Last but not least, there is no doubt that the external limits of the passage are v. 1 and v. 21. First, all commentators agree that v. 1 begins and v. 21 ends a narrative unit. Secondly, from the point of view of the dramatic action, Gen 21:1-21 is a self-contained episode. Thirdly, Gen 20:1-18 is a separate narrative about Abraham, Sarah, and king Abimelech set in Gerar (time, place, and some characters different from Gen 21:1-21). Fourthly, in Gen 21:22-34, we leave Sarah, Hagar and Ishmael, and we meet again Abimelech, this time with the commander of his army Phicol. In view of that, the purpose of v. 1 is to introduce a new episode in Sarah's and Abraham's life with a flashback to God's promises given before in Gen 15:4, 17:16, and 18:10. On the other hand, the closing vv. 20-21 provide general information about the further events of Hagar's and Ishmael's lives.[73]

It is interesting to find out what modern commentators think about the limits of Gen 21:1-21. Do we have here two independent episodes, or rather one episode comprising two or more interconnected scenes? Where does the demarcating line between the scenes go? In the case of many scholars, the delimitation they propose results from source criticism rather than from narrative analysis applied to the passage, yet a short survey of their views seems in place.[74]

Von Rad treats Gen 21:1-21 as one unit divided into two thematic parts: vv. 1-13 and vv. 14-21, since he organizes his translation of the unit in two paragraphs.[75] Speiser follows generally von Rad's approach,[76] but a significantly different solution is given by Westermann, who treats Gen 21:1-7 and 21:8-21 as two separate narratives. For Westermann, "Gen 21:1-7 is an account of the birth of Isaac to which the nar-

---

72 David W. Cotter makes a strong case for the division between vv. 8 and 9 on the basis of close parallels between chapters 15-17, on the one hand, and the whole chapter 21, on the other, as well as on the basis of the concentric structure of 21:9-21 (*Genesis*, 136-138).

73 To my knowledge, only Cotter insists that we should consider the *whole* chapter 21 as a textual unit (*Genesis*, 134-143).

74 It seems that those scholars who focus on the source division of the pericope may be prejudiced against treating v. 9 as the beginning of scene 2. Such bias can be avoided when we start the analysis of the pericope from a narrative and synchronic point of view.

75 See von Rad, *Das Erste Buch Mose*, 196-97.

76 See Speiser, *Genesis*, 153-57.

rative 21:8-21 is attached."⁷⁷ The former narrative brings to a conclusion the introduction to the Abraham cycle in Gen 11:27-32, whilst the latter "is nothing less than the classical structure of a narrative from the patriarchal period, coherent and self-contained; it is a narrative of particular finesse which can have arisen at that time and which goes back to oral tradition."⁷⁸

Other commentators provide us with the whole spectrum of possible approaches to the question of the narrative's thematic division, but their views may be presented under two headings: those scholars who discuss separately two narratives within Gen 21:1-21; and those who stress the unity of Gen 21:1-21, even if they usually distinguish a number of episodes within the narrative. Hence, first, we have authors who speak of two distinct narrative units: the first narrative unit is in vv. 1-7; the second comprises vv. 8-21. Thus, de Vaux speaks of two narratives (*récit*).⁷⁹ Sarna uses the term "two episodes."⁸⁰ Brueggemann deals with "the narrative of the two sons of Abraham in 21:1-21," but analyses the two narratives separately.⁸¹ Similarly, Hamilton discusses the two units one after the other.⁸² Secondly, we have at least six authors who stress the unity of chapter 21 and see a strong connection between the two subdivisions in vv. 1-7 and vv. 8-21. Thus, Driver,⁸³ and Skinner⁸⁴ call the whole section 21:1-21 "The birth of Isaac and expulsion of Ishmael." Gunkel examines the passage under one heading,⁸⁵ but clearly differentiates between two "Abraham legends": "Isaac's birth, 21:1-7" and "Ishmael's rejection and his deliverance at Beersheba, 21:9-21."⁸⁶ Coats approaches the topic from a different angle because of his preoccupation with structures and literary genres. He treats Gen 21:1-21 as part of the Abraham saga (saga being "a long, prose, traditional narrative" which "has typically an *episodic* structure

---

77 Westermann, *Genesis 12-36*, 331.
78 Westermann, *Genesis 12-36*, 338.
79 See de Vaux, *La Genèse*, 102.
80 Sarna, *Genesis*, 144-45.
81 See Brueggemann, *Genesis*, 177-85.
82 See Hamilton, *The Book of Genesis*, 71-86.
83 See Driver, *The Book of Genesis*, 209-13.
84 See Skinner, *A Critical and Exegetical Commentary*, 320-24.
85 See Gunkel, *Genesis: Translated and Interpreted*, 225-29.
86 Gunkel, *Genesis: Translated and Interpreted*, 158. I do not understand why Gunkel does not include v. 8 as part of the narrative of Ishmael, contrary to what he writes later in the commentary (see *Genesis: Translated and Interpreted*, 225). There is the same problem in the original German edition (see *Genesis: übersetzt und erklärt*, 159).

developed around stereotyped themes or topics,"[87]) and regards the passage as one of the three tales of family strife (besides Gen 16:1-16 and 18:1-15).[88] Moreover, he calls the whole narrative in vv. 1-21 the "Birth of Isaac," and distinguishes its five main structural elements: "general fulfilment of annunciation" in v. 1; "birth report" in vv. 2-7; "crisis rejoined" in vv. 8-13; "dénouement" in vv. 14-19; and "conclusion" in vv. 20-21.[89] Similarly to his predecessors, Coats sees the demarcation line separating the first two episodes of the story going between v. 7 and v. 8, rather than v. 8 and v. 9, as I would like to propose. In turn, Wenham gives an interpretation of the whole passage Gen 21:1-21, but clearly distinguishes two episodes: vv. 1-7 and 8-21. He also subordinates the second episode to the first by giving the whole passage the title "Isaac displaces Ishmael," and by calling the second episode a story of Isaac's weaning.[90] Lastly, Robert Alter, whose new translation of Genesis is "an experiment in re-presenting the Bible ... in a language that conveys with some precision the semantic nuances and the lively orchestration of literary effects of the Hebrew and at the same time has stylistic and rhythmic integrity as literary English,"[91] presents a translation and commentary to the whole chapter 21. He divides the text into paragraphs in the way which suggests the following demarcation: vv. 1-13 and vv. 14-21. Hence, there is no division between v. 8 and v. 9 in Alter's translation, but it is also impossible to determine whether he considers vv. 1-7 to be a separate episode.[92]

Taking into consideration the whole discussion, I strongly incline to the view of those scholars who treat the pericope as a literary unit. If we presumed that a new separate episode begins in v. 8 ("The child grew up and was weaned"), it would be difficult to explain the lack of the proper name in v. 8. Most readers would look at the beginning of that episode, and would ask: "Who is that child?" However, given the criteria of the dramatic action, as well as the unity of time, place, and characters, I believe that we should divide the episode Gen 21:1-21 into three scenes. Thus the first scene comprises vv. 1-8, whilst the second vv. 9-13, even if this goes against the grain of some scholarly opinion. The analysis of the cognitive, aesthetic, and practical dimensions of the

---

87 Coats, *Genesis*, 5.
88 See Coats, *Genesis*, 97.
89 Coats, *Genesis*, 152.
90 See Wenham, *Genesis 16-50*, 76, 78.
91 Alter, *Genesis*, ix.
92 See Alter, *Genesis*, 97-101.

pericope (in chapter 5) will show that the arguments supporting my conviction are even more numerous.

2.3. The Literary Sources of the Pericope

One of the most significant questions raised by the historical-critical method with reference to biblical texts is the problem of underlying literary sources, which were amalgamated, and which contributed to the final form of the text. As Wenham summarizes, in the case of Genesis, we may speak about three primary sources: J, E, and P. They may be differentiated on the basis of five characteristics: different names of the deity; duplicate narratives; different vocabulary; different style; and, finally, different theological viewpoints.[93] Certainly, there have been various amendments to the classical version of the source theory. Roland E. Murphy rightly states: "The modern consensus on the formation of the Pentateuch has been breached, but not replaced. ... But the distinction between J and E has always been a bone of contention, long before the current uncertainty. The present tendency is to think more in terms of expansions of J, and to recognize the role of a redactor (R)."[94] I will bear this in mind, while presenting the scholarly views on the source division of Gen 21:1-21.

To begin with, we may examine the views of Speiser, who argues that vv. 1-2a belong to J (with a possibility that 1b may belong to P because "the second half of the verse duplicates the first,"[95]) and that vv. 2b-5 are of priestly origin, whereas vv. 6-21 are added by E.[96] In this respect, Speiser follows von Rad, who suggests exactly the same attribution.[97] Driver holds a similar opinion, and states that v. 1a belongs to J,

---

93   Wenham, *Genesis 1-15*, xxvi.
94   Murphy, "Introduction to the Pentateuch," *NJBC*, 4.
95   Speiser, *Genesis*, 154.
96   See Speiser, *Genesis*, 153-57.
97   See von Rad, *Genesis*, 226-30. Strictly speaking, von Rad says that it is vv. 2a-5 which belong to P (see *Das Erste Buch Mose*, 197). The same is repeated in the English translation (see *Genesis*, 226). This seems to be a misprint because the German translation of Gen 21:1-21 provided by von Rad at the beginning of chapter 14 of his work suggests that it is vv. 2b-5 which belong to P (see *Das Erste Buch Mose*, 196-97). He distinguishes the sources using a different font for each of them. Moreover, mentioning vv. 2a-5 does not make sense (we would expect simply vv. 2-5). Furthermore, the attribution of vv. 1-2a to J and vv. 6-21 to E is an indirect conclusion drawn from von Rad's discussion of the matter. He does not specify unequivocally the character of vv. 1-2a and 6-21.

1b to P, 2a to J, and again 2b-5 to P. The remaining part of the narrative can be attributed to E.[98] Gunkel accepts Driver's belief concerning the sources in vv. 1-5, but divides v. 6 in two, and says that v. 6a belongs to E, whereas v. 6b and v. 7 to J. Beginning only from v. 8 do we have a purely Elohistic narrative.[99] The same view is supported by Skinner,[100] and largely by de Vaux (de Vaux suggests only one modification, namely that the whole of v. 1 belongs to J).[101] Martin Noth suggests the following attribution: vv. 1a and 7 are part of J, vv. 1b-5 belong to P, and vv. 6, 8-21 should be ascribed to E.[102] Vawter proposes a slightly different account of the problem. He attributes vv. 1, 6b, and 7 to J, vv. 2-5 to P, and vv. 6a, 8-21 to E.[103] In turn, Coats distinguishes only two sources, since "there is no evidence from form-critical analysis of structure that would support a clear separation between the Yahwist and the Elohist. At most, the Elohistic elements seem to be an expansion of the Yahwist's narrative, not a distinct narrative unit that has an independent form-critical integrity."[104] Thus Coats claims that vv. 1b-5 are part of P [sic], whereas vv. 1a, 6-21 belong to JE.[105] Finally, Wenham writes unconvincingly: "I prefer to suppose that the main editor J has introduced and arranged earlier materials, conventionally denoted P and E, to fit in the overall theme of the narrative. J's hand is most clear in the introductory v. 1 (note the double mention of the LORD; cf. 17:1) and possibly in the wording of the promises (vv. 13, 17-18)."[106]

For Speiser, the Elohistic character of vv. 6-21 is indisputable. First, we have "the consistent use of Elohim (6, 12, 17, 19, 20)"[107] in the narrative. Secondly, Gen 21:1-21 is parallel to Gen 16:1-16 (an account of the birth of Ishmael which is predominantly Yahwistic), but differs from Gen 16:1-16 in so many respects that it could not have been written by the same author.[108] Thirdly, from the point of view of the characterization of the personages, "E seeks to explain people and their actions, but he does so with the aid of words rather than deeds. If E's characters do

---

98 See Driver, *The Book of Genesis*, 209-10.
99 See Gunkel, *Genesis: Translated and Interpreted*, 225.
100 See Skinner, *A Critical and Exegetical Commentary*, 320-21.
101 See de Vaux, *La Genèse*, 102.
102 See Noth, *A History of Pentateuchal Traditions*, 17, 28, 35, 264.
103 See Vawter, *On Genesis*, 246-47.
104 Coats, *Genesis*, 98.
105 See Coats, *Genesis*, 98-100, 152-54.
106 Wenham, *Genesis 16-50*, 79.
107 Speiser, *Genesis*, 156.
108 See Speiser, *Genesis*, 156.

more reasoning than J's, they are also less natural and impulsive."[109] A further argument for the attribution of vv. 6-21 to E comes from the aetiology of the names of Isaac and Ishmael. In the narrative under discussion, the explanation of the meaning of the name Isaac comes in v. 6 ("Sarah said, 'God made me laugh and everybody who hears about it will rejoice with me'"), and this explanation differs from the accounts given earlier in Gen 17:17 (P), and in Gen 18:10-14 (J). Similarly, the meaning of the name Ishmael in Gen 21:1-21 is derived from v. 17: "God heard (וישמע) the voice of the boy"; whereas in Gen 16:11b (J), we read: "you shall call his name Ishmael because the Lord has given heed (שמע) to your affliction." The difference is that, in the former case, God listens to the voice of the boy, whereas in the latter, he pays attention to Hagar's pain.[110] We must add, however, that the argument concerning the three etymologies of the name Isaac is somewhat weakened in the light of Hamilton's following observation: "Source critics often cite these verses as evidence for triplicate traditions about Isaac's name: 17:17 (P); 18:12-15 (J); 21:3-7 (E). But 21:6 is entirely consistent with 17:17 and 18:12-15 if one translates ṣeḥōq as *joke*."[111] Hence, Hamilton translates 21:6a: "And Sarah said: 'God has made a joke of me.'"[112] Even if this translation seems somewhat unusual, it certainly weakens the argument of those source critics who support the "triplicate traditions" about the origin of the name Isaac. Moreover, Hamilton's translation and exegesis of Gen 21:8-21 lessens the tension between the narrative and its Yahwistic counterpart in Gen 16:1-16.[113] What follows from his discussion is, at least, the fact that we should not be too hasty in drawing far-reaching conclusions from the comparison of two similar narratives. Biblical exegesis is, to some extent, an intuitive enterprise, and it sometimes happens that an exegetical technique which is too mechanical may lead us astray.

Claus Westermann's presentation of the status quo differs from his predecessors' stance. He states that "apart from ascribing vv. 3-5 to P, everything remains questionable."[114] Thus Westermann arrives at the conviction that vv. 1-7 are the work of a redactor, who also edited the introduction to the whole Abraham cycle in Gen 11:27-32.[115] Of course,

---

109 Speiser, *Genesis*, 157.
110 See Speiser, *Genesis*, 157.
111 Hamilton, *The Book of Genesis*, 74.
112 Hamilton, *The Book of Genesis*, 72.
113 See Hamilton, *The Book of Genesis*, 75-86.
114 Westermann, *Genesis 12-36*, 331.
115 See Westermann, *Genesis 12-36*, 331.

Westermann admits that the redactor used the sources which he had at his disposal. Hence, vv. 6-7, which describe Sarah's joy at the birth of Isaac, belong only to J. To prove this, Westermann, following K. Budde, H. Gunkel, O. Procksch, and J. Skinner, suggests a transposition within vv. 6-7, and reads them in the following order: v. 6a, 7, and 6b: "Sarah said: 'God made me laugh. Who would have said to Abraham that Sarah would nurse children? Nevertheless, I have borne a son in Abraham's old age. Everybody who hears about it will rejoice with me.'"[116] Westermann is convinced that such a transposition solves the problem that v. 7 as such does not give any explanation of the name Isaac, whereas the only purpose of vv. 6-7 is to provide such an explanation. Moreover, the rearrangement of the verses clarifies and underlines the positive message in v. 6b: "Everybody who hears about it will rejoice with me." If we read v. 6b after v. 7, the phrase כל־השמע יצחק־לי can no longer be understood in the negative sense: "Everybody who hears about it will laugh at me."[117] In addition, Westermann rejects the argument that v. 6 can be attributed to E because it contains the word אלהים for God. "It is already clear," writes Westermann, "that this is a dubious criterion in 21:1-7. It looks as if the redactor is deliberately using both designations for God indiscriminately."[118]

Now, if we take into consideration Speiser's conviction that v. 6 must belong to E because it contains the aetiology of the name Isaac which differs from the explanation given in Gen 18:10-14 (J), and, as a result, it cannot belong to J, we encounter a problem. However, Westermann solves this problem through recourse to the creative work of the redactor, and emphasizes the fact that Gen 21:1-7 is a result of the redactor's skilful efforts: "The only possible explanation of all this is that the redactor chose from the many explanations of the name available from the tradition those that presupposed the birth of the child. This is a proof that besides the written works at hand to him, the redactor knew a broad oral tradition going side by side with them."[119] Hence, according to Westermann, both v. 6 and v. 7 belong to J, but they were subsequently and carefully reworked by the redactor. Moreover, Westermann does not doubt that vv. 1-2 can be attributed both to J and P, and it is now impossible to separate the two sources in vv. 1-2. Thus Westermann supports the view on the composite character of vv. 1-2

---

116 Cf. Westermann, *Genesis 12-36*, 330.
117 Cf. Westermann, *Genesis 12-36*, 333-34.
118 Westermann, *Genesis 12-36*, 333.
119 Westermann, *Genesis 12-36*, 334.

already defended by Driver.[120] The latter, however, clearly distinguishes between two sources in vv. 1-2. Westermann argues that vv. 1-2 form a conclusion to chapters 17 (P) and 18 (J), and are followed by vv. 3-5, which are "an untouched piece from P which is really a genealogical conclusion of chapter 17."[121] It seems that Westermann's views are well-balanced, and that he avoids the trap of complicating the question of the sources when it is not really necessary. By way of example, he is aware of the point made by many exegetes that v. 1 may belong to two different sources (v. 1a to J, and 1b to P), but he says that "this is not certain and need not to be pressed."[122] Hamilton's argument additionally reinforces Westermann's view: "All this speculation becomes needless, however, once it is seen that the whole verse [v. 1] is poetry, a fact reinforced by the chiasm of subject-verb – verb-subject. Also, the two statements made by the narrator in terms of Yahweh in v. 1 balance Sarah's two statements with which this unit concludes (vv. 6-7)."[123] Westermann's solution to the problem is, to a great extent, backed up by Van Seters, who distinguishes five stages of the literary development of Genesis: pre-Yahwistic first stage, pre-Yahwistic second stage, the work of the Yahwist himself, the Priestly stage, and, finally, the post-Priestly stage.[124] Van Seters is convinced that v. 1 belongs to the Yahwist, v. 2 to the pre-Yahwistic first stage, vv. 3-5 are clearly the work of P, whereas vv. 6-7, again, belong to the pre-Yahwistic first stage.[125]

Moving on now to the remaining part of the narrative, namely vv. 8-21, we must say, first, that Westermann disagrees with the well established view that vv. 8-21 belong to E. This view is supported by Driver, who points out that since Ishmael was carried by his mother, which is implied in vv. 14-15, he must have been a small child. Yet, since Gen 16:16 ("Abram was eighty-six years old when Hagar bore Ishmael to Abram") interpreted in the light of Gen 21:5, 8 suggests that Ishmael must have been at least fifteen years old, and since Gen 16:16 belongs to P, the narrative of Hagar and Ishmael exiled to the wilderness of Beer-sheba in Gen 21:8-21 must belong to E. Moreover, a possibility that Gen 21:8-21 belongs to J should be excluded because of the presence of the

---

120 See Driver, *The Book of Genesis*, 209.
121 Westermann, *Genesis 12-36*, 331.
122 Westermann, *Genesis 12-36*, 332.
123 Hamilton, *The Book of Genesis*, 73.
124 See Van Seters, *Abraham*, 313. The only text in the Abraham cycle which belongs to the post-Priestly stage is, according to Van Seters, chapter 14 (*Abraham*, 313).
125 See Van Seters, *Abraham*, 313.

word אלהים to describe God.¹²⁶ It must be noted here that, among contemporary scholars, a great defender of the Yahwistic character of vv. 8-21 is Van Seters, who argues that "the thematic concerns of 21:8-21 would strongly suggest that the author is, in fact, J."¹²⁷ Van Seters, however, remains rather isolated in this respect.

Now, Westermann convincingly proves that vv. 8-21 cannot have been added by J because they are parallel to the Yahwistic story in Gen 16:1-16, and because they consistently use the name אלהים. Yet they do not belong to E either because "a comparison of possible E texts, 20:1-18 and 21:8-21, shows that they are of such a different kind that it scarcely seems possible that they stem from the same author and the same period."¹²⁸ In view of this, Westermann concludes: "If 21:8-21 cannot have come from J then it is to be traced to an interpolator [*der Ergänzer*]."¹²⁹ To summarize Westermann's discussion of the source division in Gen 21:1-21, we have the following: vv. 1-2 belong to J and P, without a possibility that they may be clearly separated; vv. 3-5 are attributed to P; vv. 6-7 are part of J; and, finally, vv. 8-21 were added by an unknown interpolator.

In this book, I shall follow the source division of Gen 21:1-21 proposed by Westermann. In his commentary, he evaluates the views of all important scholars writing on the subject before him. He also combines the best abilities of the historical commentator with a knowledge of new trends in biblical exegesis. His rejection of the conviction that Gen 21:8-21 belongs to E seems to be an innovative yet reasonable path to explore. However, I am not persuaded of the need to make a transposition within vv. 6-7. Although Westermann is not the only one who proposes to do this, I think that the integrity and arrangement of the MT can be sacrificed only in well-justified cases.¹³⁰

---

126 See Driver, *The Book of Genesis*, 212.
127 Van Seters, *Abraham*, 202.
128 Westermann, *Genesis 12-36*, 338.
129 Westermann, *Genesis 12-36*, 338.
130 The problem of sources in Genesis (and the Pentateuch) is open to debate: "More recent research on the Pentateuch indicates that only for the Priestly Writing and Deuteronomy can one suggest a sure textual basis that is capable of gaining a consensus. ... It is not possible to apply the source hypothesis to the non-Priestly textual tradition, and to separate the two sources J and E and their redaction together (JE) cleanly" (Kratz, "The Growth of the Old Testament," *OHBS*, 482). See also Whybray (*The Making of the Pentateuch*, 111-116) for a brief assessment of E. However, Kratz's and Whybray's views do not contradict Westermann's opinion that vv. 8-21 were added by an interpolator, and so the discussion in the following section remains valid.

2.4. Synchronic versus Diachronic Approaches

Brevard S. Childs, the founding father of canonical criticism, who tries to bridge the gap between diachronic and synchronic approaches, writes in *Introduction to the Old Testament as Scripture*:

> The canonical study of the Old Testament shares an interest in common with several of the newer literary critical methods in its concern to do justice to the integrity of the text itself apart from diachronistic reconstruction. ... For theological reasons the biblical texts were often shaped in such a way that the original poetic forms were lost, or a unified narrative badly shattered. The canonical approach is concerned to understand the nature of the theological shape of the text rather than to recover an original literary or aesthetical unity.[131]

According to Childs, the common feature shared by canonical criticism and "literary" methods is doing "justice to the integrity of the text." However, Childs draws a distinct line between canonical criticism and other synchronic approaches. For Childs, the hallmark of the canonical approach is its interest in the "theological shape of the text," which can be discovered through the study of the relationship between the text and the community of faith. To justify the unique character of canonical criticism, Childs points to a situation when the aesthetic unity of a text becomes distorted because that text is shaped by a redactor in order to become a medium for communicating certain theological truths. Childs indirectly suggests that literary approaches become partially useless in this case, and it is only the canonical approach that can fruitfully accomplish the mission of elucidating the text's theological message and explaining its present structure. Yet, when we have a closer look at Childs's argument, we see that the line he draws between canonical and literary criticism is not always clear, and sometimes does not exist at all. Moreover, the transforming procedures applied to the text by a redactor do not necessarily result in damage done to its aesthetic dimension, but rather bring about a reorganization of that dimension, and Gen 21:1-21 is a case in point.

In the two preceding subchapters, we have seen that the results of the delimitation of Gen 21:1-21 are different, depending on a particular approach. For narrative criticism, the first scene of the passage comprises vv. 1-8, whilst for source criticism the demarcation line should be drawn between v. 7 and v. 8 (vv. 8-21 are added by an unknown interpolator). Thus from the vantage point of the historical critic, who fo-

---

131 Childs, *Introduction to the Old Testament*, 74.

cuses on ancient literary sources, v. 8 begins a new scene, or, strictly speaking, a new unit belonging to a different source. On the contrary, for the narrative critic, the historical sutures are no longer recognizable because he or she tends to pay attention to the dramatic action, and to the unity of time, place, and characters. Can we say that the historical critic is correct, whereas the narrative critic errs, and mistakenly applies modern narrative criteria to the ancient text? If we asked Childs to solve the problem, he would probably say that the interpolator who joined vv. 8-21 to vv. 1-7 did not care much about the original units' aesthetic dimension, and what really mattered for him was a new theological dimension which the two units acquired, even if it left them "badly shattered." In saying this, Childs would most likely show his deep commitment to the historical method, although he has so often tried to dissociate himself from his historically-oriented colleagues.

It seems to me, however, that the solution to the problem should be different. The biblical text, in its present form, is a synchronic reality, which, in most cases, shows, more or less obviously, the marks of its diachronic process of formation. In the case of Gen 21:1-21, the source division is not obvious from a narrative perspective, and to discover the stitches joining v. 7 and v. 8, we need specialized historical-critical tools. By contrast, when the narrative critic reads Gen 1-3, the presence of the two different stories may suggest to the critic the existence of two ancient sources, and the historical critic will happily confirm this hypothesis. Hence the two perspectives, the narrative and the historical, are by no means mutually exclusive. They operate, to a great extent, independently, and arrive at autonomous conclusions. Even though the conclusions can sometimes be similar, there is always an important difference between them. Narrative analysis demonstrates the presence of a break in the dramatic action or in the unity of time, place, and characters, whereas source criticism tells us about the underlying historical sources. In view of that, as regards Gen 21:1-21, the conclusions are different, but both are true. On the synchronic "surface" of the text, there is a gap between v. 8 and v. 9. When we dive into the text's historical depth we will discover that the gap exists, in fact, between v. 7 and v. 8. These two gaps, however, have different natures, being narrative in the former case, and source-critical in the latter.

To conclude, at the level of the text's historical past we meet a redactor, who, inspired by theological reasons, merged a number of accessible sources into a new text. Yet, every so often, the redactor's work results in a literary reorganization of the text, which is then recognizable by narrative analysis. As Clines reminds us, we do not need to ask, and perhaps also ought not to, whether a new textual configuration which emerges from intermingling or juxtaposing literary sources was *intended* by the redactor.[132] In this way we avoid the trap of the intentional fallacy,[133] and focus on the work as it stands before us. Therefore, what we should be interested in, and what we could establish with a degree of certainty, is the text's meaning for its original audience, and for the generations of readers that came afterwards. This line of thinking will be adopted in this book, and I shall discuss its nuances and ramifications for biblical exegesis in the following chapter.

As a result, we see that Childs's statement concerning the literary unity of a text damaged by the work of a redactor is, to a great extent, exaggerated. First, the unity of a text does not depend only on the homogeneity of its underlying historical sources. As I have already proved, from a narrative point of view, Gen 21:1-21 is a well-constructed and self-contained literary unit. On the synchronic level, such features as the plot, as well as the unity of time, place, and characters become more important for the text's integrity than its historical sources. In the case of Gen 21:1-21, Childs's notion of "damage" is illusory because of the presence of new literary patterns. The historical documents underlying Gen 21:1-21 have lost their original unity, but the resulting narrative has become an entity characterized by a new set of literary features.[134] The present shape of the text should, therefore, be fully appreciated, and its historical process of formation can always be recreated to some extent. In this way, we can embrace both the synchronic and the diachronic levels, without confusing them, or pretending that one of them is superior to the other.

---

132 See Clines, *The Theme of the Pentateuch*, 25.
133 Cf. Cuddon, *The Penguin Dictionary of Literary Terms*, 421-22.
134 Clines rightly observes that "minor alterations in the received material, to say nothing of juxtapositions of differing traditional material, can result in large-scale differences of emphasis, significance and direction" (*The Theme of the Pentateuch*, 25).

3. A General Hermeneutical Model

Exegetical praxis always rests on the foundation of a hermeneutical theory. If the theory is sound, there is a good chance that our interpretive endeavours will succeed. If we are, however, unaware of the presuppositions or the proceedings of the exegetical approach which we adopt, we risk arriving at incomplete, or even false, conclusions. The other, no less dangerous, side of the coin is sharpening the critical tools so endlessly and perfectly that this effort actually prevents us from putting them into practice. Yet it is in exegesis where we can clearly see the limitations of hermeneutics. Without applying our tools to biblical texts, we can never learn about those tools' real value. For this reason the presentation of the general hermeneutical model in this chapter will be done at the service of the exegesis of Gen 21:1-21 in the chapters to follow.

This chapter will begin by examining Wayne C. Booth's theory of the *threefold interests* in literary texts and debating its value for the exegesis of ancient Hebrew narratives. Then I shall introduce Eric D. Hirsch's distinction between *meaning* and *significance*, and combine it with the theory of literary interests. My third step, inspired by Ricoeurian hermeneutics, will consist in distinguishing the three types of the reader's *knowledge* about reality, and discussing the way in which biblical narratives mediate between the world of the reader and the transcendent world which they project. Finally, since the whole discussion in this chapter raises a number of philosophical issues, in its last section, I will propose tentative answers to the most important of them.

3.1. The Threefold Interests of the Reader in the Text

Anybody who tries to describe the main characteristics of Wayne C. Booth's approach to literature arrives in the land of rhetorical criticism. To give a short definition of rhetorical criticism, the following can be quoted: "[Rhetorical criticism] tries to analyse how the text is constructed: not just its verbal patterns or its use of imagery, but how it is articulated, how the argument carries the reader along."[1] In other words, a rhetorical critic's task is to explain how certain features of a literary work participate in the process of communication between the text and its reader. Thus, we are not surprised to see how Booth defines the main focus of *The Rhetoric of Fiction*, a book which has become a classic for students of literature: "My subject is the technique of non-didactic fiction, viewed as the art of communicating – the rhetorical resources available to the writer of epic, novel, or short story as he tries, consciously or unconsciously, to impose his fictional world upon the reader."[2]

It is worth remarking that Booth is very consistent throughout his book. Even when he discusses literary features characteristic of the reader, he always analyses these problems with reference to the text, and his approach is more or less text-centred. At the same time, he never performs his analyses in total isolation from the world of readers, and hence he breaks with the rigid principles of the New Criticism.[3] In the light of a very helpful distinction between two groups of literary critics, of which the first asks *what it is about the texts* that generates meaning, whereas the second poses the question *what it is about us* that generates meaning,[4] Booth belongs definitely to the first group, although he does not disregard issues characteristic of the second. Because of this critical attitude, scholars differ on classifying Booth's critical output. Mark A. Powell, in his introductory book on narrative criticism published in 1990, mentions Booth in a short chapter devoted to rhetorical criticism, and suggests that, in secular literary circles, Booth is considered a rhetorical critic, whereas in biblical studies, his writings are regarded as a part of narrative criticism.[5] Oddly enough, two years later Powell writes: "The most influential heir of New Criticism in the modern day is Wayne Booth. Booth, who sometimes tries to disassociate himself with the movement, has in fact moderated the approach of New Criticism in a way that continues to appeal to a wide variety of scholars."[6] Then he does not mention Booth at all, when he

---

1   Barton, *Reading the Old Testament*, 209.
2   Booth, *The Rhetoric of Fiction*, xiii. The beginning of the rhetorical approach to texts in biblical exegesis can be precisely dated to December 1968, when James Muilenberg, during his address to the Society of Biblical Literature, emphasized the need for understanding biblical texts as a whole, and not only as the sum of many independent literary units (see Barton, *Reading the Old Testament*, 199).
3   Cf. Powell, Curtis, and Gray, *The Bible and Modern Literary Criticism*, 10-11.
4   See Barton, *Reading the Old Testament*, 209.
5   See Powell, *What Is Narrative Criticism?*, 15.
6   Powell, Curtis, and Gray, *The Bible and Modern Literary Criticism*, 7.

discusses rhetorical criticism. In contrast, Susan R. Suleiman situates Booth within the reader-response movement, and she regards his approach as an example of a rhetorical variety of audience-oriented criticism.⁷ "To the rhetorical critic," argues Suleiman, "what matters primarily is the ethical and ideological content of the message. He seeks not only to formulate the set of verbal meanings embedded in the text, but above all to discover the values and beliefs that make those meanings possible – or that those meanings imply."⁸

As a result, we get a slightly perplexing set of views concerning this one critic. Is Booth a modern heir of the New Criticism, or a rhetorical critic but not a reader-response critic, or rather a reader-response theorist whose approach is rhetorical? How should we understand those who situate him within the field of narrative criticism? Is he one of those mercurial critics, like Stanley Fish, who resist any attempt to classify them? Certainly, part of the problem seems to be that narrative criticism is a very broad and eclectic category, and that it partially overlaps other fields of criticism. Since many exponents of narrative criticism make use of Booth's ideas, such as *implied author* and *reliable narrator*, he may be perceived as a critic working directly within narrative criticism. Yet Booth did not intend to create an all-inclusive theory of narrative. In the preface to *The Rhetoric of Fiction*, he clearly states that his endeavour is more limited: "I am aware that in pursuing the author's means of controlling his reader I have arbitrarily isolated technique from all of the social and psychological forces that affect authors and readers. ... I have, in short, ruled out many of the most interesting questions about fiction."⁹ Hence, although his literary concepts are useful in narrative criticism, he cannot simply be called a typical representative of the latter.

In view of that, Booth paves the way for reader-response criticism, but he is not its main proponent because he emphasizes the fundamental role of the text and its stylistic devices. As he himself admits, he is a disciple of "The Chicago School," and thus shows respect for the text's authority.¹⁰ Booth's place is, therefore, in rhetorical criticism, or, in other words, half-way between the New Criticism and various reader-response approaches. If we made a foray into the woods of reader-response criticism, we would meet Booth in a small, shady glade, just in the place where a highway leading to the woods ends, and a narrow,

---

7   See Suleiman, "Introduction," 7-11.
8   Suleiman, "Introduction," 8.
9   Booth, *The Rhetoric of Fiction*, xiii-xiv.
10 See Iser, Holland, and Booth, "Interview," 66.

winding footpath to the dense woodland begins. It is exactly where the sun of text-centred approaches starts shining more and more dimly through the dense leafage of audience-response criticism.[11]

In the first part of *The Rhetoric of Fiction*, Booth spells out rules which govern works of fiction, and which constitute their rhetorical dimension. In doing this, Booth is critical of other scholars' opinions, and never allows himself to accept their argument easily; rather, he presents different opinions to introduce his own point of view. In the book, he discusses first three rules that govern modern fiction under the headings: "True Novels Must Be Realistic," "All Authors Should Be Objective," and "True Art Ignores the Audience."[12] Then he introduces the fourth group of rules, which he calls "Emotions, Beliefs, and the Reader's Objectivity,"[13] and which provides a context for the discussion of the types of literary interests.

Hence Booth proposes the following classification of the reader's interests: "intellectual or cognitive," "qualitative," and "practical,"[14] and associates these three groups of interests with the three Platonic ideas of truth, beauty, and goodness, as Ska precisely observes.[15] As regards the first group, I prefer to call it "cognitive," since the term "intellectual," used together with "qualitative" and "practical," may inadvertently suggest that the second and third types of interests are somehow "non-intellectual." Hence the term "cognitive," even though not devoid of potential difficulties, appears to fit the tripartite structure better. Moreover, following Booth's suggestion, I shall call the second group of interests "aesthetic," which, of course, does not suggest that "a literary form using this interest was necessarily of more artistic value than one based on other interests."[16]

The cognitive interests manifest themselves in "strong intellectual curiosity about 'the facts,' the true interpretation, the true reasons, the

---

11 One must remember that any effort to classify a literary critic is often approximate. There are chapters of Booth's *The Rhetoric of Fiction* which show his New Critical background. There are other parts which testify to his deep interest in reader-response approaches. Moreover, Booth's critical attitude evolved over the years. In *The Company We Keep*, he is even closer to typical reader-response approaches.
12 See Booth, *The Rhetoric of Fiction*, 23-118.
13 See Booth, *The Rhetoric of Fiction*, 119-47.
14 Booth, *The Rhetoric of Fiction*, 125.
15 See Booth, *The Rhetoric of Fiction*, 133; see Ska, *Our Fathers Have Told Us*, 62.
16 Booth, *The Rhetoric of Fiction*, 125. Booth, speaking of the three types of literary interests, prefers using the term *interests* in the plural, rather than *interest*. By and large, I shall follow this convention because it emphasizes the plurality and complexity of the term.

true origins, the true motives, or the truth about life itself."¹⁷ The reader who pursues the cognitive interests is thus preoccupied with the discovery of different aspects of truth in literary works. Booth gives the example of Fyodor Dostoevski's *Crime and Punishment*, which arouses our curiosity "about the philosophical and religious and political battle between nihilism and relativism on the one hand and salvation on the other."¹⁸ Hence our cognitive interests engage us in analysis and reasoning, and make us pay attention to the characters of the novel inasmuch as they reveal to us diverse truths. However, according to Booth, there are not many works which are based almost solely on the reader's cognitive interests; the philosophical treatise and the purely ratiocinative detective novel are among a few examples.¹⁹

"We have, or can be made to have," writes Booth about the aesthetic interests, "a strong desire to see any pattern or form completed, or to experience a further development of qualities of any kind."²⁰ He then enumerates different types of qualities that we may seek: a cause-effect chain; conventional expectations; abstract forms, such as balance, symmetry, climax, repetition, contrast, and comparison; as well as "promised" qualities, namely qualities characteristic of each particular work (e.g. a peculiar stylistic or symbolic brilliance, an original kind of wit, irony, or convincing character portrayal).²¹ By way of illustration, in *Crime and Punishment*, "we would like more of this skill in transforming disagreeable characters into sympathetic portraits, and Dostoevski does not disappoint us."²² Booth is aware that some of the above qualities could well be discussed under the heading of the cognitive interests, but we must keep in mind that "the satisfaction we receive from the following qualities [i.e. the aesthetic qualities] is to some degree distinct from the pleasure of learning,"²³ and, in consequence, it seems justified to treat them as a separate category.

Clarifying the notion of the practical interests, Booth remarks aptly:

> If we look closely at our responses to most great novels, we discover that we feel a strong concern for the characters as people; we care about their good and bad fortune. In most works of any significance, we are made to admire or detest, to love or hate, or simply to approve or disapprove of at

---

17 Booth, *The Rhetoric of Fiction*, 125.
18 Booth, *The Rhetoric of Fiction*, 134.
19 See Booth, *The Rhetoric of Fiction*, 126.
20 Booth, *The Rhetoric of Fiction*, 125.
21 See Booth, *The Rhetoric of Fiction*, 126-28.
22 Booth, *The Rhetoric of Fiction*, 134.
23 Booth, *The Rhetoric of Fiction*, 126.

least one central character, and our interest in reading from page to page, like our judgment upon the book after reconsideration, is inseparable from this emotional involvement.[24]

Booth draws our attention to two implications of the practical interests. First, he tells us that they stimulate the emotions of hope and fear.[25] This, and the following chapters, will show that the emotional aspect of the practical interests plays an important role in the overall literary evaluation of a work because the reader's affective response to a work results from his or her practical interests. *Crime and Punishment* provides us with another example: "We sympathize with Raskolnikov in a peculiarly intense fashion from beginning to end; we wish passionately, though without much hope, for his happiness, and we fear the very punishment which our interest in cause-and-effect patterns demands."[26] Secondly, Booth objects to those critics who underplay "the role that moral judgment plays in most of our worthwhile reading."[27] He is convinced that, irrespective of our subjective judgment on the personages of a novel, we cannot avoid a general moral judgment when it comes to the evaluation of the principles upon which the personages' behaviour is based.[28] Hence he states: "We may tell ourselves that we do not condemn stupidity and viciousness, but we believe that men ought not to be stupid and vicious nonetheless. We may explain the villain's behavior by relating him to his environment, but even to explain away is to admit that something requires excuse."[29] Booth's emphasis on the moral judgment in reading, and the categories of goodness and evil associated with this judgment, will be important to the discussion in the following chapters.

The unquestionable strength of *The Rhetoric of Fiction* lies in the fact that Booth draws upon his vast knowledge of world literature. The book is full of quotations and examples, which make its theoretical dimension extremely well rooted in "literary reality," in contrast to many modern critics who often do not care about exemplifying their statements. Booth is aware of this advantage when he says that "in a time when too much criticism, pursuing 'autonomy,' floats off into the Great

---

24 Booth, *The Rhetoric of Fiction*, 129-30.
25 See Booth, *The Rhetoric of Fiction*, 125, 30. Aristotle is also interested in two kinds of emotion: fear and pity. Every well-written tragedy provokes these two emotions (see e.g. *Poet.* 1453b 1-5, *CWA* 2:2326).
26 Booth, *The Rhetoric of Fiction*, 134.
27 Booth, *The Rhetoric of Fiction*, 131.
28 See Booth, *The Rhetoric of Fiction*, 131-33.
29 Booth, *The Rhetoric of Fiction*, 131.

Inane, with never a reference to anything but its own concept-spinning, there is surely room for a criticism that is openly embedded in and respectful of the stuff that it criticizes."[30] Another feature of the book is the meticulousness of presentation combined with outstanding clarity. Even though the author's reasoning is based upon extensive literary material, the reader never loses track of what is under discussion. Seymour Chatman praises this aspect of the book: "Values, norms, beliefs – Wayne Booth's *The Rhetoric of Fiction* has dealt with these elements in the novel with such sophistication that any account can only seem a footnote to his work."[31]

Furthermore, Booth underlines that his tripartite classification of literary interests remains only one of the possible ways of organizing critical thinking about the subject, and "there are unavoidable limitations in any one choice."[32] This, however, is not a downside of his approach; it is an inevitable drawback of all possible classifications. In addition, Booth is aware that our interests in literary works partially overlap. In many cases, it is not possible to speak of the three kinds of interests in their pure form. Yet if we had always been able to distinguish sharply between the three interests, literature would have lost its intricate and multifaceted character. Eliot's cautious approach to criticism, introduced in chapter 1, which always allows a margin of imprecision, explains very well why we should not expect from Booth's theory the exactitude characteristic of the sciences.

Finally, Booth reminds us that "even though most great works embody to some degree all three types of interest, some of the particular interests under each type are incompatible with each other and with some types of rhetoric."[33] In practice, the author must sacrifice some of his or her readers' interests in order to allow other interests come to the fore. Yet, as Booth rightly remarks, it is seldom the case that any of the three interests is completely suppressed. To use Booth's own example, even the philosophical treatise and the purely ratiocinative detective novel often contain a trace of aesthetic qualities, and may trigger the reader's emotional response.

To conclude, it appears that Booth's theory is solidly rooted in the literary soil, and, since numerous literary examples verify its legitimacy and applicability, the theory is useful in literary analysis. Moreover, the

---

30 Booth, *The Rhetoric of Fiction*, xii.
31 Chatman, *Story and Discourse*, 241.
32 Booth, *The Rhetoric of Fiction*, 124.
33 Booth, *The Rhetoric of Fiction*, 134.

theory conforms well to the critical approach which I have introduced in chapter 1 as a basis for my whole argument. Booth shows convincingly that his interpretive scheme is a valuable tool for the analysis of narrative texts, and even its intrinsic limitations help to discover the complexity and art of narrative. This is why I can adopt Booth's theory for the general hermeneutical model which will be introduced on the following pages.

3.2. The Three Dimensions of Biblical Narratives

To demonstrate the validity of Booth's theory in relation to biblical exegesis, I must discuss a number of issues. The questions which need to be addressed here are: To what extent is Booth's theory applicable to exegesis of narrative biblical texts? How should we properly distinguish between the original meaning of a biblical text and different meanings discovered in this text by modern readers? This, and the next subchapter, will attempt to answer these questions.

There are at least four reasons why Booth's theory seems valuable for the exegesis of biblical narrative texts. First, as I showed in chapter 1, an exegete is entitled to use general literary hermeneutics in biblical interpretation. Secondly, Gen 21:1-21, and the whole Abraham cycle (Gen 11:27 – 25:18), are examples of a narrative text, defined by Genette as an "oral or written discourse that undertakes to tell of an event or a series of events."[34] Similarly, Booth deals with narrative fiction, predominantly with the novel, and what Booth discusses are diverse examples of "written discourses that undertake to tell of a series of events." Moreover, there are parallels between the definition of the modern novel, the characteristics of the passage under discussion, and the whole cycle to which the passage belongs. J. A. Cuddon calls the novel "a form of story or prose narrative containing characters, action and incident, and, perhaps, a plot."[35] Without making too hasty comparisons, I may say that the above definition of the novel fits well both Gen 21:1-21 and the whole Abraham cycle. Having said this, I must, of course, emphasize that the passage under discussion differs from the novel in at least three respects. The novel is usually a free-standing literary work, whereas the Abraham cycle is part of the book of Genesis. In turn, Genesis is part of the Pentateuch, and of the Hebrew Bible. In

---

34 Genette, *Narrative Discourse: An Essay*, 25.
35 Cuddon, *The Penguin Dictionary of Literary Terms*, 561.

addition, literary styles employed by the authors and editors of the Hebrew Bible and those of the modern novel are poles apart, even if the Bible has influenced, directly or indirectly, later literature. Next, in the case of Gen 21:1-21, and the whole Abraham cycle, we are dealing with a short story, whereas the modern novel is considerably longer. These differences, however, do not invalidate the idea of a basic affinity between the novel and the Abraham cycle, an affinity founded upon their narrative character, as well as upon the presence of characters, action, incident, and plot.[36] Hence Booth's analysis of the rhetoric of fiction is relevant to our biblical passage.

Thirdly, Booth's theory has a general application. Although he discusses the reader's interests concerning prose, his theory may be applied to poetry without any special adjustments. By way of example, when we read George Herbert's "Love," we discover the truth about divine love and human awareness of sin; we enjoy the poem's subtle stylistic devices; finally, we sympathize with the author, and participate in the forgiveness offered to him by Love.[37] Therefore, Booth's treatment of the reader's interests can be applied to any kind of literature, and what distinguishes the results of this application is that it focuses upon a particular type of rhetoric which distinguishes a given genre of literature. Since a commonsense judgment tells us that we may learn something from any specimen of literature, enjoy its aesthetic values, and feel concern for its characters, it is legitimate to use Booth's theory in the exegesis of biblical narrative texts without further ado.

Fourthly, an attentive reader of *The Rhetoric of Fiction* may raise an important objection here. How should we understand Booth's statement from the preface to the first edition of the book? He declares:

> I am writing about the rhetoric of fiction, I am not primarily interested in didactic fiction, fiction used for propaganda and instruction. My subject is the technique of non-didactic fiction, viewed as the art of communicating with readers – the rhetorical resources available to the writer of epic, novel, or short story as he tries, consciously or unconsciously, to impose his fictional world upon the reader.[38]

Does the Abraham cycle deserve to be called non-didactic fiction? At first glance, it seems that the opposite is the case. As I will show in

---

36 Interestingly, Cuddon is convinced that the origins of the novel can be found in the Egyptian Middle Kingdom (such texts as *The Predestined Prince* or *Sinuhe*), but he does not mention the Bible (*The Penguin Dictionary of Literary Terms*, 562). Perhaps, like Eliot, Cuddon thought that the Bible could not be regarded as literature.
37 Herbert, "Love," *PBEV*, 113-14.
38 Booth, *The Rhetoric of Fiction*, xiii.

chapter 5, from the point of view of literary genre, the Abraham cycle should be classified as a collection of "patriarchal stories" or "narratives about Israel's ancestors," which are a kind of non-historical and non-biographical fiction arising from the community of Israel's need for self-definition.[39] This need for self-definition is a sign of the didactic character of the patriarchal stories. At the same time, however, the didactic character of the patriarchal stories should not be overestimated. On the one hand, they were written and read for instruction; on the other, as literature and fiction, they retain their pure artistic value. So, they lie half way between didactic and non-didactic fiction, and thus remain within the scope of Booth's interest. What is more, the border between didactic and non-didactic fiction appears to be less clear-cut if we remember that it is hardly possible to find a specimen of non-didactic fiction which would be devoid of any instructive aspects: "the distinction between genuine literature (or 'poetry') and 'rhetoric' and 'didactic' literature is entirely misleading if it suggests that some stories, those that we seem to read just for enjoyment, are purged of all teaching."[40] Finally, Booth, in the first chapter of his book, analyses the book of Job and the two Homeric epics as examples of "direct and authoritative rhetoric,"[41] and the very fact that he deals with them proves that, in his discussion, there is room for ancient fiction, including the Bible.

I would now like to show how Booth's theory may be incorporated into a general hermeneutical model which I will propose in this chapter, and how my critical approach differs from Booth's. When we read Booth's examination of the reader's interests within the context of the whole *Rhetoric of Fiction*, we see that he begins with the analysis of the reader's various interests; he then classifies them, and demonstrates how they lead to the discovery of rhetorical devices present in the text; next, he explains how the author uses the rhetorical resources to control the reader.[42] Thus, taking into account the basic elements of the model of narrative communication, Booth's logic can be depicted in the following way:

---

39 Cf. Westermann, *Genesis 12-36*, 41-50. I explain the fictional character of the patriarchal stories in the last section of this chapter.
40 Booth, *The Company We Keep*, 151-52.
41 Booth, *The Rhetoric of Fiction*, 6.
42 I must emphasize that this is the internal logic of Booth's discussion of the three types of interests, but not necessarily of the whole book. The idea of the threefold interests is only one of the many concepts which Booth presents there.

> readers with their interests → narrative →
> implied author → real author

Booth concentrates on the distinction between *real author* and *implied author*, and says of the latter: "Even the novel in which no narrator is dramatized creates an implicit picture of an author who stands behind the scenes. ... This implied author is always distinct from the 'real man' – whatever we may take him to be – who creates a superior version of himself, a 'second self,' as he creates his work."[43]

As will soon be obvious, the main emphasis in my discussion will be placed on other elements of the model of narrative communication. First, I am interested in the concept of *implied reader*, which I have already defined in chapter 1. Secondly, I would like to emphasize the link between a particular kind of interest and its corresponding Platonic *idea of truth, beauty, and goodness*. The link is only cursorily mentioned by Booth, when he states: "We all seem convinced that a novel or play which does justice to our interest in truth, in beauty, and in goodness is superior to even the most successful 'novel of ideas,' 'well-made play,' or 'sentimental novel'"[44] I guess that Booth has not developed this topic because a discussion of the Platonic ideas would lead him too far away from criticism to philosophy. However, I shall adopt the link between the three interests and the three ideas as one of the main assumptions on which my general hermeneutical theory will be based. Following this line of reasoning, I may say that when readers pursue the three interests, they learn about different aspects of truth, beauty, and goodness, to the extent that the text's rhetoric allows them to do so. Thirdly, I would like to speak of three main *dimensions* of narrative, which correspond to the three kinds of the reader's interest. Hence I will speak of the *cognitive, aesthetic, and practical dimensions* of the text. The cognitive dimension of the text comprises a set of diverse factors, which are discovered by the reader who pursues his or her cognitive interests. These factors enable the reader to determine the different aspects of truth communicated by the text. A similar definition may be given as regards the aesthetic and practical dimensions. In view of the above, the logic of my critical approach is as follows:

> real reader → implied reader → three types of interests →
> narrative → three dimensions of narrative → three Platonic ideas

---

43   Booth, *The Rhetoric of Fiction*, 151.
44   Booth, *The Rhetoric of Fiction*, 133.

Now, I have arrived at the point where I can introduce my proposal concerning the *full theological dimension* of the text. I have shown that in the process of attentive reading of biblical narratives, the reader discovers its three dimensions: cognitive, aesthetic, and practical.[45] I would like to argue that these three dimensions constitute the full theological dimension of the text. If one considers Louis Jacobs's remark that "the whole of the Hebrew Bible has God as its concern,"[46] and if one keeps in view the "severely concrete, 'organic' nature of ancient Hebraic thought,"[47] one cannot confine the theological dimension of biblical narratives only to its cognitive aspect. There is no doubt that the importance of the cognitive ideas contained in the text should never be underestimated. Yet both the aesthetic and practical dimensions are also ways of conveying the theological message of the biblical text.

This apprehension of the theological dimension concurs with what Joseph A. Fitzmyer writes: "Narrative analysis not only recounts the story of salvation (in an 'informative' way), but also tells it (in a 'performative' way) in order to accost readers to get them to reflect existentially on the narrative salvific power for them."[48] I can only add that this salvific power becomes evident when we take into consideration all aspects of biblical narratives, which are multi-faceted, and cannot be reduced to only one dimension. Perhaps it is owing to their composite nature that biblical narratives have preserved the vital force to transform human lives. As Booth notices: "There is no reason why great novels cannot be written relying primarily on any one kind [of interests]. But it is clear that no great work is based on only one interest."[49] This is why I intend to demonstrate in this book that the Bible's literary grandeur is based on the fact that its narratives fully satisfy all the three interests in the text.

In conclusion, I would like to share my conviction that the theological dimension of the biblical text ought not to remain the last goal of our interpretive efforts, but the reader, through the act of faith, should turn to God – the ultimate source of truth, beauty, and goodness. In this context, the well-known words of St Augustine are worth quoting: "It is one thing from a wooded summit to catch a glimpse of the home-

---

45 Fowler calls the process of reading a "mysterious merger of text, reader, and context" ("Who Is the 'Reader,'" 15).
46 Jacobs, "Theology," *EJ* 15:1104.
47 Jacobs, "Theology," *EJ* 15:1105.
48 Fitzmyer, *The Biblical Commission's Document*, 61.
49 Booth, *The Rhetoric of Fiction*, 133.

land of peace and not to find the way to it. ... It is another thing to hold on to the way that leads there, defended by the protection of the heavenly emperor."[50]

3.3. Meaning and Significance

Biblical scholars of different persuasions who work in both secular and ecclesiastical contexts differ on the use of such fundamental critical terms as meaning, authorial intention, sense, and significance. As a result, their critical approaches are often incompatible with each other. A case in point is what David Jasper says about literary approaches in exegesis, which brought about "the change in focus of interest from the intention of the author and the original context of the writing, to the response of the reader in determining the meaning and significance of the text."[51] Jasper suggests that the onus is on the reader to establish meaning and significance, and that both of them result from the reader's response to the text. To give an example belonging to an ecclesiastical context, the Roman Catholic Biblical Commission's document *The Interpretation of the Bible in the Church* speaks of a certain tension between ancient exegesis, which "attributed to every text of Scripture several levels of meaning," and modern historical exegesis usually associated with "the thesis of the one single meaning."[52] The authors of the document suggest that we should speak about the literal, spiritual, and fuller senses of Scripture, by which they understand, respectively, the meaning intended by the human and the divine authors, the meaning of the text "when read, under the influence of the Holy Spirit, in the context of the paschal mystery of Christ and of the new life which flows from it,"[53] and "a deeper meaning of the text, intended by God but not clearly expressed by the human author."[54] When readers discover in the biblical text fresh meanings applicable to the contemporary context, this process is called by the authors of the document "actualization."[55] Even a brief look at the above distinctions shows a plurality of approaches to the problem of meaning. Jasper's and the Biblical Commission's intellectual frameworks differ greatly from each other. While

---

50 Augustine, *Conf.* VII. xxi (27) (transl. Chadwick, 131-32).
51 Jasper, "Literary Readings," 27.
52 Fitzmyer, *The Biblical Commission's Document*, 117.
53 Fitzmyer, *The Biblical Commission's Document*, 127.
54 Fitzmyer, *The Biblical Commission's Document*, 130.
55 See Fitzmyer, *The Biblical Commission's Document*, 170-76.

Jasper seems to situate meaning and significance in the reader's corner of the narrative communication model (author → text → reader), the Commission speaks about four kinds of meaning, which are established in many different ways, and with the aid of factors which do not belong to the communication model, such as interpretive tradition and the ecclesiastical hierarchy.

In view of that, an attempt to propose a clear definition of the above critical terms is crucial to my project. To do this, I would like to meet two criteria. First, I will give preference to a theory of meaning which is not overly elaborate. A theory of meaning which I would like to adopt in this dissertation will be only one part of a complex hermeneutical model, so it ought not to be unnecessarily complicated in order to avoid the theoretical proliferation of concepts. Secondly, I intend to use a theory applicable to both secular and ecclesiastical contexts. Thus the theory should be based upon the communication model, and it ought not to increase external interpretive factors. If a particular ecclesiastical context demands a further level of the validation of meaning, as is the case in many Christian communities, then the chosen theory of meaning should be flexible enough to add such a level.

I believe that a theory which can be adopted for the purpose of the hermeneutical model which I am proposing is Eric D. Hirsch's distinction between meaning and significance expounded in *Validity in Interpretation* and in *The Aims of Interpretation*. Hirsch defends the possibility of achieving hermeneutical knowledge, as well as the stability and determinacy of meaning. The tool with the aid of which he makes his defence is the just-mentioned distinction. Hirsch is right in saying that "if criticism is to be objective in any significant sense, it must be founded on a self-critical construction of textual meaning, which is to say, on objective interpretation."[56] He thus rightly claims that a failure to achieve an objective interpretation of a given text leads ineluctably to the potential fiasco of our critical efforts. Hirsch distinguishes between *interpretation* and *criticism*, and calls the object of interpretation the *meaning* of the text, whereas the proper object of criticism is the text's *significance*.[57] He defines meaning and significance in the following way:

> *Meaning* is that which is represented by a text; it is what the author meant by his use of a particular sign sequence; it is what the signs represent. *Significance*, on the other hand, names a relationship between that meaning and a person, or a conception, or a situation, or indeed anything imagina-

---

56 Hirsch, *Validity in Interpretation*, 210.
57 See Hirsch, *Validity in Interpretation*, 211.

ble. ... Significance always implies a relationship, and one constant, unchanging pole of that relationship is what the text means."[58]

Hirsch discusses in detail different aspects of the distinction between meaning and significance, but the core of his argument always remains the same. The meaning of the text cannot be discovered without recourse to its author, whilst the text's significance is always a function of its meaning.[59]

In the following paragraphs, I shall discuss the applicability of Hirsch's theory to biblical exegesis, and point to certain interpretive problems which that theory inevitably causes. However, before I do this, I should observe that as long as we are faithful to Eliot's approach to criticism (see chapter 1), which suggests that critical terms are guidelines rather than cut-and-dried definitions, Hirsch's categories provide us with a relatively safe tool for interpretation. After all, Hirsch is well aware of the limitations of his own theory when he states: "For most of my notions I disclaim any originality. ... If I display any argumentative intent, it is not, therefore, against the analytical movement, which I approve, but only against certain modern theories which hamper the establishment of normative principles in interpretation."[60]

The main problem concerning Hirsch's theory is that the above definition of meaning is based upon the notion of the author ("it is what the author meant"). Hirsch seems to be aware of this limitation, and, several pages later, stresses that his theory is applicable also to anonymous texts. Since most Hebrew Bible texts, including the passage under discussion, are anonymous, it seems impossible to define their meaning using the above definition.[61] Hirsch, however, finds a way out of this conundrum by saying that, in order to achieve interpretive accuracy, we are obliged to date anonymous texts as precisely as possible, and to recreate "the cultural and personal attitudes the author might be expected to bring to bear in specifying his verbal meanings."[62] As Barton reminds us, this is exactly what we look for in the historical-critical method. Historical-critical scholarship is preoccupied with the original meaning of biblical passages, places them in their original con-

---

58 Hirsch, *Validity in Interpretation*, 8.
59 See e.g. Hirsch, *The Aims of Interpretation*, 79-81.
60 Hirsch, *Validity in Interpretation*, 212.
61 Not only is the concept of the *author* hardly applicable to most ancient Hebrew texts, but we also have *non-authored* Hebrew texts, or, strictly speaking, collections, such as legal codices, proverbs, and sayings.
62 Hirsch, *Validity in Interpretation*, 240.

texts, and helps us determine what their authors might have meant.[63] As a result, the meaning of Gen 21:1-21 can be determined by applying the tools of the historical-critical method to the narrative. Yet "neither inclusion in a literary canon, nor inclusion in the biblical canon, actually changes the meaning of a text," writes Barton; "what it does is to declare that the text, in its original meaning, is a classic, which still has power to speak now, and always will have."[64] This "power to speak now" is the text's significance. In consequence, the original meaning of Gen 21:1-21, studied in isolation from any broader context, is usually different from its significance, which the unit acquires through relating it to any context different from the original one.

Having said this, we see that the original meaning of biblical texts recreated by the historical method still remains closely linked to the authorial intention: instead of claiming adamantly that we *know* what the author *meant*, we now talk cautiously about the "attitudes the author *might be expected to bring*," and what the author *might have meant*. Is this cautious approach safe enough to prevent us from falling into the trap of intentional fallacy, "the error of criticizing and judging a work of literature by attempting to assess what the writer's intention was and whether or not he has fulfilled it rather than concentrating on the work itself"?[65] I believe that it is not, and we should seek a further refinement of Hirsch's categories.[66]

Since we deal with anonymous texts, and, as a result, their authors and redactors evade our critical eyes, it appears that the definition of meaning should be based upon the notion of the text. What is more, the distinction between meaning, which relates to the text's original context, and significance, which reflects its subsequent reception, should be safeguarded in order to preserve the distance between the original and the modern reception of the text. Hence the remark made by Eco about modern literature applies also to our case: "The private life of the empirical authors is in a certain respect more unfathomable than their texts. Between the mysterious history of a textual production and the

---

63   Barton, "Historical-Critical Approaches," 10-11.
64   Barton, *Reading the Old Testament*, 178.
65   Cuddon, *The Penguin Dictionary of Literary Terms*, 421.
66   Ricoeur gives a clear reason for this: "We underestimate the phenomenon of writing if we reduce it to the simple material fixation of living speech. Writing stands in a specific relation to what is said. It produces a form of discourse that is immediately autonomous with regard to its author's intention" (*Essays*, 99). To put it another way, the author, who is a user of linguistic signs, and a creator of textual reality, discovers in the end that as soon as signs become fixated in a written form, they begin an existence which is, to a great extent, independent of their creator.

uncontrollable drift of its future readings, the text qua text still represents a comfortable presence, the point to which we can stick."[67] Eco underlines that a quest for the authorial intention is very difficult and often irrelevant to the interpretive process, and, instead, he introduces the concept of *intentio operis* (*intention of the text*), which is related to and contrasted with *intentio auctoris* and *intentio lectoris*.[68]

Eco introduces his theory in two clear steps. First, he states that *intentio operis* is not given directly, but the reader must always infer it from textual data: "since the intention of the text is basically to produce a model reader able to make conjectures about it, the initiative of the model reader consists in figuring out a model author that is not the empirical one and that, in the end, coincides with the intention of the text."[69] As we can see, in such a case, we hardly need to take the real author's intention into consideration.[70] Yet, secondly and importantly, there are cases when the real author plays an important role in the interpretive process. Taking one of Wordsworth's poems as an example, Eco stresses that "to *interpret* Wordsworth's text I must respect his cultural and linguistic background."[71] What is important, however, is that, even in this case, Eco refrains from talking about the authorial intention, but focuses on the author's cultural background.[72]

---

67 Eco, *Interpretation and Overinterpretation*, 88.
68 Eco, *Interpretation and Overinterpretation*, 25. These three concepts explain the "dialectics between the rights of texts and the rights of their interpreters." Eco adds that "in the course of the last few decades, the rights of the interpreters have been overstressed" (*The Limits of Interpretation*, 6).
69 Eco, *Interpretation and Overinterpretation*, 64. The model reader is a "sort of ideal type whom the text not only foresees as a collaborator but also tries to create" (Eco, *Six Walks*, 9). In turn, the model author is a voice "manifested as a narrative strategy, as a set of instructions which is given to us step by step and which we have to follow when we decide to act as the model reader" (*Six Walks*, 15). The terms *model author* and *model reader* are similar in meaning to Booth's *implied author* and Iser's *implied reader*.
70 Cf. Eco, *Interpretation and Overinterpretation*, 66.
71 Eco, *Interpretation and Overinterpretation*, 69.
72 Eco's theory is not devoid of philosophical problems, as, indeed, is any theory of meaning. In her review of *The Limits of Interpretation*, Bal criticizes Eco for a "casual use of key concepts," and says that the "*intentio operis* is not an intention at all, but an interpretation, personified in an image of subjective agency that is projected, ultimately and inevitably, upon the author" ("The Predicament of Semiotics," 547). Bal is right in saying that only a *person* can have a "real" *intention*, and so *intentio operis* cannot be called *intention* in the proper sense of the word. However, I believe that Eco's approach to the problem, despite its deficiencies, remains a successful attempt to free the meaning of the text from the authorial intention, and, for this reason, I can accept it here.

How should we then understand the *meaning* of biblical narratives in the light of the above discussion? As I see it, the meaning of a narrative is its *intentio operis*, which is discovered by the reader in the conjectural and circular process of interaction between a model reader and a model author, and which respects the linguistic and cultural background of its creation.[73] When that original background is removed and replaced by a different context, i.e. "another mind, another era, a wider subject matter, an alien system of values, and so on,"[74] we arrive at the text's *significance*. What is important, however, is that both meaning and significance are closely related to *intentio operis*. If we put the emphasis in our critical praxis on *intentio lectoris*, we no longer, according to Eco, *interpret* the text but we *use* it.[75] In chapter 5, I shall show examples of overinterpreting texts by certain types of reader-response criticism, which stress the importance of *intentio lectoris* at the expense of *intentio operis*.

Now, in order to root the whole discussion in the exegesis of biblical narratives, I should show how the terms *meaning* and *significance* apply to my model pericope. It appears that the pericope changed its meaning during the successive stages of its compilation. For Westermann, scenes 2 and 3 of the narrative (Gen 21:8-21) are a story about deliverance and God's salvific action.[76] Yet, as Westermann subsequently points out, "The narrative has taken on another meaning inasmuch as it has been resumed by and applied to the people of Israel. This was done by inserting the promises about the descendants of Isaac and Ishmael in vv. 12bβ-13 and 17aβ-18, thereby throwing the emphasis in the narrative on the separate destinies of the two children and their descendants."[77] It seems that the "transformation of meaning" applies to most biblical texts, and in order to explain this phenomenon in clear terms and in accordance with Hirsch's theory, it is better to speak about a set of different texts which have different meanings rather than about one text which gradually changes its meaning. Hence the process of inserting new material into a given text, or rewriting the text, results in the creation of a new text, and of a new, though sometimes only

---

73 It is my intention to dissociate the definition of *meaning* from the concepts of the *original author* and *original audience*. In the case of the Hebrew Bible, the concept of the *original author* is highly elusive, and an attempt to identify the *original audience* is also hypothetical.
74 Hirsch, *The Aims of Interpretation*, 2-3.
75 See Eco, *The Limits of Interpretation*, 57-58.
76 See Westermann, *Genesis 12-36*, 344.
77 Westermann, *Genesis 12-36*, 344.

slightly different, meaning. In our case, however, these "earlier texts" ceased to exist as a result of the process of their rewriting. Nevertheless, as long as we are discussing the stages of a text's formation, or its final form, but within its original context, we are dealing with its meaning. As soon as we leave the original context, and look at the text from a different vantage point, we arrive at the text's significance.

Certainly, we can speak of many different levels of the text's significance resulting from relating its meaning to different contexts. First, in the case of the Bible, the text acquires its significance as a part of the biblical canon.[78] Discussing the canonical shape of Genesis, Brevard S. Childs states that the central theological theme of Genesis is God's promises given to the patriarchs.[79] In Gen 12, he sees the first clear statement of two fundamental promises: the promise of posterity (v. 2, "I will make of you a great nation"), and the promise of the land (v. 7, "To your descendants I will give this land").[80] He then qualifies his statement, and writes that "within the canonical context of the book of Genesis the promises to the patriarchs have been clearly assigned a different role. ... The divine words of assurance have been set within an *eschatological pattern* [my emphasis] of prophecy and fulfilment which now stretches from Abraham to Joshua."[81] By saying this, Childs draws our attention to the fact that, in the original setting, the promises given to the patriarchs were to be fulfilled in a short period of time. Only the incorporation of the promises within the broader framework of Genesis resulted in their temporal extension: "The promises function only as a prelude to the coming exodus, and extend into the distant future."[82] The narrative Gen 21:1-21 does not contain a direct promise related to the land, but a promise regarding Abraham's progeny. The opening scene of the narrative (vv. 1-8) contains the fulfilment of the promise of the son: Sarah conceives, and gives birth to Isaac; the child is circum-

---

78 In *Biblical Theology of the Old and New Testaments*, Childs reminds us that we should read Old Testament narratives in the context of the whole Scripture. "The challenge of Biblical Theology," argues Childs, "is to engage in the continual activity of theological reflection which studies the canonical text in detailed exegesis, and seeks to do justice to the witness of both testaments in the light of its subject matter who is Jesus Christ" (78-79). Needless to say, the model pericope has its direct thematic continuation in diverse New Testament passages, which throw new light on Gen 21:1-21, and create new levels of significance. However, because this is a subject in its own right, I will not discuss it here.
79 See Childs, *Introduction to the Old Testament*, 150-52.
80 See Childs, *Biblical Theology*, 125.
81 Childs, *Introduction to the Old Testament*, 151.
82 Childs, *Introduction to the Old Testament*, 151.

cised in accordance with the divine command in Gen 17:10-14, and subsequently weaned. Then, in vv. 11-12, we encounter a promise concerning both Isaac and Ishmael: Abraham will have numerous descendants through both sons. The promise concerning Ishmael is, in turn, reiterated in v. 18. Childs's remarks help us to see the promises in Gen 21:1-21 in a new light, and since its central theological theme, which is part of the narrative's meaning, changes through the incorporation of the narrative into the whole book and into the Pentateuch, we discover the narrative's new significance.[83]

Apart from the canonical context, the narrative's significance has been changing through the centuries depending on its readers, and on various cultural circumstances. The ages of patristic and mediaeval exegesis provide us with numerous examples, which, due to this book's main objective, cannot be fully dealt with here.[84] What interests me most, however, is the narrative's significance to its modern readers. This is why the subsequent chapters of the dissertation will be a her-

---

83 Nevertheless, it appears that the contribution of the canonical approach to exegesis of Gen 21:1-21 is not as impressive as may seem to follow from the above paragraph. The theme of the promises given to the patriarchs is commonplace in the historical-critical literature of the subject. Westermann makes the same observations concerning the promises as Childs, without recourse to the canonical approach: "A distinction is to be made between those [promises] which are spoken into a situation of need or anxiety or uncertainty, such as correspond to the way of life of the patriarchs, and those which do not correspond to this situation, and whose fulfillment consequently can take place *only much later* [my emphasis]. To the first group belong the promise of a son, of new pasture lands, and of presence; to the second, the promise of the possession of the land, of an abundant posterity, and blessing in general" (*Genesis 12-36*, 112). As a result, even if, to some extent, the canonical approach broadens a theological perspective offered by other approaches, it is difficult to regard its own contribution as really significant and irreplaceable. Barr correctly states, "In some books only thin results emerge from the canonical reading: in the important book of Genesis, for instance, really rather little" ("Childs' Introduction," 17). However, a great value of canonical criticism, which undoubtedly remains despite the above criticism, and which should be taken into consideration, is its call to interpret every biblical passage in the light of the whole of Scripture.

84 There are numerous patristic commentaries on Gen 21:1-21. By way of example, Chrysostom interprets "Sarah's giving birth in her old age … as a figure of the church," and points out that Abraham's "remarkable obedience and gratitude along with God's ineffable care and considerateness provide material for moral reflection." Sarah's cruel behaviour is understood, after St Paul, allegorically as representing the "opposition between the flesh and the spirit." Even the "skin of water," according to Origen, "provides the opportunity for an allegorical contrast with the church that drinks from 'wells.'" Similarly, the inability to spot the "well of water" symbolizes our spiritual blindness. Chrysostom tells us that "God's intervention … demon-

meneutical study of the meaning and modern significance of Gen 21:1-21.

Finally, the distinction between meaning and significance throws interesting light on my principal interpretive scheme, namely reading biblical narratives through the prism of the reader's interest in truth, beauty and goodness. Hence the full theological dimension of biblical narrative texts, which comprises the cognitive, aesthetic, and practical dimensions, results from the literary interplay involving three groups of factors: first, the threefold interest of the reader in the text; secondly, the context in which the text is analysed: either the original, or the modern context; thirdly, the text's meaning and significance. As a result, the full theological dimension comprises six categories: cognitive meaning, aesthetic meaning, and practical meaning, on the one hand; cognitive significance, aesthetic significance, and practical significance, on the other (Figure 1, p. 94).[85]

These six categories should be taken into consideration when we attempt to describe the theological dimension of biblical narratives, but the above distinction needs further discussion. As Alter observes:

> One might imagine the Bible as a rich and variegated landscape, perfectly accessible to the observer's eye, but from which we now stand almost three millennia distant. Through the warp of all those intervening centuries, lines become blurred, contours are distorted, colors fade; for not only have we lost the precise shadings of implication of the original Hebrew words but we have also acquired quite different habits and expectations as readers, have forgotten the very conventions around which the biblical tales were shaped.[86]

The importance of Alter's remarks ought not to be belittled. The historical distance between the modern and ancient reader is significant in the case of ancient Hebrew narratives. While we should be able to establish the three aspects of the text's significance relatively easily, a similar task regarding the text's aspects of meanings is far from being

---

strates his loving kindness," whereas, according to Cyril of Alexandria, "Hagar, understood allegorically (following Paul) as the 'mother of the Jews,' continues to have the opportunity to draw from the fountain of living water (Christ) if she begins to weep" (all quotations from Sheridan, *Genesis 12-50*, 89-99).

85 I must emphasize that when I combine Hirsch's theory of meaning and significance with Booth's discussion of the three types of literary interests, I do it *mutatis mutandis*. In Hirsch's conceptual world both *meaning* and *significance* correspond to what I call *cognitive meaning* (or, simply, *meaning*) and *cognitive significance*. To my best knowledge, Hirsch does not examine non-cognitive dimensions of the text such as aesthetic or practical.

86 Alter, *The Art of Biblical Narrative*, 185.

straightforward and obvious. I have already mentioned that historical-critical scholarship helps us establish the text's meaning. However, we must now ask what aspects of meaning the historical method is able to highlight.

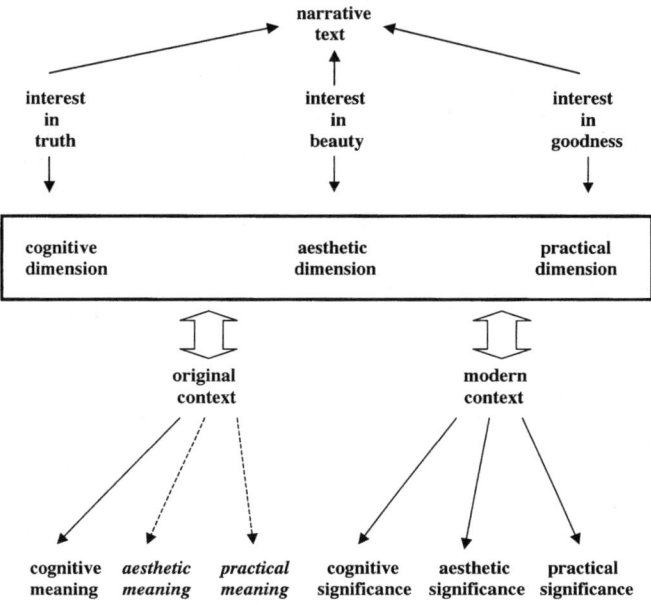

Figure 1. The full theological dimension of the text.

When we search for the aesthetic meaning of a text, we are interested in patterns, forms, and qualities of various kinds present in the text, and recognizable within the original context. Yet, in order to say which qualities were identifiable in that context, we need some ancient aesthetic criteria. What counted as *beautiful* to ancient Israelites? Since, apart from the Hebrew Bible, we have hardly any kind of ancient Hebrew literature, and, what is more, the Bible itself does not provide us with clear aesthetic criteria, this question is not easy to answer. Our expectations and conventions differ greatly from those of ancient Israelites, as Alter reminds us. Similarly, practical meaning is also difficult to establish. It is so because the text's practical dimension is not limited to its moral content. If it were, our practical interests would simply be part of or even equal to cognitive interests. What, however, distinguishes practical interests from cognitive ones is the response of the reader to the fate of literary characters. "If we look closely at our responses to most great novels," states Booth, "we discover that we *feel* [my emphasis] a strong concern for the characters as people; we care about their good and bad fortune."[87] Hence, although we can recreate the ancient Hebrews' moral sensitivity to a satisfactory extent, we cannot say much about their emotional response to biblical narratives. It is true that the reader's response to the fate of literary characters often reflects the moral judgement pronounced on those characters, and it does not seem that Hebrew readers were excluded from this rule. Yet, on the other hand, we seldom encounter black-and-white personages in works of literature, and we may sometimes empathize with the characters whose moral values are questionable. Hence while Hebrew readers' emotional commitment to the characters of a narrative was related to their system of moral values, it seems difficult to establish the degree of their emotional response in the case of a particular narrative. In other words, the aesthetic and practical meanings of Hebrew narratives have been partially eclipsed by the centuries which have passed since the moment of their literary creation.

In contrast, the cognitive meaning of Hebrew narratives is much easier to grasp and analyse. The historical-critical method helps to reconstruct the original linguistic and cultural background of those narratives, and to establish a cognitive message communicated by the text. In the case of aesthetic and practical meanings, we are dealing with extratextual factors which are difficult to ascertain, i.e. with ancient aesthetic and reader-response criteria, whereas cognitive meaning, as I have shown before, results from the text's *intentio operis* established within the original context of the text's creation. Certainly, the degree to which we can determine *cognitive* meaning is directly proportional to the historical method's ability to recreate the original *cognitive* background in which the text was created and received. It appears, however, that, given the current state of modern biblical historical criticism, we can speculate about the cognitive aspects of the original background with a degree of probability certainly higher than in the case of aesthetic and practical aspects.[88] Therefore, on the following pages, I

---

87 Booth, *The Rhetoric of Fiction*, 129.
88 Any historical reconstruction is, by virtue of its object and method, hypothetical, and, in consequence, the historical-critical method has a number of limitations. The Biblical Commission, on the one hand, praises the method for its objectivity and the ability to arrive at the text's original meaning, but, on the other, states that the method "is not concerned with other possibilities of meaning which have been revealed at later stages of the biblical revelation and history of the Church" (Fitzmyer, *The*

shall focus on the aesthetic and practical *significance* of Gen 21:1-21, and I shall not examine the aesthetic and practical *meanings* of the pericope, even if such an examination would be challenging and intriguing. Nevertheless, since the three dimensions of the text are interrelated, the aesthetic and practical aspects of meaning will be indirectly present in the discussion of the cognitive meaning.

3.4. Ricoeurian Hermeneutics

In chapter 1, drawing upon Auerbach's and Alter's literary analyses, I discussed a number of features of ancient Hebrew narratives, two of which I would like to mention again: Hebrew narratives are a sign of transcendent reality, and possess the power "to draw us out" of ourselves. God in Gen 21:1-21 is one of the narrative's personages, but he is, at the same time, a sign signifying the presence of the transcendent world existing beyond the real and narrative worlds. God either appears, or is mentioned, in vv. 1-2, 4, 6, 12-13, 17-20, which constitute half of the verses of the narrative. He appears on the narrative stage suddenly, and we do not know from where exactly he comes. Unlike the human characters, his dwelling place and his nature are veiled in mystery. In vv. 17-18, he speaks to Hagar through his angel, who "called to Hagar from heaven."

The model pericope has also the power to "draw us out" of ourselves.[89] Attentive reading of the narrative leads us to the transcendent world, and we are, to some extent, forced to "forget" about our

---

Biblical Commission's Document, 48). In the next chapter, I shall discuss two accusations levelled at the historical method by postmodern biblicists, but here I can also mention one of the bluntest critics of the method, Walter Wink, who organizes his critique under five headings: "the method as practised was incommensurate with the intention of the texts"; "the ideology of objectivism drew historical criticism into a false consciousness"; "biblical studies increasingly fell prey to a form of technologism which regards as legitimate only those questions which its methods can answer"; "biblical criticism became cut off from any community for whose life its results might be significant"; and "biblical criticism developed in a historical context which has now changed; in the present context it is, as now practiced, obsolete" (see Wink, *The Bible in Human Transformation*, 2-15). Wink goes too far in his condemnation of the method. Suffice to say that as long as historical critics are aware of the limitations of the method, and do not absolutize its conclusions, the method offers a good degree of probability. After all, we do not have a better tool for reconstructing the past.

89 Cf. Alter, *The World of Biblical Literature*, 23.

own world. Alter, introducing the idea of "drawing us out" of ourselves, states that biblical literature achieves this effect in two ways: "it scrutinizes the human condition with such a probing, unblinking gaze that is conveyed in the most subtle narrative vehicle," as well as "by the boldness with which it represents human figures confronted, challenged, confounded by a reality beyond human ken."[90] Both features are present in the passage under discussion. Genesis 21:1-21 draws before our eyes a simple but moving picture of the human condition with its best and worst manifestations. In vv. 6-7, we witness the inexpressible joy of a mother who finally gives birth to a long-awaited son. The same mother, in vv. 9-10, gives in to the feelings of jealousy and anger. Her rival, in turn, faces anguish and despair in v. 16, driven away form her hearth and home, and becomes the one who is "challenged by a reality beyond human ken."

Paul Ricoeur describes a similar phenomenon with regard to literature in general: "Through fiction and poetry, new possibilities of being-in-the-world are opened up within everyday reality. ... Everyday reality is thereby metamorphised by what could be called the imaginative variations which literature carries out on the real."[91] He suggests that when we read fiction and poetry – and, in his works, he includes the Bible in the category of "fiction and poetry" – our "everyday reality" is transformed, and some "new possibilities of being-in-the-world" emerge. Certainly, what Ricoeur is saying is not that any kind of literature unconditionally and directly points to a transcendent reality, but that literature powerfully interacts with the reader's everyday reality, creating new ways of the reader's perceiving his or her world.

I believe that Ricoeurian hermeneutics offers excellent tools to explain the interaction between the text and the reader, as well as taking into account the referential role of literature. This is why I would like to base my subsequent considerations upon the Ricoeurian analysis of the revelatory function of Scripture, and use his ideas introduced in *Hermeneutics and the Human Sciences* and *Essays on Biblical Interpretation* as a starting point for my discussion.

Ricoeur's significant contribution to philosophical hermeneutics is the idea of the four forms of *distanciation*.[92] According to John B.

---

90 Alter, *The World of Biblical Literature*, 23.
91 Ricoeur, *Hermeneutics*, 142.
92 The idea of the four forms of *distanciation* can be put simply by distinguishing its two basic levels. The first one, corresponding to the first and second phase, takes place between the text and its author, whereas the second level includes phases three and four, and occurs between the text and its receivers.

Thompson, who introduced the selection of Ricoeur's essays, the first form of distanciation "is the surpassing of the event of saying by the meaning of what is said," the second form consists in the "relation between the inscribed expression and the original speaker," the third exists "between the inscribed expression and the original audience," whilst the fourth form "concerns the emancipation of the text from the limits of ostensive reference."[93] Because of the process of distanciation the text becomes "distanced," or separated, from the circumstances of its origin, and that process always takes place, irrespective of the text's character or date of composition. Moreover, distanciation explains the differences between oral and written forms of communication. Interestingly, there is a link between the fourth form of distanciation and the referential role of the biblical text, so Ricoeur's theory provides me with a very useful framework for the presentation of my main subject.

According to Ricoeur, the first form consists in "the distanciation of the saying in the said."[94] As long as Gen 21:1-21 was part of oral tradition, the meaning of what was said was in a close relationship with the circumstances of the spoken discourse. Once the oral tradition had been written down, the meaning of the text came to the fore, and the subsequent generations of readers have not been easily able to reconstruct "the event of saying." Although with the aid of the historical-critical method we can, with a degree of probability, hypothesize about the circumstances of the oral stage, the very event of saying has become surpassed by the text's meaning. The second form of distanciation involves a "relation between the inscribed expression and the original speaker," and concerns the intention of the author versus the meaning of the text. "Writing renders the text autonomous with respect to the intention of the author," says Ricoeur. "What the text signifies no longer coincides with what the author meant; henceforth, textual meaning and psychological meaning have different destinies."[95] Of course, in the case of most Hebrew Bible texts, the category of the authorial intention is very elusive due to the complicated historical process which gave rise to those texts, and their anonymity. Instead of the *author*, we often have anonymous tradents and redactors. Whatever their intention was, it is now inaccessible because of writing down the oral discourse and its subsequent editing. In the context of the third form of distanciation, Ricoeur draws our attention to the fact that the written

---

93   Ricoeur, *Hermeneutics*, 13-14.
94   Ricoeur, *Hermeneutics*, 134.
95   Ricoeur, *Hermeneutics*, 139.

discourse goes beyond its original context and audience, and, as a result, it becomes addressed to any possible reader. "An essential characteristic of a literary work, and of a work of art in general," states Ricoeur, "is that it transcends its own psycho-sociological conditions of production and thereby opens itself to an unlimited series of readings, themselves situated in different socio-cultural conditions."[96] This is precisely what happens when modern readers peruse our model pericope. The conditions determining their reception of the text differ significantly from the historical conditions of the original audience. By way of illustration, whilst for post-exilic Jews Gen 21:1-21 may have been proof that the promises given to their forefathers are irrevocable, for readers living in Europe on the threshold of the third millennium the same text may be an invitation to rethink their faith in God's providence.

The fourth form of distanciation is a very complex idea, and to explain it, Ricoeur introduces the notion of the *reference* of a proposition: "The reference is the truth value of the proposition, its claim to reach reality."[97] Thompson comments: "Whereas the shared circumstances of the speech situation provide some degree of referential specificity for spoken discourse, in the case of written discourse these shared circumstances no longer exist."[98] Thus in the case of Gen 21:1-21, the *reference* is the degree to which the propositions of the narrative agree with the reality to which the narrative refers. Now, "in oral discourse ... reference is determined by the ability to point to a reality common to the interlocutors,"[99] and this ostensive function becomes lost when oral discourse is written down. To put it another way, as long as Gen 21:1-21 had been recounted orally, its veracity could have been proved to some extent through its listeners' memory or experience. Once the oral discourse had been written down, both the circumstances of the speech situation and the referential value of the discourse ceased to exist. In view of that, we can ask whether, for us modern readers, the truth value of Gen 21:1-21 is positive or negative. Ricoeur answers this question indirectly: "This abolition of the ostensive character of reference is no doubt what makes possible the phenomenon we call 'literature,' which may abolish all reference to a given reality."[100] Ricoeur intelligently avoids the obvious philosophical trap, which is the question of

---

96 Ricoeur, *Hermeneutics*, 139.
97 Ricoeur, *Hermeneutics*, 140.
98 Thompson, "Ricoeur, Paul," n.p.
99 Ricoeur, *Hermeneutics*, 141.
100 Ricoeur, *Hermeneutics*, 141.

the truth of literature, by introducing the notion of a *second order reference*:

> My thesis here is that the abolition of a first order reference, an abolition effected by fiction and poetry, is the condition of possibility for the freeing of a second order reference, which reaches the world not only at the level of manipulable objects, but at the level that Husserl designated by the expression *Lebenswelt* [life-world] and Heidegger by the expression "being-in-the-world."[101]

If we keep asking what a second order reference, "at the level of being-in-the-world," means, we are given the above-mentioned answer: "Through fiction and poetry, new possibilities of being-in-the-world are opened up within everyday reality."[102] Vanhoozer helps us grasp the meaning of Ricoeurian "new possibilities" when he says:

> Ricoeur sets off on the first and most important of his many detours: the final destination is still an understanding of human being, but the route now passes by symbols, myths, metaphors and texts – all of which attest to the meaning of human existence. These linguistic works are expressions of our desire to be, our passion for existence. Human existence is only reached via these works which mediate it. ... Ricoeur proposes that it is poetic or creative language which best expresses the surplus, the "more than actuality," of human being. Poetic language responds to this surplus of being with a surplus of meaning.[103]

According to Ricoeur, the principal task of a human being is to understand the mystery of human existence, and the way to this goal leads through reading literary works, which illustrate the various aspects of human existence. Hence the kernel of Ricoeur's hermeneutical project is self-interpretation through reading: "The interpretation of a text culminates in the self-interpretation of a subject who thenceforth understands himself better, understands himself differently, or simply begins to understand himself."[104]

What Ricoeur describes as an inherent feature of general literature is also true of Scripture, and he introduces his discussion of scriptural genres and their revelatory function by putting it into a broader con-

---

101 Ricoeur, *Hermeneutics*, 141.
102 Ricoeur, *Hermeneutics*, 142.
103 Vanhoozer, *Biblical Narrative*, 7-8.
104 Ricoeur, *Hermeneutics*, 158. The process of self-interpretation and self-understanding is always deeply rooted in the symbolic culture of the subject: "The journey to selfhood commences with the exegesis of the imaginary symbols and stories constitutive of one's cultural inheritance in order to equip the subject to become an integrated self by means of appropriating these symbols and stories as her own" (Wallace, "From Phenomenology," 302).

text. What is at stake is the correct understanding of the idea of *revelation*: "The way of posing the question which, more than any other, I will seek to overcome is the one that sets in opposition an authoritarian and opaque concept of revelation and a concept of reason which claims to be its own master and transparent to itself."[105] What does the authoritarian and opaque way of understanding revelation consist in? Ricoeur explains that the concept of revelation becomes obscured when we do not distinguish between or we mix up the following three meanings of revelation: "the level of the confession of faith where the *lex credendi* is not separated from the *lex orandi*"; "the level of ecclesial dogma"; and "the body of doctrines imposed by the magisterium as the rule of orthodoxy."[106] Hence Ricoeur is trying to recover the original meaning of revelation as opposed to what we call today a system of "propositions which count as 'revealed truths.'"[107] Now, Ricoeur invites us to explore the modes of discourse in Scripture through which revelation is communicated to us. There are five basic modes: prophetic discourse, narrative discourse, prescriptive discourse (legislative texts), wisdom discourse, and hymnic discourse.[108] Each of them helps us understand the revelatory feature of Scripture, and expresses some of its characteristics. However, since, in this book, I focus on biblical narratives, a brief summary of Ricoeur's treatment of narrative discourse seems to be in place.[109]

First, Ricoeur states that in the narrative genre both the author and narrator are, to a great extent, behind the scenes. What matters above all is the text, and "we should pay more attention to the things recounted than to the narrator and his prompter."[110] Secondly, this statement leads Ricoeur to the emphasis laid on events told by scriptural narrative texts: "The idea of revelation then appears as connected to the very character of these events. What is noteworthy about them is that they

---

105 Ricoeur, *Essays*, 73.
106 Ricoeur, *Essays*, 73-74.
107 Mudge, "Paul Ricoeur," 23. Ricoeur is by no means denying the validity of the magisterium or of systematic theology. He observes, however, that these two ways of theological proceedings assume the existence of revelation at "its most originary level," and this is what he tries to elucidate (see *Essays*, 74).
108 See Ricoeur, *Essays*, 75-90.
109 I am aware of the danger of "homogenizing the Bible's semantic polyphony" (Wallace, "From Phenomenology," 310) when the discussion of the revelatory feature of Scripture is limited to only one of its genres (narrative, in my case). In this book, I focus on the narrative genre, but I bear in mind that my conclusions are relevant to that genre, and are not all-inclusive.
110 Ricoeur, *Essays*, 78.

do not simply occur and then pass away. They mark an epoch and engender history. ... To speak of revelation is to qualify the events in question as *transcendent in relation to the ordinary course of history* [my emphasis]."[111] Thirdly, Ricoeur says that those events always point towards God's action in human history.[112] This is why we cannot limit the meaning of revelation to a system of theological statements. If we do, we give preference to philosophical language, which is not scriptural, and relegate the original language of a community of faith to a secondary position. Hence Ricoeur stresses that the biblical genres are not a "rhetorical façade" which hides a propositional system of truths: they belong to the "polysemic and polyphonic concept of revelation."[113]

The discussion of the five types of scriptural discourse is then linked to the concept of *poetics*, which Ricoeur defines as the "totality of these [biblical] genres inasmuch as they exercise a referential function that differs from the descriptive referential function of ordinary language and above all of scientific discourse."[114] The feature of the referential function of biblical poetics is that it redescribes our reality, and offers new fictional configurations. Ricoeur speaks of this process using two pairs of parallel terms, modern and Aristotelian: *fiction* leads to *redescription*, *mythos* paves the way to *mimesis*.[115] In this context, we can understand another Ricoeurian fundamental concept, namely *the world of the text*, which "designates the reference of the work of discourse, not what is said, but about what it is said."[116] As a result, we arrive at the conclusions similar to those discussed above as the result of the process of distanciation. The world of the text interacts with the world of the reader, and, in consequence, "new possibilities of being-in-the-world are opened up within everyday reality."[117]

---

111 Ricoeur, *Essays*, 78. Ricoeur gives an example of how biblical theology based upon tradition criticism, contributes to the subject under discussion. The case in point are von Rad's efforts to establish the most ancient Hebraic creed (*Essays*, 78-79).
112 See Ricoeur, *Essays*, 79.
113 Ricoeur, *Essays*, 92. Ricoeur notes that such a concept of revelation prevents it from being possessed or withheld by an institution (*Essays*, 95).
114 Ricoeur, *Essays*, 100.
115 See Ricoeur, *Essays*, 102.
116 Ricoeur, *Essays*, 100. The world of the text is different from both the author (or his or her intention) and the text's immanent structure (*Essays*, 100).
117 Ricoeur, Hermeneutics, 142. Wallace notes that, according to Ricoeur, "our discourse has performative force." This is why biblical texts not only communicate something, but "propel the reader into a living confrontation with the God referred to by these texts" ("From Phenomenology," 304). Boyle adds that written texts "imply the existence of the whole system in which those states of affairs occur about which things are said" (*Sacred and Secular Scriptures*, 69).

Wallace aptly summarizes three main features of the Ricoeurian approach to biblical genre, revelation, and theology. First, "biblical genre is productive of meaning"; secondly, "the content of revelation is inseparable from its literary style or form"; and, thirdly, "the task of theology is not to secure the reality of God through metaphysical arguments but to discover how that reality is enacted through the first-order language of Jewish and Christian scriptures."[118] These three features provide me with a springboard and inspiration for the hermeneutical model which I propose here. So, after having introduced the concept of the three dimensions of the text resulting from the reader's threefold interests, as well as the distinction between meaning and significance, I shall now move on to the notion of the reader's knowledge, which will be based upon Ricoeurian hermeneutics.

3.5. The Three Types of the Reader's Knowledge

T. S. Eliot begins his poem "The Hollow Men" with a penetrating confession: "We are the hollow men / We are the stuffed men / Leaning together / Headpiece filled with straw. Alas! / Our dried voices, when / We whisper together / Are quiet and meaningless / As wind in dry grass."[119] In this subchapter, I would like to read his poem as a complex metaphor for those who lack an important spiritual dimension, and, in consequence, are forced to live in a "dead land" and a "cactus land."[120] To develop this metaphor further, and to use poetic licence, I might say that this spiritual dimension, which is oft-neglected by the "hollow men" of our generation, is provided by reading Scripture. If we do not want, or cannot, read the Bible in an innovative way, which opens our eyes to the transcendent reality existing beyond the text, we risk being exiled to the "valley of dying stars."[121]

Hence I would like to argue that a prominent feature of biblical narratives is their power to become a vehicle leading the reader towards the transcendent sphere and allowing participation in that sphere. To explain this in the language of philosophy and literary criticism, I shall employ three pairs of interrelated terms: first, *immanent knowledge* based upon *actuality*; second, *narrative knowledge* of *quasi-reality*; and,

---

118 Wallace, "Can God Be Named," 301 n. 11.
119 Eliot, "The Hollow Men," 89.
120 Eliot, "The Hollow Men," 90.
121 Eliot, "The Hollow Men," 91.

third, *transcendental knowledge* founded upon *trans-reality*.[122] From a philosophical point of view, these terms belong to two distinct categories: actuality, quasi-reality, and trans-reality are certain kinds of beings, and they must be discussed from an *ontological* perspective; in turn, immanent knowledge, narrative knowledge, and transcendental knowledge are states of mind of the knowing subject, and, consequently, they must be analysed from an *epistemological* point of view. In the ensuing paragraphs, I will introduce these terms, and in subsequent chapters, they will be analysed and exemplified by my model pericope.

By *actuality*, I understand the real world of human beings and of animate and inanimate objects.[123] I assume that the existence of this world is a matter of obviousness to the reader, and this commonsense assumption is based on a number of philosophical choices, which will be presented in the next subchapter. In our case, actuality comprises texts and their readers. The epistemological counterpart of actuality is *immanent knowledge*, which I define as the horizon of readers' knowledge about the actuality to which they belong.[124] Hence immanent knowledge is what I, the reader, have in mind with reference to the world: my memories, thoughts, feelings, and mental images. Immanent knowledge is a dynamic process open to change and development. As readers become more mature and experienced, their knowledge about actuality is modified and evolves. Moreover, the immanent knowledge of modern readers is closely linked to the intellectual trends of the world in which those readers live.

The explanation of the notions of *quasi-reality* and *narrative knowledge*, which are closely linked to the text, needs much more space and

---

122 It will soon be obvious why I prefer speaking of *actuality*, *quasi-reality*, and *trans-reality*, instead of the *real world*, *narrative world*, and the *transcendent world*, even though these terms are identical. The semantic value of the former three categories will help me explain better the process of mediation between the real and transcendent worlds.

123 I prefer to use here the term *actuality* rather than *reality* because *actuality* is only part of *reality* as a whole.

124 The term *horizon* is very important in Edmund Husserl's phenomenology and Hans-Georg Gadamer's hermeneutics. For Gadamer, the *horizon* is the "range of vision that includes everything that can be seen from a particular vantage point" (*Truth and Method*, 269). Hence the understanding of a historical text involves, first, distinguishing between *the horizon of the reader* and *the horizon of the text*, and, secondly, the *fusion* of the two horizons (see *Truth and Method*, 273). In my discussion of the three types of knowledge, I apply the term *horizon* only to readers and to their knowledge of reality.

discussion. In our case, when we read biblical narratives, our first impression is that the narrative world projected by the text into our minds, unlike objective reality, is highly conventional and finite. It is conventional because it usually follows very closely a number of rules pertaining to the art of narrative composition; it is finite because, although open to diverse interpretations, it constitutes a complete corpus of writings to which nothing can be added, and from which nothing can be subtracted: readers can only endlessly return to the same text that they already know. The rules upon which these narratives are founded have been explained by numerous theoreticians and critics, and it is not necessary to present them here. In a few words, they comprise both standard features characteristic of every narrative such as the plot, characters, and settings; as well as specific narrative features such as biblical type-scenes, the techniques of repetition, or the art of reticence.[125] The presence of these rules contributes to the fact that some biblical narratives may be regarded as relatively schematized and simplified, although certainly not, ultimately, lacking in complexity.[126]

In the real world, even though conventions also form a part of the human patterns of behaviour and communication, much of what we experience takes us by surprise and is highly unconventional. Similarly, the world of our experience is by no means finite or complete: the book of real life is always full of new facts and unpredictable events. In other words, while the narrative reality is, to some extent, rigid and limited, and we may explore only its depth, the real world is a continually expanding system. Saying this, I may now define the two above notions. By *quasi-reality* I understand the conventional and finite narrative world in which readers participate through reading narrative texts, which is projected into their minds, and with which they interact. As in the case of immanent knowledge, *narrative knowledge* is the epistemological counterpart of quasi-reality, and signifies the horizon of readers' knowledge about quasi-reality. To put it another, more poetic, way, we may consider the quasi-reality of biblical narratives to be an opportunity for discovering the existence of the transcendent world. This discovery is the only way to avoid a situation when our critical efforts are

---

125 See Alter, *The Art of Biblical Narrative*, the whole book.
126 This remark does not invalidate an observation made, among others, by Auerbach that some biblical characters are developed fully and in a masterly way. Similarly, the plot of many biblical stories is complicated and replete with unexpected turns in action (cf. Auerbach, *Mimesis*, 17ff.)

"Shape without form, shade without colour, / Paralysed force, gesture without motion."[127]

Furthermore, the notion of narrative knowledge is linked to the three textual dimensions of narrative: they become three dimensions of the reader's narrative knowledge. To take the case of the aesthetic dimension for illustration, we may say that it consists of a set of various intratextual and extratextual factors, which are discovered by readers pursuing their aesthetic interests. These factors enable them to determine the different aspects of beauty communicated by the text, and to realize that this beauty is a manifestation of the universal Platonic idea of beauty (see the next subchapter). The extratextual factors belonging to the aesthetic and practical dimensions are determined by the context in which the reader interprets the text, or, in other words, by the reader's immanent knowledge. By contrast, in the case of the cognitive dimension, the extratextual factors are determined by the original context in which the text was created.

Saying this, I have arrived at the point where I can introduce the notions of *trans-reality* and *transcendental knowledge*. Their definition is analogous to the definitions of actuality and quasi-reality. Hence the term *trans-reality* signifies the transcendent sphere which readers discover through the mediation of biblical narratives, and in which they indirectly participate. *Transcendental knowledge*, in turn, stands for the horizon of readers' knowledge about trans-reality. Interestingly, trans-reality is the ontological foundation of both actuality and quasi-reality. Through the act of reading, readers communicate with the transcendent realm, which is reality in the fullest sense of the word, and the ultimate cause of everything that exists. Biblical narratives are a vehicle leading them towards trans-reality, and they discover behind biblical texts a world of impenetrable divine purposes, a world which is also the ultimate source of truth, beauty, and goodness which they pursue in narrative texts. This discovery becomes part of their transcendental knowledge. In this way readers share the experience of "Those who have crossed / With direct eyes, to death's other Kingdom."[128]

In the previous subchapter, I have clearly stated that my hermeneutical approach to reading biblical narratives benefits from and depends on Ricoeur's hermeneutics. However, while Ricoeur aims to create a universal and all-encompassing theory of interpretation, the scope of my present work is limited to ancient Hebrew narrative texts,

---

127 Eliot, "The Hollow Men," 89.
128 Eliot, "The Hollow Men," 89.

particularly to Gen 21:1-21. Because of this limitation, I can concentrate on diverse literary features typical of Hebrew narratives; in other words, I can discuss specific issues which are by no means central in the Ricoeurian hermeneutical system. Moreover, Ricoeur puts significant weight on the pure theory of interpretation, whereas I am interested in the application of interpretive theory to exegetical praxis. For this reason, I have modified the Ricoeurian basic hermeneutical model, and I have tailored it to the features of Hebrew Bible narratives. Apart from that, I have integrated the Ricoeurian theory with the concept of the three textual dimensions, which has provided me with an opportunity for showing the applicability of diverse interpretive approaches to my model pericope. However, I am well aware that I must still address four issues arising from a comparison between the Ricoeurian model and the model which I am proposing in this book.

First, the Ricoeurian idea that reading fiction and poetry has the power to metamorphize everyday reality, and leads to self-understanding, corresponds with my epistemic concepts of immanent, narrative, and transcendental knowledge, as well as with the three respective spheres of reality, which are ontological terms: actuality, quasi-reality, and trans-reality. When Ricoeur says that, through the interaction between the world of the reader and the world of fictional works, "new possibilities of being-in-the-world are opened up within everyday reality," he employs, to my best knowledge, both ontological and epistemological terms, depending on the aspect of the interaction which he wants to highlight. On the one hand, the "new possibilities" refer to the knowledge which the subject discovers about himself or herself, and about reality. On the other, both the world of the reader and the world of fictional works signify certain kinds of beings. Vanhoozer, discussing the Ricoeurian treatment of history and fiction, suggests that the fictive world of the text enjoys ontological status,[129] but, at the same time, fictions "enjoy a special epistemological role: they discover through inventing."[130] In contrast, in my project, I would like to make a distinction between the ontological and epistemological aspects of the process of reading. This is why, in the following chapters, I shall ask questions about the reader's knowledge concerning the three spheres of reality. Having said this, I must emphasize that I do not intend to push the distinction between "being" and "knowing" too far. Epistemology is linked to ontology, and the knowledge which the knowing

---

129 See Vanhoozer, *Biblical Narrative*, 98-99.
130 Vanhoozer, *Biblical Narrative*, 97.

subject gains influences that subject's being. In view of the above, I can rephrase Ricoeur's theory using my own epistemic terms, and say that, through reading biblical narratives, the reader's immanent knowledge is metamorphized by narrative knowledge, and results in the emergence of knowledge about the transcendent sphere to which those narratives refer. In consequence, within the "new possibilities of being-in-the world," the reader discovers the existence of a world, which is the ultimate cause and foundation of both the reader's actuality and the narrative world.

Secondly, I should explain the place of the Ricoeurian concept of the world of the text in my interpretive scheme. Is the world of the text a correlate of quasi-reality (and, in consequence, narrative knowledge) or, rather, trans-reality (and transcendental knowledge)? When Ricoeur introduces his concept, he states that "what is finally to be understood in a text is not the author or his presumed intention, nor is it the immanent structure or structures of the text, but rather the sort of world intended beyond the text as its reference."[131] He also gives examples of what he understands by his concept: "the proposed world that in biblical language is called a new creation, a new Covenant, the Kingdom of God, is the 'issue' of the biblical text unfolded in front of the text."[132] As I see it, Ricoeur's world of the text exhibits certain features of both quasi-reality and trans-reality. On the one hand, it is quasi-reality in which readers participate through reading texts. On the other, since trans-reality signifies the transcendent sphere discovered by readers, it is not far from such concepts as the above new creation or the Kingdom of God. Yet in my treatment of quasi-reality, I emphasize various literary structures of the text, which moves me away from the Ricoeurian views on the world of the text. Similarly, when I analyse trans-reality, I stress its absolute ontological primacy over quasi-reality and actuality, whereas Ricoeur often speaks of multiple worlds created by diverse literary texts rather than of *one and supreme* world projected by the text. The above affinities and dissimilarities between the two models stem, of course, from the different goals of our hermeneutical proceedings. Ricoeur proposes a general hermeneutical model of literary texts applicable also to Scripture, whereas I aim to introduce and apply a model which accounts for the features of ancient Hebrew narratives, Gen 21:1-21 in particular.

---

131 Ricoeur, *Essays*, 100.
132 Ricoeur, *Essays*, 103.

Thirdly, Ricoeur emphasizes that the goal of reading is the self-understanding of the knowing subject.[133] By contrast, my model proposes a different description of the process. The knowing subject, through the mediation of narrative, gains knowledge about *reality as a whole*, including its supernatural and natural dimensions. Only secondarily, and because the subject is a part of that whole reality, does he or she arrive at self-understanding.

Fourthly and finally, the presence of truth, beauty, and goodness in the text is never a key issue for Ricoeur. The conceptual framework which he uses to analyse narrative consists of such concepts as time, emplotment, mimesis, history and fiction, the world of the reader, and the world of the text. On the contrary, the central question which I pose with regard to narrative is how the reader's quest for the three universals is performed and achieved in the process of reading.[134]

Going back to T. S. Eliot's poetic image of the hollow men, who symbolize readers entangled in a closed circle of the present, and unable to communicate with the life-giving eternal, I would like to quote another meaningful phrase: "Between the idea / And the reality / Between the motion / And the act / Falls the Shadow."[135] Is it too naïve to cherish the hope that a diligent study of biblical hermeneutics may diminish the overpowering influence of the Shadow and make God's glory shine again in the hidden recesses of our minds?

3.6. A Philosophical Basis for the Hermeneutical Model

In the preceding subchapters, I have pointed out that I am aware of the existence of the philosophical assumptions on which my hermeneutical model is based. The most important of them is the ontological status of the *Platonic triad*, and of the three spheres of reality corresponding to the three kinds of knowledge which the reader acquires in the process

---

133 See Ricoeur, *Hermeneutics*, 158.
134 Boyle enumerates a number of features of Ricoeurian hermeneutics which he finds "fishy": Ricoeur does not emphasize enough the Church's authority in biblical interpretation; the Incarnation does not play an important role; the life of Jesus is equated with the concept of testimony; and his views on revelation favour Scripture at the expense of the oral Tradition. Even if some of these claims might be true, in this book, I do not make use of the whole system of Ricoeurian thought, but simply choose a few concepts, which, I very much believe, are credible (see Boyle, *Sacred and Secular Scriptures*, 74-75).
135 Eliot, "The Hollow Men," 91-92.

of reading biblical narratives. The above topic constitutes a subject in its own right, and, since this book contains a presentation and a practical application of the hermeneutical model, pursuing purely philosophical topics would lead me too far away from my subject matter. This is why, in the ensuing paragraphs, I intend only to indicate the presence of important philosophical debates underlying my interpretive theory. Moreover, the general validity of the hermeneutical model which I have introduced in this chapter does not depend on the outcome of those philosophical debates. What would really undermine my model are different forms of anti-metaphysical and postmodern critical theories which deny the possibility of acquiring certain knowledge about reality and negate the existence of a reality other than textuality itself. However, as I shall demonstrate in the next chapter, even postmodern interpretive theories have their advantages, of which I would like to make use in the presentation of the details of my model.

Readers who pursue cognitive, aesthetic, and practical interests in biblical narratives ultimately face the question of what truth, beauty, and goodness are, and in what way, if at all, they exist in the text. By way of example, when readers discover stylistic devices present in the text, they may call the text beautiful, and say, in consequence, that beauty exists in the text. On the other hand, however, beauty is considered by many to be a general category, which exists in itself. Since the dawn of philosophy, various thinkers have claimed the real existence of *pulchrum*. In view of that, how should we reconcile the two ways in which beauty, and, respectively, truth and goodness, are perceived? It appears that we are in need of a philosophical theory giving an account of the ontological status of the Platonic triad.

I believe that when readers discover the cognitive, aesthetic, and practical dimensions of the text, they cannot, strictly speaking, make a legitimate claim that truth, beauty, and goodness *are present* in the text. Rather, they should say that the text, through its narrative architecture, *communicates* different aspects of truth, beauty, and goodness. Certain truths may be communicated by the words of the personages about whom the text tells us. We may learn about good or evil when we judge the personages' behaviour. Aspects of beauty may be communicated thanks to the text's stylistic devices or literary themes. The text, however, is like a musical score, which has great potential, but which must be "played" or "performed" by the reader in order to reveal its hidden content. We would not say that a score contains music. Rather, it contains musical notation, which guides musicians when they play it. Likewise, the text contains written information, which guides its readers through the process of reading, and the communication of truth, beauty, and goodness requires the active participation of readers in the whole process. After all, the Platonic triad is discovered as a result of readers' pursuit of their own interests, and the specific outcome of this pursuit may vary from reader to reader. Hence whenever I speak of the triad's presence *in the text*, I am taking an intellectual shortcut. What I really mean is a very complex phenomenon of communication by the text and participation by the reader through which truth, beauty, and goodness are made manifest.

A different way of speaking about the Platonic triad in the context of literary texts is to regard the three ideas as the texts' properties or attributes. Bealer tells us that "properties are a kind of universal."[136] Thus, in a basic sense, truth, beauty, and goodness (we might also say: being true, beautiful, or good) are a kind of universal, or, simply, they are universals. Simon Blackburn defines a *universal* as "a property or relation that can be instanced, or instantiated, by a number of different particular things."[137] We may give other examples of universals: *redness*, understood as a property which makes things red, or *being between*, which is a relation of one thing to two other things. Philosophers differ on the matter of the existence of universals, and, according to what they believe, such philosophers may be divided roughly into three groups. *Realists* are convinced that "properties exist independently of the mind."[138] *Conceptualists* hold that "properties exist but are dependent on the mind."[139] In turn, *nominalists* maintain that "only particulars (and perhaps collections of particulars) exist; therefore, either properties do not exist or they are reducible ... to collections of particulars (including perhaps particulars that are not actual but only possible)."[140] Within the school of realism, there are two factions. "*In rebus* realism: a property exists only if it has instances. *Ante* rem realism: a property can exist even if it has no instances."[141] The latter version is as-

---

136 Bealer, "Property," *CDP*, 657.
137 Blackburn, *The Oxford Dictionary of Philosophy*, 387.
138 Bealer, "Property," *CDP*, 657.
139 Bealer, "Property," *CDP*, 657.
140 Bealer, "Property," *CDP*, 657. John C. Bigelow explains the difference between *particulars* and *universals*: "What distinguishes particulars is the fact that, while a particular instantiates properties and relations, nothing instantiates a particular. Universals both 'have' (properties and relations) and are 'had'; particulars 'have' but are not 'had.' Since a particular is not instantiated by another thing, it is sometimes said to exist 'in itself,' whereas a universal exists 'in' something else" ("Particulars," *CREP*, 659).
141 Bealer, "Property," *CDP*, 657.

sociated with Platonism, whereas the former is characteristic of the Aristotelian school of thought.[142]

Furthermore, truth, beauty, and goodness, being universals, are also called *transcendentals*. Flew and Priest understand transcendentals as "a term used by medieval philosophers to signify predicates that transcend the Aristotelian categories, for example 'exists' and 'is true.'"[143] In other words, transcendentals are properties which can be applied to all possible beings.[144] Most mediaeval metaphysicians believe that there are four transcendentals: *being* (*ens*), *one* (*unum*), *true* (*verum*), and *good* (*bonum*). Others expand the list to include *thing* (*res*), *something* (*aliquid*), and *beautiful* (*pulchrum*).[145] The philosophical doctrine of transcendentals was developed fully by Suárez, a Spanish Jesuit philosopher, who published most of his works at the turn of the sixteenth and seventeenth centuries, and whose philosophy is regarded as a bridge between mediaeval scholasticism and modern philosophy.[146] Gracia summarizes Suárez's views on transcendentals:

> Although being *qua* being has no properties that are really distinct from it, it does have properties that are conceptually distinct from it. These properties are unity, truth and goodness. They are coextensional with being because whatever is a being is also one, good and true, and whatever is one, good or true is also a being. It is the coextension of these properties with being that makes them transcendental, for they are common to the ten categories into which being is divided.[147]

Suárez's use of terminology, "really distinct" and "conceptually distinct," is a different way of saying what *The Cambridge Dictionary of Philosophy* puts: "The transcendentals are convertible (interchangeable), but they are not synonymous."[148] Moreover, what Suárez is saying proves that even long after the golden age of mediaeval philosophy the place of beauty among the transcendentals was contested.

My own stance on the matter of the existence of truth, beauty, and goodness is *realistic*, since I believe that the three universals exist independently of the mind. Moreover, I follow the Aristotelian school, and I

---

142 See Blackburn, *The Oxford Dictionary of Philosophy*, 387.
143 Flew and Priest, *A Dictionary of Philosophy*, 403.
144 See MacDonald, "Transcendentals," *CDP*, 809.
145 See MacDonald, "Transcendentals," *CDP*, 809. Interestingly, among the first scholars who listed beauty as a transcendental are Jean de la Rochelle and Bonaventure. However, the Dominican scholastics, Albert the Great and Aquinas, did not put beauty on the list (see Murphy, *Christ the Form of Beauty*, 213).
146 See Gracia, "Suárez," 462.
147 Gracia, "Suárez," 467.
148 MacDonald, "Transcendentals," *CDP*, 809.

claim the existence of the triad *in rebus* rather than *ante rem*. However, from a theological standpoint, I would say that the triad exists, in the ultimate sense, in the mind of God. This doctrine was fully developed by Aquinas, who, drawing on the philosophical tradition of Plato, Aristotle, Neo-Platonists, Pseudo-Dionysius, and Augustine, arrived at a synthesis of his predecessors' thought.[149] As Boland summarizes Aquinas's teaching on divine ideas: "Everything that is, insofar as it is, has some corresponding idea in God who is the only source of being."[150] Simultaneously, the ideas in God's mind are God: "The model, pattern, archetype, paradigm or idea for the creation: where can it be except in God and what can it be except God since whatever is in God, is God and whatever God has, God is."[151] Hence, taking into account Aquinas's views, truth, beauty, and goodness exist primarily in God's mind and, secondarily, as the properties of created beings, including literary texts.[152]

What is important for my hermeneutical model is the fact that its validity does not depend directly on the above ontological choices. Irrespective of whether readers are realists, conceptualists, or nominalists, with regard to the question of the existence of the Platonic triad, they still pursue their cognitive, aesthetic, and practical interests, and discover that narrative texts communicate diverse aspects of the triad. Readers may believe that truth, beauty, and goodness are only *mental* entities or dispositions,[153] or they may be convinced that the three words, which express the ideas, are only empty sounds, but the three-dimensional approach to narrative still holds.[154]

The next question which must be debated here is the ontological status of the three spheres of reality in my hermeneutical model: the real, narrative, and transcendent worlds. The terminology which I have used to describe them hints already at their status: quasi-reality is sub-

---

149 See esp. Boland, *Ideas in God*, 315-32.
150 Boland, *Ideas in God*, 324.
151 Boland, *Ideas in God*, 323.
152 The problem of the ideas in God's mind is complicated. Some scholars believe that Aquinas failed to achieve a synthesis of this subject because he was trying to reconcile two different kinds of ideas: the Platonic ideas of all beings such as the idea of the man, or of the horse, with the transcendental properties of being such as truth or goodness.
153 Cf. Butchvarov, "Metaphysical Realism," *CDP*, 489.
154 There has been a long literary tradition of emphasizing the unity of the three transcendentals. For Emily Dickinson, truth and beauty are "brethren" and "one" ("I Died for Beauty," 345).

ordinate to actuality, whereas trans-reality transcends both of them. What should be determined here, however, is their ontological status.[155]

To begin with, my philosophical stance on the ontological status of *actuality* can be described as *metaphysical realism*. The *Cambridge Dictionary of Philosophy* defines this option as "the view that (a) there are real objects (usually the view is concerned with spatiotemporal objects), (b) they exist independently of our experience or our knowledge of them, and (c) they have properties and enter into relations independently of the concepts with which we understand them or of the language with which we describe them."[156] Metaphysical realism expresses in philosophical terms what we normally call a commonsense understanding of reality. To adjust the above definition to literary criticism, we may say that (a) actuality comprises real readers and real texts, which have spatiotemporal qualities, and thus any process of reading happens in the real world and in real time; (b) texts are artefacts, which originate at a certain point of time, and then exist independently of their authors and readers; (c) every given text has a set of literary features which are not contingent on their interpretation; in other words, texts are, to a great extent, "masters," and they impose on their readers certain interpretive constraints due to their internal nature and structure. Similarly, I believe that the immanent knowledge of actuality is governed by the same principles of metaphysical realism. We as readers and knowing subjects encounter texts, which exist independently of us, and which are like musical scores guiding us through the process of reading. Our knowledge of them is thus always secondary to their nature, and our encounter with them does not change their nature. However, when we say that the nature of such objects as literary texts is not changed by our encounter with them, i.e. by the process of reading and interpretation, we should also remember that, in an important sense, texts which are read and interpreted are raised to the level of intelligibility. In other words, they become what they really are, and what they were intended to be, when they are actualized during the process of reading. This does not mean that the principles of metaphysical realism applied to literary texts are void, but that they must be understood in a broad

---

155 Another interesting question which arises in this context, but cannot be discussed here fully, is the complex net of relationships existing between the three spheres of reality. If we equate trans-reality with the divine sphere of God, we see clearly that the only God we know created actuality, and expressed himself in the signs of quasi-reality. Hence it is difficult to speculate on trans-reality without taking into account that it is deeply linked to actuality and quasi-reality.

156 Butchvarov, "Metaphysical Realism," *CDP*, 488.

sense. Certainly, in the case of literary works, the idea of their existence and nature independent from readers should not be taken too rigidly.

An explanation of the ontological status of *quasi-reality* needs much more space, but the tradition of analytical philosophy provides me with useful tools to discuss the subject. As I have said in the preceding subchapter, quasi-reality signifies the conventional and finite narrative world in which readers participate through reading narrative texts, which is projected into their minds, and with which they interact. As a result, quasi-reality is actualized by readers through the *act of reading*, and exists *in their minds*. The quasi-reality of a biblical narrative text may or may not be linked to some historical events, depending on that text's genre; yet, as will be signalled here, and clearly demonstrated in chapter 5, the link between the quasi-reality of Gen 21:1-21 and its corresponding historical reality is at best vague and secondary. Readers perusing Gen 21:1-21 do not have direct access to knowledge about the *historical Abraham*; they meet the *textual Abraham*, and the question to what extent the features of the textual Abraham reflect the historical Abraham's characteristics is a complicated matter. Westermann's discussion of the problem can be summarized as follows.[157] In all probability, the characters of the patriarchal stories were real people, and some of the most important events which shaped their lives, and which are recorded in Gen 12-36, really happened; but to say more than that would be to give free rein to imagination. Hence what the reader can be sure about are the features of the textual Abraham, and the distinction between the textual and the historical characters is of paramount importance for the subsequent discussion.[158]

What, then, is the ontological status of the textual Abraham and of the narrative world he inhabits? To answer this complex question, it seems worthwhile to adopt Kendall L. Walton's theory expounded in *Mimesis as Make-Believe*. Presenting the foundations of his theory, Walton states that *"representations ... are things possessing the social function of serving as props in games of make-believe."*[159] Since, in our case, Gen 21:1-21 is a representational work of art, it invites its readers to play a game of make-believe. When they open the book of Genesis, and start reading the narrative under discussion, they are made to believe that the events described in it actually happened, even if they can-

---

157 See Westermann, *Genesis 12-36*, 23-86.
158 Certainly, the gap between the historical and the textual Abraham is much bigger than, to use a topical example, between the historical Jesus and the Jesus of the Gospels.
159 Walton, *Mimesis*, 69.

not prove the historical veracity of the account, or the goal of the account is far from communicating any historical truths. Thus Gen 21:1-21 *prompts* readers' imaginings, and *generates fictional truths*.[160] Following Walton's classification, we should say that the proposition "Abraham gave a grand banquet on the day when Isaac was weaned" (21:8) is *fictional*, and "the fact that it is fictional is a *fictional truth*."[161] Now, it is important to say that Abraham's generous gesture is *fictional* in the *fictional world* created by Gen 21:1-21. If we want to be precise, we should use what Graham Priest calls "the intentional operator," and say: "In the way things are represented in Gen 21:1-21, Abraham gave a grand banquet on the day when Isaac was weaned."[162] In the real world of the patriarchal period, the banquet may or may not have happened, but that does not contradict the fictional character of the event represented in Gen 21:8. In other words, we must not confuse the actuality of the patriarchal period with the quasi-reality of the narrative world. Walton warns us not to mix up the concept of fictionality with the concept of truth: "What is true is to be believed; what is fictional is to be imagined."[163] The temptation of considering fictionality as a kind of truth would easily lead us astray. We must remember that calling a proposition fictional is not an attempt to negate or to establish its veracity. A proposition *is always fictional* within a given game of make-believe, even if it has its counterpart in a historical event. Walton argues: "*Fictional worlds* are associated with collections of fictional truths; what is fictional is fictional in a given world – the world of a game of make-believe, for example, or that of a representational work of art."[164]

Walton's philosophical stance may sound sacrilegious to those who believe that the patriarchal stories tell us the real events of Abraham's, Isaac's, and Jacob's lives, but even to those who agree that the stories give a vague account of some major events that happened to the patri-

---

160 Cf. Walton, *Mimesis*, 21.
161 Walton, *Mimesis*, 35.
162 See Priest, *Towards Non-Being*, 117 n. 2.
163 Walton, *Mimesis*, 41.
164 Walton, *Mimesis*, 69. It seems that such an approach to the historicity of events depicted by biblical narratives fits well the Ricoeurian system of thought. As Wallace remarks: "Ricoeur puts into abeyance any judgment about … the reality status of the imaginary claims made by one's orienting textual sources. This bracketing exercise is performed in order to accord to these claims the status of lived possibilities, even if they cannot be established as referring to proven realities in the world" ("From Phenomenology," 302). Similarly, Mudge points out that, according to Ricoeur, the "poetic function of biblical language suspends the criteria of falsification and verification" ("Paul Ricoeur," 25).

archs. I think that the offence is caused by the way our contemporaries understand the concept of *fiction* as opposed to *reality* and *fact*. Eagleton, discussing the nature of literature, says that "a distinction between 'fact' and 'fiction' … seems unlikely to get us very far, not least because the distinction itself is often a questionable one."[165] A given literary work can be regarded by some as fictional, and by others as factual; similarly, what we now consider to be fictional may have been conceived by its past author as factual, and the other way round. Moreover, a prosaic or poetic work can comprise both historical and imaginary elements.[166] Hence H. Porter Abbott is right in saying that "the distinction between fiction and non-fiction is often found to collapse."[167] There is no doubt, however, that we need at least a tentative means of distinguishing between works of fiction and nonfiction, or between the fictional and nonfictional elements of a given work. Walton suggests that "any work with the function of serving as a prop in games of make-believe, … qualifies as 'fiction'; only what lacks this function entirely will be called nonfiction."[168] Walton's suggestion may sound categorical, but it is, in fact, useful for our discussion. If we analyse a narrative as a whole, we may like to succumb to its fictional power, and to start playing a game of make-believe. On the contrary, when we apply the tools of the historical method to the same narrative, we will disregard its fictional dimension, and start asking questions about the historical process of its formation. What is more, Walton's remark shows clearly that the real distinction does not lie between fiction and fact, but between fiction and nonfiction.[169]

---

165 Eagleton, *Literary Theory*, 1.
166 Cf. Eagleton, *Literary Theory*, 1-2.
167 Abbott, *The Cambridge Introduction to Narrative*, 190. Eugene R. Kintgen's analysis of Elizabethan literature proves that the relationship between fictionality and veracity was well understood long ago: "Whether or not [Sir Philip] Sidney was being entirely serious in arguing that poets never lie because they nothing affirm, we can see it as an early statement of Culler's strategy of impersonality and distance, a recommendation to readers to interpret literary texts so that the poet is not asserting anything about the real world" ("Reconstructing Elizabethan Reading," 9). In "An Apologie for Poetrie," Sidney states that "the Phisitians," "the other Artists, and especially the Historian" tell us lies, yet "for the Poet, he nothing affirmes, and therefore neuer lyeth. For, as I take it, to lye, is to affirme that to be true which is false" (n.p.)
168 Walton, *Mimesis*, 72.
169 Prickett and Barnes comment: "As we all know, a fictional story may in some sense be more 'true' of a situation, an experience, or a society than any description of an actual event. We should not ask of it, therefore: did this actually happen to real people? but: is this 'true to life,' is this artistically true?" (*The Bible*, 105).

Two difficulties arise here. First, who is to decide whether a given work's purpose is to serve as a prop in games of make-believe? Walton answers that the onus is on the authors to determine the reception of their works: Charles Darwin wanted us to *believe* the propositions contained in *The Origin of Species*, whilst Jonathan Swift wrote *Gulliver's Travels* so that we could *imagine* Gulliver's adventures. As Gregory Currie puts it: "a work is fiction if its author had a certain kind of intention: the intention that readers adopt the attitude of make-believe toward the propositions of the story."[170]

Secondly, how should we classify those literary works which are either ambiguous in terms of their authorial intention, or whose authorial intention cannot be established, or which have both fictional and nonfictional features, as seems to be the case with Genesis? Walton answers this question by reminding us that there exist works of fiction which tell us fictional stories about real characters.[171] By way of illustration, we can write a novel whose protagonist is Napoleon Bonaparte, yet the novel can be properly called fictional as long as its main purpose is not to teach us the facts of Napoleon's life. In the same way, even if one day we might be able to prove beyond doubt the historicity of Abraham, some details of the Abraham cycle would remain purely fictional.

Walton, however, emphasizes that his definition of fiction is *functional*, and that the function of a particular work depends on different factors: the author's intention, the readers' reception, or a set of rules governing reading literary works. Those various factors contribute to the fact that a given work can sometimes be fiction to some, and nonfiction to others.[172] Now, if we support Westermann's claim that the patriarchal stories are rooted in long oral tradition, and that "one cannot apply the idea of history or the historical to the oral stage of transmission," as well as that "the question about the historicity of the patriarchal stories and figures is a question wrongly put,"[173] we will probably agree that there is nothing sacrilegious in calling them narrative fiction. Westermann strongly opposes those who would like to strip the patriarchal stories of their narrative identity by translating their message into the language of precise theological statements.[174] On the contrary, the most fundamental function of those stories is "to give

---

170 Currie, *The Nature of Fiction*, 196.
171 See Walton, *Mimesis*, 73-75.
172 See Walton, *Mimesis*, 91.
173 Westermann, *Genesis 12-36*, 43.
174 See Westermann, *Genesis 12-36*, 46-47.

each new generation a share in the experiences, both external and internal, of the events and dramas which the fathers themselves lived through."[175] Now, if we read Westermann's statement about the patriarchal narratives' function in the context of Walton's classification, and remember that, according to Currie, the fictionality of a given text does not depend on that text's literary genre,[176] we see that the narratives under discussion have strong fictional characteristics.

To explain the problem further, we should look at the patriarchal narratives from two different viewpoints: that of the original audience, and that of modern readers. The idea that the distinction between fiction and nonfiction may not have existed for the original audience appears to be true. Both Westermann and Walton clearly suggest such a possibility. Westermann puts it: "The question whether the event narrated is historical or not is not pertinent to the understanding of reality in these narratives, because they are told among people for whom this alternative did not yet exist."[177] When we move on to the viewpoint of modern readers, we discover that the patriarchal stories do not fit the standards of modern historical objectivity. If we seek their underlying historical truth, we must remember that "the biblical account is by no means a simple reflection of ancient reality," but "a highly ideological construction of a phenomenon that could be viewed very differently."[178] However, apart from our historical interests, we will certainly profit from reading the patriarchal stories as fiction, following Walton's advice: "When imagining is important, we may want to understand a story as fiction, as prescribing imaginings. We still need not to decide whether it is true, or even ask. This, I am suggesting, may be essentially the attitude some cultures have toward their myths."[179]

---

175 Westermann, *Genesis 12-36*, 48.
176 See Currie, *The Nature of Fiction*, 4.
177 Westermann, *Genesis 12-36*, 46. This view is supported by Prickett and Barnes: "Most critics would now accept that our categories of history, myth, and fiction are all constructs by which we attempt to make sense of our past. But to describe the Bible in any of these terms is highly misleading. It belongs, as we have seen, to a period when such essentially modern distinctions did not and could not yet exist; and in attempting to apply such models to it, we should always be conscious of what we lose in our reading of the original" (*The Bible*, 107). See also Barr's distinction between *story* and *history* in *The Scope and Authority*, 1-17.
178 Collins, *The Bible after Babel*, 129. Of course, Collins is well aware that certain biblical books are historically more reliable than others, yet as regards Genesis, he states: "The authors and compilers of Genesis may have had various intentions; it is not apparent that providing an accurate record of the past ranked high among them" (p. 38).
179 Walton, *Mimesis*, 98.

Going back to the ontological status of quasi-reality, we should now say that the quasi-reality of Gen 21:1-21 comprises fictional characters living in a fictional world. Do those characters and their world really exist? The answer which Walton gives, and which I have decided to adopt for my considerations, is straightforward: fictional worlds and fictional characters *do not exist*, and those who attribute special ontological status to quasi-reality are simply dangling empty promises in front of us. Walton's treatment of the subject can be summed up in four points.[180] First, it is true that both those who try to explain the way fictional characters exist, and those who deny fictional characters any kind of existence, face various philosophical difficulties. On the one hand, nobody would claim that Santa Claus *really* exists; on the other, how is it possible that he does not exist if we talk about him and even represent him in so many ways?[181] Secondly, Walton observes that we get entangled in difficulties with fictional entities because of our ways of speaking about them, so the core of the problem lies in *language*: people "mistake the *pretense* of referring to fictions, combined with a serious interest in this pretense, for genuine ontological commitment."[182] Thirdly, for Walton, pretence means "acts of participation in games of make-believe,"[183] and even the act of detached scholarly criticism of a literary work involves a certain degree of pretence that fictional worlds exist and contain fictional characters.[184] Yet, when we pretend that something exists, the object of our pretence cannot exist; otherwise, there would be no need for pretending. Thus, when we say that "the Lord visited Sarah according to what he had said, and he did to Sarah as he had promised" (v. 1), we start playing a game in which we state a number of fictional propositions. There is no need, however, to assume that the textual Lord and textual Sarah are real beings. It should be said again that whether the Lord is a transcendent and eternal figure, and whether the historical Sarah existed in the remote past, is a different matter belonging, in the former case, to philosophical theology, and, in the latter, to history. However, in the narrative quasi-real world, we deal with non-existent fictional entities, and we pronounce a series of propositions in which those fictional entities are mentioned.[185]

---

180 See Walton, *Mimesis*, 385-430.
181 See Walton, *Mimesis*, 385-86.
182 Walton, *Mimesis*, 390.
183 Walton, *Mimesis*, 391.
184 See Walton, *Mimesis*, 393-94.
185 Walton's theory is strongly backed up by Priest who convincingly argues that fictional objects do not exist. At first, Priest distinguishes between two classes of fic-

Fourthly and lastly, this way of explaining the ontological status of fictional worlds and characters does not need to entail nominalism. We can simultaneously disbelieve the existence of the textual Abraham, and believe in the existence of universals, as Walton aptly points out.[186] The point is in reducing the number of entities belonging to our ontological menagerie, not in getting rid of them.[187]

Finally, my philosophical presuppositions concerning the existence of *trans-reality* can be described as *classical theism*. According to Brian Leftow, classical theism claims that God is "wholly independent of all else. God is absolutely the first being. He exists before there is anything else for him to depend on. So he must need or depend on nothing in any way other than himself."[188] Moreover, we cannot properly say that God has any attributes because that would contradict his very nature. When we say that the universals of beauty, truth, and goodness exist in God, we mean that God himself is ultimate beauty, truth, and goodness. As Boland puts it: "whatever is in God, is God and whatever God has, God is."[189] God is also eternal, "alive without past or future, living a life neither containing nor located in any series of earlier and later

---

tional objects: some of them, like Napoleon, may well exist; others, which he calls "purely fictional" do not exist (*Towards Non-Being*, 116). Later, however, Priest supports the stance according to which all objects in works of fiction are purely fictional as long as we remember that some of them may have real counterparts, which Priest calls "actual." So, my distinction between the *historical* and the *textual* Abraham corresponds to Priest's distinction between the *actual* and the (purely) *fictional* Abraham (*Towards Non-Being*, 118).

186 See Walton, *Mimesis*, 390.
187 At the opposite end of the philosophical spectrum lies Amie L. Thomasson's artifactual theory of fiction. Thomasson claims existence for fictional entities by regarding them as "abstract cultural artifacts as ordinary as the works of literature in which they appear" (*Fiction and Metaphysics*, 73), and "admitting fictional objects into our ontology" (p. 74). Moreover, Thomasson is convinced that it is possible to solve philosophical conundrums characteristic of fictional objects demonstrated already by Russell and Quine (*Fiction and Metaphysics*, 55). A discussion of the validity of Thomasson's theory, albeit interesting, would go far beyond the scope of this book. It appears that the theories of Walton, Currie, and Priest are better tailored to the character of my hermeneutical project. By regarding fictional characters as non-existent, I avoid many potential philosophical problems, as well as gain an opportunity to develop the idea of literary games, which is important for the conclusion of this book.
188 Leftow, "God," n.p. As in the case of literary texts and their readers, I do not intend to push the idea of God's independence from his creation too far. After all, the only God we know is the God who created the universe out of love, and this love belongs to his very nature.
189 Boland, *Ideas in God*, 323.

events"; necessarily existent since "a being is more perfect if wholly immune to nonexistence"; and omnipresent, which means that he is "present in all space and time, though not contained by either."[190] God has also perfect knowledge, and, in consequence, fully knows everything which is knowable.[191]

When I speak about trans-reality, I mean the transcendent sphere which readers discover through the mediation of biblical narratives, and in which they indirectly participate. In view of the definition of classical theism, I should now further qualify my approach. First, trans-reality, as I understand it, is different from the divine sphere present in the narrative world of Scripture. Although Gen 21:1-21 scarcely tells the reader about the nature of the divine sphere, and simply calls God's habitation "heaven" (v. 17), there are other biblical texts which reveal more about the divine realm. Heaven is the place where God sits enthroned (Ps 2:4); he punishes the people of Sodom and Gomorrah by sending brimstone and fire from heaven (Gen 19:24); he speaks with Israel from heaven (Exod 20:22); he is not alone in heaven, but is surrounded by "all his angels" and "all his host" (Ps 148:2). At the same time, however, he transcends the highest heaven ("heaven of heavens," 1 Kgs 8:27, Neh 9:6, 2 Chr 2:6).[192] Hence the "heaven" of Hebrew texts is the place where God lives; yet, at the same time, scriptural accounts hint that God is far greater than heaven, and dwells "somewhere" beyond it. As a result, even though the divine realm portrayed in the Hebrew Bible is a textual reality, and, strictly speaking, the reader only pretends that the textual heaven exists, the textual divine sphere points towards trans-reality, which is the *real divine sphere* existing beyond the text.

Secondly, trans-reality is neither one of God's attributes, nor the place where God dwells, and in the latter sense it is different from "heaven." According to the principles of classical theism, trans-reality means God himself understood as the first and perfect being, transcending time and space, and knowing everything knowable. The need for speaking about "trans-reality" results from the human inability to comprehend God's simplicity and perfection. The reader's knowledge about God, mediated by scriptural narrative texts, is, by its very nature, multi-faceted. The reader learns from Scripture about God's nature, as well as about God's various purposes and plans. This is why our prac-

---

190 Leftow, "God," n.p.
191 See Leftow, "God," n.p.
192 See *BDB*, 1030.

tical way of speaking about the divine realm comprises different aspects, and it is better to label them as "trans-reality," without forgetting about the close ontological correspondence between trans-reality and God himself.

Nevertheless, as in the case of the ontological status of the Platonic triad, a particular philosophical model which the reader adopts to explain the nature of actuality, quasi-reality, and trans-reality does not invalidate the simple and pragmatic fact that biblical narratives play a mediatory role in the process of reading, and that they lead the reader from the sublunary world of everyday existence to the transcendent world of divine purposes. It is now the task of the subsequent chapters to explain in detail how this mediation is achieved when the reader peruses the narrative Gen 21:1-21.

4. Immanent Knowledge

Immanent knowledge, which I have defined as readers' knowledge about actuality, has a *subjective* and an *objective* aspect. The subjective aspect arises from the fact that immanent knowledge evolves as readers become more mature and experienced. This process requires time and an active intellectual approach to challenges brought about by everyday life. Readers' levels of maturity and experience determine their ways of reading texts, and biblical narratives are no exception. There is very little chance that inexperienced readers will penetrate the various meanings of the narrative world of Gen 21:1-21 as deeply as mature readers who have experienced rejection and anguish. Thus the ability of acquiring narrative knowledge is conditioned by the immanent knowledge of actuality, and, for most of us, immanent knowledge develops fully as the time span of our lives progresses. To put it another way, we might say that the extent to which real readers become implied readers of a given text depends partly on skills acquired during their lifetime.[1]

The objective aspect of immanent knowledge depends on many factors. Readers do not live on a desert island. On the contrary, they are continually influenced by the intellectual trends of contemporary culture. As regards reading and interpreting Scripture, the immanent knowledge of modern readers is influenced by presuppositions about the role which Scripture plays in modern culture. Following Fowler, I have mentioned in chapter 1 that there are two main groups of those presuppositions: modern readers recognize the power which the Bible has exerted on culture, and, at the same time, they question that power, and are ready to re-evaluate the role played by Scripture. Furthermore, modern readers are both equipped with and influenced by various literary theories, which affect their judgment of scriptural texts, and guide them through the process of reading. In other parts of this book, I reflect on some of them, and I pay special attention to the New Criticism, rhetorical criticism, structuralism and narrative analysis, reader-

---

1 I shall return to the *subjective* aspect of immanent knowledge in the last chapter, where I discuss the horizon of the reader's knowledge about reality.

response criticism, and the various approaches called collectively the historical-critical method. In view of that, I have resolved to discuss here *postmodernism*, which is another significant cultural phenomenon whose importance for the modern way of thinking cannot be underestimated.

What are the most salient features of postmodernism? The authors of *The Postmodern Bible* answer this question by referring to Jean-François Lyotard's diagnosis of the "postmodern condition."[2] Lyotard points out three main aspects of postmodernism: aesthetic, epistemological, and political. As regards the first aspect, which directly influences the arts, "the focus has been on the constructed nature of the work, the play of surfaces, the obliteration of the traditional distinction between high and mass culture, and – particularly in the visual and literary arts – a preoccupation with the ineffable."[3] The epistemological aspect involves "incredulity towards metanarratives."[4] Meta-narratives are systems of thought that synthesize our knowledge about reality such as the scientific ideology of the Enlightenment, or the theological vision of God and man in Christianity. Postmodern critics feel inherent distrust towards any system of thought which lays claim to a general description and explanation of reality; they reject all attempts to unify or universalize a body of human knowledge.[5] As Peter Barry aptly puts it, the reason for the rejection is that "these 'metanarratives' ['supernarratives'], which purport to explain and reassure, are really illusions, fostered in order to smother difference, opposition, and plurality."[6] Moreover, from a philosophical viewpoint, postmodernism "typically opposes foundationalism, essentialism, and realism,"[7] so it can be called a modern anti-metaphysical intellectual project. Finally, the third aspect of postmodernism is political. Among its concerns, I should mention here postmodernists' unease about "technology's ever-increasing hegemony in the West, particularly when that hegemony is inexorably and, perhaps, inevitably linked to an ideology of mastery and

---

2   See Aichele and Collective, *The Postmodern Bible*, 9-10.
3   Aichele and Collective, *The Postmodern Bible*, 9.
4   Lyotard quoted in Aichele and Collective, *The Postmodern Bible*, 10.
5   Cf. Barton, *Reading the Old Testament*, 234.
6   Barry, *Beginning Theory*, 86. Derrida, in his essay on the problem of translation, says that "the 'tower of Babel' ... exhibits an incompletion, the impossibility of finishing, of totalizing, of saturating, of completing something on the order of edification, architectural construction, system and architectonics" ("Des tours de Babel," 244). The tower of Babel symbolizes postmodern culture.
7   Magnus, "Postmodern," *CDP*, 634.

hence to practices of violence."[8] Postmodernists' sensitivity to potential threats connected with the development and domination of technology resulted in a whole series of articles and books regarding topical issues such as the Gulf War, consumerism, and American culture.

When we move our discussion of postmodernism into the area of literary criticism, we observe that the postmodern style of writing is characterized by a number of recurring literary features. According to Barry, they are as follows: "fiction which might be said to exemplify the notion of the 'disappearance of the real'"; "'intertextual elements' in literature, such as parody, pastiche, and allusion"; irony, which helps to revisit the past; as well as the "element of 'narcissism' in narrative technique."[9] Yet, for postmodernists, the interest in these particular characteristics is always subordinate to the main postmodern reading strategy, which is *deconstruction*, and this interest serves to achieve its ideological goals.

Deconstruction, according to Mark C. Taylor, "is postmodernism raised to method,"[10] and the term denotes post-structuralist theory applied to reading and interpreting texts.[11] "The dissolving of the distinction between philosophical and literary texts," comments Edgar McKnight, "and the observation of the different ways that philosophical texts undermine philosophy's assumption of its own serious, literal, and truthful nature has characterized contemporary deconstruction."[12] Therefore, given the text's instability and relativity, we are allowed to deconstruct the text, or, in other words, we should allow the text to deconstruct itself. It does not matter whether the text is a newspaper article, a nineteenth century novel, or a chapter from St John's Gospel. The very nature of language and writing results in internal tensions being present in the text, and owing to those tensions, the text deconstructs itself into the seemingly endless labyrinth of often contradictory meanings.[13] J. Cheryl Exum and David J. A. Clines state: "Deconstruction is an enterprise that exposes the inadequacies of texts, and shows how inexorably they undermine themselves. A text typically has a thesis to defend or a point of view to espouse; but inevitably texts falter and let slip evidence against their own cause."[14]

---

8   Aichele and Collective, *The Postmodern Bible*, 10.
9   Barry, *Beginning Theory*, 91.
10 Quoted in Aichele and Collective, *The Postmodern Bible*, 136.
11 Cf. Barry, *Beginning Theory*, 70.
12 McKnight, *The Bible and the Reader*, 88-89.
13 Cf. Barton, *Reading the Old Testament*, 224-26.
14 Exum and Clines, *The New Literary Criticism*, 19. Among the most important

Deconstruction is not, however, the only reading strategy available from the postmodern stock. Diverse streams of postmodernism offer various approaches to the text. Without any doubt Jean Baudrillard's theory of "simulacra and simulations" should be regarded as one of the most important examples. Baudrillard declares: "All of Western faith and good faith was engaged in this wager on representation: that a sign could refer to the depth of meaning, that a sign could *exchange* for meaning and that something could guarantee this exchange – God, of course."[15] In other words, the basic assumption underlying *modern* civilization, which is not shared by the theoreticians of *postmodern* civilization, is that there exists a stable relationship between a signifier and a signified, and that the process of signification ends when we arrive at the signified. This premise, according to Baudrillard, has been shattered by our times and culture: representation has been replaced by simulation, and the effect of the whole process of simulation is a simulacrum.[16] As Tim Woods puts it: "Simulation is where the image or the model becomes more real than the real: as for instance, a television soap-opera actor receiving hate mail for his role in the show."[17]

To explain the origin of the simulation and the simulacrum, Baudrillard speaks of four successive phases of the relationship between a sign and reality: "(1) It is the reflection of a basic reality. (2) It masks and perverts a basic reality. (3) It masks the *absence* of a basic reality. (4) It bears no relation to any reality whatever: it is its own pure simulacrum."[18] Baudrillard suggests that the four phases are characteristic of different cultural periods. The first and the second phases dominated the long period of time from the Renaissance to the industrial revolution of the eighteenth century. The third phase was typical of the

---

proponents of deconstructive practice, we should list Barbara Johnson, Jacques Derrida, Paul de Man, Geoffrey Hartman, and Harold Bloom. Since deconstruction is a method of criticism applicable to all texts, including the results of critical proceedings, deconstructionists can deconstruct deconstruction. By way of illustration, in *Of Grammatology*, Derrida deconstructs Rousseau's *On the Origin of Languages*; in turn, de Man deconstructs *Of Grammatology* in *The Rhetoric of Blindness* (Cuddon, *The Penguin Dictionary*, 211-12). Moreover, Derrida emphasizes that deconstruction is an inescapable consequence of the stage in cultural development when we think that we have achieved unity and universality: when the project of the tower of Babel had been finished, God decided to deconstruct it (See "Des tours de Babel," 246).

15 Baudrillard, "Simulacra and Simulations," 404.
16 See Baudrillard, "Simulacra and Simulations," 405.
17 Woods, *Beginning Postmodernism*, 26.
18 Baudrillard, "Simulacra and Simulations," 405.

industrial age, whilst the fourth has been characteristic of the present times since the 1970s.[19]

The fourth phase, when a sign "is no longer in the order of appearance at all, but of simulation,"[20] is characterized by severing the relationship between the sign and its corresponding basic reality. The reader must then be aware that, to use Derrida's famous phrase, *il n'y a pas de hors-texte*.[21] Textual reality is all we have, and the so-called "reality outside the text" is only another instance of textuality because, like the text itself, reality is governed by linguistic rules. When we reach the fourth phase of simulation, meaning is no longer stable and determinate, because every text we read provides us with a continuous play of opposite linguistic forces. In the case of Gen 21:1-21, the narrative communicates the idea of divine providence, but, concurrently, a part of the narrative negates this idea. Sarah's attitude towards Hagar and Ishmael is portrayed in a negative light, yet, at the same time, Sarah plays a positive role in the divine plan. Moreover, all interpretive norms provided by the critics who believe in the stability of meaning are themselves another example of literary text, which, inevitably, is doomed to imprecision and contradiction. As a result, the fourth phase of simulation marks the end of rational discourse. Borders between intellectual categories have been blurred; everything is at the same time good and evil, true and false. As Barry sums up: "If this second aspect of the postmodern condition, this loss of the real, is accepted as a fact, then it is hard to see a ground for literary theory to occupy, since all methods of literary interpretation ... depend upon the making of a distinction between surface and depth, between what is *seen* in the text and some *underlying* meaning."[22]

It is often believed that postmodern reading strategies offer some advantages. Barton tells us that "learning systematically to distrust texts is a necessary part of reading, just as learning to distrust our own motives is a necessary part of adult life. ... Deconstruction, despite its strange jargon and dubious philosophy, is a challenge to the way we read."[23] Thanks to this challenge, we may learn about the nature of language and text, as well as about rules governing the process of reading. In the case of Scripture, a healthy dose of scepticism may often be salutary, and may help to eliminate interpretations which have been

---

19 See Woods, *Beginning Postmodernism*, 26; Barry, *Beginning Theory*, 82, 85.
20 Baudrillard, "Simulacra and Simulations," 405.
21 See Derrida, *Of Grammatology*, 158.
22 Barry, *Beginning Theory*, 89.
23 Barton, *Reading the Old Testament*, 226.

around for a long time, but are not really based on what the biblical text actually says. It is true, as Barton puts it, that "Derrida and those who follow him alert us to aspects of the biblical text we would otherwise overlook."[24]

Another benefit of deconstruction is that this technique may be enjoyed as a kind of sophisticated intellectual game.[25] However, like any other game, it should not be taken for reality. Its place is on the shelf, between a set of Chess and a box of Scrabble, and its main task is to prepare us for solving real problems through participation in fictional situations. To use another metaphor, deconstruction is like seeing horror films at the cinema. We may enjoy this particular cinematic genre, but even if horrifying events do occasionally happen in real life, we do not expect them to happen too often, and, instead, we prefer a balanced and calm lifestyle.

Edgar V. McKnight points to three other ways in which we may profit from postmodern approaches applied to biblical texts, especially from deconstruction. First, he states that in modern biblical criticism, we are interested in combining different modes of interpretation, and we often encounter the case when one feature of a text can be given different explanations: historical, theological, or literary. "The deconstruction of the opposition between the philosophical (or theoloical or historical) and the literary," writes McKnight, "implies the deconstruction of the opposition between the literal and the metaphorical."[26] If I understand McKnight aright, the postmodern philosophical perspective sensitizes the reader to the possibility that more than one reading of a given text is justified. Secondly, deconstruction draws our attention to certain features of the text, which, albeit not central, should be seriously considered in interpretation. McKnight enumerates such features as "writing (the relationship between speech and writing), origins, presence and absence, marginality, representation, and indeterminacy."[27] Finally, McKnight is convinced that deconstruction sheds new light on the so-called structures of opposition: "the asymmetrical opposition of terms, the condensation and subversion of values in single

---

24 Barton, "Beliebigkeit," 303. John J. Collins, who is critical of certain aspects of postmodernism and deconstruction, points, at the same time, to many of their benefits. He remarks that deconstructive reading is often parallel to the efforts of historical-critical scholars to find inconsistencies and tensions in the text (*The Bible after Babel*, 21-22).
25 Cf. Barton, *Reading the Old Testament*, 222.
26 McKnight, *The Bible and the Reader*, 93.
27 McKnight, *The Bible and the Reader*, 93.

terms, the text's difference from itself, self-reference, reproduction of conflicts in texts as conflicts between readings of the text, and the subversion of essential elements of the text by marginal elements."[28] Whatever these terms really mean, because, sadly, McKnight does not define them, their presence in the biblical text is usually explained through recourse to "historical and theological explanations."[29] Yet, if we assume a deconstructionist point of view in our critical analyses, we may well explain them in a way which expands the "possibilities of meaning."[30] In consequence, the structures of opposition become an interpretive chance, and are no longer a threat which should be avoided or passed over in silence.[31]

When we look at the other side of the coin, we notice, however, that postmodern critical practice creates more problems than it solves. Those postmodern critics who regard their theory of reading as ultimate and decisive, and who believe that they are "masters of words,"[32] settle for a never-ending play of ideas and excessive subjectivism, which are typical of the postmodern intellectual manifesto. Derrida, writing about the "interpretation of interpretation," states that there are two basic models of approaching the interpretive problem, and he wholeheartedly embraces the second one:

> The one seeks to decipher, dreams of deciphering a truth or an origin which escapes play and the order of the sign, and which lives the necessity of interpretation as an exile. The other, which is no longer turned toward the origin, affirms play and tries to pass beyond man and humanism ... The second interpretation of interpretation, to which Nietzsche pointed the way, does not seek in ethnography, as Lévi-Strauss does, the "inspiration of a new humanism."[33]

In the postmodern perspective, which rejects "logocentrism" and the "metaphysics of presence,"[34] but which, in fact, places the interpreting subject at the very centre of the literary world, critics become "masters

---

28 McKnight, *The Bible and the Reader*, 94.
29 McKnight, *The Bible and the Reader*, 94.
30 McKnight, *The Bible and the Reader*, 94.
31 In *On Deconstruction*, Jonathan Culler enumerates four modes of relevance of deconstructive practice to literary theory: its "impact upon a series of critical concepts, including the concept of literature itself," as well as being a "source of themes," an "example of reading strategies," and a "repository of suggestions about the nature and goals of critical inquiry" (pp. 180-81).
32 Cf. Carroll, *The Annotated Alice*, 269.
33 Derrida, "Structure, Sign and Play," 102.
34 Both terms are crucial to Derrida's intellectual project introduced in *Of Grammatology*.

of words," since they decide what the words really mean. By contrast, in the model of biblical interpretation which I support, words are our masters, and we usually look for meanings which contribute to the text's unity rather than disunity.

Furthermore, postmodern critics often reject the straightforward readings of a given text, and tend to invent interpretations which are novel and unusual. As I have said before, such a strategy may be, in some cases, beneficial, but it is also true that it may not be helpful at all.[35] Perhaps, this strategy is a heritage coming directly from the "masters of suspicion," namely Nietzsche, Marx, and Freud, and postmodern criticism deserves to be called a "hermeneutics of suspicion," to use the well-known Ricoeurian phrase. I believe that such an approach to biblical exegesis opens the floodgates to extreme subjectivity; in the end, we might be saying that a given scriptural passage means practically everything or anything, and that it evokes the most peculiar ideas.

For that reason, there are at least two important arguments that tell us to be extremely cautious, and not to accept the postmodern way of interpreting the Bible too readily. The first argument has just been stated: a reading strategy which leads finally to the annihilation of rational discourse and critical procedures is not worth taking seriously. The second argument for vigilance in the face of postmodernism is well stated by M. H. Abrams in his essay "The Deconstructive Angel." Abrams concentrates on philosophical assumptions underlying the deconstructive practice of postmodernism, and proves that deconstruction is an internally contradictory intellectual enterprise. He draws our attention to two problems inherently characteristic of deconstruction. First, the deconstructive method is not subject to any falsification or validation. The method is too general and all-encompassing to be reliable. Abrams states: "The deconstructive method works, because it can't help working; it is a can't-fail enterprise; there is no complex passage of verse or prose which could possibly serve as a counter-instance to test its validity or limits."[36] Secondly, Abrams suggests that deconstruction

---

35   The following quotation shows clearly what this style of postmodern exegesis may look like: "A cross is also a chiasmus, a crosswise fusion in which the order established in the first instance ('whoever would *save* their life will *lose* it') is inverted in the second instance ('and whoever *loses* their life ... will *save* it'). Central to Mark is the fact of the crucifiction [sic], a fiction structured like a cross or chiasmus. Chiasmus comes from the Greek verb *chiazein*, 'to mark with the letter χ,' pronounced *chi*. And *chi* is an anagram of *ich*, which is German for the personal pronoun *I*, and the technical term in Freud" (Anderson and Moore, *Mark & Method*, 95).
36   Abrams, "The Deconstructive Angel," 249.

goes against the grain of "literary common sense." Deconstruction undermines our efforts to discover the richness of literature; instead, we learn literary techniques which ultimately lead to the text's auto-destruction. Abrams continues his argument: "It is of no avail to point out such criticism has nothing whatever to do with our common experience of the uniqueness, the rich variety, and the passionate human concerns in works of literature, philosophy, or criticism – these are matters which are among the linguistic illusions that the criticism dismantles."[37] Subsequently, Abrams launches an offensive, and puts forward the kernel of his critique: deconstructionists use two different sets of language rules. When they deconstruct a literary work, they emphasize the indeterminacy of meaning, and refuse to accept the stability of the relationship between a signifier and a signified. After that, they move to the platform of critical theory, and explain their position in clearly comprehensive categories, as if the indeterminacy of meaning did not apply in that case. In other words, the deconstructionist logic is self-contradictory.

It is also true that postmodern biblical criticism approaches the historical-critical method with suspicion, to say the least. Postmodernists accuse the historical method of committing two "crimes": first, that the method's interest in the text's original milieu results in obscuring the biblical message for our contemporaries; second, that reading the Bible in the traditional scholarly manner reinforces such sins of the *ancien régime* as enslavement, colonialism, homophobia, or the subjugation of women.[38] As regards the first allegation, it is true that a by-product of historical-critical investigations may be putting less emphasis on the existential significance of the biblical text. Yet the historical-critical method is not supposed to do this. Its main objective is clearly defined, and only because of its scientific rigour is it called a *method*. Its primary task is not to make the biblical message more up-to-date, but rather to elucidate the original meaning of the text. Hence to demand from the historical method the same results that we expect from reader-response approaches is a misunderstanding. There is no doubt, however, that the historical-critical method could exhibit a higher degree of universality in approaching the biblical text. Barton's critical remark about the method's narrowness is very accurate in the context of our discussion: "The trouble (one trouble) with historical criticism is that in its pursuits of interpretative purity it is all too often thin, chopping logic rather

---

37 Abrams, "The Deconstructive Angel," 249.
38 See Aichele and Collective, *The Postmodern Bible*, 2, 4.

than engaging with the *matter* of the text, as Luther called it, the *res scripturae*."[39]

As far as the second charge is concerned, I would argue that the case is exactly opposite. A pre-critical and naïve reading of the Bible results in regarding ancient social patterns, with their many disadvantages, as a binding model to imitate. On the contrary, the historical method helps us to recognize which aspects of the biblical message are historically conditioned, because we understand better the historical milieu in which biblical texts were produced. Again, as Barton puts it, "the cure is more criticism, not less."[40] Furthermore, the postmodern demand for a *transformed* and *transforming* biblical criticism misses the point.[41] There is no need to transform the historical method into something else. Instead, it should be *supplemented* by other approaches. The scientific paradigm of the Renaissance and the Enlightenment has not ceased to be valid. We have only realized that this paradigm is not the only and infallible one. There are other approaches to the text, which may potentially yield interesting readings, and thus complement historical-critical exegesis.

Nevertheless, since postmodern interpretive techniques are applied to all possible texts, including the sacred text of Scripture, this should provoke a considered response. In the case of biblical criticism, the response will be setting down a set of clear interpretive rules, which are to safeguard us from getting lost in the labyrinth of meanings created by deconstruction. Otherwise, we would have to admit that the Bible is only a set of various and highly questionable texts, which endlessly deconstruct themselves, producing a mesmeric aura of mutually exclusive readings. If this had been the case, the reader's immanent knowledge would have had little chance to become transformed by the encounter with the text, and the narrative knowledge would have comprised an endless play of contradictory ideas. Moreover, because of the text's inability to refer to anything except itself, the reader would not have been able to acquire transcendental knowledge.

In the next chapter, where I intend to present different readings of Gen 21:1-21 based upon the three dimensions of biblical narratives, I shall prove that I am open to reasonable suggestions coming from postmodern critical practice, as long as they respect the unique role of the historical method in establishing the text's meaning. I am firmly con-

---

39   Barton, "Beliebigkeit," 302.
40   Barton, "Historical-Critical Approaches," 17.
41   See Aichele and Collective, *The Postmodern Bible*, 2.

vinced that they may give us valuable insights into the text, but we should not regard them as the last word and the highest achievement in critical theory.[42] If they are practised uncritically, they are not the last word, but a blind alley.

---

42 Collins reminds us that the "main gain of postmodernist criticism ... is that it has expanded the horizons of biblical studies" by bringing "new 'voices from the margin' to the conversation." On the other hand, the "main danger of postmodernism is the disintegration of the conversation into a cacophony of voices" (*The Bible after Babel*, 161).

5. Narrative Knowledge

The purpose of this chapter is twofold. First, I aim to examine the aspects of the narrative knowledge which the reader gains while perusing the model pericope Gen 21:1-21. To do this, I shall analyse the *cognitive*, *aesthetic*, and *practical* dimensions of the pericope using a wide range of modern interpretive approaches. Within the discussion of the cognitive dimension, I will distinguish between the *cognitive meaning* and *significance*. However, in the case of the aesthetic and practical dimensions, I shall assume the point of view of the modern reader, and I shall elucidate only the text's *significance*. Secondly, the ideas of truth, beauty, and goodness, which are communicated by the narrative text, will be at the centre of my attention, and I will demonstrate in what way they refer readers to the divine sphere. Since "fiction is the privileged path to the redescription of reality,"[1] I intend to show in this chapter the internal power of *quasi-reality* to transform readers' *actuality* and to lead them towards *trans-reality*. This task will begin here, and will be completed in chapter 6.

5.1. The Cognitive Dimension of Gen 21:1-21

I have shown in chapter 3 that in order to avoid interpretive clashes in biblical exegesis, we should distinguish clearly between the meaning and the significance of the text.[2] Following the discussion of Hirsch,[3] and Barton,[4] I have arrived at the conclusion that if we want to establish the meaning of a given pericope, we should use various tools provided by the historical-critical method. On the contrary, those approaches which analyse the text within a context different from the original one usually elucidate the diverse aspects of the text's signifi-

---

1   Ricoeur, "Philosophy and Religious Language," 43.
2   In this subchapter, when I speak of *meaning* and *significance*, I mean *cognitive meaning* and *cognitive significance*, unless stated otherwise.
3   See Hirsch, *Validity in Interpretation*, 8, 240; Hirsch, *The Aims of Interpretation*, 79-81.
4   See Barton, "Historical-Critical Approaches," 10-11.

cance. The distinction between meaning and significance by no means entails an oversimplified view of biblical exegesis. Instead, it shows the mutual dependence and complementarity of various approaches to the text. Thus an urgent need for both "historical" and "literary" exegesis is fully met, and, at the same time, the methodological differences existing between the approaches are respected.

In this book, I am following the "synchronic to diachronic" mode of proceeding because I believe that such a direction of our interpretive efforts is better tailored to the needs of most modern readers (see chapter 2). This is why, also in this chapter, I will focus first on the *significance* of Gen 21:1-21, and suggest practical ways of establishing it. The move from the synchronic to the diachronic mode will then result in the discussion of the *meaning* of the model narrative. Even though, in principle, I will be discussing the *historical* (or *original*) meaning of the final form of the text, many factors which will help me to establish that meaning will definitely be of diachronic nature. Finally, I will raise the question of the interrelationship between the significance and meaning of the text, and indicate possible ways of answering that question. A more extensive discussion of this problem will be, however, postponed to the next chapter.

5.1.1. The Cognitive Significance of the Pericope

When we debate the modern significance of Gen 21:1-21, we are dealing with *criticism*, and, in consequence, we need appropriate critical tools.[5] I would like to argue in this section that in the case of biblical narrative, the critical tools we need are readily provided by narrative theory and rhetorical criticism. Narrative texts form "more than one third of the Hebrew Bible,"[6] and they impose their literary world on the readers using a wide variety of rhetorical devices. This is why the choice of narrative theory and rhetorical criticism seems a move in the right direction, and I believe that my choice will be justified in the light of the exegetical results presented below.[7]

In the two subsequent subsections, I will follow the same logic of presentation. To begin with, I will introduce the most important aspects of the theory which I will be using. I am aware that "theory is dif-

---

5 Cf. Hirsch, *Validity in Interpretation*, 211.
6 Bar-Efrat, *Narrative Art in the Bible*, 9.
7 Having said this, I must add that most, if not all, modern literary approaches would help elucidate the significance of biblical narratives.

ficult to read, as it is to write; it is exacting, obdurate, yawn-inducing," as Chatman notes aptly in the preface to *Story and Discourse*.[8] However, it is necessary to reconnoitre the battlefield before the real fight begins, and I hope that this necessity will justify the relative aridity of my discussion. "It is pleasanter to read about the ins and outs of indirect free style," adds Chatman, "when academic prose is mixed with dollops of Joseph Conrad."[9] Ergo, my second step will be applying the theoretical concepts to the passage under discussion.

5.1.1.1. Narratological Concepts at Work

Gerald Prince propounds the following definition: "Narratology studies the form and functioning of narrative and tries to account for narrative competence. More specifically, it examines what all narratives have in common – narratively speaking – and what enables them to be narratively different."[10] As Prince puts it in his *Dictionary of Narratology*: "Narrative competence [is] the ability to produce and to understand narratives."[11] Prince then points to three features which a mature narrative theory should necessarily have. It should be *explicit*, i.e. it ought to indicate "with a minimum interpretation left to a user, how a narrative can be produced and/or processed by utilizing certain rules."[12] It must be *complete*, by which Prince understands its applicability to all narratives and only to narratives. Finally, a good narrative theory ought to be *empirically plausible*, that is, "in line with what we know about cognitive and communicative determinants."[13]

Prince deplores the fact that many a narratologist pays no attention to the question of meaning and that narrative syntax and narrative discourse are very often their only subject of interest, at the expense of narrative semantics and pragmatics. According to Prince, the reason for

---

8   Chatman, *Story and Discourse*, 10.
9   Chatman, *Story and Discourse*, 10.
10 Prince, "Narrative Analysis," 181-82.
11 Prince, *A Dictionary of Narratology*, 61. Among the best-known fathers and theoreticians of both narrative theory and structuralism, to which narrative theory is closely related, we should mention, first, Aristotle, whose *Poetics* laid the foundations for subsequent generations. Then, among modern scholars, we have Claude Lévi-Strauss, Vladimir Propp, A. J. Greimas, Gérard Genette, Roland Barthes, and Northrop Frye (see Cuddon, *The Penguin Dictionary of Literary Terms*, 533-35; Barry, *Beginning Theory*, 224-40).
12 Prince, "Narrative Analysis," 182.
13 Prince, "Narrative Analysis," 182.

the relative lack of interest in semantics and pragmatics is twofold: first, "no adequate theory of meaning is quite available to us yet" (semantics); secondly, "our understanding of communication and cognition is still too superficial to allow for anything more than a vaguely defined pragmatic component" (pragmatics).[14] Prince, however, is deeply convinced that narrative theory can help us discover diverse meanings (or readings) contained in narrative: "Narratology not only can provide instruments for the systematic description of all and only narratives, ... but it can also help us arrive at many readings of a given narrative and it can provide a starting point for many reflections or value judgments."[15]

It appears that Prince's definition of narratology is well tailored to the needs of biblical criticism. It allows for the incorporation of semantic and pragmatic components in narrative analysis, and, as a result, it helps to establish meaning, and accounts for the relationship between the text and the reader. Alter's definition of literary analysis can be recalled here: "By literary analysis," writes Alter in the first chapter of *The Art of Biblical Narrative*, "I mean the manifold varieties of minutely discriminating attention to the artful use of language, to the shifting play of ideas, conventions, tone, sound, imagery, syntax, narrative viewpoint, compositional units, and much else."[16] I think that if we combine Alter's literary approach, which may be called *close reading*,[17] with a narrative approach as understood by Prince, we will acquire a supple analytical tool for the analysis of biblical narratives.[18]

---

14 Prince, "Narrative Analysis," 83-84.
15 Prince, "Narrative Analysis," 183. Can the terms *narratology* and *narrative theory* be used interchangeably? Genette reminds us that the term narratology was proposed by Tzvetan Todorov in 1969 (*Narrative Discourse Revisited*, 7), but through his *Narrative Discourse: An Essay in Method* and *Narrative Discourse Revisited* he does not make a distinction between *narratology* and *narrative theory*. Similarly, Prince, both in his article and dictionary, does not differentiate between these two terms. Hence I also shall treat both terms as synonymous. However, I share Seymour Chatman's reservation concerning the use of the term *narratology*: "The Anglo-American intellectual community is suspicious of free-swinging uses of *-ology*, perhaps with justification. The questionability of the name, however, should not be confused with the legitimacy of the topic" (*Story and Discourse*, 9). Another term which may cause confusion is *narrative analysis*. I would like to use it to designate the application of narrative theory to particular biblical narratives. Hence, the relation between *narrative theory* and *narrative analysis* is similar to the relation between *hermeneutics*, understood as a theory of interpretation, and *exegesis*, which is hermeneutics put into practice.
16 Alter, *The Art of Biblical Narrative*, 12.
17 Cf. Cuddon, *The Penguin Dictionary of Literary Terms*, 142.
18 In the light of M. H. Abrams's model introduced in chapter 7, narrative theory is

One of the most serious objections which may be raised to the application of narrative theory to biblical exegesis is its structuralist provenance. Broadly speaking, "Structuralism is, or was, a movement in what Continental Europeans call 'the human sciences,' which sought to explain and understand cultural phenomena ... as manifestations of underlying systems of signification, of which the exemplary model is verbal language itself."[19] With respect to the field of literary theory, structuralism "challenges the long-standing belief that a work of literature (or any kind of literary text) reflects a given reality; a literary text is, rather, constituted of other conventions and texts."[20] Given the above two definitions of structuralism, one may have the impression that a direct application of the structuralist principles to biblical exegesis may produce potentially unwanted results and interpretative problems. Since most of our exegetical efforts aim at the explanation of what a biblical text means, there is concern that the structuralist approach to the text will not help discover meanings, but, instead, it will remain on the level of the text's internal make-up. In other words, there is a danger that we will end up discussing literary engineering in place of fruitful exegesis. That this danger is not exaggerated is further confirmed by the following remark made by Jonathan Culler:

> The structuralist study of literature, associated with the names of Roland Barthes, Tzvetan Todorov, Genette, and others, sought not to interpret literature but to investigate its structures and devices. The project ... was to develop a poetics which would stand to literature as linguistics stands to language and which therefore would not seek to explain what individual works mean but would attempt to make explicit the system of figures and conventions that enable works to have the forms and meanings they do.[21]

Yet the ultimate goal of exegesis is to explain *what* a particular text means, not only to say *how* this text means, and, as a result, many exe-

---

rooted in the objective group of critical theories, but, because of its semantic and pragmatic components, it inevitably drifts towards the pragmatic group, even though it never really reaches this position. Moreover, narrative theory is highly eclectic, and borrows concepts from different schools of literary criticism. However, the unifying factor of narrative theory is the subject it investigates: narrative, the way in which narrative makes meaning, and the basic procedures characteristic of all acts of story-telling (Cf. Barry, *Beginning Theory*, 222-23).
19 Lodge and Wood, *Modern Criticism and Theory*, xi.
20 Cuddon, *The Penguin Dictionary of Literary Terms*, 869. A structuralist approach to literature can be viewed as a reaction against highly individualistic Romantic interpretation.
21 Quoted in Genette, *Narrative Discourse: An Essay*, 8.

getes treat the efforts to create a biblical structuralist poetics with deep suspicion.[22]

In "Structuralism and Literary Criticism," Genette claims that this does not always need to be the case. By making some refinements, it is possible to use the structuralist approach in interpretation, and still enjoy the benefit of making meanings explicit, along with investigating "structures and devices." In my opinion, this feature is Genette's main advantage over other practitioners of the structuralist art. He states clearly:

> Structuralist method as such is constituted at the very moment when one rediscovers the message in the code, uncovered by an analysis of the immanent structures and not imposed from the outside by ideological prejudices. This moment was not to be long in coming, for the existence of the sign, at every level, rests on the connection of form and meaning.[23]

Hence, this type of structuralism may be labelled as "structuralism open to meaning." To put it another way, I believe that a version of narrative theory which would be the most beneficial to the analysis of biblical narratives should be based upon this "soft version" of classical structuralism, a version "open to meaning." In fact, Genette's literary method expounded in *Narrative Discourse: An Essay in Method*, where he analyses Marcel Proust's *Remembrance of Things Past*, may be placed somewhere between interpretative criticism and narratology. Genette himself admits that, on the one hand, his critical work on the Proustian novel gives him an excellent opportunity for developing a narrative theory; on the other, that theory helps elucidate the literary complexity of the novel.[24]

---

22 For a comprehensive and interesting discussion of modern narrative theory, see *Narratology Revisited*, in *PT* 11.2, 4 (1990).
23 Genette, "Structuralism and Literary Criticism," 90.
24 When we read Genette's *Narrative Discourse Revisited* published eleven years after *Narrative Discourse: An Essay in Method*, in which he re-evaluates the theses of the former book, things become more complicated. In *Narrative Discourse Revisited*, he states that we speak of narratology in two different ways: *thematic* and *modal*. Thematic narratology is an "analysis of the story or the narrative content," whilst its modal counterpart consists in an "analysis of narrative as a mode of 'representation' of stories" (*Narrative Discourse Revisited*, 16). For Genette, narratology *sensu stricto* is only modal narratology (*Narrative Discourse Revisited*, 17). What Genette says about the thematic and modal narratologies in *Narrative Discourse Revisited* is, to some extent, at variance with what he wrote eleven years earlier in *Narrative Discourse: An Essay in Method*. I believe that, at least for the purpose of biblical exegesis, Genette's disparagement of thematic narratology is far-fetched, and it seems unnecessary to devalue its role.

I would now like to introduce briefly the most fundamental narrative categories presented by Gérard Genette, which will be useful for the narrative analysis of Gen 21:1-21. The basic distinction made by Genette is tripartite: he explains the term *narrative* (in French, *récit*), and talks about its three different aspects: *story*, *narrative* (sic), and *narrating*.[25] According to Genette, *narrative* signifies the "oral or written discourse that undertakes to tell of an event or a series of events."[26] *Story* refers to the "succession of events, real or fictitious, that are the subjects of this discourse, and to their several relations of linking, opposition, repetition, etc."[27] In turn, *narrating* means the "event that consists of someone recounting something: the act of narrating taken in itself,"[28] and "by extension, the whole of the real or fictional situation in which that [narrative] action takes place."[29] Hence, *narrative* is the signifier and discourse, *story* is the signified and narrative content, whereas *narrating* is the efficient cause of both *story* and *narrative*.[30] Moreover, the reader has access to *story* and *narrating* only through the mediation of *narrative*.[31] Genette emphasizes that the "analysis of narrative discourse [is] ... a study of the relationships between narrative and story, between narrative and narrating, and (to the extent that they are inscribed in the narrative discourse) between story and narrating."[32]

Following the well-established practice of labelling and classifying in narrative theory, Genette puts forward another division, borrowed partly from Todorov, and partly from verbal grammar, and he marshals all narrative categories under three main headings: *tense*, *mood*, and *voice*. The categories which deal with "temporal relations between narrative and story"[33] are discussed under the heading *tense*, whose main subdivisions are: *order*, *duration*, and *frequency*. *Mood* signifies the "modalities (forms and degrees) of narrative 'representation.'"[34] Here Genette discusses such modalities as *distance* and *perspective*. Finally, *voice* refers to the categories "dealing with the way in which the narrating itself is implicated in the narrative, narrating in the sense [of] ... the narrative situation or its instance, and along with that its two protago-

---

25 See Genette, *Narrative Discourse: An Essay*, 27.
26 Genette, *Narrative Discourse: An Essay*, 25.
27 Genette, *Narrative Discourse: An Essay*, 25.
28 Genette, *Narrative Discourse: An Essay*, 26.
29 Genette, *Narrative Discourse: An Essay*, 27.
30 See Genette, *Narrative Discourse: An Essay*, 27.
31 See Genette, *Narrative Discourse: An Essay*, 29.
32 Genette, *Narrative Discourse: An Essay*, 29.
33 *Narrative Discourse: An Essay*, 31.
34 Genette, *Narrative Discourse: An Essay*, 31.

nists: the narrator and his audience, real and implied."[35] Under the heading *voice*, we find: *the narrating instance, narrative metalepsis, narrator,* and *narratee*. Genette summarizes his classification: "*tense* and *mood* both operate at the level of connections between *story* and *narrative*, while *voice* designates the connections between both *narrating* and *narrative* and *narrating* and *story*."[36]

In *Narrative Discourse Revisited*, Genette further qualifies the fundamental categories of narrative theory, and, interestingly enough, discusses the use of the term *diegesis*, pointing to some misunderstanding to which the term is prone. Possible confusion results from using the single English word *diegesis* for two different French (but originally Greek) words: *diégèse* and *diégésis*. As regards *diégèse*, even though some suggest that Genette uses it as a different word for *story*,[37] *diégèse* and *story* are not simply interchangeable. Genette explains: "*diégèse* is indeed a *universe* rather than a train of events (a story); the *diégèse* is therefore not the story but the universe in which the story takes place – universe in the somewhat limited (and wholly relative) sense in which we say that Stendhal is not in the same universe as Fabrice."[38] *Diégésis*, in turn, is "pure narrative (without dialogue), in contrast to the *mimésis* of dramatic representation and to everything that creeps into narrative along with dialogue."[39] In view of this distinction, and in order to avoid misunderstanding, I will use the well-established term *the diegetic mode of representation* (in contrast to *the mimetic mode*).[40]

Now, I would like to examine the passage under discussion from the point of view of the mode of representation used in the narrative. What is the significance of the mimetic and diegetic parts of the discourse for its cognitive dimension? Genette introduces this concept under the heading *mood*, and explains: "Narrative can furnish the reader with more or fewer details, and in a more or less direct way, and can

---

35 Genette, *Narrative Discourse: An Essay*, 31.
36 Genette, *Narrative Discourse: An Essay*, 32.
37 See e.g. Ska, *Our Fathers Have Told Us*, 5.
38 Genette, *Narrative Discourse Revisited*, 17-18.
39 Genette, *Narrative Discourse Revisited*, 18.
40 Narrative theory attracted much criticism on account of its technicality and the use of overly specialized terminology. While these complaints are often justified, and the excessive multiplication of new terms should be avoided, there is also the other side of the coin. Barry explains that "the learnedness [of narratological jargon] reflects the narratologists' greater distance from the actual telling of stories. ... But it hardly ever seems just an empty attempt to impress, and there is an attractive concision and precision about these terms" (*Beginning Theory*, 241).

thus seem ... to keep at a greater or lesser *distance* from what it tells."[41] As we would expect, the cognitive dimension is influenced by the distance which the narrative creates. Diegetic parts of a narrative, which comprise a general description of events, bring about the impression of a certain remoteness; they are characterized by "indirection and condensation."[42] On the contrary, mimetic parts slow down the pace of narrative, and create the "illusion that we are 'seeing' and 'hearing' things for ourselves."[43] I would like to argue that from the point of view of the cognitive dimension, the information found in the mimetic parts of narrative will be more important for narrative semantics than that in the diegetic parts. In other words, to establish the significance of narrative, we should look first at what is expressed in the mimetic mode, whereas what is rendered in the diegetic mode will provide us only with supplementary information. One further point must be made clear. The distinction between the diegetic and mimetic mode is different from the differentiation between "pure narrative" and dialogue (or monologue). Dialogue as such has a mimetic character. Yet it may have different degrees of mimetic intensity. Similarly, "pure narrative," although usually less mimetic than dialogue, can have a diegetic or mimetic character. That is why, to explain and to illustrate the different degrees of mimetic intensity of both "pure narrative" and dialogue, Genette discusses the issue of narrative representation under two headings: *narrative of events* and *narrative of words*.[44]

In the narrative of words, the main criterion for deciding about its mimetic intensity lies in distinguishing between three different states of characters' speech.[45] The "most mimetic" state takes place when the author quotes literally the speech of a character. Genette calls this instance *reported speech*. By way of illustration, reported speech is: "So she said

---

41 Genette, *Narrative Discourse: An Essay*, 162.
42 Genette, *Narrative Discourse: An Essay*, 163.
43 Barry, *Beginning Theory*, 231.
44 See Genette, *Narrative Discourse: An Essay*, 164-85. Hugh C. White is, to some extent, right in saying that the main theological theme of a narrative will be the result of the tension or, on the contrary, the harmony "arising from the semantic relation of the direct discourse of the characters to the indirect discourse of the narrative framework" ("The Joseph Story," 49). In other words, to establish the semantic aspect of a narrative, we should examine and compare the line of incidents to the line of words uttered by characters. It seems, however, that Genette's approach is more refined, and accounts for the situation when certain parts of the line of words or the line of incidents are more important for the narrative's semantic aspect simply because they are rendered in the mimetic mood of representation.
45 See Genette, *Narrative Discourse: An Essay*, 171-73.

to Abraham: 'Expel this slave woman and her son because the son of this slave woman shall not share inheritance with my son Isaac'" (v. 10). *Transposed speech*, which does not appear in Gen 21:1-21, is the case when the words of a character are quoted by making them part of the whole sentence: "John told Krzysztof that he should persist in writing essays on biblical criticism." Lastly, *narrated speech*, which is the "least mimetic," is the instance when the event of speaking is reported in a general way: "Abraham gave the name Isaac to his newborn son" (v. 3). In the last case, we do not know exactly what words were uttered, but we are aware of the verbal exchange of information. In addition, in all these three states of speech, we may encounter actual words spoken by interlocutors, or we may have the case of "inner monologue" (or thoughts) of a character.

As regards the narrative of events, Genette states: "The quantity of information and the presence of the informer are in inverse ratio, mimesis being defined by a maximum of information and a minimum of the informer, diegesis by the opposite relationship."[46] Then, in the sequel to *Narrative Discourse*, he further qualifies his statement, and enumerates three main features of the mimetic narrative of events: first, the "supposed obliteration of the narrating instance";[47] secondly, the "detailed nature of the narrative";[48] thirdly, Genette develops the remark made in the previous point and says that "these details will create even more of an 'illusion' if they seem functionally useless."[49]

Equipped with these analytical tools, I can now apply them to the passage under discussion. At the beginning of scene 1, we have two diegetic verses of introduction, which relate Isaac's birth. Vv. 1-2 belong to the narrative of events, and on account of their general character and lack of detail, they should be classified as diegetic. Then, in v. 3, we encounter the first mimetic instance: "Abraham gave the name Isaac to his newborn son." This verse may be regarded as an example of narrated speech; its mimetic force, however, seems practically insignificant because v. 3 is almost imperceptibly interwoven with the diegetic narration of events concerning Isaac. Vv. 4-5 continue to tell the events, but since the action slows down here, vv. 4-5 are of more mimetic character than vv. 1-2. In vv. 6-7, Sarah exclaims her joyful "Magnificat." Her re-

---

46 Genette, *Narrative Discourse: An Essay*, 166.
47 Genette, *Narrative Discourse Revisited*, 46. The term *narrating instance* refers to the identification of the narrator, as well as to how, when, and where the narrator tells the story (cf. Genette, *Narrative Discourse: An Essay*, 212-15).
48 Genette, *Narrative Discourse Revisited*, 46.
49 Genette, *Narrative Discourse Revisited*, 46.

ported speech has a strong mimetic force. Again, v. 8 resumes telling about the events; this one verse covers the span of approximately three years and lacks detail, so it is equal in diegetic force to vv. 1-2.

The whole of scene 2 is mimetic. V. 9 begins with the words: "Sarah noticed," and is an example of *inner* narrated speech (or, narrated monologue). Then, in v. 10, we encounter Sarah's reported speech directed to Abraham. V. 11 is parallel to v. 9: here we have an instance of Abraham's narrated monologue. In turn, in vv. 12-13, we listen to God's reported speech directed to Abraham.

In scene 3, vv. 14-16a, 16c, and 19-21 are the narrative of events, whereas vv. 16b and 17-18 are the narrative of words. The whole section comprising vv. 14-19 is of a strongly mimetic nature. First, the presence of the reported speech of Hagar in v. 16b, and of God in vv. 17-18 contributes to the mimetic mood. Secondly, except v. 14b, which is of general and imprecise character, the narrative of events abounds in detail. We learn, for instance, that Abraham gets up early in the morning, and gives Hagar a skin of water; Hagar throws the child under a bush, and sits down opposite, at the distance of a bowshot; Hagar fills the skin with water. It can also be argued that the phrase in v. 19 "she noticed a well of water" should be classified as narrated monologue, which additionally emphasizes the mimetic force of this section. Finally, the remaining vv. 20-21 resume the diegetic mode of narration, and tell of the further events of the story.

The above analysis shows which verses of the narrative communicate its core message. In scene 2, we ought to pay attention to vv. 10 and 12-13, which are of strongly mimetic character. Then, in scene 3, we have mimetic reported speech in vv. 16b and 17-18, as well as mimetic events in vv. 14a, 15-16a, 16c, and 19. Finally, as regards scene 1, we should focus on vv. 6-7, which is its only clearly mimetic part. Hence from the mimetic parts of scenes 2 and 3, we learn a great deal about the human characters of the story and God's action concerning their lives. The reported speech in scene 2 depicts an envious Sarah, who acts harshly to secure her and her son's future, and demands from her husband that Hagar and Ishmael should be expelled. God, surprisingly, tells Abraham to grant Sarah's demand, but secures the future of both Isaac and Ishmael. At this point of the story, we do not know, however, in what way God's plans concerning Ishmael will be fulfilled, and how the danger of death will be prevented. The reported speech in scene 3 portrays Hagar, who, faced with a dead end, succumbs to despair. Nevertheless, God comes to her and her son's rescue, saves their lives, and promises a bright future for Ishmael. Moreover, this cognitive message is confirmed by the mimetic narrative of events in scene 3:

God provides a miraculous solution to the tragic course of action initiated by Abraham in v. 14a, and experienced by Hagar and Ishmael in vv. 15-16a and 16c. Finally, Sarah's exultant speech in scene 1 can be summarized in the following phrase: God is wonderful and performs miracles for his chosen people!

To sum up, in Gen 21:1-21, God is portrayed as the God of divine providence, who miraculously fulfils his mysterious plans, and is always ready to support those who are in trouble, and to offer solutions to the most hopeless situations. His action finds expression in creating and preserving life, and in securing the well-being of his people for long generations. The second aspect of the message concerns the human characters of the story. Even though they experience God's mercy, they are inclined to secure their happiness at the expense of other people. The effects of their ruthless actions lead to suffering and despair of their neighbours. These negative consequences are, however, overcome by God's supportive action. Although it sometimes seems that there is no hope, the Lord of the living keeps watch and averts the death of his faithful.

5.1.1.2. Rhetorical Criticism: The Use of Irony

In *A Rhetoric of Irony*, Wayne C. Booth provides his readers with an in-depth discussion of the notion of irony. The book's great advantage is that its author concentrates on particular literary examples, which become a basis for a universal theory of irony. Booth never sacrifices the truth and reality of literature on the altar of even the most sublime theory. As he clearly puts it: "The worst enemy of good reading as of good criticism is the application of abstract rules that violate the life of particular works."[50] Moreover, he encourages readers to seek different and complex kinds of irony, even those that are not always palpable. He states at the very beginning: "Every good reader must be, among other things, sensitive in detecting and reconstructing ironic meanings."[51]

Booth himself is ironic from the very first pages of his book, where he states: "I have heard it said that the two standard tutorial questions at Oxford are 'What does he mean?' and 'How does he know?' I doubt the report – no university could be that good – but I take the questions

---

50 Booth, *A Rhetoric of Irony*, 277.
51 Booth, *A Rhetoric of Irony*, 1.

as the best summary of how what I attempt here contrasts with much that is said about irony."⁵² Hence these two questions will be asked here: *What do we mean* when we say that biblical narratives are ironic? *How do we know* that they really are ironic, and that we are not reading into them our own ideas, which they do not contain?

Booth's clarification of the notion of irony is founded upon at least three assumptions, which are introduced in the preface to his book. First, he believes that we are able to work out some objective criteria which may help to elucidate this often complicated matter, and, as a result, his approach to the "large slippery subject" of irony is positive.⁵³ Secondly, he stresses that although there may be many readings of a text, some of them are always better than others because ironic texts were written in order to communicate an ironic message rather than to make decoding of the text arduous or impossible.⁵⁴ Finally, in his third assumption, Booth affirms the plurality of critical approaches and the objective validity of their critical results. He reminds us that when we discover an ironic reading of a text, we should not simultaneously rule out other readings proposed by various approaches.⁵⁵

Before I embark on the discussion of the passage Gen 21:1-21, I will broach a problem which faces every reader who claims that an ancient text contains ironic meanings. A fastidious critic will always ask whether the ancient author of the text intended the irony, or whether the irony was discernible to the text's first readers. Such a question becomes very often a hopeless trap from which it is difficult to extricate oneself. Even an elaborate argument which proves that a particular biblical text is loaded with irony can be undermined by two simple questions: "What do you know about the actual writer of this passage?" and "How can you prove that the literary sensitivity of the ancients was similar to ours?" Answering these questions may be impossible, and our reader can be accused of conjuring up meanings that do not exist. While this may be true, Booth's distinction between the real author and the implied author helps to circumvent the problem. As he puts it: "It is only by distinguishing between the author and his implied image that we can avoid pointless and unverifiable talk about such qualities as 'sincerity' or 'seriousness' in the author."⁵⁶ By making this distinction, we distance ourselves from the real author, and become interested only

---

52 Booth, *A Rhetoric of Irony*, x.
53 See Booth, *A Rhetoric of Irony*, xi.
54 See Booth, *A Rhetoric of Irony*, xi.
55 See Booth, *A Rhetoric of Irony*, xi-xii.
56 Booth, *The Rhetoric of Fiction*, 75.

in the implied author, who "is the image of the author constructed by the reader as she or he reads the narrative."[57] What is more, in the case of biblical narratives, which were composed in the remote past, we hardly have access to the implied author constructed by their original readers. Our "modern implied author" reflects our contemporary literary sensitivity, and, in consequence, we no longer need to answer the questions about the identity of the actual writer or the literary sensitivity of the ancients. Hence the whole discussion moves from the level of meaning to the level of significance.

Booth claims that irony has four general features. Irony is, first, *intended* by the author; it cannot be accidental, unconscious or unintentional. When Booth speaks about the "author" in this context, he means, of course, the implied author. Secondly, irony is *covert*, which means that it does not contain any direct suggestions made by the author that it should be decoded by the reader. *Stability* is the third characteristic of irony, by which Booth means that when readers have fixed the actual meaning of an ironic statement, they do not need to repeat this process endlessly – they are not expected to "deconstruct" the text, and to search for multiple ironic meanings. Fourthly, irony is *"finite* in application," which means that its reconstructed meanings are always limited and narrow. In other words, the finitude of irony results in "a set of completed insights," which concern a particular number of things, events, or people.[58]

Booth describes in detail how the reader should reconstruct ironic meanings, and introduces a four-step procedure. I will now apply that procedure to vv. 12 and 17 of the model passage, which, in my view, contain irony. So, the first step is made when "the reader is required to reject the literal meaning. It is not enough that he may reject that meaning because he disagrees, nor is it enough that he should add meanings. If he is reading properly, he is unable to escape recognizing either some incongruity among the words or between the words and something else that he knows."[59] How should we then interpret, in the light of Booth's words, God's reply to Abraham: "Do not regard as evil the matter concerning the boy and your slave woman. Grant Sarah whatever she asks you, since it is through Isaac that your descendants will be named"? There is incongruity in v. 12 resulting from the apparent contradiction between God's words and what we know about

---

57 Abbott, *The Cambridge Introduction to Narrative*, 191.
58 See Booth, *A Rhetoric of Irony*, 5-6. In the third and shortest part of *A Rhetoric of Irony*, Booth discusses examples of unstable and infinite ironies.
59 Booth, *A Rhetoric of Irony*, 10.

God's nature. Even if we rightly assume that one of God's attributes is omniscience, we should be utterly surprised at the words "Do not regard as evil." We are ready to accept God's decision to expel Hagar and her son because we believe that God will find a solution to this difficult situation, but we shudder when God, the giver of life and defender of the poor, suggests that Abraham should not regard as evil the apparent injustice inflicted on his wife Hagar. We would rather like to hear: "*Although your soul is exceedingly sorrowful, remember that the Lord trieth the righteous. Yet you shall not see the righteous forsaken nor his seed begging bread.* Grant Sarah whatever she asks you." Another kind of discrepancy is found in v. 17, where God, knowing well that Hagar is on the brink of despair, says: "What worries you, Hagar? Fear not, since God has heard the voice of the boy where he is." Again, the words "What worries you?" seem to be completely awkward in this context. While in v. 12 God's order contradicts his goodness, the question in v. 17 belies his omniscience. He cannot ask "What worries you?" because he knows better than anybody else the plight of Hagar and her son.[60] As a result, both verses make us reflect and search for a different and satisfying explanation.

Booth describes the second step: "Alternative interpretations or explanations are tried out – or rather, in the usual case of quick recognition, come flooding in."[61] This, in turn, leads to the third step: "A decision must therefore be made about the author's knowledge or beliefs. ... No matter how firmly I am convinced that a statement is absurd or illogical or just plain false, I must somehow determine whether what I reject is also rejected by the author."[62] The process of decoding irony ends when "having made a decision about the knowledge or beliefs of the speaker, we can finally choose a new meaning or cluster of meanings with which we can rest secure."[63] Since vv. 12 and 17 are a part of God's direct speech in the narrative, the assumption that they are ironic is even more plausible. Among four characters who speak, God is the most prominent, and belongs to the realm of transcendence. He is then privileged to speak in a way which expresses and emphasizes his advantaged position. Hence irony becomes a kind of two-edged sword in God's hands. God as a literary character communicates his ideas on two levels, direct and indirect, and his transcendent position suggests

---

60 We have a similar case in the narrative of the first sin and its punishment: "But the Lord God called to the man, and said to him, 'Where are you?'" (Gen 3:9).
61 Booth, *A Rhetoric of Irony*, 11.
62 Booth, *A Rhetoric of Irony*, 11.
63 Booth, *A Rhetoric of Irony*, 12.

what "alternative interpretations or explanations" should be tried out. In other words, any explanation which deprives God of his privileged role should be automatically considered invalid because it would violate the fundamental logic of the text, and would make the story self-contradictory.

Thus God speaks on two levels and in two directions. The first level is constituted by the literal sense of God's words, and is directed to Abraham and Hagar: Abraham learns that he should not regard Sarah's demand "as evil," whereas Hagar thinks that God has just become aware of her desperate condition, and that he must now ask about further details. This level of communication respects the limited knowledge which Abraham and Hagar have about the flow of future events. The second level is founded upon the reconstructed sense of God's words, and is directed to the reader who undertakes the effort of decoding the message. On the second level, God seems to communicate the following: "I am the supreme character of the story, and its plot is under my exclusive control. Abraham and Hagar have only limited knowledge of the flow of the events in the story. As you can see, I mercifully take the human characters' weakness into consideration, and I treat them in proportion to their actual awareness of the facts. Abraham should indeed realize the evil inflicted upon his secondary wife and her son. Yet he does not understand how powerful I am, and how skilfully I am able to direct the events. So, let him follow Sarah's mean suggestion in order that I may reveal to him the power of my providential care. Likewise, I do not need to ask Hagar what worries her, since I have known about it from the very beginning. Yet let her remember than I am always ready to protect her and her son. And you, my dear reader, you have been admitted to the internal circle of close friends who know much more than the human characters of this story. You must, however, pay your admission fee: you have to find my subtle and divine irony whenever I intend it. You may, of course, remain insensitive and lazy. You may allow yourself to be carried away by the superficial drifts of the story, and, consequently, to learn nothing, and remain as ignorant as Abraham and Hagar. But if you are clever enough to find hidden ideas under the seeming simplicity of the text, you will be greatly rewarded, and your prize shall never be taken away from you."[64]

---

64 Interestingly, this analysis may be developed with the aid of at least two concepts known in narrative theory: the *knowledge* of the reader and of the characters, as well as the *point of view* (or *focalization*). Ska rightly notices that one of the most important sources of irony in the text are differences between the levels of knowledge (see *Our*

Has the presence of irony in vv. 12 and 17 been already noticed by biblical scholars? Delitzsch, in his late nineteenth century commentary, explains v. 12: "God however requires of [Abraham] the denial of his natural feeling,"[65] but he does not take up a discussion about the meaning of v. 17. Driver, discussing v. 12, notes: "'But what a woman's jealousy impels Sarah to wish, is for other reasons in accordance with God's will' (Di.); and Abraham, when satisfied of this, sacrifices his fatherly feelings, and resigns himself to the loss of his son."[66] As far as v. 17 is concerned, Driver regards God's words directed to Hagar as an exemplification of the "divine care for the lonely and the distressed."[67] Von Rad emphasizes God's historical purpose and Abraham's obedience in v. 12,[68] but passes over the problem in v. 17 in silence. Speiser practically ignores the issue in vv. 12 and 17, apart from the short remark: "Abraham was either unable or unwilling to intervene in the bitter rivalry between two headstrong women."[69] In his commentary on Genesis, Westermann draws our attention to three points: first, God's words in vv. 12-13 contribute to the subtlety of the narrative; secondly, vv. 12-13 provide a necessary justification of Abraham's behaviour in v. 14; thirdly, when God says in v. 12: "Do not regard as evil," he also makes a promise.[70] As regards v. 17, Westermann considers the words "What worries you, Hagar?" to be part of a later insertion into the story.[71] In turn, both Robert Alter's masterly translation and commentary[72] and Cotter's commentary[73] do not mention the problem at all. Finally, Edwin M. Good in *Irony in the Old Testament*, mentions Gen 21:9-21 as an ironic passage, but the reason he gives for that is different: "the vexation he [Ishmael] causes Sarah ... provide[s] an ironic suspense to the promise of descendants."[74]

Fathers Have Told Us, 57). Similarly, Paul D. Duke quotes the criteria of irony proposed by D. C. Muecke: "all irony (1) is a double-layered or two-storied phenomenon, (2) presents some kind of opposition between the two levels, and (3) contains an element of 'innocence' or unawareness" (*Irony in the Fourth Gospel*, 13).

65 Delitzsch, *A New Commentary on Genesis*, 76.
66 Driver, *The Book of Genesis*, 211.
67 Driver, *The Book of Genesis*, 212.
68 Von Rad, *Genesis*, 227-28.
69 Speiser, *Genesis*, 157.
70 See Westermann, *Genesis 12-36*, 340.
71 See Westermann, *Genesis 12-36*, 342.
72 See Alter, *Genesis: Translation and Commentary*.
73 See Cotter, *Genesis*.
74 Good, *Irony in the Old Testament*, 92.

This short survey of scholarly opinions on vv. 12 and 17, which is by no means complete, shows at least that the presence of irony in these verses is not a widely known idea in biblical exegesis. Perhaps it is even a path which has not yet been trodden, and thus well worth further exploration. We should keep in mind Booth's astute remark made in the context of the four steps leading to the recognition of irony in the text: "Obviously these steps are often virtually simultaneous – or they may, for a given work, occupy a scholar's lifetime."[75] Thus not everything which is not immediately evident is necessarily a fallacy.[76]

Booth's book on irony abounds with ironic examples quoted from literature and taken from life. In one chapter, Booth recalls a friendly conversation he once had with a workman in France, and comments on it: "The circle of inferences was closed, and we knew each other in ways that only extended conversation could otherwise have revealed. Total strangers, we had just performed an intricate intellectual dance together, and we knew that we were somehow akin."[77] Likewise, when we discover ironies in Scripture, we are also invited to perform a sophisticated dance, which may bring the fruit of intimate and gratifying closeness with the Divine Ironist.

5.1.2. The Cognitive Meaning of the Pericope

Hirsch is right when he observes that in the case of anonymous texts, we ought to pay close attention to their date of origin, as well as to "the cultural and personal attitudes the author might be expected to bring to bear in specifying his verbal meanings."[78] To put it another way, we should recreate the diachronic literary process which gave rise to a particular biblical text, and then focus on the last stage of its redaction. The

---

75 Booth, *A Rhetoric of Irony*, 12.
76 Robert M. Fowler, convinced that Booth's *A Rhetoric of Irony* "remains the best discussion available of the rhetorical use of irony in literature and our experience of irony as readers" (*Let the Reader Understand*, 14), points also to some flaws in Booth's presentation of the subject. First, Booth discusses, in principle, only verbal irony, and he is not sufficiently concerned with dramatic irony based upon the incongruity of situations and events. Secondly, he devotes much energy to the explanation of the stable and finite kinds of irony, but he does it at the expense of unstable and infinite ironies. Finally, according to Fowler, a dichotomy between stable and finite, on the one hand, and unstable and infinite, on the other, seems artificial and far-fetched (see *Let the Reader Understand*, 13-14).
77 Booth, *A Rhetoric of Irony*, 31.
78 Hirsch, *Validity in Interpretation*, 240.

question concerning the meaning of the earlier stages of the text, or its historical sources, is no doubt interesting, but from the perspective of this book that meaning is of secondary importance. In view of that, in this section, I will concentrate on the meaning of the text's final form in its original context using the tools of the historical-critical method. According to Hirsch, such proceedings should be labelled as *interpretation*.[79]

Joseph A. Fitzmyer, in his commentary on the Biblical Commission's document *The Interpretation of the Bible in the Church*, notes that the historical-critical method begins with a number of preliminary questions concerning the text's "authorship, date and place of composition, unity or integrity, occasion and purpose of writing, literary dependence (or background), outline and contents."[80] Even if those questions do not belong to the method itself, they are an important starting point for discussion. The first step taken by a historical critic is *textual criticism*, whose main purpose is to establish "a modern form of the texts that is as close as possible to the original."[81] Then we should analyse the *grammatical and semantic aspects* of the text in order to discover the textual meaning.[82] The next step is called *source criticism*, and involves "the study of doublets, irreconcilable differences, and other indicators that reveal the composite character of a textual unit, and perhaps even the sources on which the unit depends or the separate documents from which it has been put together."[83] This in turn paves the way for *genre criticism*, which is closely related to *Formgeschichte*, whose goal is "to identify the literary form of a textual unit, its features, and its *Sitz im Leben*,"[84] as well as *tradition criticism*, "which attempts to describe the development involved in the history of the form."[85] The last step of the method is *redaction criticism*, and it "concentrates on the modifications that traditional texts have undergone as they have been edited or redacted by a biblical author for the sake of his literary or religious purpose in composing the work."[86] Some scholars would label source, genre, tradition, and redaction criticism collectively as *higher*

---

79 See Hirsch, *Validity in Interpretation*, 211.
80 Fitzmyer, *The Biblical Commission's Document*, 38.
81 Fitzmyer, *The Biblical Commission's Document*, 39.
82 See Fitzmyer, *The Biblical Commission's Document*, 40.
83 Fitzmyer, *The Biblical Commission's Document*, 41.
84 Fitzmyer, *The Biblical Commission's Document*, 41.
85 Fitzmyer, *The Biblical Commission's Document*, 42.
86 Fitzmyer, *The Biblical Commission's Document*, 42. Fitzmyer uses the term *philological analysis* for all the steps of the historical-critical method following textual criticism (see pp. 40-42).

criticism, whereas the term for establishing the original text would be *lower criticism*.[87]

In chapter 2, I have already discussed the textual criticism, the grammatical and semantic analysis, as well as the source criticism of Gen 21:1-21. Therefore, given the goal of the present section, I would now like to apply other tools of the historical-critical method to my model passage. These include, first of all, genre[88] and redaction criticism, as well as some preliminary topics such as authorship, and the date of composition.

George W. Coats, in his influential commentary, defines the narratives comprising the Abraham cycle as a family saga, and explains that saga differs from history writing "by virtue of its concern to narrate not simply the course of events dictated by the cause-effect sequence of the past, but rather the central kernel of the past that encapsulates each successive generation. It is much more symbolic than objective representation; it is an art form, not an objective scientific datum."[89] Coats's taxonomy has been adopted by many scholars, but Westermann suggests a different and apparently more precise classification. In *Genesis 12-36*, he discusses different types of narrative in Genesis, and gives a somewhat critical account of the form-critical taxonomy to which most of us have got used.

Westermann enumerates the following: the folk story (saga), the aetiological folk story, the tale, the legend, and the myth, on the one hand; as well as genealogies and itineraries, on the other.[90] Genealogies and itineraries differ from the former group because they are enumerative rather than narrative in form, and they occupy only a very small part of Genesis.[91] Westermann supports R. R. Wilson's opinion that

---

87 Barton reminds us that the term *higher criticism* is now obsolete: "If the term 'higher criticism' had survived into this century, it would have included such disciplines as form and redaction criticism; the fact that we can now equate it with 'source criticism' stems purely from the fact that this was the only form of higher, i.e. nontextual, criticism current when the term was still in general use" ("Source Criticism (OT)," *ABD* 6:164; see also Barton, *Reading the Old Testament*, 248 n. 2).

88 I am aware of the problems in translating the German term *Gattung* as *genre*, and, after Barton, I adopt the following definition of *genre*: "a conventional pattern, recognizable by certain formal criteria (style, shape, tone, particular syntactic or even grammatical structures, recurring formulaic patterns), which is used in a particular society in social contexts which are governed by certain formal conventions" (*Reading the Old Testament*, 32).

89 Coats, *Genesis*, 102. Otto Eissfeldt takes a similar stand (*The Old Testament*, 40-41).

90 See Westermann, *Genesis 12-36*, 50-58.

91 See Westermann, *Genesis 12-36*, 54.

genealogies are rooted in their oral prehistory; yet this does not help to determine their historicity. Rather than to record historical events in the modern sense of the world, genealogies "served to specify the position of the individual in the community to which he belonged."[92] Similarly, the historical value of the itineraries in the patriarchal stories is relative: "the migratory groups of the patriarchal period preserved in the itineraries their stopping places along the route. They did this probably because the routes and the stopping places described the 'history' of the group and also because it was important for related nomadic groups as well as for future generations to know these routes."[93]

As regards the narrative genres in Genesis 12-36, Westermann excludes the possibility that the text contains any myths or legends in the strict sense of the word, neither is the label "tale" appropriate for any of the patriarchal stories, in contrast to what Gunkel and Gressmann proposed. Although the patriarchal stories are not history, we should not regard them as myths either: "the alternative which would describe reality either as myth or history is questionable."[94] To call them legends, their *Sitz im Leben* would have had to be religious gatherings, and their purpose imitation of their characters.[95] The presence of some common literary motifs is not sufficient to call them tales. Moreover, ordinary tales are usually indefinite as regards time and place, they contain magical traits, as well as blur the difference between the earthly and the heavenly realm.[96] Furthermore, Westermann is uneasy about labelling the patriarchal stories as folk stories or sagas (either aetiological or non-aetiological). This term is too narrow, and does not take into consideration that "they are so different in tone, material, and language."[97] In addition, unlike in the classical saga, the emphasis in the patriarchal stories is placed on domestic life.[98]

As a result, Westermann claims that we should call the narratives in Gen 12-36 *patriarchal stories* or *narratives about Israel's ancestors*.[99] He is also convinced that none of the patriarchal stories is "a completely new

---

92 Westermann, *Genesis 12-36*, 56.
93 Westermann, *Genesis 12-36*, 57.
94 Westermann, *Genesis 12-36*, 53.
95 See Westermann, *Genesis 12-36*, 53. Interestingly, the patriarchal stories become *legends* within the context of Christian or Jewish liturgy, but this is secondary to what they are *per se*.
96 See Westermann, *Genesis 12-36*, 52-53.
97 Westermann, *Genesis 12-36*, 50.
98 See Westermann, *Genesis 12-36*, 51.
99 Westermann, *Genesis 12-36*, 50.

creation of an author."¹⁰⁰ Instead, we should speak about the redactor, who had at his disposal material which had been passed down to him, and whose influence is usually very significant. The stories which the redactor used are rooted in long oral tradition, and some parts of them may be even traced back to the patriarchal period, even though it is difficult to establish unswerving criteria for their dating.¹⁰¹

Now, to establish the meaning of the pericope under discussion, we must define its original context. In our case, it is a complex question: the narrative is rooted in oral tradition, and its structure has undergone a number of changes, as source criticism convincingly shows. Vv. 1-2 belong to J and P, vv. 3-5 to P, vv. 6-7 to J, and vv. 8-21 were added by an unknown interpolator (see chapter 2). Given that the final redactor had at his disposal two sources (J and P), as well as the work of the interpolator, it is implausible that the redaction of the narrative took place before the end of the exile.

Certainly, the *terminus a quo* of the redaction depends entirely on the dating of the Pentateuchal sources, and in modern biblical scholarship this question is a bone of contention. If we take into account the most established views, we have the sixth century B.C. for the latest possible date for J,¹⁰² and the first half of the fifth century B.C. for P (the opinion of the Wellhausen school).¹⁰³ Nicholson summarizes: "Whether it [P] was composed in the exilic or post-exilic period is difficult to determine; there are arguments in favour of both of these proposed dates. It is unlikely that it was composed earlier than the exile."¹⁰⁴ Clines also suggests the fifth century B.C. for the final edition of the Pentateuch,¹⁰⁵ but discussing its theological function, he reminds us that the Pentateuch remains an entirely exilic work, and that it serves as "the self-expression of the exiles."¹⁰⁶ Thus it follows that the *terminus a quo* should be ca. 500-450 B.C. As regards the *terminus ad quem*, a comparison of the MT and the LXX of Gen 21:1-21 (see chapter 2) shows that in two cases the LXX adds to the MT (vv. 9 and 12), and in other two emends it (vv. 16 and 20), which leads to the conclusion that the *ter-*

---

100 Westermann, *Genesis 12-36*, 34.
101 See Westermann, *Genesis 12-36*, 36-37.
102 See e.g. Van Seters, *Abraham in History and Tradition*, 310-11. Westermann strongly disagrees with Van Seter's thesis, and calls "setting the Yahwist in the exile ... extremely improbable" (*Genesis 12-36*, 46).
103 See Nicholson, *The Pentateuch*, 21.
104 Nicholson, *The Pentateuch*, 221.
105 See Clines, *The Theme of the Pentateuch*, 14.
106 Clines, *The Theme of the Pentateuch*, 104.

minus ad quem of the final redaction should be ca. 250 B.C.[107] In consequence, we should place the final redaction of Gen 21:1-21 somewhere between 450 and 250 B.C. To be more precise in this respect seems impossible.

From the point of view of historical criticism, the meaning of the whole pericope is the result of the relationship between the meanings of its two underlying constituent parts: vv. 1-7 (the work of P and J) and vv. 8-21 (the work of an interpolator).[108] As will be shown below, the meanings of the two parts are complementary, and express important aspects of God's salvific action in the history of Israel. First and foremost, the narrative in vv. 1-7 contains the fulfilment of the promise of a child given to Abraham by God. As Westermann rightly observes, the narrative brings to a conclusion the different topics present in the preceding chapters: God's promise of a son in chapters 17 and 18, God's command concerning circumcision in chapter 17, and Sarah's barrenness mentioned first at the end of chapter 11.[109] Thus the message conveyed by vv. 1-7 is about God's faithfulness aiming at the preservation of Abraham's line. God's action is miraculous: Sarah becomes a mother "in her husband's old age" (v. 2). It should be noted that even though, at first glance, Abraham and Sarah are the main characters of the story, its meaning points, first of all, to God. Although God is mentioned only in half of the verses of the narrative (1, 2, 4, and 6), he is the real main character, whereas Abraham and Sarah are only the beneficiaries of his graciousness.

Secondly, the narrative in vv. 8-21, which, according to Westermann, is deeply rooted in oral tradition, and whose prehistory may go back to the patriarchal period, deals with two difficulties experienced by ancient nomads: "family conflict and the threat of the desert."[110] As

---

107 On the dating of the LXX see e.g. Peters, "Septuagint," *ABD* 5:1093-104. I am aware, following Peters, that "while it is convenient to use BHS or BHK as a starting point for understanding what undergirded the LXX translations, it is dangerous, dishonest and wrong to assume that Leningradensis B 19A (MT) lay before the pre-Christian translators" ("Septuagint," 1100). Since it is very difficult to reconstruct the type of the MT which was at the LXX translators' disposal, at least in the case of Gen 21:1-21, which is a relatively simple text, we may assume that that textual variant was similar to the MT. After all, if the LXX adds to the MT, and the addition clarifies the meaning of the text, it is more probable that the addition did not exist in the pre-MT text rather than that the subsequent MT was shorter than the pre-MT.
108 To establish the historical meaning of the pericope, I take into account its source division, and not narrative division (see chapter 2).
109 See Westermann, *Genesis 12-36*, 331.
110 Westermann, *Genesis 12-36*, 338.

in vv. 1-7, God's providential care provides a solution to the two difficulties. In the first case, God gives preference to Sarah's son at the expense of Hagar's (v. 12). In the second, he miraculously rescues Hagar and her son from imminent death in the wilderness of Beersheba (vv. 17-19). Moreover, the narrative tells us about God's care concerning Abraham's sons. Isaac is protected by God's hand, and the joyous banquet given on the day of Isaac's weaning (v. 8) emphasizes God's providential benevolence. Similarly, in v. 20, we learn that "God was with the boy," and his presence provided Ishmael with a strong foundation for his subsequent career and family life. The binary structure of the theological motifs present in vv. 8-21 is further reinforced by two promises inserted in vv. 12bβ-13 and 17aβ-18.[111] The special blessing given to Abraham becomes reserved for the line of Isaac. However, at the same time, God cares about the second son and his progeny: Ishmael will become a great nation. Thus, on the one hand, God's plans concerning his chosen nation are confirmed, but, on the other, his generosity is unlimited, and extends to other peoples.[112]

Hence the whole pericope tells its original readers or listeners of God's *faithfulness* and *providential care*. His faithfulness manifests itself in the fulfilment of the promise given to Abraham. His providential care becomes apparent when he provides a solution to the family strife, prevents the death of Hagar and Ishmael, and is deeply concerned about the future of Abraham's sons. Such phrasing of the narrative's meaning is compatible with most ways of formulating the theme of the whole Pentateuch. By way of illustration, for Clines

> the theme of the Pentateuch is the partial fulfilment – which implies also the partial non-fulfilment – of the promise to or blessing of the patriarchs. ... The promise has three elements: posterity, divine-human relationship, and land. The posterity-element of the promise is dominant in Genesis

---

111 Westermann convincingly argues that both promises were added at a later stage of the development of the narrative since they refer to distant future rather than to the present situation (see *Genesis 12-36*, 340, 342-43).
112 Nikaido compares Gen 21:8-21 and Gen 16, and reads the two chapters in the light of three other stories: the command to sacrifice Isaac in Gen 22, Hannah's story in 1 Sam 1, and the story of Joseph and Potiphar's wife in Gen 39. He arrives at the conclusion that "in contrast to her negative role as Sarah's antagonist, Hagar is portrayed in a manner that compels us to see her as a matriarchal figure on a par with such figures as Abraham and Hannah. ... Although Ishmael is ultimately rejected as Abraham's promised heir ... the story of his birth and exile contain elements that associate him with such heroic figures as Samuel and Joseph" ("Hagar and Ishmael," 240). The interpretation of the narrative given in this chapter also emphasizes the role played by Hagar and Ishmael.

12-50, the relationship-element in Exodus and Leviticus, and the land-element in Numbers and Deuteronomy.[113]

Clines's approach to the problem is criticized by Nicholson, who chides Clines for adopting the canonical criteria instead of the criteria of literary criticism in determining the limits of the Pentateuch. If the latter were taken into consideration, the question would be more difficult to answer: perhaps we would speak of the Tetrateuch, Hexateuch, or even of a bigger literary unit containing the Deuteronomistic Corpus.[114] Apart from that, Nicholson points out that the very nature of the Pentateuch is polyvalent, and he asks rhetorically: "Is the search for such an overriding theme not destined to run into the same difficulties as the quest for a 'centre' (*Mitte*) once favoured as a way of arranging a 'theology' of the Old Testament as whole?"[115] It seems, however, that Clines defends himself against these two charges. Even if he does not discuss at length the criteria for the delimitation of the Pentateuch, and simply states that it "has been recognized as a literary entity by Jews, Samaritans, Christians and Muslims for somewhere between twelve hundred and twenty-five hundred years,"[116] his academic enterprise consists in the determination of the theme of the *Pentateuch* and nothing else. Clines does not say anywhere that if he had embarked on the analysis of the Tetrateuch or the Hexateuch his conclusions would have been exactly the same. What he has in mind is just the Pentateuch. Moreover, for the purpose of my work, which discusses only Gen 21:1-21, the question of the delimitation of the Pentateuch is secondary. Clines refutes the second argument by saying that although the Pentateuch is a patchwork of different sources, we should ask, after Noth, "whether in the final analysis the whole has not become greater than merely the sum of its parts" (cf. chapter 2).[117] In addition, in the afterword written twenty years after the first edition of his book had been published, Clines takes a postmodern stand, and even though he now does not believe in the idea of determinate meaning, he still claims

---

113 Clines, *The Theme of the Pentateuch*, 30. Undertaking a similar task, von Rad states the theological theme of the Hexateuch in the following way: "God, the Creator of the world, called the patriarchs and promised them the Land of Canaan. When Israel became numerous in Egypt, God led the people through the wilderness with wonderful demonstrations of grace; then after their lengthy wandering he gave them under Joshua the Promised Land" (*Genesis*, 13-14).
114 See Nicholson, *The Pentateuch*, 256-57.
115 Nicholson, *The Pentateuch*, 258.
116 Clines, *The Theme of the Pentateuch*, 14.
117 Clines, *The Theme of the Pentateuch*, 25.

that "the theme of the fulfilment and non-fulfilment of the threefold promise is *one* fruitful way of talking about the Pentateuch."[118]

It appears that Clines rightly situates the theme of the promise of posterity in its historical exilic (or early post-exilic) context: "To the Jewish exiles, as descendants of Abraham, the divine promises are spoken no less directly than to their forefather."[119] Hence the fulfilment of the promise given to Abraham in Gen 21:1-7, strengthened by the special role attributed to Isaac in Gen 21:12, may have been interpreted by the exiles as the confirmation of their future successful restoration of the ancient traditions destroyed by the fall of Jerusalem. We hear about it in Deutero-Isaiah: "Hearken to me, you who pursue deliverance, you who seek the Lord; look to the rock from which you were hewn, and to the quarry from which you were digged. Look to Abraham your father and to Sarah who bore you; for when he was but one I called him, and I blessed him and made him many" (51:1-2).[120] According to Watts, this Isaian passage is set in Jerusalem, shortly before the Temple was rebuilt, and it encourages the Judaeans to trust the promise given to Abraham.[121] The blessing bestowed on Abraham will be now poured upon Abraham's progeny. The official Temple cult will be reinstated, and God in his providential care will provide everything which is needed for its restoration. The strangers who inhabit Jerusalem, called by Ezra "the adversaries of Judah and Benjamin" (4:1), and who prevent the Jews from finishing the work, should be removed from power. Since God helped Ishmael, he will also help them, but they will not have a share with Abraham's chosen offspring.

The above interpretation is only conjectural, and we might suggest other exilic and post-exilic contexts which would provide a setting for the first reception of the final form of Gen 21:1-21. Nevertheless, in any chosen period of the exilic and post-exilic history of Israel, the passage under discussion could provide encouragement for the Jews who lost the Temple and were struggling to rebuild their religious and national identity. A narrative about the faithful and caring God, who, in the remote patriarchal period, had chosen Abraham and Isaac, and blessed them, and who had also extended his kindness to other peoples, was destined to arouse faith and enthusiasm for the new work that was to be done.

---

118 Clines, *The Theme of the Pentateuch*, 132.
119 Clines, *The Theme of the Pentateuch*, 105.
120 Van Seters points to a "very close relationship" between the Yahwist and Deutero-Isaiah (*Abraham in History and Tradition*, 311).
121 See Watts, *Isaiah 34-66*, 180-81, 204.

5.1.3. The Refinement of Truth

So far, I have presented the cognitive dimension of the pericope Gen 21:1-21 on three different levels. First, the analysis of the mimetic and diegetic parts of the narrative has led to the conclusion that its significance consists of two aspects. We learn about God who miraculously fulfils his mysterious plans, and is always ready to support those who are in trouble. We also learn about the human characters who are liable to secure their happiness at the expense of other people, yet the destructive effects of their ruthless actions are overcome by God's power. Secondly, this message is modified and understood in a new light when we take into account the presence of irony in the narrative. Readers are invited to decode God's message, and, in consequence, to enjoy the hidden levels of significance present in the story. They are also called to leave the world of the human characters, and assume a position reserved for the divine character. Thirdly, readers discover that the narrative, apart from its modern significance, has a long and complex literary history, and, as a result, a meaning, which is revealed only by adopting the viewpoint of its original audience. From that viewpoint, the narrative tells of God's faithfulness manifested in the fulfilment of the promise given to Abraham, as well as of God's providential care, which averts death and secures the future. What is more, the narrative encouraged its original audience to restore the traditions of pre-exilic Israel rooted in the patriarchal times, and to trust the promise and blessing given to Abraham.[122]

How are these three levels of the cognitive dimension related to each other? Even a cursory glance reveals that they are not contradictory, but complementary. Each level of criticism and interpretation, to use Hirsch's distinction, either adds to or confirms what was said on the preceding level, both as regards the divine and the human characters of the story. There is, however, much more to say about the interrelationship existing between the three levels. As I have shown in chapter 3 in the context of the discussion of *distanciation*, "an essential characteristic of a literary work ... is that it transcends its own psycho-sociological conditions of production and thereby opens itself to an unlimited series of readings, themselves situated in different socio-cultural

---

[122] My interpretation is parallel to that of Cotter. For Cotter, "Genesis 12-25 is ... primarily a theological text which uses the backdrop of the life of the first generation of the chosen family to proclaim the nature of God. ... Here [in Gen 21] God acts freely to create life, to free those without freedom, to give a home to some of the homeless, but to leave others as sojourners" (*Genesis*, 136).

conditions."[123] This is precisely what happens when modern readers peruse the narrative under discussion. The conditions determining their reception of the text differ significantly from those of the ancient Israelites to whom Gen 21:1-21 was addressed in the first place, and the continuous change in the conditions results in the existence of many cognitive levels.

However, the Ricoeurian remark about an "unlimited series of readings" should not be understood in an absolute sense. In fact, Ricoeur strongly believes that some readings are better than others.[124] The decision is made through the procedure of *validation*. Ricoeur states:

> As concerns the procedures of validation by which we test our guesses, I agree with Hirsch that they are closer to a logic of probability than to a logic of empirical verification. To show that an interpretation is more probable in the light of what is known is something other than showing that a conclusion is true. In this sense, validation is not verification. Validation is an argumentative discipline comparable to the juridical procedures of legal interpretation.[125]

To put it another way, Ricoeur invites us to an intelligent debate over the various cognitive levels which we can distinguish in the text. Even though the results of this debate cannot be assessed in the light of strict scientific procedures, in *History and Truth* Ricoeur undertakes an effort to enumerate possible criteria for distinguishing between truth and falsehood, and calls them the "tasks for the spirit in truth." Loretta Dornisch renders Ricoeur's postulates in the following way:

> One looks for a complexity correlative to the orders of truth; one respects the autonomy of scientific research insofar as it is applicable. One aims at qualitative probability by bringing diverse opinions together, and by rigorously weighing contrasting judgments. One avoids clerical, political, or personal apologetic, while striving for a unity of truth which will be realized only in an unknowable future. Finally, one applies the criterion of existential appropriation: does the interpretation disclose a world for me? does it give more meaning to my life?[126]

It seems that the three levels of the pericope's cognitive dimension meet the conditions which Ricoeur postulates. First, they follow "a log-

---

123 Ricoeur, *Hermeneutics and the Human Sciences*, 139.
124 Eco supports the same approach to the interpretation of texts, and calls it a "moderate standpoint": "I shall claim that a theory of interpretation – even when it assumes that texts are open to multiple readings – must also assume that it is possible to reach an agreement, if not about the meanings that a text encourages, at least about those that a text discourages" (*The Limits of Interpretation*, 45).
125 Ricoeur, "The Model of the Text," 549.
126 Dornisch, "Symbolic Systems," 15.

ic of probability." The meaning of the pericope has been set in the particular historical context, which validated it by simply showing, but not *proving* in a scientific sense, that it is probable. Moreover, the significance discovered by narrative theory and rhetorical criticism has been based upon a number of theoretical concepts: the mode of representation used in narrative, on the one hand, and the concept of irony, on the other. Both concepts are successfully used in general literary criticism, and their particular application to Gen 21:1-21 has followed the criteria of objectivity. This is why I can say that the cognitive levels are *probable*, and, as a result, they have been *validated*. Secondly, my readings satisfy the requirements postulated by Ricoeur in *History and Truth*. Since they are pluralistic, they reflect "a complexity correlative to the orders of truth." In addition, I have not accepted any a priori or apologetic ideas which would prejudice the results of the discussion. Finally, "the criterion of existential appropriation" has been at work. I have been asking about the narrative's meaning and significance in the context of the most important issues pertaining to human life: family, love, suffering, death, and faith in God.

What should the reader do when the debate over the text's diverse meanings does not bring positive results? According to Ricoeur, the reader must make a *wager*. Dornisch explains: "When interpretations are in conflict even after the application of the norms of truth, one must then make a commitment, wager that one interpretation will give more meaning than another; one must profess a faith."[127] The concept of wager is among the best-known Ricoeurian ideas in the field of hermeneutics.[128] As Wallace rightly observes, readers cannot have "empirical and rational certitude" about what they discover through the mediation of biblical texts. The only attitude which they can assume in such circumstances is taking risks and hoping that the wager they are making make will win the eternal prize.[129]

---

127 Dornisch, "Symbolic Systems," 15-16.
128 Detweiler and Robbins explain: *"The Symbolism of Evil* concludes with Ricoeur's widely circulated essay, 'The Symbol Gives Rise to Thought,' in which he argues the possibility of overcoming the impasse of the hermeneutical cycle (one must believe in order to understand but understand in order to believe) by his famous wager of faith. Rather than attempting objective analysis, one needs to recognize one's implication in the interpretive process, take a position and work it through in the expectation that it will produce 'goodness'" ("From New Criticism to Poststructuralism," 270).
129 See Wallace, "Can God Be Named," 301-02. Wallace comments: "A person's religious wager becomes her destiny as a moral subject: by taking the risk of becoming assimilated into the worlds of the biblical texts, one verifies the claim that a scriptur-

Going back to the idea of validation, I believe that my interpretation has been, at least to some extent, validated because it has revealed three *complementary* levels. If I had used in interpretation other approaches, such as reader-response criticism, feminist criticism, or stylistics, each of them would have added new levels to the cognitive dimension. Certainly, Ricoeur is right in saying that certain readings are better than others, yet his remark does not deny the fact that the narrative Gen 21:1-21 can be reinterpreted anew and afresh as the cultural context of its readers continually changes. Does this process of reinterpretation have an end? Probably not, as far as we answer this question from a temporal perspective. It has *the end*, however, from a philosophical standpoint. When readers analyse the cognitive dimension of the narrative, they learn about the different aspects of truth which the narrative communicates. In consequence, every new reading which is complementary to those which have been put forward provides a *refinement* and *purification* of the already appropriated aspects of truth. This process has the end, and that end is Truth in the absolute ontological sense.

5.2. The Aesthetic Dimension of Gen 21:1-21

The field of aesthetics is undoubtedly very interesting, but it is true, as John Hospers writes in his *Introductory Readings*, that "the problems of aesthetics are unusually complex and troublesome. Even in philosophy, which is notorious for difficult and insoluble problems, aesthetics is approached with diffidence"[130]. However, there are only two ways of facing aesthetic conundrums: fearful evasion or rising to the challenge. The first strategy always leads to failure, whereas the other one may bring at least a partial victory. This is why, even though I can only touch on a very few issues belonging to the subject, I shall discuss in this subchapter the various factors which contribute to the aesthetic dimension of literary texts in general, and of my model pericope Gen 21:1-21 in particular. I must emphasize that through the whole subchapter I will consistently assume the point of view of the modern reader, and, as a result, I will investigate the pericope's aesthetic significance. As I have already said before, I pay little attention, if any, to the

---

ally refigured self is the crown of a life well lived in relation to self and others" ("From Phenomenology to Scripture?," 302).
130 Hospers, *Introductory Readings in Aesthetics*, 1.

aesthetic reception of the text by its ancient readers. Even if some of the ancient readers could have shared with their modern counterparts the same or similar views on literary beauty, it seems very difficult to recreate the aesthetic sensitivity of ancient Jews. An effort to do so would no doubt lead to an interesting discussion, but, for the reasons explained in chapter 3, such a discussion would go far beyond the framework of this book.

I have defined the aesthetic dimension of the text as a set of diverse factors which are discovered by readers pursuing their aesthetic interests (see chapter 3). This brief definition suggests a number of questions which must be dealt with in this subchapter. Can we establish clear criteria by which we can judge the beauty of a literary text? What is the nature of the reader's aesthetic interest? What criteria can be called intratextual, and what are extratextual? These issues will be discussed below in the three following sections. Hence, in the first section, I shall focus on the general problems of philosophical aesthetics, and I shall introduce the aesthetic theory of Immanuel Kant, and propose the criteria for judging the beauty of literary texts suggested by Hugo A. Meynell. The analysis of Gen 21:1-21 in the light of Meynell's categories will follow here. In the second section, I will move on to the theological aesthetics of Hans Urs von Balthasar, and show its application to the model pericope. Finally, in the last section, I will compare the philosophical and theological aesthetics, and show their contribution to the understanding of beauty in biblical exegesis.

5.2.1. Literary Aesthetics

When we examine the different factors which bring about the phenomenon called *aesthetic experience*, we are faced with a very intricate task. On the one hand, we know that aesthetic experience would not be possible without the presence of a beautiful work of art. We also realize that there must exist certain objective features which make that work beautiful. On the other hand, the role played by the audience in the process of aesthetic perception cannot be ignored either. To what extent should readers or viewers distance themselves from a work of art? What happens in their minds when they appreciate a particular book or painting? Anne Sheppard reminds us about these two groups of potential questions regarding aesthetics when she writes:

> Broadly, there are two different ways of attempting to answer them [the philosophical problems of aesthetics]. One is to claim that all works of art have something in common, some defining characteristics which makes

> them especially valuable; ... Historically, different aesthetic theories have proposed different accounts of what it is that all works of art share which gives them their value. ... A second way of tackling the philosophical questions of aesthetics is to examine not the works of art ... but the interest we take in such objects.[131]

There is no doubt that both ways of discussing the complex problems of aesthetics are worth exploring, and they correspond roughly to the distinction between the intratextual and extratextual factors of the aesthetic dimension. However, because the focus of this book is on the practical application of the hermeneutical model to Gen 21:1-21, I believe that the emphasis put on the intratextual factors, i.e. on defining the features of the narrative under discussion which contribute to its aesthetic dimension, seems well-justified. Thus within the first group of approaches, Sheppard discusses four types of aesthetic theory: mimetic, expressive, formal, and qualitative. The first three explain the aesthetic quality of a work of art by recourse to, first, its imitation of things in the real world; secondly, its ability to express the artist's emotions; and, thirdly, its formal features.[132] The fourth type of theory centres on the quality of beauty which aesthetic objects share.[133] It will soon be obvious that my general approach in this subchapter corresponds to Sheppard's "formal type" of aesthetic theory. However, before I move on to a comprehensive analysis of the formal features of Gen 21:1-21, I would like to discuss briefly the nature of aesthetic interest and the concept of aesthetic distance, which belong to the "second way of tackling the philosophical questions of aesthetics."

What is the nature of our aesthetic interest? To answer this question, Sheppard introduces the philosophical theory of Immanuel Kant, "the father of modern aesthetics,"[134] expounded in his *Critique of the Power of Judgment*. Thus our aesthetic judgments are, first, *disinterested*; secondly, they make claims to *universal validity*; and, thirdly, they have a *singular nature*.[135] The *disinterestedness* of aesthetic judgments finds its classical expression in the concept of *aesthetic distance*. J. A. Cuddon defines the aesthetic distance in the following way:

> The term implies a psychological relationship between the reader (or viewer) and a work of art. It describes the attitude or perspective of a person in relation to a work, irrespective of whether it is interesting to that person. A

---

131 Sheppard, *Aesthetics*, 2.
132 See Sheppard, *Aesthetics*, 4-55.
133 See Sheppard, *Aesthetics*, 56-64.
134 Schaper, "Taste, Sublimity, and Genius," 368.
135 See Sheppard, *Aesthetics*, 68.

reader may dislike a poem, for instance, for subjective reasons but this should not vitiate his objective reaction. The reader or critic has at once to be involved with – and detached from – what he is concentrating on.[136]

Hence if we undertake the task of evaluating the biblical text, we ought to assume an appropriate attitude towards the text. Our religious commitment, or, in some cases, our prejudice against the text should not hamper the objective effort to discover and evaluate its aesthetic dimension. Cuddon reminds us that the concept of aesthetic distance is a modern one, and it was clearly stated at the end of the eighteenth century by Kant.[137] Kant writes convincingly:

> Everyone must admit that a judgment about beauty in which there is mixed the least interest is very partial and not a pure judgment of taste. One must not be in the least biased in favor of the existence of the thing, but must be entirely indifferent in this respect in order to play the judge in matters of taste.[138]

Interestingly, Kant states that our judgment about beauty should not be contingent on any interestedness in the existence of the object of our aesthetic appraisal. As Paul Guyer explains in the Introduction to Kant's *Critique*: "judgments of taste ... arise solely from the contemplation of their objects without regard to any purposes that can be fulfilled or interests that can be served by their existence."[139]

Such a conviction about the crucial role played by aesthetic distance has deeply influenced literary criticism. Booth tells us that, in modern criticism, such matters as plot or emotional involvement have sometimes been treated with suspicion. As a reaction to the excesses of "romantic emotionalism and literal naturalism," many critics preferred to emphasize the importance of aesthetic distance in the perception and evaluation of a literary work.[140] By way of example, it suffices to list the names of José Ortega y Gasset, Gustave Flaubert, and Henry James.[141] Nevertheless, Booth himself offers a more balanced stance on the matter: "Distance is never an end in itself; distance along one axis is sought for the sake of increasing the reader's involvement on some other axis."[142] Booth also underlines that literary works are complex, and it

---

136 Cuddon, *The Penguin Dictionary of Literary Terms*, 10.
137 See Cuddon, *The Penguin Dictionary of Literary Terms*, 10.
138 Kant, *Critique of the Power of Judgment*, 91. Kant calls aesthetic judgments "judgments of taste," and defines *taste* as "the faculty for the judging of the beautiful" (p. 89).
139 Kant, *Critique of the Power of Judgment*, xxviii.
140 Booth, *The Rhetoric of Fiction*, 121.
141 See Booth, *The Rhetoric of Fiction*, 119-21.
142 Booth, *The Rhetoric of Fiction*, 122-23.

would be a mistake to reduce their interpretation to only one factor or dimension. He states that "every literary work ... is in fact an elaborate system of controls over the reader's involvement and detachment along various lines of interest."[143]

When we go back to the Kantian discussion of aesthetic judgment, we see that his philosophical principles can be interpreted in a less rigid way. Guyer believes that "the disinterestedness of judgments of taste is not an uncontroversial premise for Kant's entire argument ... it had by no means been universally accepted."[144] Moreover, discussing judgments about the agreeable and the good, Kant admits that they create an interest in the existence of agreeable and good things.[145] Lucien Goldmann adds that the same kind of interest is characteristic of the judgment about the true,[146] and this is why the Kantian treatment of the issue fits Booth's above remark. There are different degrees of the reader's involvement in a literary work, depending on a given type of interest, but, ultimately, the reader must achieve a balance between engagement and detachment. Sheppard remarks: "Aesthetic appreciation will fail if we are too much involved personally in the events on the stage ... On the other hand, if we distance ourselves too far, the object will simply leave us cold, as happens in melodrama where we do not feel involved with the characters at all."[147] The reader's distance should be strongest in the case of aesthetic interests, whilst cognitive and practical interests may entail a much lesser degree of detachment. This seems obvious even from a commonsense point of view. If readers are to be moved by some bad fortune which befalls their favourite characters, they must not be indifferent to those characters, but sympathize with them, and engage emotionally in the events described in a story.

Secondly, our aesthetic judgments make claims to *universal validity*. Kant argues that, unlike in the case of the agreeable and the good, our interest in beauty makes universal claims: "If he [the judging person] pronounces that something is beautiful, then he expects the very same satisfaction of others: he judges not merely for himself, but for everyone, and speaks of beauty as if it were a property of things."[148] If I make

---

143 Booth, *The Rhetoric of Fiction*, 123.
144 Kant, *Critique of the Power of Judgment*, xxviii.
145 See Kant, *Critique of the Power of Judgment*, xxviii, 91-94. Kant explains: "The agreeable is that which pleases the senses in sensation. ... That is good which pleases by means of reason alone, through the mere concept" (pp. 91, 92).
146 Goldmann, *Immanuel Kant*, 183.
147 Sheppard, *Aesthetics*, 68-69.
148 Kant, *Critique of the Power of Judgment*, 98.

claims that the narrative Gen 21:1-21 is beautiful, I thereby communicate to my readers that they also should discover beauty in that narrative. I am not only saying that the passage is beautiful *for me*. I am trying to persuade *them* to discover beauty in the passage. Without their universal validity, our aesthetic judgments would not be communicable, and all discussion of the aesthetic dimension would be futile. This conviction forms the very foundation of this subchapter.

Finally, our aesthetic judgments are *singular*: what matters in aesthetic appreciation is the given object which is judged. If I call my model passage Gen 21:1-21 beautiful, I do not automatically formulate rules concerning other passages. Aesthetic experience is always linked to a particular object. Now, it often happens that on the basis of the judgment of various objects, we arrive at a number of general conclusions about beauty. For Kant, however, such conclusions do not pertain to aesthetic judgment only: "The judgment that arises from the comparison of many singular ones [roses], that roses in general are beautiful, is no longer pronounced merely as an aesthetic judgment, but as an aesthetically grounded logical judgment."[149] Kant's distinction between aesthetic and logical judgments is of great value for my discussion. As will soon be obvious, I will choose a particular formal theory of beauty as a basis for the aesthetic appreciation of Gen 21:1-21. This theory, however, which can be summarized by the words "every literary work with such and such features should be called beautiful," does not belong only to the level of aesthetic judgment. However, its application to a particular text allows me to pass aesthetic judgment on that text.

Certainly, the Kantian taxonomy sheds interesting light on the issue of aesthetic experience, but, as Sheppard rightly remarks, it does not provide satisfactory answers to all questions arising in the field of aesthetics. "The problems of how aesthetic disputes may be resolved, how aesthetic judgment may be justified, and how aesthetic comparisons are possible," argues Sheppard, "all become particularly acute in relation to works of art," and Kant does not always help us to solve them.[150] In view of the fact that, in this subchapter, I am particularly interested in justifying my aesthetic judgment of Gen 21:1-21, or, in other words, in establishing a convincing set of criteria which will serve as a touchstone for the aesthetic dimension of my model narrative, I will have to go beyond Kantian aesthetics in my search for satisfactory solutions.

---

149 Kant, *Critique of the Power of Judgment*, 100.
150 Sheppard, *Aesthetics*, 75.

Historically, there have been numerous, and often very interesting, philosophies of beauty, but since I am dealing here with the modern aesthetic significance of the text, I should adopt a modern aesthetic theory which gives a relatively unsophisticated[151] yet sufficient account of the formal features contributing to the aesthetic dimension of a literary work.[152] I believe that the theory developed by Meynell in *The Nature of Aesthetic Value* provides me with such an account, and so I would like to ground the following considerations in his aesthetic theory.

Meynell aims to create a theory suitable for the aesthetic judgment of works of literature, visual art, and music, and this is why he makes the following general statement:

> Each type of art is a matter of *manipulation of a medium* (a) to provide a *structure* (b) which is a means to satisfaction through *exercise and enlargement of consciousness*. ... It is at least characteristic of literature and the visual arts that they exercise and enlarge consciousness through *representation* (c); and that such representation is more deeply satisfying when it involves some kind of reference to what is of *central importance in human life* (d).[153]

The above four characteristics are then applied to novels, plays, and other works of literature, and Meynell proposes the following criteria for assessing the aesthetic value of literary works:

> [They] are deemed to be of value in proportion to (i) their illustration and demonstration of what is of central importance for human life; (ii) the originality of their use of language and their treatment of plot, character, situation and so on; (iii) their just representation of people, things and circumstances; and (iv) their overall unity in variety of substance and effect. It will be seen that these features correspond respectively to (d), (a), (c) and (b) above.[154]

Meynell himself shows that the above four features fit well such different works as Tolstoy's *Anna Karenina* and Homer's epics,[155] and, in consequence, his theory is comprehensive enough to be applied to literary

---

151 I am interested in a "relatively unsophisticated" aesthetic theory for practical reasons. An overly complex aesthetic theory would not fit the limited framework of this book.
152 A selection of works on aesthetics from Socrates to Robert Bridges can be found in *Philosophies of Beauty* (ed. E. F. Carritt). Gesa E. Thiessen in *Theological Aesthetics* presents the most influential authors writing within the Christian tradition. Part I of *Theological Aesthetics* (ed. Gaut and Lopes) is an excellent source of information on the most influential philosophers writing in aesthetics as well as on chosen periods in aesthetic theory.
153 Meynell, *The Nature of Aesthetic Value*, 45.
154 Meynell, *The Nature of Aesthetic Value*, 45.
155 See Meynell, *The Nature of Aesthetic Value*, 49-50.

works of different periods, and to serve well the analysis of biblical narratives. Moreover, Meynell's theory harmonizes with Booth's analysis of the reader's interests in beauty, which is the basis for my whole discussion. It should be noted, however, that Meynell offers much broader criteria of aesthetic value than Booth does. The latter, discussing aesthetic interests, enumerates the following literary characteristics: a cause-effect chain; literary conventions, whether closely followed or violated; abstract forms such as balance, symmetry, climax, repetition, contrast, and comparison; as well as "promised" qualities which are the distinctive features of a particular work such as a peculiar stylistic, symbolic brilliance, an original kind of wit, a unique sublimity, irony, ambiguity, illusion of reality, profundity, and convincing character portrayal.[156] The traits in Booth's classification belong, roughly, to Meynell's categories (ii) and (iii), and this is why Meynell's theory is more exhaustive than Booth's.

Furthermore, before I begin the analysis of Gen 21:1-21, I should say that Meynell's theory, even though applicable primarily to the aesthetic dimension of literature, relates to other dimensions of literary works. In the preceding subchapter, where I discussed the cognitive dimension of the model pericope, I was looking for such "promised" qualities of the pericope as irony, ambiguity, and wit. They contributed to the cognitive dimension, but, at the same time, they are part of the aesthetic dimension of the pericope. Similarly, in the next subchapter, where I will establish the practical dimension of the narrative, I will pay close attention to the characters of the story. Again, the way the characters are represented in Gen 21:1-21 is directly linked to its aesthetic value. In view of that, I must emphasize that, first, the three kinds of readers' interests are linked to each other and intertwined. Secondly, an analysis of one type of interest elucidates another type. I shall return to this observation in the final chapter.

"That a great novel or play should deal with important rather than trivial matters," writes Meynell about the first aesthetic feature of literature, "seems to conform to common-sense notions of what it is for a work of literature to be great."[157] What are the important matters raised by Gen 21:1-21, and in what way are they central to human life? I believe that, in the first place, the narrative under discussion introduces the theme of family life and familial rituals which appear in the first scene (vv. 1-8), and return in the third (vv. 14-21). In vv. 1-8, we read

---

156 See Booth, *The Rhetoric of Fiction*, 126-28.
157 Meynell, *The Nature of Aesthetic Value*, 50.

about the conception, birth, and naming of Abraham's and Sarah's son, as well as the child's circumcision, growing up, and a festive banquet laid on to celebrate the day when the child was weaned. Similarly, at the end of the third scene, we learn about Ishmael, who grows up into adulthood, acquires archery skills, and is given an Egyptian wife by his mother (vv. 20-21). Certainly, the various events and rituals of family life depicted in scenes 2 and 3 are by no means limited to the personages of the story, but they happen in everyone's life. And this is what makes them universal and central to the lives of readers perusing the narrative. Moreover, the theme of family life corresponds to one of the central theological themes of the Pentateuch, namely the promise of posterity.[158] This is again proof that certain cognitive strands of the narrative under discussion contribute to its aesthetic dimension, and that both dimensions are interrelated.

Another familial theme, which depends on the preceding, consists in portraying the family fold as a place of domestic safety and bliss. The first scene of the narrative is permeated by bucolic motifs, which greatly emphasize its message: the basic patterns of family life constitute a solid base for a tranquil, merry, and secure existence. The theme recurs, in a very restrained way, in the two last verses of scene 3: Ishmael, who was expelled by his own father, and whose life was miraculously saved, sets up his own hearth and home by wedding an Egyptian woman. What has been lost is now restored. Family life is not only inseparable from personal happiness, but, in the circumstances of nomadic life, provides means to survive.

The next example of what is of central importance for human life is the image of wilderness present in the third scene, which has a clear symbolic meaning for a modern reader. The literary function of wilderness changes through the scene. In v. 14b, it creates the effect of suspense and uncertainty, which quickly gives way to hopelessness and despair in vv. 15-16. Then, in vv. 17-19, the overall ambience of wilderness changes, and is now pervaded with God's saving presence. God helps Hagar to discover a well of water, and both Hagar and Ishmael are rescued. Finally, in vv. 20-21, wilderness becomes a place where the mother and child start a new life. As a result, the image of wilderness has a double symbolic dimension. First, it refers to the common human experience of being abandoned by others, or even, from a human perspective, by God. Such an experience is usually accompanied by feelings of being misunderstood or rejected, which may lead to despair.

---

158 Cf. Clines, *The Theme of the Pentateuch*, 30.

Secondly, and surprisingly, wilderness is a place where a lost wanderer is visited and given a new meaning to life by the merciful God.

Another important theme conveyed by the story is that a quarrel in the family brings about suffering and a danger of death. Sarah's envious and aggressive reaction, sparked off by the two children playing together in v. 9, becomes apparent in v. 10, and leads to the expulsion of Hagar and her child in v. 14. In consequence, Hagar finds herself bereft of any rights and privileges, and faces a danger of death from thirst in vv. 15-17. This theme corresponds to a reality experienced by some people, and feared by most: a risk of undeserved, and often cruel, suffering or death caused by unexpected factors. The fear brought about by that risk is very different from the fear of having to face the difficulties of old age and passing away. While the latter cannot be avoided, the former can be escaped by many, and the resulting "gap of possibility" usually causes apprehension, or at least discomfort. Even if our faith in divine providence may, to some extent, alleviate this fear, it is not possible to eliminate it completely. What is more, it happens that a potentially unwanted course of events may be triggered off from within the family circle, as was the case in the family of Abraham, Sarah, and Hagar.[159]

In opposition to death stands the gift of life, and this theme is clearly present in the first and third scenes of the narrative. Vv. 1-8, apart from the theme of family life and its rituals, provide the reader with the concept of the gift of life, which is realized and manifested in every family. Yet, what is more, the gift of life is also among the most important motifs in vv. 14-21. Life is symbolized here by water, one of the four classical elements. Thus the full skin of water given to Hagar in v. 14 represents a possibility of preserving life, whilst the empty skin in v. 15 betokens the imperilment of life. Hagar's and Ishmael's lives are subsequently saved through water. In v. 19, God opens Hagar's eyes so that she may see a well of water, refill the skin, and give the child water to drink. The play on the motif of water illustrates different aspects of the gift of life, and contributes directly to the aesthetic dimension of the narrative.

Last but not least, we encounter in Gen 21:1-21 the theme of nation and land, which is a basic category in every society. The term *nation* in the Hebrew Bible (גוי in Gen 21:13, 18) signifies a people regarded as a

---

[159] Interestingly, the theme of Homer's *Iliad* is not so much the Trojan War as the tragic consequences of a quarrel between two men, Achilles and Agamemnon (see H. D. F. Kitto quoted in Meynell, *The Nature of Aesthetic Value*, 50). That theme is shared by both Homer's epic and my model narrative.

political, racial, or territorial group.¹⁶⁰ The term *land* (אֶרֶץ) appears only once in this text, in v. 21, yet it is an important underlying theme for two reasons. First, the family of Abraham inhabits the land of Canaan as strangers and nomadic wanderers until, in Gen 23, Abraham buys his first parcel of land to bury his wife. Secondly, the promise of land is one of the central themes of the Pentateuch, and is clearly present in Genesis.¹⁶¹ Abraham's descendants, among whom the new-born Isaac is the first, will one day own the land of Canaan: "And I will give to you, and to your descendants after you, the land of your sojournings, all the land of Canaan, for an everlasting possession; and I will be their God" (Gen 17:8). Gen 21:1-21 presents the theme of nation and land from a triple perspective. First, in vv. 9-10, we observe a growing tension between Sarah and Hagar. The latter is an Egyptian, and a stranger in Abraham's family, whereas the former, not only a wife but also closely related to Abraham (Gen 20:12), wants to decide about the future of her family and, in a broad perspective, of her nation. Secondly, vv. 13 and 18 bring the divine promise of creating a new nation of "the son of the slave woman" and, at the same time, in v. 13, of Isaac – the idea introduced by the adverb *also*. Thirdly, in vv. 20-21, God's pledge begins to be fulfilled, and the new nation of Ishmaelites discreetly emerges on the scene of history. While the first two perspectives show the land of Canaan, which will later become the land of Israel, the third one is linked to the wilderness of Paran, which is to become the homeland for the Ishmaelites.

In summary, when we consider the aesthetic value of Gen 21:1-21 from the point of view of how it contributes to the illustration of what is important for human life, we have the following list of ideas: family life and its rituals; safety brought about by the family institution; abandonment and deliverance; family strife resulting in affliction; the gift of life; as well as nation and land. All these ideas have a universal and archetypal value in practically all cultures and, in consequence, the aesthetic features of Gen 21:1-21 can be apprehended by an exceptionally broad audience.¹⁶² The long history of the influence of Genesis on European culture (its *Wirkungsgeschichte*) is the best proof of this. Moreover, if one short narrative like Gen 21:1-21 contains at least six

---

160 See Clements and Botterweck, "Gôy," *TDOT* 2:426-27.
161 Cf. Clines, *The Theme of the Pentateuch*, 37-40.
162 Cuddon enumerates the following archetypes relating to human existence: "birth, growing up, love, family and tribal life, dying, death, not to mention the struggle between children and parents, and fraternal rivalry" (*The Penguin Dictionary of Literary Terms*, 53).

different archetypal concepts, the whole book of Genesis must be an inexhaustible source of such ideas. Thomas L. Brodie is then right in saying: "Genesis is like an encyclopedia of life; it reflects all of human existence. As life is a many-splendored thing, so too is Genesis; it radiates in many directions."[163]

Meynell's second and third criteria for assessing the aesthetic value of literature are closely related to each other. The way in which the plot and characters are constructed in a work influences its just representation of people and things. Hence I will discuss both criteria together. First, when we analyse the literary motifs present in Gen 21:1-21, we see that scenes 1 and 3 of the narrative contain a number of contrasting themes, which results in the two scenes composed symmetrically, and containing opposite motifs, with the second scene inserted between the two. The following list shows this:

living at home (vv. 1-8) – living in the wilderness (vv. 14-21)
family life celebrated (vv. 1-8) – family life destroyed (vv. 14-16)
Isaac's safe life (vv. 2-8) – Ishmael's endangered life (vv. 15-16)
Abraham welcomes his son (v. 3) – Hagar parts from her son (v. 15)
parental joy and pride (vv. 6-8) – grief and despair (vv. 15-16)
joy and laughter (v. 6) – horror and weeping (vv. 16-17)

Therefore, the scenes of the narrative are arranged according to the simple pattern A – B – A'. The second scene does not have a counterpart, and occupies the central place.[164] This observation is important for the discussion of the unity of Gen 21:1-21.

Secondly, the plot of the narrative under discussion meets the requirements proposed by Meynell: "Plot and character are effective largely to the degree that incidents and actions are unforeseeable before they occur, and seem wholly appropriate afterwards."[165] Most of us know the plot very well, but if we imagine reading the narrative for the first time, whether as a separate episode or with the knowledge of the preceding twenty chapters, we should agree that the incidents are not easily predictable. The reader who learns about Abraham's and Sarah's happiness in scene 1 can hardly envisage the dramatic course of further events. The reaction of Sarah depicted in vv. 9-10 is so surprising that many commentators have suggested that we read "mocking" instead of

---

163 Brodie, *Genesis as Dialogue*, 112.
164 It should be noted that only the first motif ("living at home" – "living in the wilderness") pervades the whole scene 1 and 3 respectively. The other motifs are present in different verses of both scenes. Nevertheless, the contrast between the scenes is clear.
165 Meynell, *The Nature of Aesthetic Value*, 56.

"playing" in v. 9 in order to justify her harsh words. God astonishes the reader, and, in spite of his protective attitude towards Hagar in Gen 17, this time he orders Abraham to expel his concubine. The plot in scene 3 is also well crafted. Only after the narrative's climax in vv. 15-16 does God come to Hagar's rescue, and no premature solution is offered to her. Hagar and Ishmael are actually on the brink of despair and death. What is more, although it is God who saves the characters from death, the turning point in the story is not deus-ex-machina-like. If God had been absent in the last verses of the narrative, the happy ending would have been equally conceivable. Sarah could have noticed a well which had always been there, and this surprising coincidence would have brought the story to its closure. At the same time, the incidents "seem wholly appropriate afterwards." The reader understands that the two children had to be separated to secure God's promise given to Abraham. Sarah remains an imperious matriarch, yet God uses her morally questionable behaviour in order to bless Ishmael, and to help him begin a new life as an independent adult. Thus Booth's comment applies well to the pericope: "All good works surprise us, and they surprise us largely by bringing to our attention convincing cause-and-effect patterns which were earlier played down."[166] In v. 12, we learn that Hagar must be expelled. V. 13 gives us a hint that God will somehow help her and her son. Yet the "divine cause" is subsequently played down by the tragic events in vv. 14-16, and re-emerges in vv. 17-18. It is worth remembering that we should not naively assume that every biblical narrative must have a happy ending. In the world of biblical stories, God is a powerful suzerain: he bestows blessing on his people, but also withdraws it if there is a good reason. The Flood Story, the life of Esau, or King Saul falling into decadence are among the best examples of God's impenetrable purposes. Hagar *could* die, and we *should* be surprised that she did not.

The third feature contributing to the aesthetic value of the model pericope is its portrayal of characters. "It is a prime function of an unusual or original treatment of character and situation," writes Meynell, "to shock us into a perception of how things really are, so far as this is concealed by our conventional judgments and expectations."[167] In our story, we are shocked by both Sarah and God. We cannot easily find an explanation of her behaviour in v. 10, and nor are we able to predict what God will do to fulfil his promise given in v. 13. However, there

---

166 Booth, *The Rhetoric of Fiction*, 127.
167 Meynell, *The Nature of Aesthetic Value*, 56.

exists a purpose for such treatment of both the characters and the situation. Because readers are shocked, they are invited to go beyond their expectations, and to enquire into the real message communicated by the narrative. As a result, they may learn that, given the historical circumstances of the story, Sarah's reaction is not as despicable as it looks at first glance. Similarly, God's acquiescence in her demand serves his divine plan of salvation. Again, as was the case before, we see that our aesthetic and cognitive interests sometimes intertwine. An original treatment of characters, which is an aesthetic feature, makes us ponder the message of the story, and thus satisfies our interest in truth.

Fourthly, the use of language in Gen 21:1-21 has at least two features. In the subchapter on the cognitive dimension of the text, I have shown the presence of irony in the narrative resulting from the difference between the two levels of knowledge: that of God (and the reader) and that of the human characters of the story. Moreover, the Hebrew text contains two paronomastic allusions to the name Isaac. In v. 6, Sarah exclaims: צחק עשה לי אלהים, whereas in v. 8 she sees Ishmael מצחק with Isaac. If we keep in mind the obvious presence of the biblical paratactic style, as well as such well constructed and symmetrical phrases as in the opening v. 1:

ויהוה פקד את־שרה כאשר אמר ויעש יהוה לשרה כאשר דבר:

we arrive at the conclusion that the narrative, despite its simplicity and dignified austerity, contains a number of stylistic devices which directly contribute to its aesthetic dimension.

To move now on to Meynell's fourth criterion of aesthetic value, we should look for an overarching and central theme which unifies the above aesthetic features of Gen 21:1-21. Introducing this concept, Meynell reminds us of an apt remark of Percy Lubbock: "What was the novelist's intention, in a phrase? If it cannot be put in a phrase it is no subject for a novel; and the size or complexity of the subject is in no way limited by that assertion."[168] Of course, we should remember that in the case of the book of Genesis, we cannot speak of the authorial intention, and the reasons for that have already been given in chapter 3. However, when we place our discussion in the modern context, we have the right to ask about a *unifying theme* which the modern reader discovers in the narrative, and which provides a frame for its sundry sub-themes. What then, in a phrase, is the unifying theme of the model pericope?

---

168 Meynell, *The Nature of Aesthetic Value*, 41-42.

I have observed above that scenes 1 and 3 of the narrative are symmetrical to each other, and contain opposite motifs. Interestingly, none of those motifs can be regarded as central to the story because each of them is linked to its negative counterpart. By way of example, the pericope tells us about the value of family life, but, at the same time, draws a piercing image of its destruction. Joy and laughter are balanced by horror and weeping. Vv. 1-8 are set in the safety of the nomadic home, whereas the scene for vv. 14-21 is the ominous wilderness of Beersheba. In view of that, we should look for a unifying theme in scene 2 rather than 1 or 3. Scene 2 occupies the central part in the narrative's structure, and, what is more, in the second scene only, all the human and divine personages of the pericope meet and interact with each other. Hagar and Ishmael are absent from scene 1. Scene 3 does not feature Sarah and Isaac.

Now, there is no doubt that the foremost character in scene 2 is God. He intervenes and commands Abraham to grant Sarah's wish (vv. 12-13). His words build up the tension in the narrative. His knowledge surpasses the knowledge of the human personages. This is why, in our quest for the unifying theme, we should look at God's words in vv. 12-13. In brief, God's words reveal his transcendent and divine purpose which partly agrees with and partly contradicts the particular objectives of the human characters. God orders Abraham to fulfil Sarah's wish, and confirms his promise concerning Isaac, yet, at the same time, he sides with Hagar, and blesses her. Hence God's purpose is portrayed as the ultimate force which, on the one hand, helps the humans to achieve their goals, but, on the other, subdues them, and introduces a divine plan, which is often at variance with the objectives of the individuals. In view of that, I believe that the central and unifying theme of Gen 21:1-21 is *God's supreme purpose* ordering and organizing the world of human objectives and archetypal ideas according to his divine plan. For practical reasons, the unifying theme of the aesthetic dimension of Gen 21:1-21 is illustrated in the following chart (Figure 2, p. 181).

The chart needs a brief clarification. Within the main rectangle which stands for the narrative world represented in Gen 21:1-21, there are two pairs of arrows. The first pair symbolizes the different human objectives found in the story. Hence, in our case, we have the action of Abraham who takes part in the upbringing of Isaac (vv. 3-8), who also intends to prevent Sarah from expelling Hagar (v. 11), but who finally gives in to God's order (vv. 12-14). We observe Sarah's maternal care (vv. 1-7), and then her unexpected and harsh action taken against Hagar (vv. 9-10).

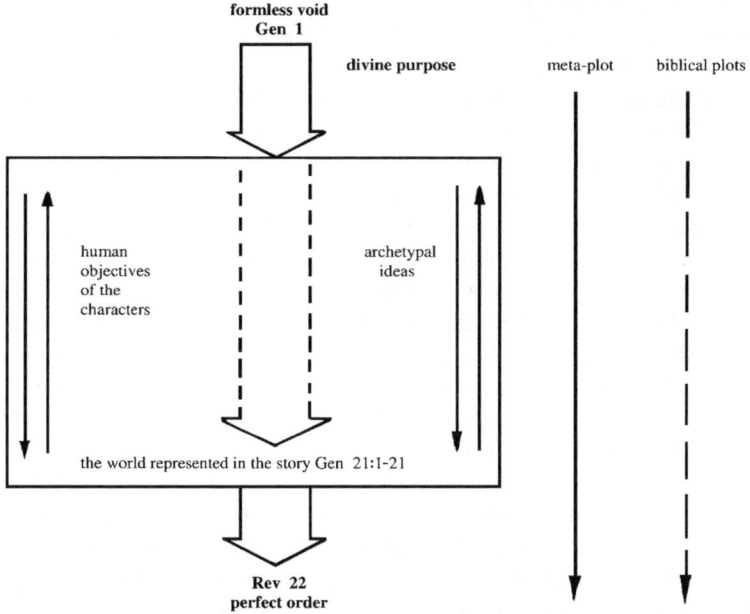

Figure 2. The unifying theme of Gen 21:1-21.

In turn, Hagar is portrayed here as an innocent victim (v. 14), who succumbs to despair (vv. 15-16), but, finally, experiences God's mercy and blessing (vv. 17-21). In brief, Sarah's and Abraham's objectives contradict Hagar's purpose. The second pair of arrows betokens the archetypal ideas present in the text: family life and its rituals; safety brought about by the family institution; abandonment and deliverance; family strife resulting in affliction; the gift of life; as well as nation and land. Some of these ideas are contradictory (abandonment and deliverance), some reinforce each other (family life and safety). There is also an interaction between the human objectives and the archetypal ideas. For instance, Sarah's intention to secure her son's future is related to her family life and its rituals, whilst Hagar finds a well of water which symbolizes the gift of life.

However, both the human objectives and the archetypal ideas are subordinate to God's purpose, which either challenges or takes advantage of them. Hence the block arrow within the rectangle, which is marked with a broken line, depicts God's purpose pervading the narrative world of Gen 21:1-21, and organizing the human objectives and the archetypal ideas according to his plan. The plan is to fulfil the promise of posterity given to Abraham in Gen 12:2 (and, subsequently, in many other places), and to Hagar in Gen 16:10. At the same time, in view of the further development of salvation history, God's purpose is to separate the line of Isaac from the line of Ishmael: "It is through Isaac that your descendants will be named" (21:12).

Furthermore, the story of Gen 21:1-21 is only a part of the long story of salvation recounted in the Bible. It begins in Gen 1, where "the earth was without form and void, and darkness was upon the face of the deep" (v. 2), and ends in Rev 22, where we see "the river of the water of life ... flowing from the throne of God and of the Lamb through the middle of the street of the city" (vv. 1-2).[169] Thus we may paraphrase this universal story of salvation as a motion from the formless void to the perfect and divine order; a motion initiated, carried on, and completed by God's all-powerful purpose (see the chart). Within this meta-motion and meta-plot, there is space for the history of the universe and humanity, for the events of modern times and yesteryear, for the life of Abraham as well as for the life of the modern reader of Scripture. The presence of the biblical meta-plot in the Christian Bible is well expressed by Josipovici: "It is a magnificent conception, spread over thousands of pages and encompassing the entire history of the universe. There is both perfect correspondence between Old and New Testaments and a continuous forward drive from Creation to the end of time."[170]

To summarize the discussion in this section, I should say that Gen 21:1-21 clearly illustrates a number of archetypal ideas which are of central importance for human life. The pericope has also a well-constructed structure, plot, and characters, as well as using the language in

---

[169] When we read the last chapter of Revelation, we can hardly resist the thought that it announces a certain kind of continuation: "He who testifies to these things says, 'Surely I am coming soon.' Amen. Come, Lord Jesus!" (22:20) Perhaps, when these words have been fulfilled, a new chapter of salvation history will be open before our eyes.

[170] Josipovici, *The Book of God*, 42. Josipovici compares the Christian Bible with the Hebrew Bible in terms of the presence of an all-encompassing theme, and arrives at the conclusion that "where the Christian Bible moves in a firm arch from beginning to end, the Hebrew Bible is very much more concerned with getting the beginning right than the ending" (*The Book of God*, 47). He observes that various links between the books of the Hebrew Bible are thematic rather than chronological (see p. 46), and remarks that "the essential history of Israel, unlike that of the nations surrounding it, was one not of small beginnings leading to a triumphal climax, but of perpetual exile and defeat" (p. 47).

a manner characteristic of literature. Finally, its beauty is discovered when the reader observes the interplay between the human objectives, the archetypal ideas, and the overriding purpose of God who leads the whole universe to final transformation and fulfilment.[171] We ought also to remember that the aesthetic effect of ancient Hebrew narratives is achieved through a relative simplicity of plot, economy with words and stylistic devices, as well as through the presence of uncomplicated paratactic structures. In consequence, the narrative art of the Hebrew Bible is even more worth our attention because it communicates various aspects of beauty using a relative paucity of literary means. Had we been unaware of this feature of the narratives, we would probably have missed one of their most interesting qualities.

5.2.2. Theological Aesthetics

Hans Urs von Balthasar is considered by many to be the greatest Catholic theologian of the twentieth century, and, because of the scope of his work, he should be counted among the most prominent thinkers the Church has ever had. As he openly acknowledges, he owes his inspiration not only to the Church Fathers and mediaeval theologians, but, importantly, to Karl Barth's *Church Dogmatics*, the works of Henri de Lubac, to Silesian-born Erich Przywara, as well as to the visions and insights of a medical doctor and mystic Adrienne von Speyr.[172] Balthasar's greatness was partially founded on his disagreement with the status quo of Catholic theology which he had to study as a young Jesuit, and which he correctly identifies as "Suárezianism."[173] His early dissatisfaction and "a grim struggle with the dreariness of theology, with what men had made out of the glory of revelation"[174] led him to the heights of a totally new theological vision.

---

171 We should not think that Scripture can be analysed only in the light of the aspects of *order* and *concordance*. There are numerous instances of *disorder* and *discordance* in the sacred text. Nevertheless, as the case of Gen 21:1-21 confirms, there is also unity and order in the sacred text. As Josipovici rightly observes, looking for order is so appealing "because it corresponds to a profound need in each of us for closure and for a universe shaped according to a clearly comprehensible story" (*The Book of God*, 47).
172 See Kerr, *Twentieth-Century Catholic Theologians*, 129-31; Nichols, *The Word Has Been Abroad*, xiii-xvii.
173 See Kerr, *Twentieth-Century Catholic Theologians*, 124.
174 Kerr, *Twentieth-Century Catholic Theologians*, 122; see also Nichols, *The Word Has Been Abroad*, xii.

In this section of the book, I shall focus on *Herrlichkeit*, or, in English translation, *The Glory of the Lord*, which is Balthasar's tour-de-force, and an attempt to re-create modern theological aesthetics. Since Balthasar deals with *pulchrum* within a theological and biblical context, his work is of utmost importance for everybody who wants to go beyond mere philosophical and literary aesthetics. Balthasar's *Herrlichkeit* is a seven-volume enterprise, and so, taking into account the limited space I can devote to it, I shall concentrate mainly on two volumes: volume 1 entitled *Seeing the Form* (*Schau der Gestalt*), and volume 6, *Theology: The Old Covenant* (*Theologie: Alter Bund*).[175]

What a reader of Balthasar's *magnum opus* on theological aesthetics usually realizes first is the direction of his theological thought. Balthasar puts the main emphasis on the intellectual movement from God to the world. Because the purpose of God's salvific action is to bring the world and man back to the realm of God's glory, the accent is always on the Creator's revelatory and salvific acts. Balthasar, charmed by the spiritual beauty of the Christmas Eucharistic preface, uses the ancient liturgical formula of the preface as a basis for his theological project: "*Quia per incarnati Verbi mysterium nova mentis nostrae oculis lux tuae claritatis infulsit: ut dum visibiliter Deum cognoscimus, per hunc in invisibilium amorem rapiamur.*"[176] Hence his theological aesthetics comprises:

> 1. *The theory of vision* (*Erblickungslehre*) (or fundamental theology): "aesthetics" in the Kantian sense as a theory about the perception of the form of God's self-revelation.
>
> 2. *The theory of rapture* (*Entrückungslehre*) (or dogmatic theology): "aesthetics" as a theory about the incarnation of God's glory and the consequent elevation of man to participate in that glory.[177]

In both "theories," or "phases," which Balthasar considers to be inseparable, the emphasis is placed on God's glory and self-revelation: "no theological perception is possible outside the *lux tuae claritatis* and outside the grace which allows us to see."[178]

Aidan Nichols suggests that in order to understand theological aesthetics properly, we should learn the fundamentals of Balthasarian

---

175 Apart from *Herrlichkeit*, the two other works belonging to the trilogy written by Balthasar are: *Theo-Drama: Theological Dramatic Theory* (*Theodramatik*) and *Theo-Logic: Theological Logical Theory* (*Theologik*). In the original, *Herrlichkeit* is divided into four volumes (I, II, III/1, III/2), with volume II in two parts, volume III/1 in two parts, and volume III/2 in three parts.
176 Balthasar, *Seeing the Form*, 119-20.
177 Balthasar, *Seeing the Form*, 125.
178 Balthasar, *Seeing the Form*, 125.

theological logic, which "is important for its expression of certain general principles of Christian thought later presupposed by the theological aesthetics and dramatics, and for introducing us for the first time to some of the root philosophical concepts set to theological use in those works."[179] Thus the following quotation from Balthasar's *General Introduction to Theo-logic* seems to be in place here:

> The world as it concretely exists is one that is always already related either positively or negatively to the God of grace and supernatural revelation. There are no neutral points or surfaces in this relationship. ... Of course, insofar as it works in a relative abstractness that prescinds from creaturely nature's embedding in the supernatural, philosophy can indeed highlight certain fundamental natural structures of the world and knowledge. ... Nevertheless, the closer philosophy comes to the concrete object and the more fully it makes use of the concrete knowing powers, the more theological data it also incorporates. ... After all, the supernatural takes root in the deepest structures of being, leavens them through and through, and permeates them like a breath or an omnipresent fragrance.[180]

In saying this, Balthasar challenges the very possibility of making a clear distinction between the *secular* and the *sacred*, the *philosophical* and the *theological*. This distinction exists only in theory. If we reflect on some aspects of reality extracted for the purpose of analysis from a greater whole, we may not take into consideration the existence of theological data. When we make an attempt at synthesis, however, the existence of theological data is not only indisputable but prevailing.

I should now turn to the presentation of Balthasar's concept of beauty, which is central to *Herrlichkeit*. In the introduction to his work, Balthasar tells us that "beauty (*Schönheit*) is the word that shall be our first," yet, at the same time, "beauty is the last thing which the thinking intellect dares to approach, since only it dances as an uncontained splendour around the double constellation of the true and the good and their inseparable relation to one another."[181] It seems that the concept of beauty is best explained in the chapter on aesthetic theology and theological aesthetics,[182] which is, in my view, crucial for understanding the Balthasarian approach to the subject.

As regards aesthetic theology, Balthasar surprises us by saying that the term *aesthetic* understood in its general and prevalent sense "cannot seriously be considered as a Biblical value at all."[183] To defend this

---

179 Nichols, *Say It Is Pentecost*, 1.
180 Balthasar, *Truth of the World*, 11-12.
181 Balthasar, *Seeing the Form*, 18.
182 See Balthasar, *Seeing the Form*, 79-117.
183 Balthasar, *Seeing the Form*, 79.

point of view, Balthasar claims that, although the effort to analyse Scripture as a work of art is deeply rooted in the history of theology, especially in Romantic theology,[184] its proponents "failed because of a deep theological inadequacy, namely, that it did not sufficiently distinguish between creation and revelation," and because they "foundered on a kind of aesthetic and religious monism."[185]

How does Balthasar think we can escape that monism? The answer to this question, and its corollaries, are expounded in the seven volumes of *Herrlichkeit*. In brief, he suggests that we should refine aesthetic theology, and transform it into theological aesthetics, by which he means "a theology which does not primarily work with the extra-theological categories of a worldly philosophical aesthetics (above all poetry), but which develops its theory of beauty from the data of revelation itself with genuinely theological methods."[186] It seems to me that Balthasar's intention is not to denounce the efforts of "aesthetic theologians." On the contrary, he rather points to the fact that if we want to preserve the dualism of creation and revelation, which is a fundamental theological principle, we should use primarily the concepts of theological aesthetics. This, I believe, does not exclude a possibility that we may be inspired by the achievements of "secular poetics." What Balthasar postulates is that we should keep in mind the other, more important, side of the coin: the prolific presence of the supernatural which pervades the natural. To put it another, more poetic, way, Balthasar says that what really gives *form* and *colour* to our literary endeavours to fathom the secrets of Scripture is our constant attention to the divine dimension in exegesis; and this is the only way to eschew a situation when our efforts are "Shape without form, shade without colour, / Paralysed force, gesture without motion."[187]

Nichols presents Balthasar's objections to aesthetic theology in a similar way, and says: "First, the beautiful, *pulchrum*, is here removed from its original position as a total reading of Being (a transcendental), and reduced to a separate object with a (limited) science all its own. And secondly, this partly coincides with, and partly reflects, the abandonment of the attempt to see the biblical revelation within the total form of a theology that *includes* philosophy."[188] According to Nichols,

---

184 Balthasar gives a survey of the works of Johann G. Hamann, Johann G. Herder, René de Chateaubriand, Alois Gügler, and Matthias J. Scheeben.
185 Balthasar, *Seeing the Form*, 104.
186 Balthasar, *Seeing the Form*, 117.
187 Eliot, "The Hollow Men," 89.
188 Nichols, *The Word Has Been Abroad*, 14.

aesthetic theology should provoke the following concerns: aesthetic theology results in aesthetic and religious monism, and may blur a disparity between creation and revelation; *pulchrum* is analysed in isolation from its transcendental counterparts; finally, biblical revelation is discussed in purely philosophical terms, instead of using a theological-philosophical method, which is the only approach that guarantees a high degree of objectivity. In this context, Balthasar writes emphatically:

> The analogy between natural and supernatural aesthetics again emerges, an analogy which gives the divine Spirit the freedom of space to place all human forms of expression at the service of *his* kind of poetics. … We must, then, always see clearly where the competence of the philological and archaeological method really lies and where it must be complemented and even surpassed by a special method suited to the uniqueness of its object.[189]

So it follows that Balthasar does not belittle the validity of natural aesthetics. He rather points to its obvious limitations. When it comes to biblical exegesis, aesthetic theology must be "complemented or even surpassed" by theological aesthetics. Otherwise, we may easily misunderstand the scriptural message.

To introduce Balthasar's approach to the Old Testament, I ought to explain other two crucial terms, which are indispensable for understanding the theological vision of *Herrlichkeit*. These terms are *form* and *splendour*. Balthasar admits that "our point of departure was very much a layman's insight into the beautiful. For the present, however, it would be incorrect for us to go beyond this unreflected concept lest we should prejudice our inquiry either philosophically or theologically."[190] This is why he adopts two traditional terms characteristic of general aesthetics, and, after Thomas Aquinas, he calls them "*species* (or *forma*) and *lumen* (or *splendor*) – form (*Gestalt*) and splendour (*Glanz*)."[191] By way of illustration, every beautiful object appears to a beholder in a particular shape, which is its *form*, and it appears beautiful because of its particular quality, which is its *splendour*. Balthasar is convinced that we may regard the form as being beautiful "only because the delight that it arouses in us is founded upon the fact that, in it, the truth and goodness of the depths of reality itself are manifested and bestowed."[192] By saying this, he underlines that he considers the three transcenden-

---

189 Balthasar, *Seeing the Form*, 43-44.
190 Balthasar, *Seeing the Form*, 117.
191 Balthasar, *Seeing the Form*, 118.
192 Balthasar, *Seeing the Form*, 118.

tals to be inseparable and interconnected. What is more, he speaks about the relational function of aesthetic experience: "We 'behold' the form; but, if we really behold it, it is not as a detached form, rather in its unity with the depths that make their appearance in it. We see form as the splendour, as the glory of Being."[193]

Obviously, within the Balthasarian theological context, there is ample room for studying Scripture because it is through the Scriptures (and the Church) that the supreme and objective form of revelation is "mediated" to us.[194] Balthasar states that "from the earliest days Holy Scripture has been regarded and extolled as a masterpiece of God which bears on its forehead the seal of its author. This not only with regard to its validity and authority, nor only on account of its power to impose itself, but also because of the form that it comprises."[195] He then adds that the presence and influence of this form is so clear and strong that in the past centuries it led to the underestimation of the role played by human authors of the Bible.[196] For Balthasar one thing is absolutely indisputable: if readers cannot discover the radiation of God's form in the Scriptures, they simply miss the most central biblical message. In addition, he emphasizes the crucial role that Scripture and biblical theology play in establishing a set of criteria by which all our theological endeavours should be evaluated: "Only biblical theology can and must necessarily become the standard by which to judge the whole range of the historical developments in question, and by using this standard we can see that not all these systems have remained in equal proximity to the source."[197]

The legitimate question that should now be raised is how Balthasar applies this way of reasoning to the analysis of the Old Testament.[198] First of all, he states that the person of Jesus Christ is the supreme form of revelation, and that "if this form really is the crowning recapitulation of everything in heaven and on earth, then it also is the form of all forms and the measure of all measures, just as for this reason it is the glory of all glories of creation as well."[199] We should not be surprised at the Christ-centred character of Balthasarian Old Testament exegesis. In

---

193 Balthasar, *Seeing the Form*, 119.
194 See Balthasar, *Seeing the Form*, 527-56.
195 Balthasar, *Seeing the Form*, 533.
196 See Balthasar, *Seeing the Form*, 533.
197 Balthasar, *Theology: The Old Covenant*, 20.
198 In the context of Balthasarian theology, the term *Old Testament* should be preffered to the *Hebrew Bible*.
199 Balthasar, *Seeing the Form*, 432.

this respect, he only follows the well-established conviction of St Augustine, for whom "the New Testament lies hidden in the Old and the Old Testament is unveiled in the New."[200] Balthasar deals also with the problem of the interrelationship between the Old and New Testaments.[201] He states that "the Old and New Testaments form the indispensable relational system, the geometric field of co-ordinates, the supernatural table of categories."[202] Then he adds that if we read both Testaments *in unison*, we discover the following three dimensions: "what man and the world are and mean ... for God," "what the last destiny of man and the world is to be before God and through God," and "what God himself is for the world."[203] Nichols aptly summarizes the Balthasarian approach: "For Balthasar Christ is the centre of the form of revelation: that is, he alone makes the total form of supernatural revelation coherent and comprehensible."[204]

Yet the Old Testament, being itself a prefiguration of Christ, needs to be interpreted, and its theology synthesized in one way or another. To do this, Balthasar proposes three terms, which provide the reader of the Elder Testament with an opportunity to arrive at an all-embracing theological vision of the Old Covenant. They are: *glory* (*Herrlichkeit*), *image* (*Bild*), and *grace* (*Gnade*).[205] Balthasar introduces them at the very beginning of the sixth volume of *Herrlichkeit*,[206] and, subsequently, he scrutinizes Old Testament passages in the light of this tripartite classification.

This is exactly where the Balthasarian postulate of creating the theological aesthetics of the Old Testament finds its fulfilment. Instead of implementing a system of extra-theological categories to discuss the *pulchrum* present in the Bible, he finds three pearls in the biblical treasury, and sets them in the diadem of his theological aesthetics. He chooses *glory* because, in his view, *glory* is a fundamental and recurring biblical topic. In addition, God's *glory* is "precisely what constitutes the distinctive property of God, that which for all eternity distinguishes

---

200 Augustine, *Quaest. Hept.* 2.73, PL 34, 623.
201 See Balthasar, *Seeing the Form*, 618-59.
202 Balthasar, *Seeing the Form*, 647.
203 Balthasar, *Seeing the Form*, 647-48.
204 Nichols, *The Word Has Been Abroad*, 43.
205 The third category used by Balthasar for his project is *grace*, but he often speaks about *grace and covenant*. In fact, the third category comprises "the whole realm delimited by concepts such as grace, covenant and justification" (*Theology: The Old Covenant*, 15). To simplify discussion, and following most of the commentators, I use the term *grace* to cover that "whole realm."
206 See Balthasar, *Theology: The Old Covenant*, 9-27.

him from all that is not God."²⁰⁷ The second category is *image*, and signifies a human being, who is "God's creaturely partner, who from the first pages of Scripture is referred to as his 'image and likeness,'"²⁰⁸ and who, in consequence, is a recipient of God's *glory*. Finally, Balthasar proposes the third fundamental theme, *grace* or, strictly speaking, *grace and covenant*, not least because "the entire disclosure of God is grace."²⁰⁹

How should we understand the above three categories in the context of the model pericope? First, God's glory cannot be anything else than his divinity, as Nichols rightly remarks,²¹⁰ so in order to find the manifestations of glory in Gen 21:1-21, we should pay attention to the moments when God reveals, by word or action, his divinity to the human characters. We see this at very beginning of the passage, in v. 1, where "the Lord visited Sarah according to what he had said." The divine name יהוה beginning the narration leads us to the very centre of God's mystery, which comprises both disclosure and concealment, and uses the dialectical language of paradox.²¹¹ However, through the passage, the Tetragrammaton is no longer used, and gives way to אלהים. This usage is consistent with the development of events in the story. At the very beginning, in vv. 1-2, God does not speak, but mysteriously fulfils the promise given to Abraham, and makes the impossible real: an old woman conceives and gives birth to a son. This miracle reveals the glory of יהוה, and is as astonishing and inscrutable as the divine name itself. Then, when God starts communicating with the human characters, and, in consequence, plays his own part on the narrative stage, his name becomes more generic, and he is referred to as אלהים.

Balthasar enumerates various *topoi* in which God's glory is revealed in the Elder Testament, but stresses that the common denominator for them is the divine "I": "We must now concentrate our attention on the subject of this manifestation, namely, the divine 'I,' which in the Bible reveals itself on its own initiative as both *a speaking and an acting agent* [my emphasis]. ... By speaking and acting, [God] discloses something of his unique being, which is infinitely exalted above everything worldly."²¹² In view of that, we learn about God's glory by looking at his deeds and hearing his words. Genesis 21:1-21 is a good example of

---

207 Balthasar, *Theology: The Old Covenant*, 10.
208 Balthasar, *Theology: The Old Covenant*, 15.
209 Balthasar, *Theology: The Old Covenant*, 149.
210 See Nichols, *The Word Has Been Abroad*, 187.
211 See Nichols, *The Word Has Been Abroad*, 193; Balthasar, *Theology: The Old Covenant*, 37-38.
212 Balthasar, *Theology: The Old Covenant*, 53-54.

this. Scene 1 depicts God's action in the life of Abraham and Sarah: the child is born, and the family's life is totally transformed. In scene 2, we hear God's words, and they announce that a crucial and irrevocable decision about Abraham's progeny has been made in the divine sphere: Hagar and Ishmael must go because "it is through Isaac that your descendants will be named" (v. 12).[213] God's word always demands acquiescence, and Balthasar is right in saying: "Assent is required because, in a most effortless way, the word possesses the quality of glorious lordliness and proclaims a will which takes hold of man beyond all appeal."[214] Finally, in scene 3, both aspects of God's glory are combined: God speaks and acts. He assures Hagar of the promise given to Ishmael (vv. 17-18), helps her to find a well of water (v. 19), and then acts as Ishmael's chaperone to secure his future (v. 20). Scene 3 then shows that God's word results in his protection given to the hearer: "God's word always undergirds its hearer's whole existence; it orders individual aspects of his life only by directing the entire course of his life."[215]

Moving on now to the category of image, we see that it is closely related to the concept of glory: "The beautiful does not live on splendour alone; it also needs figure (*Gestalt*) and image (*Bild*), even if what figure (*Ge-stalt*) does is to attest to him who set it up (*der Stellende*), even if image (*Ge-bild*) is beautiful only as the imaging forth of that splendour which is beyond all images (*überbildlich*)."[216] Thus God's image, which is humankind (cf. Gen 1:26-27), depends on the Creator, but, at the same time, enjoys freedom and autonomy.[217] What seems useful for the analysis of Gen 21:1-21 in the light of Balthasarian theology is his discussion of "the suspension of the image," or, in other words, the image's provisional character. Balthasar is convinced that Old Testament texts clearly show the instability and suspendedness of the image, and only in the New Covenant is the theology of image perfected and fulfilled. In consequence, the unity between the Testaments is once more emphasized, and the need to "supplement" the Elder with the Younger strongly put forward.

---

213 In his *Theo-Drama*, Balthasar discusses the Isaac/Ishmael duo, and says that the theological idea of Isaac symbolizing the "God-given son" and Ishmael, "who was begotten in an earthly manner," culminates in the theme of the *remnant* (*The Dramatis Personae*, 373).
214 Balthasar, *Theology: The Old Covenant*, 58.
215 Balthasar, *Theology: The Old Covenant*, 58.
216 Balthasar, *Theology: The Old Covenant*, 87.
217 See Balthasar, *Theology: The Old Covenant*, 88.

As regards Gen 21:1-21, the four kinds of suspension of the image proposed by Balthasar oscillate around four pairs of theological themes: man and woman, nature and grace, being and act, as well as Adam and Christ. First, as Nichols aptly puts it, we encounter in the Old Testament a tension between two statements: "male and female are to exist for one another, and yet man is to be the partner of God."[218] The tension is clearly present in the model passage. God speaks to Abraham, and initiates him into his divine purposes. The preceding chapters of Genesis show that Sarah and Hagar, to some extent, are also in dialogue with the Creator (Gen 16, 18). At the same time, however, man and woman are made for each other, and Abraham's happiness lasts as long as his two wives live peacefully in one household. The last verses of the model passage show the same situation with regard to Ishmael. He also is a beneficiary of God's promise, and God is constantly with him (vv. 18-20), yet, when he reaches maturity, he marries an Egyptian woman (v. 21). The economy of the New Covenant brings this tension to an end because, as Balthasar writes: "marriage transcends itself to become the virginal and eucharistic reciprocity between Christ as the Man and the Church as the Woman."[219]

Secondly, "the God of the Hebrew Bible has often to charge man with his sinful condition, yet no return to Paradise is possible."[220] The drama of Abraham's family caused by Sarah's envy (vv. 9-10) can be partially justified by the historical circumstances of her decision. Nevertheless, her arrogant action brings about suffering, and even God's miraculous intervention in vv. 17-19 only temporarily solves the consequences of human sin. Ishmael himself, being the rejected child, will carry the wound inflicted on him by Sarah, and will keep hurting others: "He shall be a wild ass of a man, his hand against every man and every man's hand against him; and he shall dwell over against all his kinsmen" (Gen 16:12; cf. also Gen 25:18 about Ishmael's descendants). It appears that the vicious cycle of sin and suffering will accompany the human race forever. However, as in the case of the first suspension, Christ will solve the paradox of the human sinful condition by bringing the definitive image which will "gather up into itself the meaning of all suspended fragments of the image that is man."[221]

The third kind of suspension involves "a disparity between on the one hand man's fundamental constitution (the Old Testament never in-

---

218 Nichols, *The Word Has Been Abroad*, 197.
219 Balthasar, *Theology: The Old Covenant*, 100.
220 Nichols, *The Word Has Been Abroad*, 197.
221 Balthasar, *Theology: The Old Covenant*, 101.

dicates that the Fall has *destroyed* the image) and on the other human agency which is grossly impaired."[222] In the passage under discussion, with the exception of the two children, the actions of the human characters are indeed impaired. Abraham is unable to prevent the conflict between his two wives, which first appears in Gen 16, and then in Gen 21 gains its momentum. Sarah, moved by the anxiety about her own and her son's future, decides to use whatever force is possible to get rid of her rival (vv. 9-10). Hagar, who is apparently a victim of the familial strife, loses faith and succumbs to despair in v. 16. None of these three acts according to God's primeval plan revealed in Gen 1:28: "Be fruitful and multiply, and fill the earth and subdue it." Abraham and Sarah are unable to multiply because of Sarah's infertility. Sarah subdues Hagar, but only because she is controlled by negative feelings. Finally, it is the earth and the wilderness which subdue Hagar and Ishmael, and are about to put an end to their lives. Hence humankind in Gen 21 finds itself in a desperate condition. They are created in God's image, but act like weak and sinful humans. Yet when Christ comes, the tension between being and act is fully and ultimately resolved in him.[223]

Fourthly, Balthasar states that the final suspension exists between Adam and Christ. Adam was told to rule and subdue the earth, but "how can one who has been appointed not only to dispose things fully, but even to rule, at the same time be wholly pliant to God and a servant?"[224] From the perspective of Old Testament theology this is impossible. Only Christ can fully rule and, at the same time, be subject to the Father (cf. Phil 2:9-11). In Gen 21:1-21, we see this paradox in the person of Abraham. He is a son of Adam (cf. Gen 5; 11:10-26), and thus takes part in Adam's mission to rule. Certainly, the first task Abraham has to perform is to rule as the head of his family, and in this task he fails. The idea of protecting his firstborn son Ishmael is against the wishes of Sarah (v. 11). Nor does God allow Abraham to proceed with the natural course of action. Abraham must subdue his fatherly feelings to God's will, and trust the promise concerning Ishmael (vv. 12-13). Abraham's mission to rule is postponed because of factors beyond his control. He must step aside when God takes the initiative. In the New Testament, however, there will be no contradiction between the acts of God's image and the will of God. Christ becomes God's image in the

---

222 Nichols, *The Word Has Been Abroad*, 197.
223 See Balthasar, *Theology: The Old Covenant*, 102.
224 Balthasar, *Theology: The Old Covenant*, 103.

fullest possible sense, and perfectly exercises his mission to rule while being totally obedient to his Father.

When Balthasar discusses the autonomy and freedom of the image, he already assumes the presence of grace: "Only when this autonomy of the image has been sufficiently pondered can we then go on to the third leading concept: namely, grace, the offer of the covenant, the initiative of divine love toward the image of himself that he had formed."[225] Nichols is right in pointing out that, in Balthasar's theological aesthetics, grace is not primarily a quality possessed by the human soul, but rather the fact that God "bends down to the earth and raises man up to himself ... in, that is to say, an act of 'rapture.'"[226] Genesis 21:1-21 conforms to this understanding of grace: "The Lord visited Sarah according to what he had said, and he did to Sarah as he had promised" (v. 1). The human personages of the story do not have to do anything to become recipients of God's grace. God himself visits his people, and fulfils his promises. At the same time, his grace is not an abstract gift, but visible and concrete reality: it has the face of the long-awaited child Isaac.[227]

Moreover, another visible sign of God's grace is the covenant made with his people,[228] and we may say that the narrative action in Gen 21:1-21 is a materialization of the covenant God made with Abraham in Gen 15 and 17. In 15:5 and 17:2-6, Abraham is given the promise of numerous descendants, and we see the first sign of the fulfilment of that promise in the birth of Isaac in 21:2. In 17:9-14, God demands that every male belonging to Abraham's household should be circumcised, and while this order is fulfilled immediately in 17:23-27, Isaac is circumcised in 21:4. In addition, God gives his blessing to Ishmael in 17:20, repeats that in 21:13, 18, and then puts his promise into action in 21:19-20. The special destiny of Isaac foretold in 17:19, 21 becomes reality when God tells Abraham to dismiss Hagar and Ishmael in 21:12. As a result, we see that the theme of the covenant is indirectly yet clearly present in the passage under discussion.

In the last section devoted to the concept of grace, Balthasar describes Israel's response to God under the heading "Integration of Glorification": "God's glory, integrated in the grace of the covenant, exists for Israel: 'His splendour is over Israel.' But Israel itself is integrated in its own answer, viz. thankfulness as glorification: 'My mouth is full of

---

225 Balthasar, *Theology: The Old Covenant*, 88.
226 Nichols, *The Word Has Been Abroad*, 200; cf. Balthasar, *Theology: The Old Covenant*, 149.
227 Cf. Balthasar, *Theology: The Old Covenant*, 144.
228 See esp. Balthasar, *Theology: The Old Covenant*, 149-58.

thy praise, of thy splendours all the day' (71:8)."[229] The Old Testament is one long story recounting God's grace, but, at the same time, it overflows with texts illustrating and expressing the gratitude of God's people for his grace. The model pericope is no exception. Sarah's joyful declaration in v. 6: "God made me laugh, and everybody who hears about it will rejoice with me" is part of the long hymn of grace pervading almost every chapter of the Elder Testament. Similarly, the mention of the "grand banquet on the day when Isaac was weaned" (v. 8) tells us of Israel's constant readiness to celebrate every gift she receives as proof of God's grace.

What is, in brief, the result of the application of the Balthasarian categories to the model passage? God shows his glory by revealing his divinity to Abraham and Sarah, and the Tetragrammaton at the very beginning of the narrative symbolizes God's mysterious revelation. The human personages of the pericope are also dazzled and deeply influenced by God's glory manifested in his actions and words. At the same time, each of them represents God's image, but this image is limited in four different ways. This limitation becomes apparent when we analyse their words and actions through the prism of the following terms: man and woman, nature and grace, being and act, as well as Adam and Christ. Balthasar makes a strong claim that the only way of overcoming those limitations is reading the New Testament as the fulfilment and perfection of the Old. Hence when we meditate on the Old Testament characters, we discover that they point to Jesus Christ who is the only and supreme image of God.[230] Finally, the idea of grace permeates Gen 21:1-21. The narrative depicts the God who bends down to his creation, and invites them to participate in his divine purposes. The covenant made with Abraham finds its realization in the passage under discussion. Israel's song of thanksgiving for her Creator's goodness finds its expression in the joy of Sarah as well as the festive celebration on the day of Isaac's weaning. These three theological categories, glory, image, and grace, are clearly recognizable in the narrative, and they constitute the text's theological aesthetic dimension.

---

229 Balthasar, *Theology: The Old Covenant*, 204.
230 This feature of Balthasar's approach will resonate with those modern readers who are Christians, and who would have been less interested in the Old Testament if the New had not existed.

5.2.3. Beauty in Scripture

The two perspectives of looking at Gen 21:1-21, which have been introduced in this subchapter, should now be analysed in terms of the interpretive results to which they lead. There is no doubt that they differ from each other by virtue of their presuppositions. Philosophical aesthetics examines the sacred text as any other literary text, and is not directly interested in the origin, nature, and the purpose of the passage. In contrast, theological aesthetics and its analytical tools depend entirely on the answers to the questions of origin, nature, and purpose. For a theologian, Gen 21:1-21 was written under divine inspiration. It is God's word and self-communication. Its purpose is to communicate divine love to man and woman, to purify God's image in humankind, and to open them to the reality of God's eternal glory. Moreover, philosophical aesthetics does not arrive at the categories proposed by its theological counterpart, nor is the latter interested in the "worldly beauty" of the biblical language. The issues of plot, characterization of the personages, and stylistic devices are entirely peripheral to the theological discussion. At the same time, however, both approaches are, to a great extent, independent. They operate according to their own presuppositions, and as long as we accept their assumptions and the ways they arrive at conclusions, we can look at them as two reliable modes of approaching the text. A philosopher may not accept the notion of divine revelation as a decisive factor in interpretation. A theologian, on the other hand, may regard the analysis of plot and characters as a secondary issue. Nevertheless, their conclusions are not contradictory, and stem from two different methodologies.

Even Balthasar himself, who challenges the distinction between the *philosophical* and the *theological,* and states that "the supernatural has impregnated nature so deeply that there is simply no way to reconstruct it in its pure state (*natura pura*),"[231] grants philosophy a certain kind of independence as long as we remember about the basic inseparability of philosophy and theology. For Balthasar, the unity of philosophy and theology is "the Christian option," and it allows us "to describe the truth of the world in its prevalently worldly character, without, however, ruling out the possibility that the truth we are describing in fact includes elements that are immediately of divine, supernatural provenance."[232] Similarly, as I have shown above, when Bal-

---

231 Balthasar, *Truth of the World*, 12.
232 Balthasar, *Truth of the World*, 12.

thasar discusses natural and supernatural aesthetics, he does not get rid of the former, but rather points to its limitations, and to the need for it to be complemented by supernatural aesthetics in the case of a "supernatural object," which is Scripture.[233]

Having said this, however, we cannot ignore the fact that there are at least two points of convergence between the approaches represented by Meynell and Balthasar. By and large, Meynell's philosophical aesthetics applied to Gen 21:1-21 arrives at the conclusion that the supreme character of the story, God, controls and orders the world of human objectives and archetypal ideas. Balthasar's theological method, in turn, explains this process in detail by focusing on the biblical category of image. In other words, Balthasar begins where Meynell ends, and the conclusions of the latter are developed by the former in the language of biblical revelation. Balthasar summarizes the stories of the David cycle:

> This is indeed the theatre of the world; the action, however, is enveloped by a God who not only remains a spectator of the play, in order afterwards to reward and to punish, but a God who, in the actions of his "images," remains the archetype that also participates in the action, both in hidden and manifest ways. He lets man explore the extremest possibilities of his freedom, and yet he conducts events as a play of his manifold elections and directions.[234]

Similarly, in Gen 21:1-21, God does not remain a passive spectator, but, without violating the rights of the human characters, he directs the whole play "both in hidden and manifest ways." Sarah is granted what she demands, yet it is God's purpose which finally prevails in the story. As "David can become the father of all those who sing and glorify the glory of God,"[235] likewise, in the model pericope, we hear the song of thanksgiving sung by Abraham, Sarah, and Hagar. This is precisely where Balthasar's approach transcends Meynell's. We not only observe the interplay between the actions of the "images" and God's overriding purpose. We see a process which leads to the glorification of God by his "images," and is a response which the image gives to God when it beholds his glory and experiences his grace.

Secondly, the move from philosophical to theological aesthetics corresponds with the general interpretive approach which I have adopted in this book. Its main goal is to make the richness of Scripture accessible to a wide circle of modern readers. In chapter 2, I have sugges-

---

233 Cf. Balthasar, *Seeing the Form*, 43-44.
234 Balthasar, *Theology: The Old Covenant*, 113-14.
235 Balthasar, *Theology: The Old Covenant*, 114.

ted a "synchronic to diachronic" mode of critical proceedings to meet the expectations of most well-read modern readers. Here I would like to propose a "philosophical to theological" route in the discussion of beauty. It seems that such a route fits the mentality of modern readers better than the opposite direction because of its safe philosophical basis. Those readers who are unwilling to embrace the data of revelation in their reflection will accept the first philosophical stage of the discussion, and will then be given an opportunity to see in what way the theological stage complements the conclusions of the philosophical one. On the other hand, those whose intellectual standpoint allows for both philosophical and theological data will be offered first a philosophical perspective followed by Balthasarian theological aesthetics, and, in consequence, their expectations will also be fully satisfied.

Furthermore, even if we look at both aesthetic approaches separately, we see that each of them clearly points to the idea of beauty. When we analyse the model pericope from the point of view of philosophical aesthetics, we are often convinced that there must exist a reality, a realm of beauty, which goes beyond the literary text itself. I agree with Władysław Stróżewski, a disciple of Roman Ingarden, who says that although all beautiful things have a transient and temporary value, the beauty of these things is eternal and permanent.[236] Stróżewski justifies this belief in the following way:

> Our language is able to distinguish between two different things: "a beautiful work of art" and "the beauty of a work of art." ... We take the greatest delight in the beauty to which the work leads us and in which this work participates. We experience this beauty by the medium of the work, but we also touch it somehow directly in its existence which transcends the work. The *esse* of beauty is "stronger" than the *esse* of the work.[237]

When we read biblical narratives as literature, we discover that the beauty they communicate is not simply equal to the sum of their particular aesthetic features. Those features comprise various ideas, stylistic figures, and structures, but we would not say that they *are* beauty. They are *beautiful* because they *reveal beauty*. Now, whether we regard beauty as independent of beautiful things is conditioned by the philosophical choices we make, yet even if we follow the school of nominalism or conceptualism, we agree that we can at least *talk* about beauty as different from beautiful things, and as existing, par excellence, in God's mind because God himself is its eternal source.

---

236 See Stróżewski, *O wielkości*, 280.
237 Stróżewski, *O wielkości*, 277 (my translation from Polish).

Theological aesthetics leads to the same conclusion even more directly. It consists, first, in seeing God's glory, and, secondly, in the consequent elevation of humankind to partake of that glory.[238] I have demonstrated above the ways in which the biblical characters perceive God's glory, and how they respond to it. The same can be said about the reader of Gen 21:1-21, and there is little doubt that this narrative was written in order to invite its original listeners and readers to identify themselves with its personages,[239] and to accept the promise given to Abraham as their own. Modern readers, of course, because of the different historical circumstances, are no longer the addressees of the narrative in the same way its first audience was. However, the story of Gen 21:1-21 is not devoid of existential value to modern readers either. Pursuing their interests in beauty, they are invited to see God's glory in order to be subsequently "drawn out" of themselves,[240] and elevated to the divine sphere from where Beauty in its absolute ontological sense takes its origin.

In addition, and in a way parallel to the cognitive dimension, the move from philosophical to theological aesthetics shows the reader that *pulchrum* emanating from the model pericope is multi-dimensional, and that it can be perceived on different levels. In this subchapter, I have shown the application of only two aesthetic theories to the biblical text. I am sure, however, that most of the aesthetic theories which have been formulated in the long history of philosophy, and those which are yet to come, have the potential for showing even more aspects of beauty communicated by literary texts, including the model pericope. Hence the process of the reinterpretation of Gen 21:1-21 in the light of various aesthetic theories never ends simply because "in every age interpreters ask different questions, and so different aspects of the text's meaning emerge."[241] The only keystone in the process of aesthetic evaluation is the idea of beauty itself, which emanates from the text in diverse ways, but, at the same time, provides our interpretive efforts with one common denominator.

It is my firm conviction, however, that when we discover the aesthetic dimension of the biblical text, we should not simply stop and contemplate beauty contained therein. It is far more gratifying to continue the journey because beauty is only a signpost which leads us

---

238 See Balthasar, *Seeing the Form*, 125.
239 See chapter 5 ("The Cognitive Meaning of the Pericope").
240 See Alter, *The World of Biblical Literature*, 23.
241 Barton, "Introduction," *The Cambridge Companion*, 1.

farther away,²⁴² and which shows the way to God – the ultimate and infinite source of beauty. Following J. R. R. Tolkien with a bit of poetic licence, I would say that the reader should finally leave the Grey Havens of aesthetic experience bathed in the moonlight, embark on the ship of faith, and set sail for the West where he will behold the white shores of eternal beauty under a swift sunrise.²⁴³

5.3. The Practical Dimension of Gen 21:1-21

As lovers of classical music know very well, an exquisite piece of music played by an orchestra with excellent strings, but devoid of woodwind, brass, percussion, and keyboards, would be only a deplorable imitation of the original, and every connoisseur would reject such a performance without hesitation. Likewise, an interpretation of the biblical text which ignores the text's various dimensions, and limits itself to one of them only, will certainly fail to unveil all treasures hidden in Scripture. This is why, following the discussion in the two previous subchapters, I will now move on to the subject of the practical dimension of biblical narratives. I have already quoted Eliot's strong conviction that "it is impossible to fence off *literary* criticism from criticism on other grounds, and that moral, religious or social judgments cannot be wholly excluded."²⁴⁴ In this subchapter, I intend to show that moral judgments not only cannot be excluded, but form an integral part of literary criticism of biblical texts. To do this, I shall first introduce four Aristotelian categories, which are useful for the analysis of narrative texts. Those categories will be then applied to the model pericope. Next, I will demonstrate and critically evaluate the validity of reader-response approaches in biblical criticism, using Wolfgang Iser's concept of *gaps* as an example.

An interesting question arises here. I have said in chapter 3 that my discussion of the practical dimension of biblical narratives will be limited to their practical significance established in the modern context, in view of the difficulty of recreating the degree of the ancient Hebrew reader's emotional response to the fate of literary characters. Do I contradict myself when I use ancient Aristotelian categories to explain the modern practical significance of Gen 21:1-21? By no means. There are at

---

242 See Lewis, *Surprised by Joy*, 238.
243 Cf. Tolkien, *The Return of the King*, 377-78.
244 Eliot, "To Criticize the Critic," 25.

least two reasons why I am allowed to do this. First, Aristotle is the most important precursor of modern narratologists, and examples of successful use of Aristotelian categories in narrative criticism abound. In fact, it is difficult to find a book presenting the tenets of narrative theory which would be devoid of references to Aristotle and his foundational works.[245] Secondly, although the categories which I employ are of ancient origin, they are used to explain the practical interests and emotional involvement of the *modern* reader. Perhaps the response of the ancient reader to the model pericope might not have been very different from the response of his modern counterpart, yet it is not the subject of the discussion in this subchapter. I am preoccupied here with determining the reception of the text by the modern reader, and Aristotle provides me with tools suitable for this goal.

In brief, since the practical dimension of the text is closely linked to readers' interests in goodness, and to their emotional involvement with the characters of a story, I shall show what triggers the emotional response of the reader perusing Gen 21:1-21.[246] Then, I will spell out the elements comprising the practical dimension of the model narrative, and discuss the relationship existing between the reader and the text's practical dimension.

---

245 An interesting recent application of Aristotle's theory to the analysis of classical and modern fiction, cinema, TV, and even cyberspace is *Aristotle in Hollywood* by Ari Hiltunen.

246 See Booth, *The Rhetoric of Fiction*, 129-30. This is why, in this subchapter, I will pay close attention to the characters of Gen 21:1-21 because they play a crucial role in determining readers' practical interests. The following remark made by Alter is helpful in the context of my discussion: "Now, in reliable third-person narrations, such as in the Bible, there is a scale of means, in ascending order of explicitness and certainty, for conveying information about the motives, the attitudes, the moral nature of characters. Character can be revealed through the report of actions; through appearance, gestures, posture, costume; through one character's comments on another; through direct speech by the character; through inward speech, either summarized or quoted as interior monologue; or through statements by the narrator about the attitudes and intentions of the personages, which may come either as flat assertions or motivated explanations" (*The Art of Biblical Narrative*, 116-17). I am also aware that if I undertake the critical task, I must not yield to the temptation of putting too much emphasis on the characters, and thereby on the psychological aspects of literature. Eliot states that many critics failed in their efforts to evaluate Shakespeare's *Hamlet*, simply because they put too much stress on the analysis of the play's protagonist (see "Hamlet," 141-42). However, after having dealt with the cognitive ideas and aesthetic qualities of the model pericope, I can now safely move to a type of criticism which is more focused on the characters.

5.3.1. An Analysis of the Plot

In *The Poetics*, Aristotle analyses the plot of tragedy, and speaks about *anagnorisis* (αναγνώρισις, a *discovery*), *peripeteia* (περιπέτεια, a *reversal*), and *pathos* (πάθος, a *calamity*, or *suffering*). He calls *anagnorisis* and *peripeteia* the "most powerful elements of attraction in Tragedy."[247] *Peripeteia* is "the change of the kind described from one state of things within the play to its opposite ... in the probable or necessary sequence of events."[248] In turn, *anagnorisis* is a "change from ignorance to knowledge, and thus to either love or hate, in the personages marked for good or evil fortune. The finest form of discovery [*anagnorisis*] is one attended by reversal [*peripeteia*]."[249] Both terms usually refer to the characters of tragedy; in the first case, the change concerns a character's general situation in terms of good or bad fortune; in the second, a character's knowledge or ignorance. The third constituent of the plot, the *pathos*, is defined by Aristotle in the following words: an "action of a destructive or painful nature, such as murders on the stage, tortures, woundings, and the like."[250] This term refers to one or more events of the plot, and usually involves the characters.

Surprisingly enough, Peter Barry, introducing the above three Aristotelian categories in *Beginning Theory*, speaks about *anagnorisis*, *peripeteia*, and *hamartia*. The last term means, according to Barry, a "'sin' or 'fault' (which in tragic drama is often the product of the fatal character-defect which came to be known as the 'tragic flaw')."[251] Barry's tripartite distinction is different from what Aristotle writes: "Two parts of the plot, then, reversal and discovery, are on matters of this sort. A third part is suffering [*pathos*]."[252] Aristotle does indeed use the term *hamartia* in chapter 13 of *The Poetics*, where he characterizes a typical protagonist of tragedy. Aristotle says that "there remains, then, the intermediate kind of personage, a man not preeminently virtuous and just, whose misfortune, however, is brought upon him not by vice and depravity but by some fault [δι' ἁμαρτίαν τινά]."[253] Hence, strictly speaking, and in contrast to what Barry states, the third basic constituent of the plot is *pathos*, yet *pathos* happens as a result of a character's *hamartia*. The

---

247 Aristotle, *Poet.* 1450a 32-33 (*CWA* 2:2321).
248 Aristotle, *Poet.* 1452a 22-24 (*CWA* 2:2324).
249 Aristotle, *Poet.* 1452a 30-32 (*CWA* 2:2324).
250 Aristotle, *Poet.* 1452b 11-12 (*CWA* 2:2324).
251 Barry, *Beginning Theory*, 224.
252 Aristotle, *Poet.* 1452b 10-11 (*CWA* 2:2324).
253 Aristotle, *Poet.* 1453a 6-10 (*CWA* 2:2325).

whole discussion becomes more complicated in the light of what Barnes writes about tragedy in Aristotle. Barnes broadens the meaning of *hamartia*: "It is reasonably plain that a *hamartia* is not a defect of character – a *hamartia* is an event, an action, something that you do when you go wrong in some way. ... A tragic *hamartia* is simply a mistake."[254] Nevertheless, Barnes's remark does not invalidate the fact that the third element of the plot is *pathos* rather than *hamartia*.

To apply these three Aristotelian categories to Gen 21:1-21, I should first discuss the six characters of the story. As in most, if not all, narratives, the characters are not of equal importance for the plot of the story, but make up a hierarchical structure. This structure, in turn, helps readers not to lose their way "in the fictional woods" of the narrative, to use the title of Eco's suggestive book on the concepts of narrative fiction. For the purpose of my model narrative, I would like to propose two sets of criteria to establish the hierarchy of the characters: first, whether a character speaks or is silent in the story; secondly, whether a character is active or passive, i.e. whether he or she performs action, or is only a passive object of action. Of course, the more active a character is, the higher his or her place in the hierarchy. Conversely, silent characters are relegated to a less important position.[255] The application of these criteria results in the following list of characters in the order of their appearance through the story:

God	speaks (vv. 12-13, 17-18); active (vv. 1, 12-13, 17-20), never passive
Sarah	speaks (vv. 6-7, 10); both passive (v. 1) and active (vv. 2, 6-7, 9-10)
Abraham	silent; both passive (vv. 2, 5, 10, 12-13) and active (vv. 3-4, 8, 11, 14)
Isaac	silent; passive (vv. 2-5, 8-9), never active
Ishmael	silent; both passive (vv. 9, 14-15, 17, 19-21) and active (vv. 16, 20-21)
Hagar	speaks; both passive (vv. 14, 17, 19) and active (vv. 14-16, 19, 21)

A close analysis of the above list shows that the hierarchy among the characters of the passage is plainly drawn. First of all, we have God, who speaks and never plays a passive role. Secondly, we encounter

---

254 Barnes, "Rhetoric and Poetics," *CCA*, 280.
255 Such an approach to biblical texts has been formalized in *discourse analysis*. On discourse analysis, see e.g. *Discourse Analysis* by W. R. Bodine (ed.) and *The Grammar of Discourse* by R. E. Longacre.

two women, Sarah and Hagar, who speak and are both passive and active. Thirdly, there are Abraham and Ishmael, who are silent, but both passive and active. The last place in this list is occupied by Isaac, who does not speak at all, and is a totally passive character.

Hence the character who controls all the action is God. He exercises his divine power from the very beginning (v. 1), where he grants Sarah the long-awaited child. His words directed to Abraham in scene 2 (vv. 12-13) create the complication of the plot, whilst his action in scene 3 (v. 19) constitutes the plot's turning point. In other words, God controls the plot of the story, and we cannot speak of any change regarding his situation or knowledge: he is omnipotent and omniscient. In consequence, the terms *peripeteia* and *anagnorisis* do not apply to him.

The next category of characters comprises Sarah and Hagar, who play in the narrative both a passive and active role, and who speak, in contrast to their husband and children. Sarah gradually builds up her important position: in v. 1 she is childless, but through the divine intervention she conceives, gives birth to a son (v. 2), and effectively eliminates her rival and her rival's son from the "family competition" through her action in v. 10. Hence we may say that the *peripeteia* of Sarah begins in v. 1 and ends in v. 10. Her fortune is radically and positively changed, and she regains her due status of first wife and mother in this nomadic family. Sarah's *peripeteia* is accompanied by her *anagnorisis*. She realizes two things. First, she again believes in God's omnipotence. Her sceptical laughter in Gen 18:12 ("So Sarah laughed to herself, saying: 'After I have grown old, and my husband is old, shall I have pleasure?'") is now replaced by the joyful outburst of laughter in v. 6: "God made me laugh and everybody who hears about it will rejoice with me." Secondly, Sarah becomes fully aware of her prominent role in the family. She gave her husband the son who had been promised. She now must preserve and develop what has been granted her. Sarah's harsh conduct towards Hagar is partially rooted in this *anagnorisis*, but also in the way she is portrayed as an uncompassionate woman. Moreover, it is worth recalling in this context Aristotle's definition: "The finest form of discovery [*anagnorisis*] is one attended by reversal [*peripeteia*]."[256] In Sarah's case, there is a close concurrence of *anagnorisis* and *peripeteia*.

Sarah's fate intertwines with her opponent's. In the case of Hagar, however, we see two instances of *peripeteia* and *anagnorisis*. Although, in scene 2, Hagar's fate hangs in the balance, her inevitable ordeal be-

---

256 Aristotle, *Poet.* 1452a 32 (*CWA* 2:2324).

gins only in v. 14, where she appears on the narrative stage. So the first *peripeteia* of Hagar reaches its negative climax in v. 16, where the woman faces the reality of death in the desert. A further *peripeteia*, being a reversal of Hagar's fortune from defeat to victory, begins in v. 17, and is announced by the words of the angel: "What worries you, Hagar? Fear not." Hagar's life is saved, she returns to normal life, and resumes motherly duties. Hagar's desperate emotional reaction in v. 16 proves that there are also two kinds of *anagnorisis* in her case. First, in vv. 14-16, she learns about the cruelty of Sarah and Abraham, and is prepared to die in the wilderness. Secondly, in vv. 17-21, she regains hope, and, like Sarah, discovers that God is the only Lord of death and life. In addition, the image of the well in v. 19 marks the turning point of Hagar's *peripeteia* and *anagnorisis*.

Another group of characters comprises Abraham, Ishmael, and Isaac. Isaac is a totally passive character and does not speak at all. The second child, Ishmael, is also silent through the narrative, and only at the very end of the narrative (vv. 20-21) plays a quasi-active role. Neither child moves the action forward, which, of course, does not mean that they are unimportant to the story. On the contrary, the children's play in v. 9 becomes a source of conflict. Yet it seems justified that, even though the categories of *peripeteia* and *anagnorisis* apply partially to Ishmael and Isaac, I do not need discuss them at length here. Isaac disappears from the stage in v. 10, whereas the fate of Ishmael is strictly parallel to his mother's. As far as Abraham is concerned, he, like Isaac and Ishmael, is also silent in the narrative, yet he plays a clear and important role: he is one of the central characters in scenes 1 and 2, and, obedient to God's words, he initiates Hagar's painful ordeal in scene 3. Abraham's *peripeteia* begins in v. 2 and ends in v. 14. In scene 1, Abraham participates in the important stages of his new-born son's life, which are subsequently crowned by the sumptuous banquet in v. 8. Although, in scene 2, a new and unexpected problem arises, Abraham's moral dilemma does not signify any reversal of his situation. He expels Hagar in v. 14, and this very act confirms his privileged position in the family. There is, however, a major change concerning his knowledge, and, because of this, we can speak about two stages of Abraham's *anagnorisis*. Like Sarah, in scene 1, Abraham discovers and experiences God's omnipotence and fidelity to his people. Hence his *anagnorisis* moves from ignorance to knowledge. In scene 2, we observe an opposite movement. Abraham must abandon his natural attachment to his secondary wife and firstborn son. He receives God's promise concerning Ishmael, yet he is not given a clear explanation of how this promise will be fulfilled (vv. 12-13). In consequence, we observe another cognitive shift, this time from knowledge to ignorance.

The above considerations may be represented in the following chart (Figure 3):

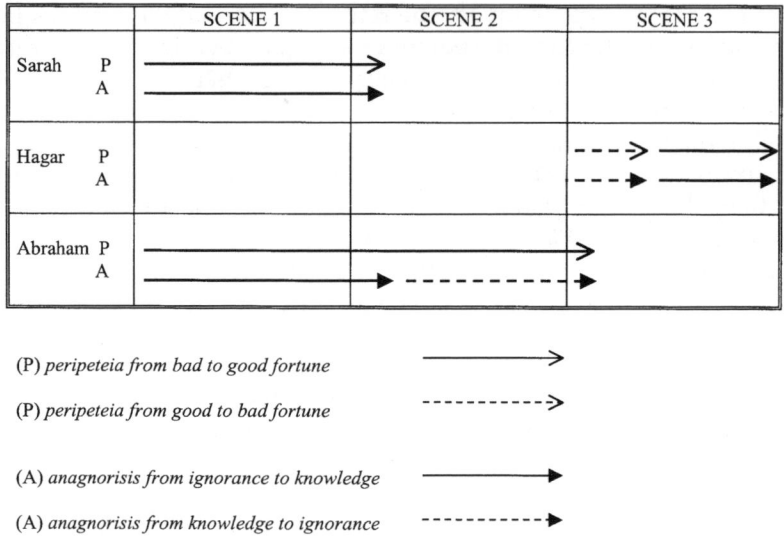

Figure 3. *Peripeteia* and *anagnorisis* in Gen 21:1-21.

The chart helps explain emotional tension present in the story. Since, according to Aristotle, *anagnorisis* and *peripeteia* are the "most powerful elements of attraction in Tragedy,"[257] the presence of both categories contributes to the emotional tension. Thus, in scene 1, we have two "positive" instances of *peripeteia*, as well as two "positive" instances of *anagnorisis* concerning Sarah and Abraham. The overall emotional ambience of scene 1 is positive, and the reader is likely to respond to the text with a set of positive feelings. Scene 2 is characterized by the presence of Abraham's "positive" *peripeteia*, but his *anagnorisis* is "negative" here, which may result in the growing perplexity of the reader. The first part of scene 3 (vv. 14-16) is supposed to provoke the strongest emotional tension; both the *peripeteia* and *anagnorisis* of Hagar are "negative" here, and the parallel fate of Ishmael additionally intensifies the psychological effect of the story. The reader is expected to respond to

---

257 Aristotle, *Poet.* 1450a 32-33 (*CWA* 2:2321).

vv. 14-16 with the feelings of apprehension and pity. Finally, the second part of scene 3 (vv. 17-21) brings about a sense of relief and joy, owing to the "positive" *peripeteia* and *anagnorisis* of Hagar (and Ishmael).

In his analysis of tragedy in *The Poetics*, Aristotle is interested mostly in two kinds of emotion: fear and pity. A well-written tragedy should always provoke these two emotions. Aristotle's remarks concerning the cause of fear and pity help further explain the emotional impact of the passage under discussion. He writes:

> Let us see, then, what kinds of incident strike one as horrible, or rather as piteous. ... Now when enemy does it on enemy, there is nothing to move us to pity either in his doing or in his meditating the deed, except so far as the actual pain of the sufferer [*pathos*] is concerned; and the same is true when the parties are indifferent to one another. Whenever the tragic deed, however, is done among friends – when murder or the like is done or meditated by brother on brother, by son on father, by mother on son, or son on mother – these are the situations the poet should seek after.[258]

In view of this Aristotelian remark, Gen 21:1-21 is precisely what "the poet should seek after." Although neither God, nor Abraham, nor Sarah intend to kill Hagar and Ishmael, the reader has the justified impression that the result of the three characters' action may be the death of Hagar and Ishmael. This is fairly obvious before the turning point in v. 17, which is brought about by divine intervention. In consequence, we may call a part of the narrative, namely Gen 21:9-16, a tragedy. This micro-tragedy is preceded by a pastoral idyll in vv. 1-8, and followed by a happy ending in vv. 17-21. Thus if we venture to classify the pericope in modern literary terms, we will say that Gen 21:1-21 is a biblical family story which contains celebratory motifs at the beginning, a tragic narrative in the middle, and which ends with a strong theological note emphasizing unfailing divine providence.

Now, what are the *pathos* and *hamartia* of the story? As Aristotle defines it, *pathos* is an "action of a destructive or painful nature, such as murders on the stage, tortures, woundings, and the like."[259] It seems obvious that the *pathos* of the passage is evoked in vv. 14-16. Hagar is expelled from her hearth and home; she hopelessly wanders in the wilderness, carrying her child; finally, she despairs and awaits inevitable death. J. A. Cuddon aptly remarks that *pathos* is "that quality in a work of art which evokes feelings of tenderness, pity or sorrow."[260] The first

---

258 Aristotle, *Poet.* 1453b 14-21 (*CWA* 2:2326).
259 Aristotle, *Poet.* 1452b 11-12 (*CWA* 2:2324).
260 Cuddon, *The Penguin Dictionary of Literary Terms*, 651.

part of scene 3 provokes the strongest emotional response, and the three components of the plot contribute to this tension: vv. 14-16 tell the story's *pathos*, and both the *peripeteia* and *anagnorisis* change here from good fortune and knowledge to bad fortune and ignorance.

Moreover, *pathos* is clearly linked to *hamartia*. If we remember that *hamartia* is "some fault,"[261] we should point towards Sarah.[262] She is imperious and jealous, but also apprehensive. In v. 10, she demands from Abraham an immediate expulsion of Hagar; the sight of her son playing with Ishmael floods her heart with envious feelings; the prospect of living under the same roof with Hagar provokes insecurity concerning her own position in the family. Even if, according to the historical-critical analysis of the event in vv. 9-10, Sarah acts like a typical member of ancient nomadic society, from the point of view of the plot, Sarah's *hamartia* is a flaw of her character which triggers subsequent events. Furthermore, if we broaden the definition of *hamartia*, following Barnes's interpretation ("an event, an action, something that you do when you go wrong in some way. ... a mistake"),[263] we must say that the *hamartia* of the story is the event related in vv. 9-10. Sarah notices the two children playing together, yields to her apprehensive thoughts, and reacts angrily to what she witnesses.[264]

In addition, the tragic quality of both scene 2, and the first part of scene 3, is emphasized by the two child characters. Following Adele Berlin's classification of characters that includes *full-fledged characters*, *types*, and *agents*,[265] we should call both Ishmael and Isaac by the last term. Giving the examples of Bathsheba in 2 Sam 11-12 and Abishag in 1 Kgs 1-2, Berlin describes *agents* thus: "They are not important for themselves, and nothing of themselves, their feelings, etc., is revealed to the reader. ... They are necessary for the plot, or serve to contrast with or provoke responses from the characters."[266] This description is ideally suited to characterize Ishmael and Isaac. Both children do not say anything in the story and are either totally passive (like Isaac) or

---

261 Aristotle, *Poet.* 1453a 10 (*CWA* 2:2325).
262 W. Hamilton Fyfe translates *hamartia* as "some flaw of character" (in Aristotle, *The Poetics*, trans. W. Hamilton Fyfe, 47).
263 Barnes, "Rhetoric and Poetics," *CCA*, 280.
264 Aristotle does not define *hamartia* clearly enough. This is why the *hamartia* of the narrative under discussion may be Sarah's flaw of character, Isaac's and Ishmael's play, or the simple fact that Hagar and Ishmael are Sarah's and Isaac's potential future rivals. If we understand *hamartia* as closely related to the tragic protagonist, then the second and third interpretation should be preferred.
265 See Berlin, *Poetics and Interpretation*, 23.
266 Berlin, *Poetics and Interpretation*, 32.

only seldom active (like Ishmael). Nonetheless, their importance for the plot and for the emotional response of the reader should not be underestimated. Without Isaac, scene 1 could not exist because all its events revolve around his birth and upbringing. Without Ishmael, the emotional impact of scene 3 would be significantly diminished. Without both children playing together at the beginning of scene 2, Sarah's *hamartia* would not manifest itself and provide the inciting moment of the plot.

The role played by the child characters is interesting also from the point of view of literary motifs present in the tragic part of the narrative (vv. 9-16). Ishmael and Isaac symbolize the innocence of childhood. Their childish play triggers Sarah's *hamartia*, and from now on the point of gravity of the action moves to the world of guilty adults. The subsequent events bring about despair and the danger of death: two realities of which children are unaware, but of which adults are frightened. The development of the incidents adds to the emotional impact of vv. 9-16: paradoxically, the fact that Hagar and Ishmael face cruel deaths has its indirect cause in the innocent play of the oblivious children. To summarize this stage of discussion, it seems right to quote Barry's remark: "Aristotle's three categories are essentially to do with the underlying themes and moral purposes of stories, being very much about what might be called 'deep content,' since in an important sense they all concern 'inner events' (a moral defect, the *recognition* of its existence, and the *consequences* of its existence)."[267]

Aristotle's conceptual system provides us with another path to explore, which, however, will be only briefly mentioned here because it constitutes a subject in its own right. As we could see from Booth's definition of practical interests, they are linked to the rise of readers' emotions, and here we can see a point of connection between Booth's theory of literary interests and the remarks of Aristotle concerning the concept of *catharsis*, or *purgation*. Unfortunately, we have only two scarce passages on this subject in Aristotle's works, but they have been attracting the attention of scholars for many centuries, and they are still provoking debate. In *The Politics*, Aristotle says:

> We maintain further that music should be studied, not for the sake of one, but of many benefits, that is to say, with a view to education, or *purgation* [κɑθάρσις, my emphasis] (the word "purgation" we use at present without explanation, but when hereafter we speak of poetry, we will treat the sub-

---

267 Barry, *Beginning Theory*, 226.

ject with more precision); music may also serve for intellectual enjoyment, for relaxation and for recreation after exertion.[268]

Having enumerated the three aims of music, which are also, as Aristotle's explanatory remark shows, characteristic of poetry, and thus literature, he continues:

> For feelings such as pity and fear, or, again, enthusiasm, exist very strongly in some souls, and have more or less influence over all. Some persons fall into a religious frenzy, and we see them restored as a result of the sacred melodies – when they have used the melodies that excite the soul to mystic frenzy – as though they had found healing and *purgation* [my emphasis]. Those who are influenced by pity or fear, and every emotional nature, must have a like experience, and others in so far as each is susceptible to such emotions, and all are in a manner purged and their souls lightened and delighted.[269]

Here Aristotle explains that the emotions which are aroused while listening to music or, by analogy, reading literature bring about *catharsis*, which leaves listeners or readers "lightened or delighted." Moreover, *catharsis* is effectuated by the emotions of pity and fear; however, it indirectly follows from the above quotation that other kinds of emotion, such as enthusiasm, may bring about the same experience.

I agree with the opinion of those scholars who suppose that the subject of *catharsis* announced in *The Politics* must have been treated in the second part of *The Poetics*, which was eventually lost,[270] since in the first part of *The Poetics* we find only a very short remark about *catharsis*:

> A tragedy, then, is the imitation of an action that is serious and also, as having magnitude, complete in itself; in language with pleasurable accessories, each kind brought in separately in the parts of the work; in a dramatic, not in a narrative form; with incidents arousing pity and fear, wherewith to accomplish its catharsis of such emotions.[271]

In the light of the above three passages, we see that not only do we lack a precise definition of *catharsis* (at best, the definition can be regarded as ostensive), but we do not know what precisely is the object of *catharsis*. The translation of the passage from *The Poetics* is only one of the possible renderings of the Greek original. Is it readers or listeners who are purged, or rather their emotions, or, as Leon Golden suggests in his

---

268 Aristotle, *Pol.* 1341b 35 – 1342a 1 (*CWA* 2:2128).
269 Aristotle, *Pol.* 1342a 4-15 (*CWA* 2:2128-29).
270 See e.g. the discussion by Janko in Aristotle, *Poetics I, with the Tractatus Coislinianus*, xvi, 82.
271 Aristotle, *Poet.* 1449b 24-28 (*CWA* 2:2320).

translation of *The Poetics*, the object of purgation are the incidents of the plot?[272] We do not know this for certain.

The meaning of *catharsis* in the Aristotelian system is debatable,[273] but I incline towards its interpretation proposed by Janko. He understands Aristotelian *catharsis* as one of the three aims of literature. It comes up through representation (*mimesis*), works on emotions, and brings their purification, as well as teaching us how to respond emotionally in a correct way.[274] This interpretation is supported by Ricoeur, who sees *catharsis* as effectuated by the plot,[275] by F. L. Lucas,[276] G. E. Lessing,[277] Norman Gulley,[278] and also, to some extent, by Barnes.[279] In view of that, it is the *pathos* of Gen 21:1-21 evoked in vv. 14-16 which brings about *catharsis*. The reader empathizes with Hagar and her child, and is fully aware of Hagar's "negative" *peripeteia* and *anagnorisis*. Hence v. 16, which constitutes the emotional climax of the narrative, makes the reader feel pity and fear, whereas the turn of action in v. 17 and the subsequent verses bring about the *catharsis* of the reader's emotions. What is the nature of the cathartic experience? Lucas explains: "In fine, 'the *catharsis* of such passions' does *not* mean that the passions are purified and ennobled, nice as that might be; it does *not* mean that men are purged of their passions; it means simply that the passions themselves are reduced to a healthy, balanced proportion."[280] As a result, Gen 21:1-21 and, indeed, most biblical narratives are conducive to restoring the reader's emotional balance. In this context, it seems

---

272 See Aristotle, *Poetics: A Translation and Commentary*, trans. Leon Golden and O. B. Hardison, 11.
273 Cf. Cuddon, *The Penguin Dictionary of Literary Terms*, 115.
274 See Aristotle, *Poetics I, with the Tractatus Coislinianus*, 200.
275 See Ricoeur, *Time and Narrative* 1:50-51, 242 n. 43.
276 See Lucas, *Tragedy*, 35-78.
277 Quoted in Bernays, "Aristotle on the Effect of Tragedy," 155.
278 See Gulley, "Aristotle on the Purposes of Literature," 171.
279 See Barnes, *Aristotle*, 84; Barnes, "Rhetoric and Poetics," *CCA*, 277-79. This way of understanding Aristotelian *catharsis* has its opponents. O. B. Hardison supports the so-called "clarification theory" (in Aristotle, *Poetics: A Translation and Commentary*, trans. Leon Golden and O. B. Hardison, 114-20, 133-37), and argues that the term *catharsis* does not concern emotions in any way, but rather "the techne of tragedy" (p. 117), and applies to the incidents of the plot. Hardison understands *catharsis* as *clarification*, and argues that the tragic poet presents the incidents of the plot "in such a way as to bring out the probable or necessary principles that unite them in a single action and determine their relation to this action as it proceeds from its beginning to its end" (p. 117). In consequence, the incidents become clarified, and, according to Hardison, this is what Aristotle describes by the term *catharsis*.
280 Lucas, *Tragedy*, 38-39.

worthwhile to quote another remark of Booth's concerning the practical interests:

> We will accept destruction of the man we love, in a literary work, if destruction is required to satisfy our other interests; we will take pleasure in combinations of hope and fear which in real life would be intolerable. But hope and fear are there, and the destruction or salvation is felt in a manner closely analogous to the feelings produced by such events in real life.[281]

Therefore, the nomadic story of Gen 21:1-21 brings about the *catharsis* of our emotions, and teaches us how to balance our emotional response in the circumstances of everyday life. When we close the book of Scripture, and open the book of day-to-day existence, the scriptural quasi-reality and the cathartic experience are still there, and they influence our thoughts and emotions.

5.3.2. The Concept of Gaps

The Aristotelian categories are focused, to a great extent, on the formal features of a literary work. Fyfe observes that Aristotle's "dissection discovers all except the principle of life, and while we deplore the capital omission, we must admit that he has taught all later critics more than they can ever afford to forget."[282] Although, as is obvious from the preceding section, Aristotle is interested in the reader's emotions, most of his considerations can be labelled as a text-centred type of literary criticism, and this is probably the reason why the Aristotelian concepts have been so popular among the modern practitioners of narrative theory. In this section, however, I intend to move on to a critic whose approach is classified as a reader-centred type of criticism. Wolfgang Iser and his concept of *gaps* will be now the subject of discussion. To introduce Iser's approach, I shall first place it on the map of general criticism. Having done this, I shall introduce and explain the concept of *gaps*, and I shall apply it to my model pericope. I am aware that the applicability of different reader-response literary techniques to the exegesis of scriptural texts is a much debated issue, and, among biblical critics, we can find both fierce enemies and enthusiastic supporters of this type of criticism. This is why I shall also reflect on the advantages and downsides of reader-response approaches for biblical criticism, and spell out the conditions of their use in the biblical field.

---

281 Booth, *The Rhetoric of Fiction*, 130.
282 See Aristotle, *The Poetics*, trans. W. Hamilton Fyfe, xv-xvi.

In order to discuss different schools within reader-response criticism, we should first define this literary movement. Mark A. Powell's approach to the problem is both simple and practical when he characterizes reader-response criticism as "a pragmatic approach to literature that emphasizes the role of the reader in determining meaning. ... [It] represents a compendium of approaches that define this role in various ways."[283] Powell then qualifies his statement, and adds a remark about a role played by reader-response critics who "study the dynamics of the reading process in order to discover how readers perceive literature and on what bases they produce or create a meaning for any given work."[284] It is worth emphasizing that both parts of the definition neither point to nor exclude a potential role played by the author and by the text itself in determining the text's meaning. Powell leaves this question open, and, in consequence, his definition seems flexible enough to be adopted for our discussion. Thiselton notes: "From the point of view of biblical interpretation a potentially positive contribution is offered by any theoretical hermeneutical model which places an emphasis on *the role of readers as participatory and active*."[285] Fortunately, this contribution has been provided by numerous scholars, who have developed a new paradigm of literary interpretation, and whose works may be of great value for exegetes struggling to re-evaluate biblical texts in the light of contemporary shifts in literary theory.

Although the theoretical suppositions of reader-response theories should be carefully evaluated,[286] we cannot ignore the simple fact that reader-response criticism gives us helpful tools to explain the obvious difference between the impact of many biblical passages on ancient and contemporary readers. By way of example, a modern appraisal of Sarah's behaviour in Gen 21:1-21 differs from the ancient one. The modern reader confronted with Sarah's action born out of envy tends to react with dislike and shock. Yet the ancient reader's reaction, as Westermann convincingly demonstrates,[287] was probably much more balanced. In contrast to the modern reader, the ancient one perceived Sarah's action as a necessary and natural move aiming to secure the future welfare of herself and her son Isaac. Over the many centuries during which this passage has been known to readers, a shift has taken place in both life circumstances and ethics. Reader-response criticism,

---

283 Powell, *What Is Narrative Criticism?*, 16.
284 Powell, *What Is Narrative Criticism?*, 16.
285 Thiselton, *New Horizons in Hermeneutics*, 515.
286 Cf. Thiselton, *New Horizons in Hermeneutics*, 515ff.
287 See Westermann, *Genesis 12-36*, 339.

which analyses the text from the point of view of the reader, is able to shed light on that shift, and explain how it determines our reading of the story.

Powell distinguishes seven reader-response approaches, and groups those under three headings. The criterion for classification is the relationship between the reader and the text.[288] He calls the first group of approaches *the reader in the text*, and includes here *narrative criticism* and *structuralism*. The reader is considered to be "in the text" because he or she is "encoded within it" or "presupposed by it."[289] Powell notes rightly that narrative criticism and structuralism, which, in turn, embrace a number of sub-approaches, are considered by biblical scholars to be independent methods, which are separate from but parallel to other reader-response approaches. The second group in Powell's classification includes *phenomenological criticism* practised by Wolfgang Iser, and *affective stylistics* developed in the early works of Stanley Fish. Powell calls this group *the reader with the text*, for the reason that "the relationship of reader and text is dialectical, so meaning should not be viewed as something a reader creates out of a text but rather as the dynamic product of the reader's interaction *with* the text."[290] In the third group, Powell places the *theory of interpretive communities* invented by Fish in his later works, *transactive criticism* exemplified by the works of Norman N. Holland, and *deconstruction* practised by Derrida. These three approaches are placed under the heading *the reader over the text*, and explained in the following way: "Since meaning is largely subjective, readers are not ultimately constrained by literary dynamics or authorial intention in their interpretation of a work."[291] Powell adds that deconstruction should be regarded as standing outside the basic model of reader-response approaches and, in consequence, treated independently. To sum up, according to Powell, we have seven types of reader-response criticism, but if we treat narrative criticism, structuralism, and deconstruction separately, what remains is: phenomenological criticism, affective stylistics, the theory of interpretive communities, and transactive criticism.[292]

---

288 See Powell, *What Is Narrative Criticism?*, 16.
289 Powell, *What Is Narrative Criticism?*, 18.
290 Powell, *What Is Narrative Criticism?*, 17-18.
291 Powell, *What Is Narrative Criticism?*, 17.
292 A different categorization is provided by Susan R. Suleiman. She puts forward six varieties of audience-oriented criticism: *rhetorical*; *semiotic and structuralist*; *phenomenological*; *subjective and psychoanalytic*; *sociological and historical*; and *hermeneutic* ("Introduction," 6-7). According to her classification, the *rhetorical* approach is represen-

It seems, however, that the above attempt to classify different schools within reader-response criticism has one serious limitation. The diversity and multiplicity of approaches are difficult to categorize into a list containing a few headings. Powell's categorization helps to throw light on the complicated area of reader-response approaches, yet the price that we must pay for that is double: either we have difficulty finding a place for mercurial critics such as Fish, or we are forced to apply Procrustean techniques, and to lop off those features of a particular approach which do not fit our labelling. In consequence, I think that it is better to discuss individual critics rather than to make often futile efforts aimed at placing a given critic under a particular category. However, all reasonable and not overly complicated endeavours to classify the works of various critics are always of importance.

Moving on now to Iser, one of the central themes of his literary theory is the concept of *Leerstellen*, which may be rendered in English as *gaps* or *blanks*.[293] Iser, commenting on Virginia Woolf's complimentary remarks on the novels of Jane Austen, writes:

> What is missing from the apparently trivial scenes, the gaps arising out of the dialogue – this is what stimulates the reader into filling the blanks with projections. He is drawn into the events and made to supply what is meant from what is not said. What *is* said only appears to take on significance as a reference to what is not said; it is the implications and not the statements that give shape and weight to the meaning.[294]

At first glance Iser's observation seems accurate: it is hardly possible to give an example of a literary text which does not leave any space for the reader's imagination and projections. Curious and interested readers always ask questions and find answers whenever they come across discontinuities in dialogues, narration, or other structures constituting a narrative. Hence the presence of gaps and blanks results from the very nature of communication. As far as terminology is concerned, it

---

ted by Wayne C. Booth, among others, whereas the works of A. J. Greimas, Gérard Genette, and the early Roland Barthes reflect the *semiotic and structuralist* variety. The tenets of the *phenomenological* approach may be grasped, according to Suleiman, by studying the works of Iser, whilst the most typical representative of scholars using the *subjective and psychoanalytic* approach is Holland. Finally, the *sociological and historical* variety is represented by Lucien Goldmann and Hans-Robert Jauss, whereas the *hermeneutic* variety is present, in its negative version, in the works of Geoffrey Hartman and Derrida.

293 Cf. Barton, *Reading the Old Testament*, 212; McKnight, *The Bible and the Reader*, 79; Thiselton, *New Horizons in Hermeneutics*, 517. Among other important concepts proposed by Iser are: *implied reader* and *anticipation and retrospection*.
294 Iser, *The Act of Reading*, 168.

seems reasonable to adopt a suggestion made by Ska, who, following Sternberg's discussion of the poetics of biblical narrative,[295] proposes that we should differentiate *gaps* from *blanks* on the basis of their significance to narration: the former are relevant to narration, whereas the latter are not.[296] I intend to follow this differentiation here, and I shall deal only with gaps, which are all "empty literary spaces" relevant to narration.

It appears that the first important gap in my model passage Gen 21:1-21 is found in vv. 9-10. The reader does not know why Sarah behaves in this particular way, and what is the reason why she aims to get rid of Abraham's concubine and her son. Even in the light of the prior events described in Genesis, Sarah's action seems partly incomprehensible. In Gen 16:1-16, a story parallel to Gen 21:1-21, Sarah gives her maid to Abraham to "obtain children by her" (16:2). Subsequently, the reader witnesses growing tension between the two women, which finally makes Hagar escape from her hearth and home. Yet the ending of the story in Gen 16:1-16 tells us that Hagar returned to Abraham, and the first scene of Gen 21 (vv. 1-8) does not hint at the possibility of a new strife in this nomadic family. The reader rightly thinks that the conflict has been effectively headed off. Moreover, in the light of Gen 17:19 ("Sarah your wife shall bear you a son, and you shall call his name Isaac. I will establish my covenant with him as an everlasting covenant for his descendants after him"), we see that the primacy of the younger brother Isaac over his step-brother Ishmael has been confirmed by the divine authority, and the rights of Isaac cannot be violated in the future. Although the reader should not underestimate the impact of Sarah's apprehension, it is difficult to justify the cruelty of her action taken against Hagar. Unlike the ancient reader, his modern counterpart cannot clearly explain the connection between the cause in v. 9 (two children playing together) and the effect in v. 10 (Sarah's demand to expel Hagar). As a result, the gap between v. 9 and v. 10 remains, and the reader must supply an explanation for Sarah's behaviour in order to preserve the logic of narration. Had the reader not found a satisfactory explanation, he or she would have had to embrace an apparent contradiction. What is more, the differentiation between *gaps* and *blanks* mentioned above can be clearly grasped here. When we ask: "Why did Sarah react in such a peculiar way?," we encounter a gap in narration, whilst the questions: "Where did Sarah exactly see the

---

295 See esp. Sternberg, *The Poetics of Biblical Narrative*, 235-37.
296 See Ska, *Our Fathers Have Told Us*, 8-9.

son of Hagar?," or "Did she talk to her husband immediately or after a while?" are blanks because they are not directly relevant to narration.

To discuss the gap in vv. 9-10 more closely, we may profit from a definition proposed by Sternberg: "A gap is a lack of information about the world – an event, motive, causal link, character trait, plot structure, law of probability – contrived by a temporal displacement. ... What happened (or existed) at a certain temporal point in the world may be communicated in the discourse at a point earlier or later, or for that matter not at all."[297] In the light of this definition, in vv. 9-10, we encounter a gap caused by lack of information about Sarah's motive for expelling Hagar, by lack of a clear causal link between v. 9 and 10, and by lack of knowledge concerning Sarah's personality traits. It is also worth noting that the gap is not totally filled in any later point of the passage. The divine intervention in vv. 12-13 comes after Sarah's action in vv. 9-10, and may be understood as God's attempt to make use of the morally questionable decision taken by Sarah for the purpose of the divine plan. However, this interpretation of vv. 12-13 does not give us a desired explanation of Sarah's motive either. Following vv. 9-10, Sarah is no longer mentioned in the story and disappears from the narrative stage; only in Gen 23:2 does the reader learn that Sarah died in Hebron at the age of one hundred and twenty-seven. As a result, the reader is supposed to provide a justifying or accusatory explanation of Sarah's behaviour. Did Sarah act out of envy? Was she moved by apprehension about her and Isaac's future? Was her decision caused by a serious flaw in her character, or was she just affected by a sudden emotion? Whatever the reader's projections are, they are neither confirmed nor negated by the flow of subsequent events. A key to the mystery was buried together with Sarah in the cave of Machpelah, east of Hebron.[298]

Another example of a narrative gap in the text under discussion is found in v. 13, where God assures Abraham: "I will also make the son of the slave woman a nation because he is your offspring." The pledge is reiterated again in v. 18: "I will make him a *great* nation." In vv. 14-16, the reader is given a brief description of Hagar's expulsion, and of her hopeless wandering in the wilderness. A gap arises from two obvious questions: "How will the child be saved?" and "How will he become the father of a nation?" The answer to the first question is provided in the story: vv. 17-19 recount God's intervention. Yet the second question remains unanswered. The fact that the son of Hagar

---

297 Sternberg, *The Poetics of Biblical Narrative*, 235.
298 See Gen 23:19.

had been rescued and given a wife from Egypt does not automatically imply that he subsequently became the forefather of a great nation. When we turn the pages of Genesis, we read in 21:22-34 about a covenant between Abraham and Abimelech; chapter 22 brings a moving narration of Abraham's sacrifice; in Gen 23 we witness Sarah's death and burial; and Gen 24 recounts a long story leading to the marriage between Isaac and Rebekah. Only in Gen 25:12-18, after the narrative of Abraham's remarriage and death, is our curiosity satisfied by the passage mentioning twelve children of Ishmael, Abraham's son, who became princes and progenitors of twelve tribes. Hence in this case, unlike in Gen 21:9-10, we encounter a situation when a gap is solved by a subsequent analepsis.[299]

Turning now to an assessment of the applicability of Iser's theory to biblical exegesis, I would like to discuss some advantages of his theory. It appears that its strength lies in the emphasis placed on the active role of the reader. Iser's approach shows, as Thiselton aptly remarks, that "reading the biblical text should constitute not an exercise for passive spectators, but an *eventful and creative process*."[300] To highlight this advantage, Iser, inspired by Roman Ingarden's philosophical analyses, introduces an important distinction between *text* and *work*. In general, the *text* becomes the *work* through its realization, which is the equivalent of creative reading:

> One must take into account not only the actual text but also, and in equal measure, the actions involved in responding to the text. ... The work is more than the text, for the text only takes on life when it is realized, and furthermore the realization is by no means independent of the individual disposition of the reader – though this in turn is acted upon by the different patterns of the text.[301]

It appears, however, and I will demonstrate this in subsequent paragraphs, that when we speak about the text's realization, we should distinguish clearly between the different levels upon which this process happens. By way of illustration, two readers may *realize* the same text in two different ways because their *emotional* response to the text differs. Can we say the same about the *cognitive* level of the text? Does the "intellectual" message communicated by the text depend on its readers,

---

299 See Ska, *Our Fathers Have Told Us*, 9. Ska defines *analepsis* as the "telling of events after the moment in which, chronologically, they took place" (p. 8). According to biblical chronology, Ishmael must have had a number of sons before Abraham died (cf. Gen 21:5, 25:7).
300 Thiselton, *New Horizons in Hermeneutics*, 515.
301 Iser, *The Implied Reader*, 274-75.

or, rather, is it governed by the text's semantic structure? Iser's approach to this issue does not provide us with clear answers.

Iser's concept of gaps is also suitable for the analysis of most biblical narratives because of their syntactical features. Robert M. Fowler in *Let the Reader Understand* rightly notes that the presence of gaps in the Gospel of Mark is caused by its paratactic-episodic style.[302] The author of the Gospel consistently employs paratactic structures on the level of sentences, whereas on the level of literary units, the episodes are usually simply juxtaposed to each other. Such literary strategy, according to Fowler, leads inevitably to the presence of numerous gaps and blanks, and this feature was observed by many scholars in the past.[303] The indications are that exactly the same can be said about ancient Hebrew narratives. The use of parataxis, which is their common feature, as well as the picaresque style of presenting events, result in a large number of gaps, which must, in turn, be filled in by the reader.[304]

Furthermore, Iser reminds us that readers, confronted with gaps in narration, must use their imagination in order to provide information lacking in the text. As a result, every act of reading is slightly different in terms of personal response because every reader's imagination is different. "The reading of narrative is a fine tissue of insertions like this that we make as we move from point to point," writes H. Porter Abbott, "and though this can often lead to overreading, it also gives the experience of narrative much of its power. In other words, the energy narrative draws on is our own."[305] Thus a literary critic who can demonstrate convincingly how readers interact with gaps encountered in the text may do us an invaluable favour, and may teach us to be more sensitive to potential reading strategies, and to use our imaginative abilities. In consequence, our interest in biblical narratives may be rekindled and the pleasure of reading intensified.

So far so good, but we also must look at the other side of the coin. A close examination of Iser's theory shows that there are a large num-

---

302 See Fowler, *Let the Reader Understand*, 134-35.
303 See Fowler, *Let the Reader Understand*, 135-36.
304 One has to remember a remark made by Robert Alter: "Biblical narrative prose exhibits a good deal of variation from parataxis to hypotaxis, according to the aims of the writer and the requirements of the particular narrative juncture" (*The Art of Biblical Narrative*, 27). This remark does not, however, invalidate the fact that, on the purely syntactical level, parataxis is overwhelming: "So pervasive is *wə* that the discourse is largely organized around this single particle, which, it should be noted, has other roles to play, notably as the particle joining nouns in sequence" (Waltke and O'Connor, *Introduction*, 647).
305 Abbott, *The Cambridge Introduction to Narrative*, 84.

ber of potential problems which arise when one tries to apply his ideas without any modification to biblical criticism. The first problem caused by his theory is the exaggeration of the role played by gaps in the interpretation of the text. By way of example, Iser says: "What *is* said only appears to take on significance as a reference to what is not said."[306] If we apply Iser's reasoning to Gen 21:1-21, we have to agree that if the two gaps in the story were filled in, then "what is said" would become less significant. Let us imagine that in v. 10 Sarah says: "Expel this slave woman and her son because the son of this slave woman shall not share inheritance with my son Isaac. *I know very well that if they remain in our household, the rights of my son Isaac will surely be neglected, and it will bring down my grey hairs with sorrow to Sheol.*" Similarly, v. 13 could read: "I will also make the son of the slave woman a nation because he is your offspring. *And he and his future wife will live happily in the wilderness of Paran. And he will beget twelve sons and the sons of his sons will be many, since I will surely fulfil the promise which I am now giving to you.*" Could we agree that "what is said" now becomes less significant? As I have already shown, in Gen 21:1-21, God miraculously fulfils his mysterious plans, and is always ready to support those who are in trouble. On the other hand, the human characters are inclined to secure their happiness at the expense of other people, yet the destructive effects of their ruthless actions are overcome by God's power. This is "what is said." The imaginary filling of the two gaps reinforces, in fact, the picture of God as the God of providence: his saving action is presented in a more detailed way. At the same time, Sarah's action against Hagar does not become less evil. However, the story without the gaps demands less emotional involvement from the reader. Again, we would say that Iser's statement should be more nuanced. The cognitive significance of the story under discussion does not depend on the gaps to the extent that Iser suggests. What, however, does depend on the gaps is our emotional involvement in the narrative world.

Furthermore, Iser's analyses contain a large number of remarks which would smack of exaggeration if they were applied to biblical criticism. By way of example, Iser states: "Even in the simplest story there is bound to be some kind of blockage, if only because no tale can ever be told in its entirety. Indeed, it is only through inevitable omissions that a story gains its dynamism."[307] I do not intend to argue against the general correctness of this observation. The problem, how-

---

306 Iser, *The Act of Reading*, 168.
307 Iser, *The Implied Reader*, 279-80.

ever, lies in details: "it is *only* [my emphasis] through inevitable omissions." Every experienced reader of biblical narratives is able to give a long list of literary devices that make a story dynamic. It is sufficient to enumerate here such devices as unexpected changes in the order of chronological events, different ways of constructing the plot, slowing down or speeding up narrative time, and creating complex types of personages. Yet even the most inevitable omissions cannot be regarded as the *only* way of making a story more dynamic.

A similar overstatement takes place when Iser says: "Whenever the reader bridges the gaps, communication begins. The gaps function as a kind of pivot on which the whole text-reader relationship revolves."[308] Iser suggests indirectly that the communication between the reader and the text does not begin until the reader encounters gaps in the text. Yet communication actually begins when the reader starts reading the text; the gaps may only help to *intensify* the communication. Iser's statement should be rephrased: "The gaps function as *one of many possible kinds of pivots* on which *part of* the text-reader relationship revolves." In fact, Iser qualifies his statement: "There is, however, another place in the system where text and reader converge, and that is marked by the various types of negation that arise in the course of the reading. Blanks and negations both control the process of communication in their own different ways."[309] Nevertheless, by saying this, Iser is still trying to convince us that these two literary notions, blanks and negations, constitute the most important way of stimulating the whole relationship existing between the text and the reader, which, again, appears to be an exaggeration.

In addition, Iser does not distinguish clearly between the *meaning* of a text and a particular *reading* of the same text. As I have shown earlier, the meaning of a text is a relatively stable concept, whereas various readings differ greatly depending on individual readers and the presence of gaps. Those different readings, however, can be validated according to a "logic of probability," to use a Ricoeurian phrase,[310] and some of them are better than others. Yet Iser links the gaps (or blanks) of a text with its meaning:

> The blank in the fictional text appears to be a paradigmatic structure; its function consists in initiating structured operations in the reader, the execution of which transmits the reciprocal interaction of textual positions into consciousness. The shifting blank is responsible for a sequence of colliding

---

308 Iser, *The Act of Reading*, 169.
309 Iser, *The Act of Reading*, 169.
310 Ricoeur, "The Model of the Text," 549.

> images, which condition each other in the time flow of reading. ... The images hang together in a sequence, and it is by this sequence that the meaning of the text comes alive in the reader's imagination.[311]

I believe that if we equate a particular reading of a text with its meaning, we run the risk of importing the most outlandish ideas into that text, and we may finally end up saying that a text has as many meanings as there are readers. Barton expounds it in a few fitting words:

> The reader-response critic is to a great extent the text's master, *deciding* within what context of expectations he will read the text and so make sense of it. In this system of thought, there are no correct interpretations of texts, only "readings" which are more or less interesting, illuminating, novel, or valuable; the question what the text "actually means" is seen as unbelievably naive.[312]

Furthermore, different authors writing in the field of literary theory criticize Iser for his ambiguity, and this critique is often well deserved. Suleiman notes aptly:

> On the one hand, Iser asserts the primacy of the reader's creative role in realizing the text, thus allowing for a high degree of "free" variations; on the other hand, he suggests that it is ultimately the text itself which directs the reader's realization of it. ... The question of how much freedom a reader has is eluded, or rather answered in contradictory ways.[313]

Likewise, Thiselton reminds us that Iser was censured by both *objectivists*, who stress the primacy of the text in determining the meaning, and *pluralists*, who believe that it is the reader's expectations which determine the meaning of the text.[314] In my view, Iser would have avoided much criticism, if he had described his position in a more definitive way. Yet because he tries to manoeuvre his literary boat between the Scylla of the text and the Charybdis of the reader, he finally runs aground without a possibility of reaching a safe haven.

I agree with H. Porter Abbott who says that "narratives by their nature are riddled with gaps,"[315] so the interaction between the text and the reader is inevitable. However, I do not naively think that readers are totally free to create out of gaps everything they can possibly imagine. It is very often the case that the text imposes very strict limitations upon the reader. By way of illustration, in the passage Gen 21:1-21, the gap concerning the future of Ishmael must be filled in with projections,

---

311 Iser, "Interaction between Text and Reader," 119.
312 Barton, *Reading the Old Testament*, 212-13.
313 Suleiman, "Introduction," 23, 24-25.
314 See Thiselton, *New Horizons in Hermeneutics*, 522.
315 Abbott, *The Cambridge Introduction to Narrative*, 83.

but it would be against the grain of the text if those projections contradicted the ending of the narrative in vv. 20-21. What is more, Abbott, discussing a passage from Milton's *Paradise Lost*, observes: "If narrative comes alive as we fill in its gaps, it also gains life by leaving some of them unfilled. In the art of narrative, less can be more."[316] This seemingly paradoxical remark illustrates the frequent case when leaving a gap void may increase tension in the narrative, and make it more intriguing and alive. If the reader of Gen 21:1-21 leaves the gap concerning Sarah's action in vv. 9-10 open, the text will not become a tedious story. On the contrary, even after closing the book, the reader will be puzzled by the question: "Why did Sarah react in such a way?," and may finally decide to return to reading in order to solve the mystery.

To sum up the assessment of Iser's theory, I should say that although many of Iser's concepts may be of some use in general criticism, his literary theory as a whole cannot be safely applied to the analysis of Gen 21:1-21, nor, most probably, to other biblical narratives. If we accepted all the tenets of Iser's theory, we would open the floodgates to more radical forms of reader-response criticism. Eventually, this type of criticism would cease to be *reader-response* because there would be nothing to respond to. What would remain would be the self-centred world of the reader, for whom an encounter with the text is only an opportunity to express his or her narcissistic world of self-awareness.[317] In other words, an unavoidable corollary of Iser's theory are different forms of more extreme reader-response approaches such as those of Stanley Fish or Norman N. Holland.

Having said this, I am also convinced that *it is* possible to make moderate use of Iser's concept of gaps without accepting the other elements of his theory. As I have shown in the previous paragraphs, the concept of gaps is useful for detecting and explaining the emotional involvement of the reader in the story. When the issues of the relationship between the text and the reader are settled in a way which does not violate the basic determinacy of meaning, Iser's ideas provide us with an extra tool with which we can predict and gauge the "emotional temperature" of the narrative, and, in consequence, the reader's practical interests in the text.

---

316 Abbott, *The Cambridge Introduction to Narrative*, 85.
317 Eco observes in a jocular manner: "Undoubtedly the universe of literary studies has been haunted during the last years by the ghost of the reader" (*The Limits of Interpretation*, 46).

5.3.3. Goodness in the Bible

I will now demonstrate in what way the analysis of Gen 21:1-21, inspired by Iser's concept of gaps, complements the application of the classical Aristotelian terms to the same text. In other words, I will show that, within the discussion of the text's practical dimension, the Aristotelian approach, which forms a basis for modern narrative criticism, can be profitably supplemented by those theories which lay emphasis on the role played by the reader in interpretation.

The first gap in vv. 9-10, which tells about Sarah's action against Hagar, and makes the reader fill it in with projections, contains, at the same time, the *hamartia* of the story. Sarah's "flaw of character" provokes a strong emotional response because the reason for her behaviour remains mysterious. If we had known why exactly she wanted to expel Abraham's concubine, we might have found excuses for her action. However, since the reasons are disguised, we must use our imagination to supply them, and, in consequence, our emotional involvement becomes stronger. Secondly, the gap in vv. 12-13, where God commands Abraham to grant his wife's demand, and promises to make Ishmael a nation, accompanies the feeling of growing perplexity in the story resulting from Abraham's "negative" *anagnorisis* in scene 2. At the same time, it introduces the *pathos* of the story, which follows immediately in vv. 14-16. Thirdly, the gap in v. 18, where the reader is again faced with the question: "How is it possible for Ishmael to become a great nation?," ends Hagar's "negative" *peripeteia* and *anagnorisis*, and prepares the reader for the narrative's resolution and dénouement, which bring a partial answer to the gap in v. 18. Hence it seems that the role which the gaps play in the narrative reinforces the reader's emotional involvement resulting from the presence of the characters' *peripeteia* and *anagnorisis*.

Booth reminds us that "if we look closely at our responses to most great novels, we discover that we feel a strong concern for the characters as people; we care about their good and bad fortune."[318] This is what constitutes our practical interests in the text. In view of that, what exactly does the practical dimension of Gen 21:1-21 consist of? In chapter 3, I have defined the practical dimension of the text by saying that it comprises a set of diverse factors which enable us to determine the different aspects of goodness communicated by the text. As in the case of the aesthetic dimension, those factors are of both an intratextual

---

318 Booth, *The Rhetoric of Fiction*, 129.

and an extratextual character. The discussion in this subchapter has shown that among the intratextual factors we should enumerate the classical Aristotelian categories present in the narrative: *peripeteia, anagnorisis, hamartia,* and *pathos*. The analysis of the response of the reader based upon Iser's theory helps, in turn, to spell out the extratextual factors, which are the reader's projections brought about by the presence of gaps. There is, however, one element missing in this whole picture. What precisely are the *aspects* of goodness divulged by the narrative? Booth tells us that readers' practical interest in goodness is inseparable from a "concern for the characters as people" and "their good and bad fortune." Hence I must again turn to the personages of Gen 21:1-21 in order to discover the aspects of goodness disclosed by the narrative.

Three personages can be excluded from our discussion here. On the one hand, we have God, who controls the narrative world of Gen 21:1-21, and who is not at all influenced by either bad or ill fortune. On the other hand, we have Isaac and Ishmael, the silent agents who play a secondary role from the point of view of the plot. As a result, it is Abraham and the two women who deserve our close attention, and who embody the various aspects of goodness. To be more precise, those aspects of goodness are different *moral values* or *qualities* which become manifest when we analyse the personages' actions and fortunes. All moral values are, basically, of double nature: positive or negative, good or evil; yet this binary categorization does not preclude the existence of the whole spectrum of qualities, whose positive or negative "intensity" may vary. By way of example, the good qualities are happiness, success, prosperity, and life. On the contrary, the negative qualities comprise grief, failure, poverty, and death. Each positive quality has its negative counterpart, and it is the *interplay between different moral qualities* in the story which ultimately reveals the aspects of goodness (or its lack), and contributes to the practical dimension of the narrative.

Equipped with these distinctions, we should first analyse the qualities embodied by Sarah. In scene 1, she experiences the exuberant joy of maternity, which is granted to her by God after the long years of barrenness. In the following scene, however, she displays negative moral qualities: envy, apprehension, and aggression towards her rival Hagar. The opposite set of values can be observed in the case of Hagar. In the first part of scene 3, she is humiliated and expelled from her hearth and home to meet death in the wilderness, where she succumbs to despair. Her fortune is, however, reversed in v. 17, where God grants her salvation and the partial fulfilment of the promise concerning her son. Abraham, in turn, experiences in scene 1 the joy of parenthood, and his trust in God's presence and action in his life is apparently strengthened. He is then put to the test in scene 2, where he finds himself torn apart by the conflict between the love of his wife, on the one hand, and the love of his concubine and her son, on the other. God solves this conflict, but Abraham must face another drama. The future of Ishmael is secured by God's promise, yet the necessity to part with Hagar inflicts another blow on Abraham's emotional life. He needs to sacrifice one value to save another, and that need constitutes the tragic dimension of his existence.

Therefore, when we pay attention to the personages of the story and to the vicissitudes of their lives, we witness a very complex and ever-changing pattern of diverse, positive and negative moral qualities, which appear and pass away, which influence each other, and which, eventually, contribute to the practical dimension of the story. One character only is undisturbed by this flux of values. It is God, whose divine status excludes him from being influenced by any turn of fortune, but who often enters the earthly stage to execute his decrees. He is the supreme source of goodness, yet, at the same time, he clearly communicates to the characters of the story that his divine goodness is different from goodness understood in human terms. The decision to expel Hagar to the wilderness is evil in Abraham's eyes, yet it helps fulfil God's purposes, and, ultimately, it brings happiness and success to Hagar and Ishmael. In consequence, from the perspective of modern readers, the human understanding of goodness becomes purified in order to fit its divine counterpart, and to enable the communication between the actuality of the readers and the trans-reality of God.

The interplay between moral qualities contributing to the practical dimension of the text has two corollaries for readers. First, they recognize that their own lives are reflected in the narrative world, and this is what makes the latter so alluring. The narrative world, albeit conventional and finite, provides readers with a suggestive synthesis of many issues comprising the tissue of everyday life. Secondly, readers are influenced by the narrative world, and one aspect of this influence has already been mentioned in this subchapter. The *catharsis* of emotions effectuated by literary texts helps readers keep a healthy emotional balance in the circumstances of everyday life. Apart from that, every work of literature exerts moral influence on its readers, even if certain modern trends in criticism are very unwilling to admit it.[319] Booth labels the

---

319 See Booth, *The Company We Keep*, 3-8, 25-46.

discussion of the moral value of literary works *ethical criticism*, and explains:

> Ethical criticism attempts to describe the encounters of a story-teller's ethos with that of the reader or listener. Ethical critics need not to begin with the intent to evaluate, but their descriptions will always entail appraisals of the value of what is described: there are no neutral ethical terms, and a fully responsible ethical criticism will make explicit those appraisals that are implicit whenever a reader or listener reports on stories about human beings in action.[320]

Literary texts, including Gen 21:1-21, are written to move their readers deeply, to make them think about various truths, and to appreciate their aesthetic qualities. The readers' ethos is influenced, and often changed, by the ethos of the literary works they peruse. However, in the case of biblical narratives, this change may be more profound, and may involve leaving the sublunary sphere of everyday experience in search of the transcendent world which will never pass away. It is now the goal of the next chapter to explain how this process may be achieved.

---

320 Booth, *The Company We Keep*, 8-9.

6. Transcendental Knowledge

The main argument of this book is that the reader, who is immersed in the real world called *actuality*, participates indirectly in the *trans-reality* of God through the mediation of the *narrative world* of biblical stories. To put it another way, we would say that the reader's *immanent knowledge* is augmented by *narrative knowledge*, and, in consequence, a new epistemic horizon emerges, which is called *transcendental knowledge*, and which stands for the reader's knowledge about trans-reality. Using the model pericope Gen 21:1-21 as an example, it is the purpose of this chapter to explain in detail in what way the reader gains transcendental knowledge about the divine reality, and what that knowledge comprises.

The very fact that Scripture plays a mediatory role in the process of reading is based on the fundamental feature which it shares with other sacred texts, namely that it enables us to participate in divine revelation. Whereas that feature may also be characteristic of certain general literary texts, it is always essential for calling a text *sacred*. Hence, by their very nature, scriptural texts point to a transcendent reality, and invite the reader to participate in the divine sphere (see chapter 3). However, when we note this trait of scriptural texts, we must clarify in what way the communication between the profane and the sacred is achieved, and what are the other aspects of the biblical text which facilitate the emergence of transcendental knowledge. I shall explain this issue in two steps. First, I will show the importance of the three dimensions of narrative knowledge for the surfacing of transcendental knowledge in the mind of the reader. In other words, I will clarify in what way truth, beauty, and goodness, communicated by biblical narratives, lead the reader to the divine sphere. Secondly, following Ricoeur's masterly analysis of the temporal character of narrative, I will show how the narrative under discussion approximates the concept of eternity, which is a distinguishing feature of the divine realm. In brief, a discussion of the role played by the Platonic triad in the biblical texts, as well as the relationship between time and eternity will be the last step taken to explain the general hermeneutical model proposed here.

6.1. The Platonic Triad and Its Divine Source

In the three preceding subchapters, I have discussed the cognitive, aesthetic, and practical dimensions of Gen 21:1-21, and the discussion of each dimension was followed by general considerations regarding the ideas of truth, beauty, and goodness, and the role they play in the process of reading. I shall now summarize this discussion, and show the ways in which the three Platonic ideas make the communication between actuality and trans-reality possible, or, in other words, in which they lead the reader from his or her own world to the divine world. To do this, I shall propose five levels on which that communication takes place.

First, and generally, the various manifestations of truth, beauty, and goodness which we can observe in the world around us point inevitably to a deeper reality, and often trigger some kind of existential experience. By way of illustration, R. S. Thomas in his evocative poem "The Bright Field" tells us about a link between certain natural phenomena and a deeper awareness of the purpose of life: "I have seen the sun break through / to illuminate a small field / for a while, and gone my way / and forgotten it."[1] The poet quickly realizes that what he had seen gave him an insight into the reality of human life, and, surprised by the intensity of his spiritual perception, he exclaims: "[Life] is the turning / aside like Moses to the miracle / of the lit bush, to a brightness / that seemed as transitory as your youth / once, but it is the eternity that awaits you."[2] It is true that many natural events and phenomena may give rise to an experience of this or similar kind; yet, at the same time, one of the most privileged moments when such an experience may occur is when we read Scripture, the book of divine mysteries, which opens our eyes to invisible reality. The world of biblical narratives has a suggestive power, and brings images and associations which open the reader's mind to existential experience. The sinister image of the wilderness and of God's salvific action depicted in Gen 21:14-19 may shed light on those moments of the reader's life when he or she also experienced abandonment and loneliness, and may become a source of strength and hope. This level of reading Scripture seems to fit what Thiselton generally labels "the hermeneutics of pastoral theol-

---

1 Thomas, *Laboratories of the Spirit*, 60.
2 Thomas, *Laboratories of the Spirit*, 60.

ogy," and discusses under the heading "biblical symbols: productive and spiritual reading."[3]

However, the analysis of the three dimensions of the biblical text, which forms the core of my argument, opens other levels of the communication between the profane and the divine. I also believe that the reader may become indirectly conscious of some of those levels of communication without actually verbalizing any of them. Yet, to comprehend them fully, a deep reflection on the presence of, and the role played by, the Platonic triad in the text is needed. The reader must also approach the biblical text within the broad context of literary theory, and pay attention not only to the text itself, but also to the complex net of relationships existing between the text, the reader, and the world.

In view of that, the second level of communication consists in the fact that each of the transcendentals communicated by the biblical text usually has as many complementary aspects as many there are interpretive approaches used in the exegesis of the text. I have called this phenomenon *the refinement of truth, beauty, and goodness*. Hence, even within the limited framework of this book, which focuses on only one Hebrew narrative, and applies to that narrative a few chosen interpretive approaches, I have proved that the refinement of ideas is a potential feature characteristic of all biblical texts, and the rationale for that refinement is provided by the changing character of the questions asked by the interpreter. From the historical perspective, the process of reinterpretation and refinement will last as long as we undertake our critical efforts. From the philosophical standpoint, however, the various aspects of truth, beauty, and goodness point to Truth, Beauty, and Goodness in the absolute ontological sense.

Moreover, and thirdly, the analysis of Gen 21:1-21 has shown that there is a significant "twist" between the aspects of each transcendental, which represents a change of perspective from human to divine. When readers recognize different levels on which the text communicates the Platonic triad, they also become aware that biblical narratives often juxtapose human and divine ways of expressing what is true, beautiful, and good. By way of example, and as regards truth, the limited knowledge which Abraham has about God as a faithful protector of his people, and which is confirmed by the events recounted in scene 1, is challenged and surpassed by God's unexpected decision concerning Hagar and Ishmael in vv. 12-13. God's eternal truth triumphs over human, limited truth. Similarly, the beauty resulting from the presence

---

3   Thiselton, *New Horizons in Hermeneutics*, 575-82.

of the archetypal ideas and the human objectives in the narrative under discussion is brought under control by the beauty of God's purposes ordering and organizing the human reality according to his divine plan. Finally, divine goodness is different from goodness understood in human terms. The decision to expel Hagar to the wilderness is morally questionable in Abraham's eyes, yet it helps fulfil God's purposes, and, ultimately, it brings happiness to Hagar and her son. As in the case of truth and beauty, the human understanding of goodness becomes purified in order to fit its divine counterpart, and to enable the communication between the actuality of the reader and the trans-reality of God. This "twist," which is discoverable in Gen 21:1-21, is certainly not a feature of all biblical narratives without exception, yet the figure of the powerful God who transcends the human ideas about what is true, beautiful, and good is present in most of them, and is undoubtedly a feature of Scripture understood as a whole. It finds its clear expression in the well-known Isaian passage 55:8-9: "For my thoughts are not your thoughts, neither are your ways my ways, says the Lord. For as the heavens are higher than the earth, so are my ways higher than your ways and my thoughts than your thoughts."

Fourthly, the presence of the three transcendentals contributes to the feature of biblical narratives which is called by Alter "the power to 'draw us out' of ourselves."[4] Alter argues that biblical narratives exhibit this feature because they, in a very convincing manner, "scrutinize the human condition," and "represent human figures challenged by a reality beyond human ken."[5] Balthasar comments on the same feature: "the biblical scenes we have enumerated show only by way of example what applies to every hearer of God's word: he perceives God by being transported outside of himself."[6] Auerbach, in turn, speaks about biblical narratives' "claim to absolute authority," and the ability "to overcome our reality."[7] I believe that my analyses in chapter 5 have shown that the cognitive, aesthetic, and practical dimensions of Gen 21:1-21 are conducive, in a direct way, to the above features mentioned by Alter, Balthasar, and Auerbach. We learn about the truth of the human condition. We are transported outside of ourselves when we see God's beauty revealed in the dazzling light of his glory. The interplay of goodness and evil in the characterization of the personages convinces us of their humanity, and of the challenge they had to face in their

---

4   Alter, *The World of Biblical Literature*, 23.
5   Alter, *The World of Biblical Literature*, 23.
6   Balthasar, *Theology: The Old Covenant*, 13.
7   Auerbach, *Mimesis*, 15.

lives. In consequence, we not only witness Sarah's inexpressible joy in vv. 6-7; we ourselves are given a chance to forget about the reality surrounding us, and to get a glimpse of divine trans-reality which brings eternal joy.

The above four levels on which the communication between the profane and the sacred is achieved do not necessarily require that the reader's philosophical stance should be theistic with respect to the existence of God, or realistic with respect to the existence of transcendentals. Even those readers who are agnostics or atheists, on the one hand, or conceptualists or nominalists, on the other, can accommodate the four levels introduced so far with only one exception. Nominalists would reject the conclusion of the second level, namely that the various aspects of truth, beauty, and goodness point to Truth, Beauty, and Goodness in the absolute ontological sense. For nominalists, transcendentals do not exist at all. However, the rest of the argument stands, and the only concession which non-theists and non-realists would like to be made by theists and realists is the assumption that trans-reality is actually a theoretical concept invented to explain the object of the reader's transcendental knowledge, and transcendental knowledge itself is only an imaginary horizon within the reader's knowledge about reality. Nevertheless, and in contrast to the preceding four levels, the next level, on which we speak of God as the metaphysical source of the three transcendentals, demands that the reader should be a theist and a realist.

So finally, and fifthly, we can say that truth, beauty, and goodness communicated by the biblical text point to their metaphysical source. I have already broached this topic in chapter 3, where I mentioned Aquinas's views on ideas in God, following the analysis of his works by Boland. Aquinas is convinced "that there must be ideas in God, that there must be a plurality of ideas in God and that whatever has being in any way must have some corresponding idea in God,"[8] and his views on the divine ideas are presented in *Scriptum super libros Sententiarum, Questiones Disputatae de Veritate,* and *Summa Theologiae.*[9] Since "whatever is in God, is God and whatever God has, God is,"[10] also truth, beauty, and goodness *are in* God and *are* God. In consequence, when the reader discovers these three transcendentals in the biblical text, the

---

8   Boland, *Ideas in God,* 196.
9   See Boland, *Ideas in God,* 200.
10 Boland, *Ideas in God,* 323.

way leading from actuality through the mediation of quasi-reality to trans-reality is wide open.[11]

Obviously, the transcendental knowledge of the reader perusing biblical narratives does not consist only in the reader's awareness that trans-reality exists, and, as will be shown in the following subchapter, that trans-reality is eternal. The reader acquires some *specific* knowledge about trans-reality through the mediatory role played by quasi-reality. The analysis of the three textual dimensions in chapter 5 has shown that the reader learns about God's various attributes. As a result, this knowledge becomes part of transcendental knowledge. In the case of the model narrative, the reader finds out that God miraculously fulfils his mysterious plans, and is always ready to support those who are in trouble. His faithfulness is manifested in the fulfilment of the promise given to Abraham, and his providential care averts the danger of death and secures the future. God's supreme purpose orders the world of human objectives and archetypal ideas according to his divine plan, and we see God's beauty in his glory communicated to people. Furthermore, even if the practical dimension of the narrative does not bring any specific knowledge about God, it points indirectly towards God's omnipotence and omniscience. Now, the reader realizes that this knowledge about God is primarily narrative knowledge. It is gained through participation in the fictional world of Gen 21:1-21. Nonetheless, it foreshadows the full knowledge in which the reader will participate when he or she reaches finally the eternity of God. In other words, we should say that the relationship between the narrative knowledge about God and the transcendental knowledge which is yet to come is parallel to the relationship between the aspects of truth in the narrative and Truth in the absolute sense, or between time, which already carries the seeds of eternity, and God's absolute eternity. To use the imagery employed by St Paul in 1 Cor 13:12: "Now we see in a mirror dimly, but then face to face. Now I know in part; then I shall understand fully, even as I have been fully understood." The reader knows that the eternal trans-reality exists, but the knowledge of its nature is shadowy, and still to be completed by God himself.

---

11   The problem of the ideas in God's mind, and the status of the Platonic triad, are very complex in the theology of Aquinas. In contrast, such Platonic Christian theologians as Augustine or Pseudo-Dionysius emphasize the link between the triad and God much more than Aquinas. For Augustine, God *is* truth, beauty, and goodness. See e.g. Augustine, *Conf.* II. vi (12), X. xxiv-xxvii (35-38) (transl. Chadwick, 30-31, 200-201).

To sum up, another question should be raised. Are the above five levels of communication Scripture-specific, or should we rather think of them as common to general literature? A quick analysis shows that all levels of communication apply to general literature. Having said this, we must remember that although not all literary works exhibit these features to the same extent, it is not unusual for many of them to mediate between the world of the reader and some kind of transcendent, and even divine, world. A good literary example is the persona of Harry Haller a.k.a. Steppenwolf in the famous novel by Hermann Hesse. Steppenwolf recalls his dream of Goethe, in which he accuses Goethe of betraying the knowledge of the dark side of human existence, and replacing it with an optimistic vision: "giving utterance to faith and optimism and spreading before yourself and others the illusion that our spiritual strivings mean something and endure."[12] In reply, Goethe teases Steppenwolf mercilessly, and tells him what his biggest mistake is: "We immortals do not like things to be taken seriously. We like joking. Seriousness, young man, is an accident of time. … In eternity, however, there is no time, you see. Eternity is a mere moment, just long enough for a joke."[13] Later, Steppenwolf reflects on his dream, and understands its true meaning: Goethe's laughter "was that which is left over when a true man has passed through all the sufferings, vices, mistakes, passions and misunderstandings of men and got through to eternity and the world of space. And eternity was nothing else than the redemption of time, its return to innocence, so to say, and its transformation again into space."[14] We see that this passage from Hesse's novel provokes a deep existential reflection. Its cognitive, aesthetic, and practical aspects are multiple and complex. There exists a "twist" representing a move from Steppenwolf's outlook on life and that of Goethe's. The beauty of Hesse's poetic prose has undoubtedly the power to "draw readers out" of themselves. Finally, the reader who reflects on the process of reading is able to recognize that the presence of the three transcendentals in the novel, manifested through its literary dimensions, point directly to the source of all ideas – eternal God inhabiting the divine sphere.

In view of that, can we still claim that Scripture is a privileged medium of communication between actuality and trans-reality? The answer to this question is positive as long as we agree that being *privileged*

---

12   Hesse, *Steppenwolf*, 113.
13   Hesse, *Steppenwolf*, 115-16.
14   Hesse, *Steppenwolf*, 181.

is not the same as being *exclusive*. As I have shown in chapter 1, an attempt to place scriptural exegesis within a general hermeneutics of literary texts is fully justified. To explain the way in which scriptural texts lead their readers to trans-reality, we do not need to invent any "special" or "divinely inspired" hermeneutics. Moreover, general literary hermeneutics shows that Scripture has a number of distinct features, but, again, none of them is reserved to biblical literature alone. However, the Bible remains unique by virtue of the distinctive configuration of both its contents and features.

6.2. Time and Eternity in Narrative

In "Burnt Norton," the poem opening T. S. Eliot's sophisticated and evocative "Four Quartets," we read: "Time present and time past / Are both perhaps present in time future / And time future contained in time past. / If all time is eternally present / All time is unredeemable."[15] Eliot points here to the central existential problem concerning time, which his poetic imagination finds insurmountable. As Denis Donoghue explains, the key problem, which permeates the whole of "Four Quartets," is how to make sense of time, which seems to be "eternally present and therefore unredeemable because it excludes history, process, and the flux."[16] If the present cannot be transcended, and if only the present moment really exists, we seem trapped in a paralyzing snare. Since the present is so often full of misery, and it cannot be transcended or redeemed, we all are beings-towards-death, to use the famous Heideggerian phrase. The ultimate horizon of our actuality is death, which brings an end to the pointless domination of the present. Our efforts to think or speak of eternity are only a naive dream, which brings disillusionment when we are wide awake.

The question of the relationship between time and eternity, broached by T. S. Eliot in "Four Quartets," seems urgent when we read biblical narratives. Those narratives have a clear temporal structure, and they tell events that happened in time.[17] Yet they also point to the

---

15 Eliot, "Four Quartets," 189.
16 Donoghue, *Words Alone*, 230-31. Helen L. Gardner supports this interpretation of "Four Quartets" ("Four Quartets: A Commentary," 61).
17 I am aware that the problem of time and eternity in Scripture is very complex. Ricoeur reminds us that "narrative and the time of narrative – with their apparent linearity – constitute only its most visible framework" ("Biblical Time," 179). When we take into account other genres of the Hebrew Bible, the concept of time becomes

divine sphere, and try to convince the reader that the human and the perishable are inextricably interwoven with the divine and the imperishable. How are these two spheres related to each other, and how do biblical narratives refer to eternity? To answer this question, I shall first introduce the biblical definition of eternity, followed by the discussion of how the ancient Hebrew reader could understand the model passage Gen 21:1-21 in the light of that definition. Next, I shall propose a modern definition of eternity, and examine the same issue from the viewpoint of the modern reader.

It appears justified to discuss first the meaning of the noun עולם, which is the closest Hebrew equivalent of the term *eternity*.[18] Even a cursory comparison of the Hebrew text and its modern translations reveal that עולם is very often translated as "eternity." In Qoh 3:11 ("he has put eternity into man's mind"), the Hebrew word for eternity is העלם. In Isa 45:17, the phrase עד־עולמי עד is rendered as "to all eternity." In Gen 49:26, the expression גבעת עולם is translated as "everlasting hills," whilst in Jer 20:11 the phrase כלמת עולם means "eternal dishonour." I might, of course, multiply the examples, but I think that the above four instances clearly exemplify the case. When we encounter in our modern Bible translations the words *eternity*, *eternal*, or *everlasting*, we can safely assume that, in the majority of cases, the underlying Hebrew term is עולם. Nonetheless, it must be clearly stated that the above comparison between the original and the translations does not solve the problem of whether biblical authors meant by עולם the same concept which we now express by the word *eternity*. Hypothetically, we might assume that modern biblical translations of the Hebrew passages containing עולם are to some extent imprecise. Therefore, we must first establish the original meaning of the term עולם.

The noun עולם does not occur at all in the pericope under discussion. It is, however, found in Genesis several times. By way of example, the RSV translates the phrase אל עולם in Gen 21:33 as the "Everlasting God." The etymology of עולם is not certain, but the basic meaning of the noun is "long time" or "farthest, remotest time."[19] As the example from Gen 21:33 clearly shows, the noun is often used attributively in combination with other words, which is proof of its non-abstract char-

---

multidimensional, and the seeming opposition between the Hebrew and Greek understanding of time (*linear* versus *cyclical*) must be critically revisited (see "Biblical Time," 167-180).

18   22 times in the Hebrew Bible, we found its variant spelt without the mater lectionis: עלם (see Preuss, "Ôlām," *TDOT* 10:531).
19   See Preuss, "Ôlām," *TDOT* 10:531.

acter.²⁰ Hence Hans W. Wolff is right in saying after Ernst Jenni that עולם "means primarily the time that is furthest away from us, both in the past and in the future."²¹ Since the meaning of the noun refers to "remotest time," עולם is used in the Hebrew Bible with regard to the furthest past, and, four times more often, with regard to the distant future. In the first case, it may mean "time immemorial," "antiquity," or "distant past." In the second, it may be rendered as "perpetual duration," "forever," and it may also intensify expressions relating to the future, and may mean, simply, "for a long time."²² Obviously, the meaning of עולם varies greatly, depending on the context, and, in some cases, its actual translation is a very moot question. In consequence, the noun is a complex and multidimensional concept. It could, however, be argued that עולם very often denotes an idea that transcends the concept of time understood as the mere "here and now" of a human being.

Even if, within the boundaries of Hebraic thought, עולם is closely linked to the concept of time and depends directly on it, it appears that, for the ancient Hebrews, *eternity* was not just a different kind of *time* or *time in its totality*. It meant much more. Barr convincingly proves that we may regard *eternity* as being different from *time*, at least in a number of cases attested in the Hebrew Bible. Barr opposes a method in biblical theology which is grounded only in philological analyses. In order to have justified opinions regarding Hebrew words and concepts, we have to look at what the Bible really says: "Theological assertions, which are not based upon what the Bible says but upon the linguistic resources which it uses, must be regarded with caution."²³ Barr aptly summarizes his well-balanced opinion about the meaning of עולם:

> While accepting the value of Jenni's basic sense of "the remotest time," I should venture to suggest that at some points this is best supplemented with the sense "perpetuity," or something like it. ... Conversely, the range of "the remotest time" has to be qualified by the observation that certain contexts, which would seem natural from this rendering, such as "in the remotest time, before man was created, such and such happened," do not occur for *'olam* at all, and as far as we can tell are impossible for this word. We might therefore best state the "basic meaning" as a kind of range

---

20 See Preuss, "Ôlām," *TDOT* 10:532.
21 Wolff, *Anthropology of the Old Testament*, 89. The majority of scholars discussing the noun עולם refer to the article by E. Jenni, "Das Wort 'ôlām im AT," *ZAW* 64 (1952) and 65 (1953).
22 Cf. Preuss, "Ôlām," *TDOT* 10:533-36.
23 Barr, *Biblical Words for Time*, 162.

between "remotest time" and "perpetuity," and existing only in certain contexts at that.²⁴

Thus Barr suggests that although עולם may have several meanings, we cannot exclude the possibility that one of those meanings refers to an idea which equals to time in its greatest extent, or to time being far beyond the experience of the human being. Moreover, Barr states: "Eternity is not something above or outside time; but what else is possible when it has been assumed that language moves from the finite to the infinite and bases its terms for the latter upon the former, and that the process of linguistic derivation reflects more or less exactly the process of knowing the subject."²⁵ In the light of the above two remarks made by Barr, I believe that in the Hebrew Bible we may observe the process of refinement of the notion of eternity. In numerous cases, the noun עולם signifies only a remote period of time in the past or in the future. There are, however, examples of usage when עולם appears to designate time understood in its broadest and ultimate sense. Yet, owing to the organic and non-abstract nature of the Hebrew language, none of the meanings of עולם really transcends the boundaries of the concept of time. Hence, in the Hebrew Bible, *eternity* in its refined meaning should be regarded as "remotest time," "time without beginning or end," and "perpetuity."

Certainly, we must be very cautious about making judgments concerning the authorial intention in the cases when the biblical author uses expressions containing עולם. John R. Wilch seems to be right, when he says:

> The term [עולם] was first especially employed for "ecclesiastical" language by Deutero-Isaiah with respect to history as the world of God and his activity. ... Then, apocalyptic appropriated it as an attribute of the world beyond. ... Although the occasional reference to the idea of eternity may well have had its Hebrew origin in the historical concept of Dt.-Isa., the convincing repudiation of all Greek influence in Ecc. by Oswald Loretz leads to caution in this point.²⁶

Thus caution must be exercised when we discuss the meaning of עולם for the ancient Israelites. Nevertheless, we should keep in mind that there are examples of expressions containing עולם which seem to be very much in favour of the refined meaning of the term. In Ps 90:2 we read: ומעולם עד־עולם אתה אל, which is rendered as "from everlasting to everlasting thou art God." The phrase is preceded by "before the

---

24 Barr, *Biblical Words for Time*, 69 n. 1.
25 Barr, *Biblical Words for Time*, 93.
26 Wilch, *Time and Event*, 18.

mountains were brought forth, or ever thou hadst formed the earth and the world." In this context, even a very cautious interpretation suggests that עולם refers to the greatest imaginable time-span, which is equal to the time-span of the existence of uncreated God. Similarly, in Dan 12:2, we read: "And many of those who sleep in the dust of the earth shall awake, some to everlasting life, and some to shame and everlasting contempt." Two Hebrew phrases which employ עולם are: לחיי עולם and לדראון עולם. In both cases, the idea of time that has no end seems to be intended here.

In the pericope under discussion, the term עולם does not occur at all. As a result, Gen 21:1-21 does not speak directly about eternity. Nevertheless, I would like to argue here that the content of the pericope points *indirectly* yet *clearly* towards the concept of eternity perceived as perpetuity and temporal totality without beginning or end. To prove this statement, I have to make an observation concerning the accumulation of human-time expressions in the first scene of the passage (vv. 1-8). By "human-time expressions" I understand the phraseology which refers to units of time characteristic of human life and everyday experience. Thus, "two days" is a human-time expression, whereas "two centuries" is not. Interestingly enough, the first scene of the discourse has several human-time expressions, which do not occur later in the story. So, in v. 2, we encounter זקנים ("old age") and מועד ("appointed time"). In v. 4, we have בן־שמנת ימים ("eight days old"), followed by בן־מאת שנה ("hundred years old") in v. 5. In v. 7, the noun זקנים is repeated. Finally, in v. 8, we read ביום הגמל ("on the day of weaning"). In consequence, in the first scene of the pericope, we have five human-time expressions in contrast to only one human-time expression in both the second and third scenes (in v. 14 we come across בבקר, "in the morning").

Now, I would like to demonstrate how the pericope Gen 21:1-21 points indirectly towards the Hebrew concept of eternity. This is achieved in at least three different ways: through a symbolic development of time in the story, through the notion of fidelity, and owing to the presence of the divine name in the narrative. First, as I have shown in the discussion of the cognitive and aesthetic dimensions, the narrative abounds with the literary motifs of life. A deeper analysis shows, however, that the theme of life is closely linked to the theme of time. The life of the narrative's characters is not only saved, but, first and foremost, prolonged. Abraham's, Sarah's, and Hagar's lives are symbolically continued in the lives of their progeny, Isaac and Ishmael. Isaac faces the prospect of secure life, when his potential rival Ishmael is expelled. Ishmael, in turn, also enjoys God's presence and blessing:

he grows up, acquires skills, and marries an Egyptian. In other words, as the story develops, an ample amount of time in its different aspects is granted to each of the characters. Moreover, when we proceed from the exposition of the story to its climax and resolution, human-time expressions are no longer used in the narrative, and yield to a narrative strategy which avoids clear-cut time expressions. In the second and third scenes, we hear a divine promise concerning both Isaac and Ishmael. In consequence, the narrative's centre of gravity moves towards the future: Abraham's descendants will be named through Isaac (v. 12), and Ishmael will become a great nation (vv. 13, 18). Moreover, the narrative is open-ended: the reader is left in suspense as regards the further events and the end of Hagar's and Ishmael's lives. Bearing these all narrative features in mind, I believe that we may see a certain kind of symbolic development in the story. The human-time expressions in scene 1, which emphasize the "here and now" of the characters, give way to a narrative strategy which is no longer limited by precise time designations. The second and the third scenes are less definite and open to the unpredictable yet secure future. God's action and words in vv. 12-13 and 17-20 make divine time present within the human time of the characters. In conclusion, as the story develops, the overall concept of time becomes less precise and more divine, as well as more oriented towards the future. In this way, the narrative points indirectly to the notion of עולם. Time in the story is developed and transfigured: the more we approach the end of the narrative, the more it approximates perpetuity and temporal totality without end.

Secondly, the idea of eternity is approximated by the notion of fidelity. Ricoeur speaks about this approximation in the conclusion of his tripartite work. He says that the most precious sense of Exodus 3:14a (*ehyeh asher ehyeh*), a sense which is untranslatable into modern languages, is "expressed by the idea of fidelity."[27] He then adds: "The eternity of Jahweh is above all else the fidelity of the God of the Covenant, accompanying the history of his people."[28] Calling both Genesis and Exodus books of "beginnings" (the beginning of creation in Gen 1:1, the beginning of the history of election in Gen 12:1, and the beginning of the story of the exodus from Egypt in Exod 1:1), he states: "All these beginnings speak of eternity inasmuch as a certain fidelity is found rooted in them."[29] Therefore, in the context of our passage, we

---

27 Ricoeur, *Time and Narrative* 3:265.
28 Ricoeur, *Time and Narrative* 3:265.
29 Ricoeur, *Time and Narrative* 3:265.

should now investigate whether the idea of fidelity is contained also in Gen 21:1-21.

I would like to argue that the pericope under discussion expresses God's fidelity in many ways. Yet, in order to see this clearly, the reader must read Gen 21:1-21 within the context of the whole Abraham cycle (Gen 12:1 (or even 11:27) – 25:18). First and foremost, the pericope under discussion begins with the clear statement: "The Lord visited Sarah according to what he had said, and he did to Sarah as he had promised" (v. 1). God is faithful to his own promise given in Gen 17:16: "I will bless her [i.e. Sarah], and moreover I will give you a son by her; I will bless her, and she shall be a mother of nations; kings of peoples shall come from her." Similarly, in Gen 18:10 we read: "The Lord said, 'I will surely return to you in the spring, and Sarah your wife shall have a son.' And Sarah was listening at the tent door behind him." God is also faithful to Sarah's husband Abraham: "This happened at the appointed time promised to Abraham by God" (v. 2b). Again, a flashback to earlier events recorded in Gen 17 and 18 explains the narrator's words. Moreover, the theme of God's faithfulness to Isaac is also briefly introduced in the story: "Grant Sarah whatever she asks you, since it is through Isaac that your descendants will be named" (v. 12b). These words are a reiteration of the promise given already in Gen 17:19: "Sarah your wife shall bear you a son, and you shall call his name Isaac. I will establish my covenant with him as an everlasting covenant for his descendants after him." In addition, the climax and the resolution of the story concern directly God's fidelity to Hagar and Ishmael. God's promise is stated twice in vv. 13 and 18, and, even if we have to wait until Gen 25:12-18 to read about its fulfilment, the events recorded in Gen 21:19-21 give us a foretaste of God's faithfulness.

The presence of the theme of God's fidelity is even more obvious when we read the pericope under discussion within the framework of the whole Pentateuch. Ricoeur rightly states that "any exegesis of Exodus 3:14 must take into account the declaration that follows it."[30] Accordingly, in Exod 3:15 we read: "Say this to the people of Israel, 'The Lord, the God of your fathers, the God of Abraham, the God of Isaac, and the God of Jacob, has sent me to you': this is my name for ever, and thus I am to be remembered throughout all generations." The Abraham cycle, whose integral part is Gen 21:1-21, introduces the idea of the God of Abraham and the God of Isaac. Then the same idea is revealed to Moses during the encounter at the burning bush. Moses learns that

---

30 Ricoeur, *Time and Narrative* 3:333 n. 30.

God, whose name is אהיה אשר אהיה, is the faithful God of his ancestors. Finally, in the last chapter of Deuteronomy, God again speaks to Moses: "This is the land of which I swore to Abraham, to Isaac, and to Jacob, 'I will give it to your descendants'" (34:4a). God's fidelity, revealed in the Abraham cycle, and confirmed in the story of the Exodus, is now reinforced on Mount Nebo. And, according to Ricoeur, inasmuch as these texts express God's faithfulness, they approximate eternity understood as perpetuity and time without end.

Thirdly, after having said that eternity is approximated by fidelity in the Pentateuch, Ricoeur briefly remarks on two other loci of eternity: in hymnic and wisdom literature (by which Ricoeur understands principally the Psalms), as well as in the sayings of Qoheleth. The former opposes "the eternity of God to the transitory character of human life," whilst the latter "sees human life as dominated by ineluctable times ... and by an unending return of the same events."[31] Ricoeur then summarizes the discussion: "This variety of tonalities agrees with an essentially nonspeculative, nonphilosophical mode of thinking, for which eternity transcends history from within history."[32] He gives an example of how this process of transcendence is mediated in the Hebrew Bible, and says: "The unpronounceable name of JHWH designates the vanishing point common to the suprahistorical and the intrahistorical. Accompanied by the prohibition against graven images, this 'name' preserves the inscrutable and sets it at a distance from its own historical figures."[33]

To put it another way and to apply to our pericope, every time we encounter in the narrative the unpronounceable divine name, we move from the intrahistorical dimension (human time) to the suprahistorical dimension (עולם as the time equal to the existence of God). What is more, the divine name יהוה helps us clearly distinguish between the impenetrable essence of God, which cannot be comprehended by the reader, and a particular literary incarnation of God, which plays its role on the narrative stage together with human characters. This is how we should understand the above Ricoeurian remark: "this 'name' preserves the inscrutable and sets it at a distance from its own historical figures." Apart from that, Ricoeur calls the divine name the "vanishing point common to the suprahistorical and the intrahistorical" because it refers to the reality which, although it can be spoken of, is not accessi-

---

31 Ricoeur, *Time and Narrative* 3:266.
32 Ricoeur, *Time and Narrative* 3:266.
33 Ricoeur, *Time and Narrative* 3:333 n. 31.

ble to the human mind. By way of illustration, in Gen 21:1-21, we encounter the divine name once, at the very beginning of the discourse: ויהוה פקד את־שרה (v. 1). This is precisely the moment when readers face the inscrutable. The Lord, who dwells in the divine עולם, visits Sarah, whose existence is confined to the human "here and now." This divine visitation constitutes a descending movement portrayed at the outset of the narrative. Readers, however, are invited to perform a reverse intellectual movement. They should mentally transcend the temporal circumstances, which they share with Sarah, and proceed in the direction of the divine and eternal עולם.

To carry forward the discussion, I must now change the main vantage point which I have adopted for my analyses. So far, I have been trying to demonstrate how the ancient reader, through the mediation of Gen 21:1-21, could approximate the concept of eternity understood as עולם. From now on, I shall change the perspective, and discuss the same problem from the point of view of the modern reader. To do this, I shall propose a definition of eternity tailored to the needs and mentality of the modern reader. The two thinkers whose definition I would like to adopt are Augustine and Karl Barth. It is fortunate that Augustine's meditation on time and eternity in his *Confessions* is the starting point for Ricoeur's discussion in *Time and Narrative*.[34] Similarly, Barth, who discusses the eternity and glory of God in his *Church Dogmatics*, is another important author for Ricoeur. Even if some scholars strongly deny the Barthian character of Ricoeur's hermeneutical project, they cannot reject the simple fact that Ricoeur himself confesses his dependence on Barth.[35]

Augustine states that the idea of eternity can be assigned to God only: "Lord, eternity is yours, so you cannot be ignorant of what I tell you. Your vision of occurrences in time is not temporally conditioned."[36] According to Augustine, the distinctive feature of eternity is that, in contrast to time, it does not include either the past or the future: "Take the two tenses, past and future. How can they 'be' when the past is not now present and the future is not yet present? Yet if the present were always present, it would not pass into the past: it would not be time but eternity."[37] Hence, for Augustine, eternity means "timeless

---

34 S. H. Clark's *Paul Ricoeur* is a good and critical introduction to *Time and Narrative*, and, indeed, to the whole philosophical output of Ricoeur.
35 The best-known opponent of the idea of Ricoeur's intellectual affinity with Barth is Hans Frei (see Vanhoozer, *Biblical Narrative*, 148-89).
36 Augustine, *Conf.* XI. i (1) (transl. Chadwick, 221).
37 Augustine, *Conf.* XI. xiv (17) (transl. Chadwick, 231).

present." Genevieve Lloyd rightly observes that Augustine echoes here the views of Plotinus found in *Enneads*: "So eternity, in contrast to time, involves stable existence, neither in process of change nor having changed – 'pure being in eternal actuality.' Here there is no future, for every then is a now. Nor is there any past, for nothing here has ever ceased to be."[38]

Even this quick look at Augustine's views shows a fundamental difference between his concept of eternity and the Hebraic one. Eternity, as conceived by Augustine, is non-temporal and par excellence stable, whereas עולם, even in its most refined meaning, is entirely temporal and ever-changing (the idea of perpetuity emphasizes the ever-changeability of eternity). However, a common feature of eternity to be found in both systems of thought is the emphasis on divinity: according to Augustine, only God is eternal; for ancient Israelites, עולם also refers either to God's existence or his attributes and actions.

According to Barth, eternity is God's attribute and a "quality of His freedom."[39] At the very beginning of his exposition, Barth discloses the theological sources of his doctrine: The Old and New Testaments, Augustine, Anselm of Canterbury, Polanus, Boethius, and Aquinas.[40] Barth subsequently defines eternity in contrast with time: "Time is distinguished from eternity by the fact that in it beginning, middle and end are distinct and even opposed as past, present and future. ... Eternity has and is the duration which is lacking to time. It has and is simultaneity. Eternity is not, then, an infinite extension of time both backwards and forwards."[41] This definition shows that Barth, like Augustine, sets eternity in contrast to time, and, in this respect, departs radically from the Hebrew notion of eternity. However, through his exposition, he qualifies this statement and says that "it is a poor and short-sighted view to understand God's eternity only from the standpoint that it is the negation of time."[42] Thus, Barth introduces the notion of the negative and positive quality of eternity. The former is its non-temporality; the latter is its duration, which has beginning, succession, and end. "That [God's eternity] is duration without separation between beginning, succession and end," says Barth, "is true only against the background of the decisive and positive characteristic that as true duration, the duration of God Himself is *the* beginning, succession and

---

38   Lloyd, "Augustine," 58.
39   Barth, *Church Dogmatics*, 608.
40   See Barth, *Church Dogmatics*, 608-40.
41   Barth, *Church Dogmatics*, 608.
42   Barth, *Church Dogmatics*, 610.

end."⁴³ Therefore, Barth explains that God's eternity comprises the past, the present, and the future; yet, these three realities are simultaneous and irreversible.

To clarify the Barthian views on eternity, I should quote another statement from *Church Dogmatics*:

> Eternity does not lack absolutely what we know as present, as before and after, and therefore as time. Rather this has its ultimate and real being in the *simul* of eternity. Eternity simply lacks the fleeting nature of the present, the separation between before and after. ... Eternity is the negation of time only because and to the extent that it is first and foremost God's time and therefore real time.⁴⁴

As Barth himself concedes, his concept of eternity lacks the Augustinian emphasis on the contrast between time and eternity, but it much better tallies with biblical language and imagery.⁴⁵ In my view, we may regard the Barthian definition of eternity as an attempt to adjust the meaning of עולם to the prevailing ideas of modern theology moulded by twenty centuries of reflection. Concurrently, his definition appears very well balanced, owing to its binary structure: Barth does not deny differences between human time and divine eternity (negative quality), yet, at the same time, he underlines the fact that time is rooted in eternity, and that there is a deep analogy between the divine and human realms.

Interestingly enough, Vanhoozer points to a link between the Barthian notion of eternity and Ricoeurian narrative theory: "Thanks to the configurative dimension of narrative, temporality need not be limited to chronology. The configurative dimension makes a whole out of a beginning, middle and end; as in Barth's understanding of eternity, there is both simultaneity and ordered succession."⁴⁶ In the final part of this subchapter, I shall then investigate how the narrative under discussion approximates the notion of eternity understood in terms of Barthian theology. I shall do this in two steps: first, I would like to discuss the topic of the refiguration of monumental time; secondly, I will introduce the concept of the limits of narrative.

---

43 Barth, *Church Dogmatics*, 610.
44 Barth, *Church Dogmatics*, 613.
45 See Barth, *Church Dogmatics*, 610. The whole Barthian discussion concerning eternity and time is very extensive and beyond the scope of this book. Barth discusses the concept of eternity in the light of Trinitarian theology, and introduces the ideas of *pre-temporality, supra-temporality,* and *post-temporality* of eternity (see *Church Dogmatics*, 615-40).
46 Vanhoozer, *Biblical Narrative*, 212.

In the second volume of *Time and Narrative*,[47] Ricoeur examines the fictive experience of time, by which he understands the "temporal aspect of this virtual experience of being-in-the-world proposed by the text."[48] To put his highly abstract considerations into practice, he sets to work on three novels: *Mrs Dalloway* by Virginia Woolf, *The Magic Mountain* by Thomas Mann, and *Remembrance of Things Past* by Marcel Proust. Ricoeur justifies his choice in the following words:

> Each of the three works under consideration, freeing itself in this way [of imaginative variations] from the most linear aspects of time, can, in return, explore the hierarchical levels that form the depth of temporal experience. Fictional narrative thus detects temporalities that are more or less extended, offering in each instance a different figure of recollection, of eternity in or out of time, and, I will add, of the secret relation between eternity and death.[49]

As regards the first novel, whose narrated time is only one day, it tells the story of Clarissa Dalloway, an upper-class woman who is to give a party that evening, and young Septimus Warren Smith who commits suicide on the very same day in the afternoon. The two characters show two different ways of responding to what Ricoeur calls monumental time, symbolized in the novel by the striking of bells and clocks. About Septimus's experience of time Ricoeur writes: "Septimus's worldview expresses the agony of a soul for whom monumental time is unbearable."[50] In turn, Clarissa responds to monumental time in a way totally different from the young Septimus's: "What maintains her fragile equilibrium between mortal time and the time of resolution in the face of death … is her love of life, of perishable beauty, of changing light, her passion for 'the falling drop.'"[51]

Vanhoozer suggests that we may read Virginia Woolf's novel as an example showing how "meaningful human experience … becomes possible only by taming the intimidating and awful reality of cosmic time with a different temporal orientation."[52] We learn from the novel that Septimus turns out to be helpless in the face of cosmic, monumen-

---

47   Rhiannon Goldthorpe rightly summarizes the starting point of *Time and Narrative*: "Fiction may be capable of resolving the aporias of time which … have effectively resisted the solutions offered by philosophical speculation. … Our most fundamental mode of resolving them is through the poetic, rather than theoretical, mediation of narrative" ("Ricoeur," 85).
48   Ricoeur, *Time and Narrative* 2:100.
49   Ricoeur, *Time and Narrative* 2:101.
50   Ricoeur, *Time and Narrative* 2:109-10.
51   Ricoeur, *Time and Narrative* 2:110.
52   Vanhoozer, *Biblical Narrative*, 190.

tal time. Clarissa, by contrast, "humanizes" time, and notices the beauty of its fleeting moments. She succeeds in finding meaning in the apparently meaningless flow of monumental time. What is more, in the context of Barth's concept of eternity, Clarissa can be regarded as somebody who "makes a meaningful whole out of a beginning, middle and end of monumental time; as in Barth's understanding of eternity."[53] Through the refiguration of monumental time, she makes it meaningful human time, and, in consequence, she prefigures the experience of eternity.

I will argue that we may say the same about the characters of Gen 21:1-21. To demonstrate how monumental time faced by Abraham and Sarah is reflected in the story, we again must take into account its broad literary context. Owing to the conciseness and the non-abstract character of Hebrew narratives, monumental time is depicted either by the narrative's imagery, or by describing an impact that it has on the characters' lives. To the best of my knowledge, Ricoeur does not clearly define *monumental time*. We may, however, understand this concept as the objective flow of time reflecting the invariable and absolute laws of nature governing the universe.

In Gen 15, God makes a covenant with Abraham, and both before and during the rite of the covenant Abraham faces a number of natural phenomena, such as the starry sky (v. 5), the sun setting (v. 12), darkness (vv. 12, 17), fire and smoke (v. 17). Abraham's reaction is rendered: "a dread and great darkness fell upon him" (v. 12). We may interpret his fear as a response in the face of Yahweh's theophany, manifested through natural signs. These signs symbolize a reality upon which a human being has no influence. A person standing in the presence of the starry sky, the setting sun, darkness, and fire experiences the transience of his or her life, which is only an episode within the flow of cosmic and monumental time. The confrontation between ephemeral human time and overwhelming cosmic time in this narrative is additionally emphasized by God's oracle in vv. 5b, 16, and 18b. Abraham learns that his descendants will be as numberless as stars in the sky, that they will come back to the promised land only in the fourth generation, and that the whole region, "from the river of Egypt to the great river," will be theirs. The scope of this promise is far beyond the limits of one human life, it extends into furthest generations, and, in consequence, reminds Abraham about his transience in the face of history governed by humanly uncontrollable processes. Moreover, both Abraham and Sarah

---

53   Cf. Vanhoozer, *Biblical Narrative*, 212.

experience the inevitability of death which comes as a last mournful chord of their childless lives. The laughter of Abraham in Gen 17:17, and of Sarah in Gen 18:12, may be interpreted as the laughter of old people who have become disillusioned with life and discovered the futility of its mesmeric promises. Nothing new or unexpected can any longer happen because the clock of monumental time is about to strike the very last hour.

Similarly, Hagar and her child must face a sinister monumental time when they are expelled to the wilderness of Beersheba in Gen 21:14-16. Surprisingly, the monumental time in these verses is not measured in years or generations but in hours. Every passing hour, corresponding to the sun moving up or down in the sky, is an evil omen of approaching death. The inescapability of monumental time, which portends the imminent catastrophe, is additionally strengthened by the narrative's imagery: the wilderness (v. 14), water in the skin running out (v. 15), Hagar's hopeless abandonment of her child (v. 15), and her final outburst of despair (v. 16). She is powerless to stop the cruel clock striking the hours of monumental time. As in the case of Abraham and Sarah, the very last hour seems to be nigh.

At the same time, in the story of Gen 21:1-21, the intimidating reality of monumental time is tamed by a different temporal orientation.[54] In the case of Abraham and Sarah, the refiguration begins in vv. 1-2 (Sarah conceives and gives birth to a son), whereas Hagar and Ishmael experience the refiguration only in vv. 17-18. In both cases, and unlike in Mrs Dalloway, the monumental time perceived by the characters is transformed by God's initiative and action.[55] God makes human perception of time meaningful. Abraham's and Sarah's time is "humanized" because the long-awaited promise is finally fulfilled. In turn, Hagar is also saved from the danger of meaningless death, and is freely given new meaning to life: to establish a new home for her son and his future wife (v. 21). In consequence, we may say that God "makes a meaningful whole out of a beginning, middle and end of the character's monumental time."[56] His unfathomable eternity is projected onto the character's lives, and in this way the approximation of eternity in the narrative is finally achieved. Furthermore, to use a Ricoeurian phrase, the reader learns from the narrative about a "secret relation

---

54 Cf. Vanhoozer, *Biblical Narrative*, 190.
55 We may say that, in a way, the whole Bible is a story about God's continuous action aiming at the refiguration of meaningless *monumental time* through a different temporal orientation leading towards the horizon of *eternity*.
56 Cf. Vanhoozer, *Biblical Narrative*, 212.

between eternity and death."[57] Even if in the case of the narrative's characters, the reality of physical death is not overcome, they experience the refiguration of monumental time, which is a temporal reflection of divine eternity or, in Barthian terms, God's real time.

Secondly, Ricoeur clearly states: "The Hebrew Bible can be read as the testament about time in its relations to divine eternity."[58] The fact that the Bible is a testament about time and eternity, apart from the sense just presented in the preceding paragraphs, results also from what Ricoeur calls "limit-experiences of narrative."[59] Here Ricoeur climbs the heights of his philosophical analysis. According to him, every narrative, owing to its temporal characteristics, is restricted by two kinds of limits: internal and external. Ricoeur explains: "By an internal limit, we mean that the art of narration exceeds itself to the point of exhaustion, in attempting to draw near the inscrutable. By an external limit, we mean that the narrative genre itself overflows into other genres of discourse that, in their own ways, undertake to speak of time."[60]

When we apply the concept of internal limits to the narrative under discussion, we see that the very fact that the narrative speaks indirectly about eternity creates its limits: "Fiction multiplies our experiences of eternity in these kinds of ways, thereby bringing narrative in different ways to its own limits."[61] When narrative reaches its final temporal point, and approximates the notion of eternity, it cannot go any farther. Nothing more can be achieved because of the impassable barrier between human temporality and divine eternity. Time reaches its own horizon, its own "limiting idea."[62] Hence, even if the narrative under discussion does not speak directly of eternity, the idea of eternity is deeply rooted therein: it is the ultimate horizon of temporality. As regards the approximation of eternity in the narrative, we may argue that some other possibilities of exploring time and eternity hypothetically exist. We cannot, however, expect that the narrative will lead us towards eternity farther than it really does. When it approximates the concept of eternity, it "exhausts itself." It suddenly dies out, dazzled by the brilliant flash of the eternal.

---

57 See Ricoeur, *Time and Narrative* 2:101.
58 Ricoeur, *Time and Narrative* 3:272.
59 See Ricoeur, *Time and Narrative* 1:22-23, 3:270-71.
60 Ricoeur, *Time and Narrative* 3:270-71.
61 Ricoeur, *Time and Narrative* 3:271.
62 See Ricoeur, *Time and Narrative* 2:22-23.

As regards the external limits of the narrative, they point to other possible ways of nonnarrative literary communication, which speak of eternity according to their own limitations. For Ricoeur, this is one of the reasons for which the Hebrew Bible comprises other genres. Thus, in order to understand fully the biblical message, we need the nonnarrative texts of the Law, as well as the poetic passages of the Prophets and wisdom literature.[63] "Narrative is not the only way of speaking about time's relation to its other [i.e. eternity]," states Ricoeur. "Whatever the scope of narrative contained therein, it is always in conjunction with other genres that narrative functions in the Hebrew Bible."[64]

I have now reached the point where I can summarize my considerations. The analysis of Gen 21:1-21 from the point of view of the ancient reader and the Hebrew concept of eternity has resulted in the conclusion that the narrative positively approximates the concept of eternity. This is achieved through the symbolic development of time in the story, through the underlying concept of fidelity, as well as through the presence of the divine name in the text. Similarly, the modern reader whose notion of eternity is based upon Barthian theology is also able to discover the concept of eternity: as the result of the refiguration of meaningless monumental time, and owing to the internal limits of narrative. Although the ancient reader, for obvious reasons, could not participate in the reading available to his or her modern counterpart, the latter can share the experience of the former. Since the Barthian concept of eternity in its positive aspect corresponds to the Hebrew concept of eternity, the ways to explore the symbolic development, the concept of fidelity, and the significance of the divine name are open before the modern reader. Moreover, the whole discussion in this subchapter has not given a purely conceptual answer to the problem of time and eternity. Vanhoozer is right when he declares that "Ricoeur believes that narratives offer a poetic rather than conceptual response to the relation of time and eternity. Narrative tales about time can imaginatively 'approximate' eternity thanks to their configurative dimension that aims at a time 'deeper' than chronology. Indeed, it is precisely in the 'depths' that 'eternity' is to be found."[65]

Going back to the question of the redemption of time signalled at the beginning of this subchapter, I may say that, surprisingly enough,

---

63 See Ricoeur, *Time and Narrative* 3:334 n. 37.
64 Ricoeur, *Time and Narrative* 3:272.
65 Vanhoozer, *Biblical Narrative*, 209.

Eliot's poetic imagination provides us with ways of thinking which are parallel to those presented here. The question of the redemption of time can be finally taken up again. Eliot says in the fifth part of "Little Gidding" that time is redeemed when we discover hidden meaning present in our lives yet coming from "outside." Donoghue comments: "Our words are not the Logos, but if we resist our self-engrossing fancies and try to apprehend 'the meaning' … instead of imposing our own, then 'every phrase and every sentence is an end and a beginning.'"[66] This is exactly the way of solving the problem which I have introduced here: through the symbolic development of time, the idea of fidelity, and the mediation of the divine name, I have arrived at the modern understanding of eternity. Subsequently, I have demonstrated that both the internal limits of narrative and the refiguration of time which narrative offers approximate the concept of eternity. If we do not reduce temporality to sheer chronology, we are able to discover the meaning offered by narrative, which transforms meaningless monumental time into meaningful human time. In consequence, time becomes redeemed for us, and we find out that "What we call the beginning is often the end / And to make an end is to make a beginning."[67] This experience is of profound existential value, and has the power to refigure our lives according to fresh and original guidelines. Perhaps this experience corresponds to what Eliot describes in the five last lines of "Four Quartets": "And all shall be well and / All manner of thing shall be well / When the tongues of flames are in-folded / Into the crowned knot of fire / And the fire and the rose are one."[68]

---

66   Donoghue, *Words Alone*, 244.
67   Eliot, "Four Quartets," 221. This interpretation of "Four Quartets" seems to be confirmed in the light of Murray's following remark: "The real contemplative task and the vocation, therefore, of the saint, is not to transcend or to escape from the horror and the burden of 'time past and time future,' but rather 'to apprehend the point of intersection of the Timeless with time' – a task which cannot be fulfilled without the assistance of divine grace" (Murray, *T. S. Eliot and Mysticism*, 260).
68   Eliot, "Four Quartets," 223.

7. The General Hermeneutical Model: Corollaries

In this final chapter, it is my intention to summarize the whole argument, but I intend to do it from a point of view which has not yet come to the fore. Reading literary works can give us a multifaceted knowledge about reality. It may reveal before our eyes previously unnoticed existential truths, surprising aspects of beauty, and a constant interplay taking place between good and evil. In view of that, the first task to approach in this chapter will be to show that reading biblical narratives can be a lifelong existential experience leading the reader to enlightenment. Since the exegesis of the model pericope Gen 21:1-21 has been governed by a tripartite distinction between the reader's literary interests, I had to use in my discussion of the biblical text a number of various exegetical approaches. What is more, each of those approaches has been rooted in different types of critical theory. For this reason, and secondly, I would now like to spell them out, and ask in what way they are interrelated. Are they at odds with each other, or do they have a common denominator and form a conceptual unity? Given the variety of approaches in modern exegesis, what should be the most profitable way of unravelling the mysteries of the biblical text whenever its readers peruse the pages of Scripture?

7.1. The Horizon of the Reader's Knowledge

The nature of the hermeneutical model introduced and expounded in chapters 3, 4, 5, and 6 is three-dimensional. First, there is a diversity of concepts characteristic of each of the textual dimensions; secondly, those concepts are interrelated; thirdly, the reading process always has a temporal nature. By way of example, the source of our aesthetic delight concerning the pericope under discussion is provided by a dynamic interaction between the human objectives, archetypal ideas present in the narrative, and the overriding purpose of God, who leads the whole universe to final transformation and fulfilment. Moreover, the concepts constituting the three dimensions are linked to each other. One of the archetypal ideas contributing to the beauty of the passage is family strife and affliction. A similar idea is discovered within the cognitive dimension of this narrative, when the reader learns that the human characters of the story are inclined to secure their happiness at the expense of other people. In like manner, the characterization of the personages of the narrative, which is another feature contributing to its aesthetic dimension, plays a crucial role in establishing its practical dimension, and becomes important in the analysis of the narrative through the prism of the Aristotelian categories of *anagnorisis*, *peripeteia*, *hamartia*, and *pathos*.

What is interesting, however, and has not yet been discussed at length, is that the process of reading based on the analysis of the three textual dimensions is of a temporal nature. First, when the reader attentively peruses the text, its different dimensions become gradually apparent. The surprising and incomprehensible divine intervention in vv. 12-13 finds its explanation only in the final part of the narrative, where the reader learns that God saved Hagar and her son from cruel death, and, subsequently, bestowed on them his blessing. This was not obvious either at the beginning or in the middle of the story; hence, the reader needs time to explore the whole dynamics of the narrative system. Secondly, the complexity and ultimate meaning of the narrative are brought to light when the reader finishes reading and starts ruminating upon the story. In consequence, the reader may decide to read the narrative again in order to explore its complexity further, and to arrive at a higher level of understanding. It may happen that even after many years the reader notices some previously ignored details of biblical narratives, and becomes conscious of meanings overlooked earlier. To take a typical case, it is easy to pass over the remark of the biblical author in Gen 21:21 saying that "his mother took a wife for him from the land of Egypt." This seemingly unimportant information becomes significant only later, when the reader learns about other examples of the relationships between biblical characters and Egyptians: Joseph marries an Egyptian noblewoman, and has two sons, Ephraim and Manasseh, with her (Gen 41:50-52); similarly, Solomon marries Pharaoh's daughter (1 Kgs 3:1). With the benefit of hindsight, the reader may realize that Ishmael's marriage was a harbinger of a later kinship and alliance between prominent Israelites and Egyptians. Thirdly, as the reader becomes more mature and experienced, his or her immanent knowledge, which stands for the horizon of the reader's knowledge about actuality, also changes and develops, and, as a result, directly affects the process of reading. A reader who knows the taste of suffering and abandonment, or who has even experienced a scorching day in the wilderness of Beersheba, will read the narrative more deeply than a novice who has not yet learnt much about the vicissitudes of human life. Accordingly, in the case of the experienced reader, the whole interaction between actuality, quasi-reality, and trans-reality will be a more dynamic and fruitful process.

In view of that, as the reader makes progress in reading Scripture in the three ways mentioned above, his or her knowledge about reality grows continually, and encompasses new ideas. In other words, the reader's cognitive horizon progressively embraces previously unexplored dimensions of reality, and proceeds from the state of limited awareness of the nature of reality to the full although finite state of comprehending that reality. In consequence, we may speak of the expanding horizon of the reader's knowledge about reality. I understand *reality* as the sum total of everything that exists. Hence, from a theological perspective, reality comprises God and all his creatures. Certainly, the entire reality is not accessible to the human mind, and the reader, in a given moment, is able to comprehend only a little fragment of it. However, as Balthasar rightly points out, "there are no neutral points or surfaces" in the relationship between "the world as it concretely exists" and "the God of grace and supernatural revelation," because "the supernatural takes root in the deepest structures of being ... and permeates them like a breath or an omnipresent fragrance."[1] This is why reality encompasses both the supernatural and the natural, and is represented in my hermeneutical model by natural actuality and quasi-reality, on the one hand, and supernatural trans-reality, on the other. In turn, the three horizons of the reader's knowledge, immanent, narrative, and transcendental, belong, at the beginning, to the natural order, and are subsequently permeated by the divine and supernatural light of revelation.

Furthermore, the nature of the reading process can be explained in terms borrowed from St John's Gospel and the works of Gregory of Nazianzus, one of the Cappadocian Fathers. The Gospel says: "In [the Word] was life, and the life was the light of men. The light shines in the darkness, and the darkness has not overcome it. ... The true light that enlightens every man was coming into the world" (John 1:4-5, 9).[2] Hence the whole reality, with its constituent parts, as well as the three horizons of the reader's knowledge become saturated by God's eternal and divine light, which is identical with his nature. In this context, the words of the Christmas preface, which form a basis for Balthasar's the-

---

1 Balthasar, *Truth of the World*, 11-12.
2 The Gospel of John abounds with the symbolism of light. See e.g. John 3:19-21, 8:12, 11:9-10, 12:35-36.

ological project in *Herrlichkeit*, become very significant: "*Quia per incarnati Verbi mysterium nova mentis nostrae oculis lux tuae claritatis infulsit: ut dum visibiliter Deum cognoscimus, per hunc in invisibilium amorem rapiamur.*"³ The reader perceives God's light shining in the scriptural quasi-reality, and is transported to trans-reality, where that light radiates with its full power. Thus the expanding horizon of the reader's knowledge about reality brings, in consequence, his or her enlightenment. Through the mediation of the biblical sacred text, the reader becomes more open to the divine light, and although, at the beginning, the sphere of knowledge about reality is limited and tenebrous, it becomes luminous, effulgent, and full of divine light as this process of reading and understanding comes to its fulfilment. A link with Gregory of Nazianzus's thought becomes clear in this context. "Salvation comes primarily through enlightenment," writes Anthony Meredith, "and it is, therefore, no surprise to find that 'light' is the characteristic term Gregory uses for referring to God. ... Evil, then, is darkness; God is light; and in the centre of Gregory's thinking lies a basic soteriological concern ... [which] expresses itself in terms of enlightenment."⁴ As Gregory himself speaks in *Oration* 2.7:

> For nothing seemed to me so desirable as to close the doors of my senses, and ... to live superior to visible things, ever preserving in myself the divine impressions pure and unmixed with the erring tokens of this lower world, and both being, and constantly growing more and more to be, a real unspotted mirror of God and divine things, *as light is added to light, and what was still dark grew clearer* [my emphasis], enjoying already by hope the blessings of the world to come.⁵

Thus Gregory's existential experience is parallel to the experience of the reader of Scripture. Reading the Bible combined with the understanding of its mediatory role may be a part of the reader's spiritual growth and salvific movement towards the Creator.

7.2. The Diversity and Unity of Critical Approaches

How should we classify different approaches within literary and biblical criticism? An excellent answer to this question has been given by Abrams in *The Mirror and the Lamp*.⁶ Abrams organizes his model

---

3   Balthasar, *Seeing the Form*, 119-20.
4   Meredith, *The Cappadocians*, 43.
5   Schaff and Wace, *A Select Library* 7:206.
6   See Abrams, *The Mirror and the Lamp*, 3-29.

around four main coordinates: *work, artist, universe,* and *audience*.⁷ In consequence, he distinguishes four groups of critical theories: *mimetic* (the work of art is analysed *principally* with reference to the *universe*), *pragmatic* (with reference to the *audience*), *expressive* (with reference to the *artist*), and *objective* (the work of art is analysed as it is, without recourse to any external points of reference).⁸ Barton, in *Reading the Old Testament*, uses Abram's model and replaces its coordinates with terms characteristic of biblical criticism. Thus we have: *text; author or authors, or community; historical events or theological ideas;* and *reader*.⁹ As a result, we get a convenient model that helps explain the main features of biblical critical theories: the historical-critical method, the canonical approach, structuralism, post-structuralism, and all their varieties.¹⁰ First, Barton notices that the main criterion for distinguishing between diverse approaches is the question: "What are their proponents reading the Old Testament … *as*"?¹¹ Secondly, another crucial comment is: "Biblical 'methods' are *theories* rather than methods: theories which result from the formalizing of intelligent intuitions about the meaning of biblical texts. … Instead of asking which method is 'right,' we might ask what is really going on in the reader when he is using each of them, what kind of reading they belong to."¹²

If we apply these two observations to the four main types of criticism, we have the following list of questions. Within the mimetic group of theories we may ask: What can we *directly* learn from the Hebrew Bible as regards the history of Israel and the theology of the pre-Christian era of revelation? Pragmatic theories are supposed to ask: Can we understand the biblical text better if we analyse the influence and effect that the text exerts on the reader? In turn, expressive theories ask: What features of the text help us discover the history of the text's development and the milieu in which its author operated? Lastly, within the circle of objective theories we may ask: What are the formal structures of the text and how do these structures influence the text's meaning? Thus to explain the biblical text fully means to use all four approaches, and their sundry varieties, or at least to be aware of them in the process of reading. I shall now show in what way those approaches have been used in the exegesis of Gen 21:1-21 presented in chapter 5.

---

7   See Abrams, *The Mirror and the Lamp*, 6.
8   See Abrams, *The Mirror and the Lamp*, 8-29.
9   See Barton, *Reading the Old Testament*, 240.
10 See Barton, *Reading the Old Testament*, 240-42.
11 Barton, *Reading the Old Testament*, 238.
12 Barton, *Reading the Old Testament*, 244, 46.

For all practical purposes, we may equate the mimetic reading of the pericope with what we call *pre-critical reading* in view of Abrams's comment: "the mimetic orientation – the explanation of art as essentially an imitation of aspects of the universe – was probably the most primitive aesthetic theory."[13] In this model of approaching the text, we are interested in the historical events and ideas which the text conveys, but we do not bother to ask any critical questions. We assume that the story is a faithful imitation of what happened to Abraham, Sara, Hagar, and their children in a remote period of Israelite history. The historical events happened exactly or almost exactly as they are told in the story. When Sarah uttered her joyful *Magnificat* in vv. 6-7, her words were quickly remembered and passed on to later generations. There is, however, a problem concerning Ishmael. From chapter 17 we learn that when Abraham was 99 years old, Ishmael was 13 years old (Gen 17:24-25). Therefore, in our story, Ishmael should be more than 14 years old (see 21:5). If we want to be faithful to our theory of reading, we must assume that Ishmael must have suffered from malnutrition if his mother was able to carry him and even to throw him under a bush (vv. 14-15). As we know, source criticism, which is non-mimetic and belongs to critical reading, solves this problem in the twinkling of an eye by positing two different sources for the pericopes under discussion. Nevertheless, although I do not use mimetic approaches in this book, I do not want to create the impression that they should be underestimated or even neglected. The majority of exegetical commentaries written before the seventeenth century reflect the mimetic approach to the text. It is true that "most Christian exegesis viewed the Bible as … a report of events that were independent of their cultural and historical milieux."[14] Yet only a completely ignorant person would devalue biblical commentaries by Jerome or Origen, even if their authors do not apply the rules of higher criticism to the texts upon which they comment.

"This way of thinking," writes Abrams, "in which the artist himself becomes the major element generating both the artistic product and the criteria by which it is to be judged, I shall call the expressive theory of art."[15] The historical-critical method results from the application of this theory to the biblical field. Regardless of the diverse and minute problems which we often discuss in historical criticism, we always put em-

---

13   Abrams, *The Mirror and the Lamp*, 8. Abrams reminds us, however, that although the most primitive aesthetic theories were based on imitation, mimesis itself cannot be regarded as a simple concept (p. 8).
14   Suelzer and Kselman, "Modern Old Testament Criticism," *NJBC*, 1114.
15   Abrams, *The Mirror and the Lamp*, 22.

phasis on the original meaning of the text and its socio-historical milieu. To establish them, we use various critical tools provided by textual criticism, source criticism, genre criticism, tradition criticism, and redaction criticism. Hence the historical-critical method has been used in chapter 2 to fix the original text of the pericope under discussion and discuss its literary sources. Then, in chapter 5, with the aid of genre and redaction criticism, I have discussed the oral stage of the pericope's formation, its meaning, and the socio-historical setting for its fist reception in written form. As the result of the application of these expressive approaches, I have been able to establish the cognitive dimension of the pericope from the point of view of its original reader.

The objective approach analyses text as it is, with a minimal recourse to any external points of reference. It looks at the text, as Abrams puts it, "as a self-sufficient entity constituted by its parts in their internal relations, and sets out to judge it solely by criteria intrinsic to its own mode of being."[16] A classical example of this reading strategy in general literary theory is structuralism and narrative analysis. To present the cognitive significance of Gen 21:1-21, I have used tools characteristic of modern narratology, namely the diegetic and mimetic modes of representation, which are of structuralist provenance. Another objective type of approach, from which I have greatly profited, has been the approach through philosophical aesthetics, which focuses on such features of the text as the presence of ideas which are of importance for human life, its use of language, the treatment of plot, the representation of characters, and the overall unity of the text. Similarly, theological aesthetics has been based on the concepts of glory, image, and grace, and on the various meanings communicated by those three concepts within the narrative world of the text. What is more, the first step leading to establishing the practical dimension of the pericope was also objective in character. My purpose was to elucidate the reader's interest in goodness, and to do this, I have used the Aristotelian terms *anagnorisis*, *peripeteia*, *pathos*, and *hamartia*.

Finally, in my discussion of the reader's narrative knowledge, there have been two instances when I have benefited from the pragmatic type of literary theories. Abrams comments: "the central tendency of the pragmatic critic is to conceive a poem as something made in order to effect requisite responses in its readers; ... to ground the classification and anatomy of poems in large parts on the special effects each

---

16 Abrams, *The Mirror and the Lamp*, 26.

kind and component is most competent to achieve."[17] Hence, to show the presence of irony in Gen 21:1-21, which influences its cognitive significance, I have used rhetorical criticism, an approach which lies halfway between objective and pragmatic theories. I have observed that rhetorical criticism very clearly emphasizes the role of the reader in discovering ironic meanings. In turn, within the discussion of the practical dimension, I have introduced W. Iser's concept of *gaps*, which, even more than in the case of rhetorical criticism, stresses the active role of the reader in the reading process, and the necessity of filling the gaps in narration with the reader's projections.

Are the above four groups of critical theories sufficient to cover the whole map of modern biblical criticism? Where is the place for the approaches which emphasize the mediatory role of the text such as the hermeneutical model proposed in this book, inspired by Ricoeurian hermeneutics? It appears that none of the four critical models applies to those approaches which speak of the self-understanding of the reader, and in which "fiction opens new possibilities of being-in-the-world within everyday reality." Therefore, in order to find a place for such approaches, we should look again at Ricoeurian hermeneutics, which is paradigmatic for all critical theories underlining the role of the creative reading of the text.

Thiselton is right when he outlines Ricoeur's hermeneutical project: "What remains central for Ricoeur is the double function of hermeneutics: the hermeneutics of suspicion which unmasks human wish-fulfilments and shatters idols, and the hermeneutics of retrieval which listens to symbols and to symbolic narrative discourse."[18] As stated by Ricoeur, the hermeneutics of suspicion is reductive in character, and among the classical modern representatives of this approach to interpretation we find Freud, Marx, and Nietzsche, the three well-known masters of suspicion. The hermeneutics of retrieval is restorative, and it is the style of interpretation practised by Ricoeur himself, who pays attention to the symbolic dimension of the text.[19] In addition, the hermeneutics of suspicion is characterized by the conviction that "language can distort rather than reveal the world,"[20] whilst in the hermeneutics of retrieval "the interpreter applies explanatory techniques to a text in

---

17 Abrams, *The Mirror and the Lamp*, 15.
18 Thiselton, *New Horizons in Hermeneutics*, 372.
19 Cf. Dornisch, "Symbolic Systems," 6.
20 Vanhoozer, *Biblical Narrative*, 109.

order to pass from a surface interpretation to a depth interpretation, from a first to a second naiveté."[21]

I believe that we may successfully apply the "suspicion-retrieval" key to the area of biblical interpretation. By and large, the pre-critical stage in biblical interpretation, characteristic of early Christian exegesis, may be called a first naiveté – the biblical text is accepted as such, the principle of mimesis is applied uncritically to the text, and the text plays the role of a mirror reflecting the truth about the world. The historical-critical method, which tries to distil from the text its original meaning, and to reconstruct the stages of the text's development, is, to a considerable extent, an example of the hermeneutics of suspicion, because it seeks the truth hidden under the illusory surface of the text.[22] So called "literary methods" of analysis, and their preoccupation with the text conceived as a self-contained system, or with the reader's response to the text, may be partially placed within the category of the hermeneutics of retrieval. However, according to Ricoeur, only the discovery of the symbolic meaning of the biblical text, based upon a new and transformed concept of mimesis understood as "the creative imitation of reality,"[23] allows us to cultivate a really imaginative kind of biblical exegesis.[24]

As a result, when we consider the four groups of theories in Abram's model and Ricoeur's hermeneutical approach, we make an *interpretive circle*, moving from the *pre-critical stage* (a relation to the *world*), through the *critical stage* (a relation to the *author*, the *text*, and the *reader*), to the *post-critical stage* (a relation to the *world*).[25] Yet the post-critical

---

21 Vanhoozer, *Biblical Narrative*, 166.
22 See Dornisch, "Symbolic Systems," 7.
23 Vanhoozer, *Biblical Narrative*, 10.
24 The move from the pre-critical stage in interpretation to the hermeneutics of suspicion, and the postulate to apply the hermeneutics of retrieval to biblical narratives, parallel Frei's ideas expressed in *The Eclipse of Biblical Narrative*. As Boyle summarizes: "Frei argues that an instinctive understanding of the Bible ... as 'realistic narrative' was eclipsed in the course of the eighteenth century and replaced by a view of these texts as (reliable or very unreliable) documentary evidence for historical propositions" (Boyle, *Sacred and Secular Scriptures*, 59). We cannot reduce biblical narratives to their informational content, but we should take into account their "narrativity" (see Barton, *Reading the Old Testament*, 163).
25 I must stress here that the nature of this interpretive circle is *logical* rather than *chronological*. I believe that at the past pre-critical stage in biblical interpretation, we had examples of approaches characteristic of the modern critical stage. Similarly, there are modern examples of biblical exegesis which are pre-critical and naive. Barton rightly states: "This makes me wary of the expression 'precritical,' and I have proposed that biblical study should be distinguished as 'critical' or 'noncritical,' avoid-

stage is founded upon a new kind of *creative mimesis*. Furthermore, the *world* to which we return is not equal to the point of our departure, but it is rather a *metamorphized reality,* or the *world projected by the text,* or, in the case of my model, *trans-reality.* The general approach to interpretation characteristic of the post-critical stage may be called a *second naiveté.*[26]

To summarize the discussion in this chapter, I should say that the general hermeneutical model which I have proposed here meets four basic conditions. First, it is *pluralistic.* It allows the use of various approaches belonging to different groups of critical theories, and, in consequence, broadens the spectrum of possible questions which we may ask, and satisfies the diverse interests which we as readers always pursue. None of the approaches is totally sufficient when it comes to the analysis of a literary text, and the more of them we use in our critical praxis, the closer we get to the full elucidation of the text's richness.[27] Secondly, before we decide to use a particular approach in biblical exegesis, we should examine its *assumptions, limitations, and its general suitability* for dealing with the ancient text of the Bible. There are many critical approaches which can be safely and profitably used in exegesis, such as the historical-critical method or narrative theory, as long as we are aware of their own methodological limitations. In contrast, there are critical theories which are better tailored to modern literature than to biblical narratives, such as Iser's theory of gaps, but even those theories may, under certain conditions, be used to highlight a particular aspect or feature of the biblical text. Thirdly, in this book, I have been trying to show the *mutual interrelationship and complementarity* of critical approaches. None of them operates in a critical vacuum, and, although the conclusions at which they arrive belong to different levels of analysis, they help us understand the complexity of biblical literature because they approach the same text from different angles. Fourthly, and

---

ing the chronological emphasis of the common terminology" (*The Nature of Biblical Criticism*, 189). In view of this I might render the above three categories as: *noncritical, critical,* and *creative.*

26 See Dornisch, "Symbolic Systems," 7. Barton rightly observes that, for Ricoeur, the post-critical move to a *second naiveté* does not mean rejecting the critical stage, but using a critical approach to the text as the source of new possibilities of being-in-the-world (see Barton, *The Nature of Biblical Criticism*, 182-183).

27 It is true, as Thiselton points out, that *pluralism* can become authoritarian if practised in an ideological way (*New Horizons in Hermeneutics*, 612). Susan Gillingham is then right in saying that the "Bible cannot be constrained by any one system of reading. ... The [biblical] texts will always be something of a mystery; and herein lies the challenge of biblical studies as an academic discipline" (*One Bible, Many Voices*, 247).

finally, I believe that in order to avoid methodological clashes between different approaches, we should always use them within a *broader hermeneutical model*, which orders them and clearly shows their advantages and limitations for the specific critical tasks we want them to perform. Such a model provides a common denominator for our critical efforts, and shows the basic unity of various methods of interpretation.

I can only cherish the hope that the general hermeneutical model presented here belongs to a type of biblical interpretation which is consciously counter-reductionist and inter-disciplinary, and which encourages the reader to undertake a creative dialogue with other fields of the humanities. Such a style of practising biblical interpretation resembles an intellectual game, or, I might say, the *Glass Bead Game*. I am evoking here the leitmotif of Hesse's novel because it corresponds in an interesting way with the subject under discussion. In the opening chapter of *Magister Ludi*, Hesse describes the principles of the Game:

> The Glass Bead Game is thus a mode of playing with the total contents and values of our culture; it plays with them as, say, in the great age of the arts a painter might have played with the colors on his palette. ... All that subsequent periods of scholarly study have reduced to concepts and converted into intellectual property – on all this immense body of intellectual values the Glass Bead Game player plays like the organist on an organ.[28]

In this kind of Game, we can play with theological ideas, as Hesse himself states: "one of the principles of the Creed, a *passage from the Bible* [my emphasis], a phrase from one of the Church Fathers, or from the Latin text of the Mass could be expressed and taken into the Game just as easily and aptly as an axiom of geometry or a melody of Mozart."[29] For this very reason, every kind of biblical interpretation which is open to other fields of the humanities, including philosophy, theology, literature, and cultural anthropology, deserves the comparison to the Glass Bead Game. In addition, in this Game, we put special emphasis on seeking an interrelationship between diverse scholarly areas rather than on a simple juxtaposition of ideas belonging to different academic fields. Again, the analogy between a counter-reductionist, inter-disciplinary variety of biblical interpretation and the Glass Bead Game is very striking. Hesse describes a meeting between the Master of the Game Joseph Knecht and a Benedictine monk Father Jacobus. The two talk about Johann Albrecht Bengel, a German theologian, and the founder of eighteenth century Pietism. In the context of their conversa-

---

28 Hesse, *Magister Ludi*, 6.
29 Hesse, *Magister Ludi*, 31.

tion, Knecht says: "What Bengel meant was not just a juxtaposition of the fields of knowledge and research, but an interrelationship, an organic denominator. And that is one of the basic ideas of the Glass Bead Game."[30] Hence the Glass Bead Game, a "symbol of the human imagination," and an "act of mental synthesis through which the spiritual values of all ages are perceived as simultaneously present and vitally alive,"[31] can be played profitably by an exegete equipped with diverse approaches of biblical criticism. However, whether the goal of the Game, which is enlightenment and cheerful serenity, will finally be achieved depends only on the skills and creative work of the player himself.

---

30 Hesse, *Magister Ludi*, 149.
31 Ziolkowski, "Foreword," ix.

Conclusion

At the end of a long journey, it is always good to look back at what we have traversed. In the same way, I have now reached the point where I can summarize the argument presented in this book, and draw wider conclusions concerning the interpretation of biblical narratives. Hence, in chapter 1, I established that Scripture can be called *literature* in the strict sense of the term because it meets the following four criteria: it is significant to its readers in a way not restricted only by its content; it conveys information, but also effectuates *catharsis*, and provides entertainment; it demands constant reinterpretation; and, finally, it exhibits aesthetic features. Next, I moved on to the discussion of the features of biblical narratives, and I showed that the most important of them is the ability of those narratives to point to a transcendent reality, or, in other words, their *revelatory function*. This observation allowed me to specify *the nature of biblical hermeneutics*. First, biblical hermeneutics is a subtype of the general hermeneutics of literary texts, and, in consequence, in biblical interpretation, we can make use of the same approaches which we employ in the interpretation of general literature. Secondly, biblical hermeneutics must account for the revelatory character of Scripture, and this is why "secular" approaches should be modified in such a way that the transcendental feature of biblical narratives can be taken into account. In the last section of the first chapter, I discussed *the nature of biblical criticism*, and, following T. S. Eliot, I emphasized that criticism is an "instinctive activity of the civilized mind,"[1] and that it cannot be separated from "moral, religious or social judgments."[2] Then I introduced the requirements which *good critics* should meet: they ought to be objective, and should use two basic critical tools, which are comparison and analysis.

Equipped with these fundamental distinctions, in chapter 2, I established the *critical text* and the *translation* of the pericope Gen 21:1-21, which I adopted as my model text. I paid special attention to v. 9 of the pericope, and I arrived at the conclusion that it should be translated in

---

1 Eliot, "To Criticize the Critic," 19.
2 Eliot, "To Criticize the Critic," 25.

a way which does not impute any evil intentions to Ishmael. Then, using the tools of *synchronic narrative analysis*, I divided the pericope into three scenes: vv. 1-8, 9-13, and 14-21. I also noticed that *diachronic source criticism* is in favour of a different delimitation, and it suggests that v. 8 should begin a new unit. This discrepancy was briefly discussed, and I indicated that on the level of synchronic analysis, which is normally the first level accessible to the modern reader, such literary features as the plot and the unity of time, place, and characters are more important for the narrative's integrity than its historical sources. Nevertheless, the diachronic analysis should also be attempted, and both levels, synchronic and diachronic, should be embraced.

In chapter 3, I organized my argument under six headings. Thus, first, I presented Booth's treatment of *literary interests*, and then, secondly, I showed that the application of Booth's theory to scriptural narratives results in distinguishing their *three basic dimensions*: *cognitive*, *aesthetic*, and *practical*. I posited the concept of *the full theological dimension of the text*, which comprises the three basic dimensions. Thirdly, I defined the *meaning* of the text as its *intentio operis*, which is discovered by the reader in the conjectural and circular process of interaction between a model reader and a model author, and which respects the linguistic and cultural background of its creation. When that original background is replaced by a different context, we arrive at the text's *significance*. Next, when I linked the concept of the three textual dimensions with meaning and significance, I came to the conclusion that the full theological dimension of biblical narratives comprises three types of meaning and three types of significance (in both cases: cognitive, aesthetic, and practical). However, owing to the historical distance between the ancient and the modern reader, and given that, in our critical praxis, we should arrive at conclusions which have a satisfactory degree of probability, I decided to focus on four components of the full theological dimension: (cognitive) *meaning, cognitive significance, aesthetic significance*, and *practical significance*. Fourthly, and importantly, I put forward the most important tenets of Ricoeurian hermeneutics, and pointed out that his idea of *revelation* and *the world of the text* satisfy the need for a biblical hermeneutics which gives account for a revelatory character of Scripture. Following the path trodden by Ricoeur, and fifthly, I introduced and defined three pairs of terms which help to explain the mediative function of Scripture. Hence I defined *actuality* as the real world of human beings and of animate and inanimate objects, and the horizon of the reader's knowledge about actuality I called *immanent knowledge*. In turn, by *quasi-reality* I understood the conventional and finite narrative world in which readers participate through reading narrative texts, whereas its epistemological counterpart I labelled *narrative knowledge*. I also established that, in the process of reading, the three textual dimensions become the intrinsic components of narrative knowledge. Then, I defined *trans-reality* as the transcendent sphere which readers discover through the mediation of biblical narratives, and *transcendental knowledge* as the horizon of reader's knowledge about trans-reality. Finally, and sixthly, I briefly discussed a number of philosophical issues underlying my hermeneutical model. Hence I established that the Platonic triad of truth, beauty, and goodness is *communicated* by the text rather than present therein. Next, I claimed that truth, beauty, and goodness can be called both *universals* and *transcendentals*; that they exist *independently* of the mind, and *in rebus*; and that, ultimately, they exist in God's mind. I also debated the *ontological status* of actuality, quasi-reality, and trans-reality. As regards the first sphere of reality, I adopted the viewpoint of metaphysical *realism*. Then I introduced the concept of *fiction* and *fictional worlds*, and I demonstrated that, from the viewpoint of the modern reader, the patriarchal narratives can be read as fiction. What is more, I showed that, from an ontological perspective, the quasi-reality of Gen 21:2-1 comprises fictional characters living in a fictional world, and those characters and that world *do not exist*. Then, as regards trans-reality, I adopted *classical theism* as my philosophical stance.

Since the reader's *immanent knowledge* is shaped by the intellectual trends of contemporary culture, and since many of those trends were discussed in other parts of the book, in chapter 4, I introduced and assessed *postmodernism* and *deconstruction*. In my evaluation of postmodern biblical criticism, I pointed out some of its advantages, such as its ability to teach us more about the nature of language, text, and the process of reading, but I also mentioned certain problems inherent in postmodern critical praxis. I made a claim that if a postmodern theory of reading is practised uncritically, it leads to excessive subjectivism, a self-contradictory logic, and the annihilation of rational discourse. However, I also stated that we should be open to certain insights coming from postmodern criticism as long as they do not undermine the foundations of the hermeneutical model which I proposed.

The theoretical assumptions introduced in chapters 1 and 3 were put into exegetical practice in chapter 5. Therefore, and first, to establish the *cognitive significance* of Gen 21:1-21, I used the narratological concepts of the *diegetic* and *mimetic mode of representation* (borrowed from Genette), and the rhetorical concept of *irony* (borrowed from Booth). The conclusion at which I arrived can be summed up in the following words: from the narrative under discussion, we learn about

God who fulfils his mysterious plans, and is ready to support those who are in trouble; we also learn about the human characters who often want to achieve their happiness at the expense of other people, but whose negative actions are thwarted by God's power; finally, we are invited to decode God's ironic message, and to enjoy the hidden levels of significance in the story. Next, using the tools of the historical-critical method, I established the narrative's *genre, original context*, and *meaning*. Hence I proved that the original readers and listeners of the narrative learnt about God's faithfulness manifested in the fulfilment of the promise given to Abraham, as well as of God's providential care which averts death and secures the future. In its original context, the narrative also encouraged its audience to restore the traditions of pre-exilic Israel, and to trust the promises given to Abraham.

Secondly, to demonstrate the *aesthetic significance* of the pericope, I looked at it from two different angles: that of *literary aesthetics*, and that of *theological aesthetics*. As regards the first angle, after having established the *nature of aesthetic interest* following Kant, I applied the criteria for assessing literary aesthetics suggested by Meynell to the model pericope. This led me to the conclusion that Gen 21:1-21 illustrates a number of archetypal ideas which are of central importance for human life. Moreover, it has a well-constructed structure, plot, and characters, and its language is characterized by artistic merits. The beauty of the narrative is also discovered when the reader observes an interplay between the objectives of the human characters, the archetypal ideas, and the overriding and ordering purpose of God. Next, I moved on to theological aesthetics, and I showed in what way the Balthasarian categories of *glory, image*, and *grace* become manifest in the pericope. God shows his glory by revealing his divinity to Abraham and Sarah by word and action. Each of the human personages of the story represents God's image, which is limited in four different ways. God's grace becomes obvious when he bends down to his creation, and invites them to participate in his divine purposes.

Thirdly, I established the *practical significance* of the narrative in two steps. The Aristotelian categories of *anagnorisis, peripeteia*, and *pathos*, which constitute the plot of tragedy, were observed in Gen 21:1-21, and their presence and function helped to explain the emotional tension present in the story, and the reader's response to it. What is more, I also showed that the narrative brings about the *catharsis* of the reader's emotions, which is effectuated by the narrative's *pathos*. The discussion of the practical significance would not be complete without having a look at *reader-response criticism*. This is why I put forward Iser's concept of *gaps*, and I analysed two important gaps present in the narrative.

These are precisely the moments of the plot when the reader is invited to participate in the story, and to fill the gaps with projections. I then rounded off the discussion with an evaluation of Iser's theory. I showed that Iser places the emphasis on the active role played by the reader, and clearly helps to explain the practical dimension of the biblical text. Nevertheless, biblical exegetes cannot accept all the elements of his theory because Iser overestimates the role of gaps in interpretation, and does not distinguish clearly between the meaning and a particular reading of the text.

Each of the three subdivisions of chapter 5 were followed by a short section aimed at summarizing the conclusions concerning the cognitive, aesthetic, and practical dimensions of the pericope under discussion, and the role played by truth, beauty, and goodness in interpretation. Therefore, in chapter 6, I further developed this topic. First, I demonstrated that the *Platonic triad* communicated by biblical narratives leads the reader to the divine sphere, and facilitates *the emergence of transcendental knowledge*. Since this happens on many different levels, even those readers whose philosophical stance is not theistic or realistic can benefit from reading biblical narratives, and can gain transcendental knowledge. Secondly, I explained in what way Gen 21:1-21, but also other ancient Hebrew narratives, approximate the concept of *eternity*. The ancient Hebrew reader was able to discover the concept of eternity through the symbolic development of time in the narrative, through the idea of fidelity, and the presence of the divine name in the text. Likewise, the modern reader can have the same experience through the refiguration of meaningless monumental time, and owing to the internal limits of narrative. In consequence, the mediatory role played by biblical narratives is unquestionable: they invite the reader to leave his or her actuality, and to focus on the divine trans-reality.

Lastly, in chapter 7, I emphasized that the process of reading biblical narratives is a *lifelong experience*. I showed that active reading may potentially lead the reader from the state of limited awareness of the nature of reality to the full although finite state of comprehending that reality. In addition, and from a theological perspective, I showed that reading Scripture which is accompanied by the understanding of its mediatory role can become an important part of the reader's spiritual growth and salvific movement towards God.

In this book, I have assessed and applied a number of interpretive approaches, and so the discussion of their interrelationship has been crucial to my project. Thus I have demonstrated that the Ricoeurian double function of hermeneutics, which consists of the hermeneutics of *suspicion* and the hermeneutics of *retrieval*, provides a useful tool to organize the existing approaches, and to show how they proceed from the pre-critical to the post-critical phase of development, or, to put it better, from the noncritical to the creative mode of interpretation. I have also stated that the hermeneutical model proposed here meets four important conditions: it is pluralistic; it uses various approaches in a critical way, and allows for their assessment in the light of their suitability for scriptural exegesis; it shows the interrelationship and the complementarity of the approaches used in biblical interpretation; and it provides a broad interpretive framework which orders the approaches, and prevents methodological clashes.

Going back to one of the fundamental questions underlying this whole work, I should ask again: can we still profit from reading biblical narratives, or, like some other great literary works, do they already belong to the passé world of antiquarian documents? It is my strong conviction that we not only can still benefit from those narratives, but that by not doing so, we deprive ourselves of a privileged medium of communication between our temporal actuality and the eternal world of trans-reality. However, when we follow the path of truth, beauty, and goodness, we may discover far-off lands of which we now only have an inkling. That path is accessible to believers and non-believers alike, and to all who can read Scripture with an open and unprejudiced mind. And, perhaps, in those far-away lands, we will meet that part of ourselves which we often seek to little avail in our temporal reality.

Bibliography

Abbott, H. Porter. *The Cambridge Introduction to Narrative*. Cambridge: Cambridge University Press, 2002.
Abrams, M. H. "The Deconstructive Angel." Pages 242-53 in *Modern Criticism and Theory: A Reader*. Edited by David Lodge and Nigel Wood. Harlow: Longman, 2000.
---. *The Mirror and the Lamp: Romantic Theory and the Critical Tradition*. New York: W. W. Norton, 1958.
Ackroyd, Peter. *T. S. Eliot*. London: Hamish Hamilton, 1984.
Aichele, George, and Bible and Culture Collective, eds. *The Postmodern Bible*. New Haven: Yale University Press, 1995.
Alter, Robert. *The Art of Biblical Narrative*. London: George Allen & Unwin, 1981.
---. *Genesis: Translation and Commentary*. New York: Norton, 1996.
---. *The World of Biblical Literature*. London: SPCK, 1992.
---, and Frank Kermode, eds. *The Literary Guide to the Bible*. London: Fontana Press, 1987.
Anderson, Janice Capel, and Stephen D. Moore. *Mark & Method: New Approaches in Biblical Studies*. Minneapolis: Fortress Press, 1992.
Aristotle. *The Poetics*. Translated by W. Hamilton Fyfe. Edited by E. Capps, T. E. Page, and W. H. D. Rouse. LCL 199. London: William Heinemann, 1927.
---. "Poetics." Pages 2316-40 in *The Complete Works of Aristotle: The Revised Oxford Translation*. Translated by I. Bywater. Edited by Jonathan Barnes. Vol. 2. Princeton: Princeton University Press, 1984.
---. *Poetics I, with the Tractatus Coislinianus, a Hypothetical Reconstruction of Poetics II, the Fragments of the On Poets*. Translated and edited by Richard Janko. HC. Indianapolis: Hackett, 1987.
---. *Poetics: A Translation and Commentary for Students of Literature*. Translated and edited by Leon Golden and O. B. Hardison, Jr. Englewood Cliffs: Prentice-Hall, 1968.
---. "Politics." Pages 1986-2129 in *The Complete Works of Aristotle: The Revised Oxford Translation*. Translated by B. Jowett. Edited by Jonathan Barnes. Vol. 2. Princeton: Princeton University Press, 1984.
Audi, Robert, ed. *The Cambridge Dictionary of Philosophy*. Cambridge: Cambridge University Press, 1995.
Auerbach, Eric. *Mimesis: The Representation of Reality in Western Literature*. Translated by Willard R. Trask. Princeton: Princeton University Press, 1953.
Augustine. *Confessions*. Translated by Henry Chadwick. Oxford: Oxford University Press, 1991.

Bacon, Francis. *The Philosophical Works*. Edited by John M. Robertson. London: Routledge, 1905.
Bal, Mieke. *Narratology: Introduction to the Theory of Narrative*. 2nd ed. Toronto: University of Toronto Press, 1997.
---. "The Predicament of Semiotics." *PT* 13.3 (1992): 543-52.
Balthasar, Hans Urs von. *The Dramatis Personae: The Person in Christ*. Translated by Graham Harrison. *Theo-Drama: Theological Dramatic Theory*. Vol. 3. San Francisco: Ignatius Press, 1992.
---. *Seeing the Form*. Translated by Erasmo Leiva-Merikakis. Edited by Joseph Fessio and John Riches. *The Glory of the Lord: A Theological Aesthetics*. Vol. 1. Edinburgh: T&T Clark, 1982.
---. *Theology: The Old Covenant*. Translated by Erasmo Leiva-Merikakis and Brian McNeil. Edited by John Riches. *The Glory of the Lord: A Theological Aesthetics*. Vol. 6. Edinburgh: T&T Clark, 1991.
---. *Truth of the World*. Translated by Adrian J. Walker. *Theo-Logic: Theological Logical Theory*. Vol. 1. San Francisco: Ignatius Press, 2000.
Bar-Efrat, Shimon. *Narrative Art in the Bible*. Translated by Dorothea Shefer-Vanson. Edited by David J. A. Clines and Philip R. Davies. JSOTSup 70. Sheffield: Almond Press, 1989.
Barnes, Jonathan. *Aristotle*. PM. Oxford: Oxford University Press, 1982.
---, ed. *The Complete Works of Aristotle: The Revised Oxford Translation*. 2 vols. BS 71, 2. Princeton: Princeton University Press, 1984.
---. "Rhetoric and Poetics." Pages 259-85 in *The Cambridge Companion to Aristotle*. Edited by Jonathan Barnes. Cambridge: Cambridge University Press, 1995.
---, Malcolm Schofield, and Richard Sorabji, eds. *Articles on Aristotle*. 4 vols. London: Duckworth, 1979.
Barr, James. *Biblical Words for Time*. SBT 33. London: SCM, 1962.
---. "Childs' Introduction to the Old Testament as Scripture." *JSOT* 16 (1980): 12-23.
---. *Holy Scripture: Canon, Authority, Criticism. The Sprunt Lectures Delivered at Union Theological Seminary, Richmond, Virginia, February 1982*. Oxford: Clarendon Press, 1983.
---. "Reading the Bible as Literature." *BJRL* 56.1 (1973): 10-33.
---. *The Scope and Authority of the Bible*. SCMC. London: SCM, 2002.
Barry, Peter. *Beginning Theory: An Introduction to Literary and Cultural Theory*. 2nd ed. Manchester: Manchester University Press, 2002.
Barth, Karl. *Church Dogmatics*. Edited by Geoffrey William Bromiley and Thomas Forsyth Torrance. Vol. 2.1. Edinburgh: T&T Clark, 1957.
Barthes, Roland. *Image, Music, Text*. Translated by Stephen Heath. London: Fontana, 1993.
Barton, John. "Beliebigkeit." Pages 301-03 in *Derrida's Bible: Reading a Page of Scripture with a Little Help from Derrida*. Edited by Yvonne Sherwood. New York: Palgrave Macmillan, 2004.
---. "Historical-Critical Approaches." Pages 9-20 in *The Cambridge Companion to Biblical Interpretation*. Edited by John Barton. Cambridge: Cambridge University Press, 1998.

---. "Introduction." Pages 1-6 in *The Cambridge Companion to Biblical Interpretation*. Edited by John Barton. Cambridge: Cambridge University Press, 1998.
---. "Introduction to the Old Testament." Pages 5-12 in *The Oxford Bible Commentary*. Edited by John Barton and John Muddiman. Oxford: Oxford University Press, 2001.
---. *The Nature of Biblical Criticism*. Louisville: Westminster John Knox Press, 2007.
---. "Reading the Bible as Literature: Two Questions for Biblical Critics." *JLT* 1.2 (1987): 135-53.
---. *Reading the Old Testament: Method in Biblical Study*. 2nd ed. London: Darton Longman & Todd, 1996.
---. "Source Criticism (OT)." Pages 162-65 in *The Anchor Bible Dictionary*. Edited by David Noel Freedman. Vol. 6. New York: Doubleday, 1992.
---, and John Muddiman, eds. *The Oxford Bible Commentary*. Oxford: Oxford University Press, 2001.
Bateson, F. W. "Criticism's Lost Leader." Pages 1-19 in *The Literary Criticism of T.S. Eliot: New Essays*. Edited by David Newton-De Molina. London: Athlone Press, 1977.
Baudrillard, Jean. "Simulacra and Simulations." Pages 404-12 in *Modern Criticism and Theory: A Reader*. Edited by David Lodge and Nigel Wood. Harlow: Longman, 2000.
Bealer, George. "Property." Pages 657-58 in *The Cambridge Dictionary of Philosophy*. Edited by Robert Audi. Cambridge: Cambridge University Press, 1995.
Berlin, Adele. "On the Bible as Literature." *Proof* 2.3 (1982): 323-27.
---. *Poetics and Interpretation of Biblical Narrative*. BLS 9. Sheffield: Almond Press, 1983.
Berlinerblau, Jacques. "What's Wrong with the Society of Biblical Literature?" No pages. Cited 18 Nov. 2006. Online: http://www.ultraviolet.co.uk/whats-wrong-with-the-society-of-biblical.html.
Bernays, Jacob. "Aristotle on the Effect of Tragedy." Pages 154-65 in *Articles on Aristotle: Psychology and Aesthetics*. Edited by Jonathan Barnes, Malcolm Schofield, and Richard Sorabji. Vol. 4. London: Duckworth, 1979.
Bigelow, John C. "Particulars." Pages 658-59 in *Concise Routledge Encyclopedia of Philosophy*. Edited by Edward Craig. London: Softback Preview, 2000.
Blackburn, Simon. *The Oxford Dictionary of Philosophy*. Oxford: Oxford University Press, 1994.
Bodine, Walter R., ed. *Discourse Analysis of Biblical Literature: What It Is and What It Offers*. SBLSS. Atlanta: Scholars Press, 1995.
Boland, Vivian. *Ideas in God According to Saint Thomas Aquinas: Sources and Synthesis*. SHCT 69. Leiden: Brill, 1996.
---, ed. *Watchmen Raise Their Voices: A Tallaght Book of Theology*. Dublin: Dominican Publications, 2006.
Booth, Wayne C. *The Company We Keep: An Ethics of Fiction*. Berkeley: University of California Press, 1988.
---. *The Rhetoric of Fiction*. 2nd ed. Chicago: Chicago University Press, 1983.
---. *A Rhetoric of Irony*. Chicago: Chicago University Press, 1974.

Botterweck, G. Johannes, and Helmer Ringgren, eds. *The Theological Dictionary of the Old Testament*. 15 vols. Grand Rapids: Eerdmans, 1977-2006.
Boyle, Nicholas. *Sacred and Secular Scriptures: A Catholic Approach to Literature*. Notre Dame: University of Notre Dame Press, 2005.
Brodie, Thomas L. *Genesis as Dialogue: A Literary, Historical, and Theological Commentary*. New York: Oxford University Press, 2001.
Brown, Francis, S. R. Driver, and Charles A. Briggs. *The Brown-Driver-Briggs Hebrew and English Lexicon: With an Appendix Containing the Biblical Aramaic*. Peabody: Hendrickson, 2005.
Brown, Raymond E., D. W. Johnson, and Kevin G. O'Connell. "Texts and Versions." Pages 1083-112 in *The New Jerome Biblical Commentary*. Edited by Raymond Edward Brown, Joseph A. Fitzmyer, and Roland Edmund Murphy. Englewood Cliffs: Prentice Hall, 1990.
Brueggemann, Walter. *Genesis*. IBC. Atlanta: John Knox Press, 1982.
Butchvarov, Panayot. "Metaphysical Realism." Pages 488-89 in *The Cambridge Dictionary of Philosophy*. Edited by Robert Audi. Cambridge: Cambridge University Press, 1995.

Carritt, E. F., ed. *Philosophies of Beauty from Socrates to Robert Bridges Being the Sources of Aesthetic Theory*. Oxford: Clarendon Press, 1931.
Carroll, Lewis. *The Annotated Alice: Alice's Adventures in Wonderland and through the Looking Glass, with an Introduction and Notes by Martin Gardner*. Revised ed. Harmondsworth: Penguin, 1970.
Chatman, Seymour Benjamin. *Story and Discourse: Narrative Structure in Fiction and Film*. Ithaca: Cornell University Press, 1978.
Childs, Brevard S. *Biblical Theology of the Old and New Testaments: Theological Reflection on the Christian Bible*. Minneapolis: Fortress Press, 1992.
---. *Introduction to the Old Testament as Scripture*. London: SCM, 1979.
---. "Response to the Reviewers of Introduction to the Old Testament as Scripture." *JSOT* 16 (1980): 52-60.
Clark, S. H. *Paul Ricoeur*. CTC. Edited by Christopher Norris. London: Routledge, 1990.
Clements, Ronald E., and G. Johannes Botterweck. "Gôy." Pages 426-33 in *The Theological Dictionary of the Old Testament*. Translated by John T. Willis. Edited by G. Johannes Botterweck and Helmer Ringgren. Vol. 2. Grand Rapids: Eerdmans, 1975.
Clines, David J. A. *The Theme of the Pentateuch*. 2nd ed. JSOTSup 10. Sheffield: Sheffield Academic Press, 2001.
Coats, George W. *Genesis, with an Introduction to Narrative Literature*. FOTL 1. Grand Rapids: Eerdmans, 1983.
Collins, John J. *The Bible after Babel: Historical Criticism in a Postmodern Age*. Grand Rapids: Eerdmans, 2005.
Cotter, David W. *Genesis*. BOS. Collegeville: Liturgical Press, 2003.
Craig, Edward, ed. *Concise Routledge Encyclopedia of Philosophy*. London: Softback Preview, 2000.
Crane, Ronald S. *The Languages of Criticism and the Structure of Poetry*. Toronto: University of Toronto Press, 1953.

Cuddon, J. A. *The Penguin Dictionary of Literary Terms and Literary Theory*. Revised by C. E. Preston. Harmondsworth: Penguin, 1999.
Culler, Jonathan. *On Deconstruction: Theory and Criticism after Structuralism*. London: Routledge & Kegan Paul, 1983.
Currie, Gregory. *The Nature of Fiction*. Cambridge: Cambridge University Press, 1990.

Dalman, Gustaf. *Aramäisch-Neuhebräisches Handwörterbuch*. Götingen: Eduard Pfeiffer, 1938.
Delitzsch, Franz. *A New Commentary on Genesis*. Translated by Sophia Taylor. 2 vols. CFTLN. Edinburgh: T&T Clark, 1889.
Derrida, Jacques. "Des tours de Babel." Pages 244-53 in *A Derrida Reader: Between the Blinds*. Edited by Peggy Kamuf. New York: Columbia University Press, 1991.
---. *Of Grammatology*. Translated by Gayatri Chakravorty Spivak. Baltimore: The Johns Hopkins University Press, 1976.
---. "Structure, Sign and Play in the Discourse of the Human Sciences." Pages 89-103 in *Modern Criticism and Theory: A Reader*. Edited by David Lodge and Nigel Wood. Harlow: Longman, 2000.
Detweiler, Robert. "What Is a Sacred Text?" *Semeia* 31 (1985): 213-30.
---, and Vernon K. Robbins. "From New Criticism to Poststructuralism: Twentieth-Century Hermeneutics." Pages 225-80 in *Reading the Text: Biblical Criticism and Literary Theory*. Edited by Stephen Prickett. Oxford: Blackwell, 1991.
Dickinson, Emily. "I Died for Beauty." Page 345 in *Anthology of American Poetry*. Edited by George Gesner. New York: Gramercy Books, 1983.
Donoghue, Denis. *Words Alone: The Poet T. S. Eliot*. New Haven: Yale University Press, 2000.
Dornisch, Loretta. "Symbolic Systems and the Interpretation of Scripture: An Introduction to the Work of Paul Ricoeur." *Semeia* 4 (1975): 1-19.
Doyle, Arthur Conan. *The Adventures of Sherlock Holmes*. London: The Folio Society, 1993.
Driver, S. R. *The Book of Genesis with Introduction and Notes*. WC. Edited by Walter Lock and D. C. Simpson. 14th ed. London: Methuen, 1943.
Duke, Paul D. *Irony in the Fourth Gospel*. Atlanta: John Knox, 1985.
Dumm, Demetrius. "Esther." Pages 576-79 in *The New Jerome Biblical Commentary*. Edited by Raymond Edward Brown, Joseph A. Fitzmyer, and Roland Edmund Murphy. Englewood Cliffs: Prentice Hall, 1990.

Eagleton, Terry. *Literary Theory: An Introduction*. 2nd ed. Oxford: Blackwell, 1996.
Eco, Umberto. *The Limits of Interpretation*. ASem. Bloomington: Indiana University Press, 1990.
---. *Six Walks in the Fictional Woods*. CENL 1993. Cambridge, Mass.: Harvard University Press, 1994.
---, Jonathan Culler, Richard Rorty, and Christine Brooke-Rose. *Interpretation and Overinterpretation*. Edited by Stefan Collini. Cambridge: Cambridge University Press, 1992.

Eissfeldt, Otto, ed. *Liber Genesis*. In *Biblia Hebraica Stuttgartensia*. Edited by Karl Elliger, Wilhelm Rudolph, Hans P. Rüger, and Adrian Schenker. Editio quinta emendata. Stuttgart: Deutsche Bibelgesellschaft, 1997.
---. *The Old Testament: An Introduction*. Translated by Peter R. Ackroyd. New York: Harper, 1965.
Eliot, T. S. "Four Quartets." Pages 189-223 in *Collected Poems 1909-1962*. London: Faber and Faber, 1963.
---. "The Function of Criticism." Pages 23-34 in *Selected Essays*. 3rd enlarged ed. London: Faber and Faber, 1999.
---. "Hamlet." Pages 141-46 in *Selected Essays*. 3rd enlarged ed. London: Faber and Faber, 1999.
---. "The Hollow Men." Pages 89-92 in *Collected Poems 1909-1962*. London: Faber and Faber, 1963.
---. "The Metaphysical Poets." Pages 281-91 in *Selected Essays*. 3rd enlarged ed. London: Faber and Faber, 1999.
---. "Religion and Literature." Pages 388-401 in *Selected Essays*. 3rd enlarged ed. London: Faber and Faber, 1999.
---. "To Criticize the Critic." Pages 11-26 in *To Criticize the Critic, and Other Writings*. London: Faber and Faber, 1988.
---. *The Varieties of Metaphysical Poetry: The Clark Lectures at Trinity College, Cambridge, 1926 and the Turnbull Lectures at the Johns Hopkins University, 1933*. Edited by Ronald Schuchard. London: Faber and Faber, 1993.
---. "What Dante Means to Me." Pages 125-35 in *To Criticize the Critic, and Other Writings*. London: Faber and Faber, 1988.
"The Epic of Gilgamesh." Pages 72-99, 503-07 in *Ancient Near Eastern Texts Relating to the Old Testament*. Edited by James B. Pritchard. 3rd ed. Princeton: Princeton University Press, 1969.
Elliger, Karl, Wilhelm Rudolph, Hans P. Rüger, and Adrian Schenker, eds. *Biblia Hebraica Stuttgartensia*. Editio quinta emendata. Stuttgart: Deutsche Bibelgesellschaft, 1997.
Epstein, Isidore, ed. *The Babylonian Talmud: A Translation and Commentary*. 35 vols. London: Soncino Press, 1935-1952.
Exum, J. Cheryl, and David J. A. Clines. *The New Literary Criticism and the Hebrew Bible*. JSOTSup 143. Sheffield: JSOT Press, 1993.

Fiddes, Paul. *Freedom and Limit: A Dialogue between Literature and Christian Doctrine*. Macon: Mercer University Press, 1999.
Fitzmyer, Joseph A., ed. *The Biblical Commission's Document "The Interpretation of the Bible in the Church": Text and Commentary*. SubBi 18. Roma: Pontificio Istituto Biblico, 1995.
Flew, Antony, and Stephen Priest. *A Dictionary of Philosophy*. London: Pan Books, 1979.
Fowler, Robert M. *Let the Reader Understand: Reader-Response Criticism and the Gospel of Mark*. Minneapolis: Fortress Press, 1991.
---. "Who Is the 'Reader' in Reader Response Criticism?" *Semeia* 31 (1985): 5-23.
Freedman, David Noel, ed. *The Anchor Bible Dictionary*. 6 vols. New York: Doubleday, 1992.

---, B. E. Willoughby, H. Ringgren, and H.-J. Fabry. "Mal'āk." Pages 308-25 in *The Theological Dictionary of the Old Testament*. Translated by Douglas W. Stott. Edited by G. Johannes Botterweck, and Helmer Ringgren. Vol. 8. Grand Rapids: Eerdmans, 1997.

Frei, Hans W. *The Eclipse of Biblical Narrative: A Study in Eighteenth and Nineteenth Century Hermeneutics*. New Haven: Yale University Press, 1974.

Frye, Northrop. *The Great Code: The Bible and Literature*. London: Routledge & Kegan Paul, 1982.

Gadamer, Hans-Georg. "The Eminent Text and Its Truth." Pages 337-67 in *The Horizon of Literature*. Edited by Paul Hernadi. Lincoln: University of Nebraska Press, 1982.

---. *Truth and Method*. London: Sheed & Ward, 1975.

Gall, August Freiherrn von, ed. *Der Hebräische Pentateuch der Samaritaner*. 5 vols. Giessen: Verlag von Alfred Töpelmann, 1914.

Gamble, Harry Y. "Canon: New Testament." Pages 852-61 in *The Anchor Bible Dictionary*. Edited by David Noel Freedman. Vol. 1. New York: Doubleday, 1992.

Gardner, Helen L. "Four Quartets: A Commentary." Pages 57-77 in *T. S. Eliot: A Study of His Writings by Several Hands*. Edited by B. Rajan. London: Dennis Dobson, 1966.

Gaut, Berys, and Dominic McIver Lopes, eds. *The Routledge Companion to Aesthetics*. 2nd ed. London: Routledge, 2005.

Genette, Gérard. *Narrative Discourse: An Essay in Method*. Translated by Jane E. Lewin. Ithaca: Cornell University Press, 1980.

---. *Narrative Discourse Revisited*. Translated by Jane E. Lewin. Ithaca: Cornell University Press, 1988.

---. "Structuralism and Literary Criticism." Pages 89-93 in *Twentieth-Century Literary Theory: A Reader*. Edited by K. M. Newton. 2nd ed. Basingstoke: Macmillan Press, 1997.

Gesenius, Wilhelm. *Gesenius' Hebrew Grammar*. Edited by E. Kautzsch. Translated by A. E. Cowley. 2nd ed. Oxford: Oxford Clarendon Press, 1910.

Gesner, George. *Anthology of American Poetry*. New York: Gramercy Books, 1983.

Gillingham, Susan E. *One Bible, Many Voices: Different Approaches to Biblical Studies*. London: SPCK, 1998.

Goldmann, Lucien. *Immanuel Kant*. Translated by Robert Black. London: NLB, 1971.

Goldthorpe, Rhiannon. "Ricoeur, Proust and the Aporias of Time." Pages 84-101 in *On Paul Ricoeur: Narrative and Interpretation*. Edited by David Wood. London: Routledge, 1991.

Good, Edwin M. *Irony in the Old Testament*. London: SPCK, 1965.

Gracia, Jorge. "Suárez (and Later Scholasticism)." Pages 452-71 in *Medieval Philosophy*. Edited by John Marenbon. Vol. 3. London: Routledge, 1998.

Gulley, Norman. "Aristotle on the Purposes of Literature." Pages 166-76 in *Articles on Aristotle: Psychology and Aesthetics*. Edited by Jonathan Barnes, Malcolm Schofield, and Richard Sorabji. Vol. 4. London: Duckworth, 1979.

Gunkel, Hermann. *Genesis: Translated and Interpreted*. Translated by Mark E. Biddle. MLBS. Macon: Mercer University Press, 1997.
---. *Genesis: übersetzt und erklärt*. GHAT. Göttingen: Vandenhoeck & Ruprecht, 1917.
Guyer, Paul, ed. *The Cambridge Companion to Kant*. Cambridge: Cambridge University Press, 1992.

Hamilton, Victor P. *The Book of Genesis: Chapters 18-50*. NICOT. Grand Rapids: Eerdmans, 1995.
Herbert, George. "Love." Pages 113-14 in *The Penguin Book of English Verse*. Edited by John Hayward. Harmondsworth: Penguin Books, 1956.
Hernadi, Paul, ed. *The Horizon of Literature*. Lincoln: University of Nebraska Press, 1982.
Hesse, Hermann. *Magister Ludi (The Glass Bead Game)*. Translated by Richard and Clara Winston. New York: Bantam Books, 1969.
---. *Steppenwolf*. Translated by Basil Creighton. PMC. Harmondsworth: Penguin Books, 1965.
Hiltunen, Ari. *Aristotle in Hollywood: The Anatomy of Successful Storytelling*. Bristol: Intellect Books, 2002.
Hirsch, E. D., Jr. *The Aims of Interpretation*. Chicago: University of Chicago Press, 1976.
---. *Validity in Interpretation*. New Haven: Yale University Press, 1967.
The Holy Bible: Revised Standard Version Containing the Old and New Testaments with the Apocrypha/Deuterocanonical Books. Expanded ed. New York: Collins, 1973.
Hospers, John, ed. *Introductory Readings in Aesthetics*. New York: Free Press, 1969.
Hynes, Samuel. "The Trials of a Christian Critic." Pages 64-88 in *The Literary Criticism of T.S. Eliot: New Essays*. Edited by David Newton-De Molina. London: Athlone Press, 1977.

Iser, Wolfgang. *The Act of Reading: A Theory of Aesthetic Response*. London: Routledge & Kegan Paul, 1978.
---. *The Implied Reader: Patterns of Communication in Prose Fiction from Bunyan to Beckett*. Baltimore: Johns Hopkins University Press, 1974.
---. "Interaction between Text and Reader." Pages 106-19 in *The Reader in the Text: Essays on Audience and Interpretation*. Edited by Susan R. Suleiman and Inge Crosman. Princeton: Princeton University Press, 1980.
---, Norman N. Holland, and Wayne C. Booth. "Interview: Wolfgang Iser." *Diacritics* 10.2 (1980): 57-74.

Jacobs, Louis. "Theology." Pages 1103-10 in *Encyclopaedia Judaica*. Vol. 15. Jerusalem: Encyclopaedia Judaica / Macmillan, 1972.
Jasper, David. "Literary Readings of the Bible." Pages 21-34 in *The Cambridge Companion to Biblical Interpretation*. Edited by John Barton. Cambridge: Cambridge University Press, 1998.
Josipovici, Gabriel. *The Book of God: A Response to the Bible*. New Haven: Yale University Press, 1988.

Joüon, Paul, and T. Muraoka. *A Grammar of Biblical Hebrew*. SubBi 14/1-2. Roma: Pontificio Istituto Biblico, 1991.

Kamuf, Peggy, ed. *A Derrida Reader: Between the Blinds*. New York: Columbia University Press, 1991.

Kant, Immanuel. *Critique of the Power of Judgment*. Translated by Paul Guyer and Eric Matthews. Edited by Paul Guyer and Allen W. Wood. CEWIK. Cambridge: Cambridge University Press, 2000.

Kelley, Page H., Daniel S. Mynatt, and Timothy G. Crawford. *The Masorah of Biblia Hebraica Stuttgartensia: Introduction and Annotated Glossary*. Grand Rapids: Eerdmans, 1998.

Kerr, Fergus. *Twentieth-Century Catholic Theologians*. Malden: Blackwell, 2007.

Kintgen, Eugene R. "Reconstructing Elizabethan Reading." *SEL* 30.1 (1990): 1-18.

Köhler, Ludwig, Walter Baumgartner, and J. J. Stamm. *The Hebrew and Aramaic Lexicon of the Old Testament*. Translated and edited by M. E. J. Richardson. 5 vols. Leiden: Brill, 1994-2000.

Kratz, Reinhard G. "The Growth of the Old Testament." Pages 459-88 in *The Oxford Handbook of Biblical Studies*. Edited by J. W. Rogerson and Judith M. Lieu. Oxford: Oxford University Press, 2006.

Kugel, James. "On the Bible and Literary Criticism." *Proof* 1.3 (1981): 217-36.

Leftow, Brian. "God, Concepts of." No pages. *Routledge Encyclopedia of Philosophy*. Edited by E. Craig. Cited 2 Nov. 2006. Online: http://www.rep.routledge.com/article/K030SECT6.

Lewis, C. S. *Reflections on the Psalms*. Glasgow: Collins, 1961.

---. *Surprised by Joy: The Shape of My Early Life*. New York: Harcourt Brace, 1955.

Lloyd, Genevieve. "Augustine and the 'Problem' of Time." Pages 39-60 in *The Augustinian Tradition*. Edited by Gareth B. Matthews. Berkeley: University of California Press, 1999.

Lodge, David, and Nigel Wood, eds. *Modern Criticism and Theory: A Reader*. 2nd ed. Harlow: Longman, 2000.

Longacre, Robert E. *The Grammar of Discourse*. New York: Plenum, 1996.

Lubbock, Percy. *The Craft of Fiction*. London: J. Cape, 1928.

Lucas, F. L. *Tragedy: Serious Drama in Relation to Aristotle's Poetics*. London: The Hogarth Press, 1961.

MacDonald, Scott. "Transcendentals." Pages 809-10 in *The Cambridge Dictionary of Philosophy*. Edited by Robert Audi. Cambridge: Cambridge University Press, 1995.

Magnus, Bernd. "Postmodern." Pages 634-35 in *The Cambridge Dictionary of Philosophy*. Edited by Robert Audi. Cambridge: Cambridge University Press, 1995.

Mann, Thomas. *The Magic Mountain*. Translated by John E. Woods. EL. New York: Alfred A. Knopf, 2005.

Matthews, Gareth B., ed. *The Augustinian Tradition*. PTr 8. Berkeley: University of California Press, 1999.

McKnight, Edgar V. *The Bible and the Reader: An Introduction to Literary Criticism*. Philadelphia: Fortress Press, 1985.
Megillah. In *The Babylonian Talmud: Seder Moed*. Translated by Maurice Simon. Edited by I. Epstein. Vol. 4. London: Soncino Press, 1938.
Meredith, Anthony. *The Cappadocians*. OCTh. London: Geoffrey Chapman, 1995.
Meynell, Hugo A. *The Nature of Aesthetic Value*. London: Macmillan, 1986.
Migne, Jacques-Paul, ed. *Patrologia Latina*. Paris, 1844-1855, 1862-1865.
Mlakuzhyil, George. *The Christocentric Literary Structure of the Fourth Gospel*. AnBib 117. Rome: Pontificio Istituto Biblico, 1987.
Moore, Carey A. "Esther." Pages 633-43 in *The Anchor Bible Dictionary*. Edited by David Noel Freedman. Vol. 2. New York: Doubleday, 1992.
Mudge, Lewis S. "Paul Ricoeur on Biblical Interpretation." Pages 1-40 in *Essays on Biblical Interpretation*. Edited by Lewis S. Mudge. Philadelphia: Fortress Press, 1980.
Murphy, Francesca Aran. *Christ the Form of Beauty: A Study in Theology and Literature*. Edinburgh: T&T Clark, 1995.
Murphy, Roland E. "Introduction to the Pentateuch." Pages 3-7 in *The New Jerome Biblical Commentary*. Edited by Raymond Edward Brown, Joseph A. Fitzmyer, and Roland Edmund Murphy. Englewood Cliffs: Prentice Hall, 1990.
Murray, Paul. *T. S. Eliot and Mysticism: The Secret History of Four Quartets*. Basingstoke: Macmillan, 1991.

Narratology Revisited. In *PT* 11.2, 4 (1990).
New Revised Standard Version: Catholic Edition. London: DLT, 2005.
Newsom, Carol A. "Angels: Old Testament." Pages 248-53 in *The Anchor Bible Dictionary*. Edited by David Noel Freedman. Vol. 1. New York: Doubleday, 1992.
Newton, K. M., ed. *Twentieth-Century Literary Theory: A Reader*. 2nd ed. Basingstoke: Macmillan Press, 1997.
Newton-De Molina, David, ed. *The Literary Criticism of T.S. Eliot: New Essays*. London: Athlone Press, 1977.
Nichols, Aidan. *Say It Is Pentecost: A Guide through Balthasar's Logic*. IHUB. Edinburgh: T&T Clark, 2001.
---. *The Word Has Been Abroad: A Guide through Balthasar's Aesthetics*. IHUB. Edinburgh: T&T Clark, 1998.
Nicholson, Ernest. *The Pentateuch in the Twentieth Century: The Legacy of Julius Wellhausen*. Oxford: Clarendon Press, 1998.
Nikaido, S. "Hagar and Ishmael as Literary Figures: An Intertextual Study." *VT* 51.2 (2001): 219-42.
Norton, Gerard J. "The Old Testament Words of God." Pages 15-31 in *Watchmen Raise Their Voices: A Tallaght Book of Theology*. Edited by Vivian Boland. Dublin: Dominican Publications, 2006.
Noth, Martin. *A History of Pentateuchal Traditions*. Translated by Bernhard W. Anderson. Englewood Cliffs: Prentice-Hall, 1972.

Oden, Thomas C., ed. *Ancient Christian Commentary on Scripture: Old Testament*. Downers Grove: InterVarsity Press, 2001-.

Parkinson, G. H. R., and Stuart Shanker, eds. *Routledge History of Philosophy*. 10 vols. London: Routledge, 1993-1999.
Peters, Melvin K. H. "Septuagint." Pages 1093-104 in *The Anchor Bible Dictionary*. Edited by David Noel Freedman. Vol. 5. New York: Doubleday, 1992.
Powell, Mark Allan. *What Is Narrative Criticism?* GBSNTS. Minneapolis: Augsburg Fortress Press, 1990.
---, Melissa C. Curtis, and Cecile G. Gray. *The Bible and Modern Literary Criticism: A Critical Assessment and Annotated Bibliography*. BIRS 22. New York: Greenwood Press, 1992.
Preuss, H. D. "Ôlām." Pages 530-45 in *The Theological Dictionary of the Old Testament*. Translated by Douglas W. Stott. Edited by G. Johannes Botterweck, and Helmer Ringgren. Vol. 10. Grand Rapids: Eerdmans, 1999.
Prickett, Stephen, ed. *Reading the Text: Biblical Criticism and Literary Theory*. Oxford: Blackwell, 1991.
---, and Robert Barnes. *The Bible*. LWL. Cambridge: Cambridge University Press, 1991.
Priest, Graham. *Towards Non-Being: The Logic and Metaphysics of Intentionality*. Oxford: Clarendon Press, 2005.
Prince, Gerald. *A Dictionary of Narratology*. Aldershot: Scolar Press, 1988.
---. "Narrative Analysis and Narratology." *NLH* 13.2 (1982): 179-88.
Pritchard, J. B., ed. *Ancient Near Eastern Texts Relating to the Old Testament*. 3rd ed. Princeton: Princeton University Press, 1969.
Proust, Marcel. *Remembrance of Things Past*. Translated by C. K. Scott Moncrieff. London: Chatto & Windus, 1957-70.

Rad, Gerhard von. "The Beginnings of Historical Writing in Ancient Israel." Pages 166-204 in *The Problem of the Hexateuch and Other Essays*. Translated by E. W. Trueman Dicken. Edinburgh: Oliver & Boyd, 1966.
---. *Das Erste Buch Mose: Genesis*. Göttingen: Vandenhoeck & Ruprecht, 1958.
---. *Genesis: A Commentary*. Translated by John H. Marks. OTL. London: SCM, 1961.
Rajan, B., ed. *T. S. Eliot: A Study of His Writings by Several Hands*. London: Dennis Dobson, 1966.
Ricoeur, Paul. "Biblical Time." Pages 167-80 in *Figuring the Sacred: Religion, Narrative, and Imagination*. Translated by David Pellauer. Edited by Mark I. Wallace. Minneapolis: Fortress Press, 1995.
---. *Essays on Biblical Interpretation*. Edited by Lewis S. Mudge. Philadelphia: Fortress Press, 1980.
---. *Hermeneutics and the Human Sciences: Essays on Language, Action and Interpretation*. Edited by John B. Thompson. Cambridge: Cambridge University Press.
---. *History and Truth*. SPEP. Evanston: Northwestern University Press, 1965.
---. "The Model of the Text: Meaningful Action Considered as a Text." *SR* 38.3 (1971): 529-62.

---. "Philosophy and Religious Language." Pages 35-47 in *Figuring the Sacred: Religion, Narrative, and Imagination*. Translated by David Pellauer. Edited by Mark I. Wallace. Minneapolis: Fortress Press, 1995.

---. "The 'Sacred' Text and the Community." Pages 68-72 in *Figuring the Sacred: Religion, Narrative, and Imagination*. Translated by David Pellauer. Edited by Mark I. Wallace. Minneapolis: Fortress Press, 1995.

---. *Time and Narrative*. 3 vols. Chicago: University of Chicago Press, 1984.

Rogerson, J. W., and J. M. Lieu, eds. *The Oxford Handbook of Biblical Studies*. Oxford: Oxford University Press, 2006.

Rosenberg, A. J., ed. "The Judaica Press Complete Tanach with Rashi." No pages. Cited May 3, 2007. Online: http://www.chabad.org/library/article.asp?AID=15782.

Roth, C., and G. Wigoder, eds. *Encyclopaedia Judaica*. 16 vols. Jerusalem: Encyclopaedia Judaica / Macmillan, 1972.

Sanders, James A. "Canon: Hebrew Bible." Pages 837-52 in *The Anchor Bible Dictionary*. Edited David Noel Freedman. Vol. 1. New York: Doubleday, 1992.

Sarna, Nahum M. *Genesis (Bereshit): The Traditional Hebrew Text with the New JPS Translation*. JPSTC. Philadelphia: Jewish Publication Society, 1989.

Schaff, Philip, and Henry Wace, eds. *A Select Library of Nicene and Post-Nicene Fathers of the Christian Church: Second Series*. Vol. 7. Grand Rapids: Eerdmans, 1983.

Schaper, Eva. "Taste, Sublimity, and Genius: The Aesthetics of Nature and Art." Pages 367-93 in *The Cambridge Companion to Kant*. Edited by Paul Guyer. Cambridge: Cambridge University Press, 1992.

Scholes, Robert. "Stillborn Literature." Pages 53-69 in *The Horizon of Literature*. Edited by Paul Hernadi. Lincoln: University of Nebraska Press, 1982.

Sheppard, Anne. *Aesthetics: An Introduction to the Philosophy of Art*. Oxford: Oxford University Press, 1987.

Sheridan, Mark, ed. *Genesis 12-50*. ACCSOT 2. Edited by Thomas C. Oden. Downers Grove: InterVarsity Press, 2002.

Sherwood, Yvonne, ed. *Derrida's Bible: Reading a Page of Scripture with a Little Help from Derrida*. New York: Palgrave Macmillan, 2004.

Sidney, Philip. "An Apologie for Poetrie." No pages. Cited: 2 June 2007. Online: http://gateway.proquest.com/openurl?ctx_ver=Z39.88-2003&res_id=xri:eebo&rft_id=xri:eebo:citation:99846470.

Ska, Jean Louis. *"Our Fathers Have Told Us": Introduction to the Analysis of Hebrew Narratives*. SubBi 13. Roma: Pontificio Istituto Biblico, 1990.

Skinner, John. *A Critical and Exegetical Commentary on Genesis*. ICC. Edinburgh: Clark, 1910.

Speiser, E. A. *Genesis*. AB 1. Garden City: Doubleday, 1964.

Sperber, Alexander. *The Pentateuch According to Targum Onkelos*. BABOM 1. Leiden: Brill, 1959.

Steiner, George. "'Critic'/'Reader.'" *NLH* 10.3 (1979): 423-52.

Sternberg, Meir. *The Poetics of Biblical Narrative: Ideological Literature and the Drama of Reading*. ISBL. Bloomington: Indiana University Press, 1987.

Stróżewski, Władysław. *O wielkości: Szkice z filozofii człowieka*. Kraków: Znak, 2002.
Suelzer, Alexa, and John S. Kselman. "Modern Old Testament Criticism." Pages 1113-29 in *The New Jerome Biblical Commentary*. Edited by Raymond Edward Brown, Joseph A. Fitzmyer, and Roland Edmund Murphy. Englewood Cliffs: Prentice Hall, 1990.
Suleiman, Susan R. "Introduction: Varieties of Audience-Oriented Criticism." Pages 3-45 in *The Reader in the Text: Essays on Audience and Interpretation*. Edited by Susan R. Suleiman and Inge Crosman. Princeton: Princeton University Press, 1980.

Thiessen, Gesa Elsbeth, ed. *Theological Aesthetics: A Reader*. London: SCM, 2004.
Thiselton, Anthony C. *New Horizons in Hermeneutics*. London: Harper Collins, 1992.
Thomas, Ronald Stuart. *Laboratories of the Spirit*. London: Macmillan, 1972.
Thomasson, Amie L. *Fiction and Metaphysics*. CSP. Cambridge: Cambridge University Press, 1999.
Thompson, John B. "Ricoeur, Paul." No pages. *Routledge Encyclopedia of Philosophy*. Edited by E. Craig. Cited 11 December 2004. Online: http://www.rep.routledge.com/article/DD058SECT3.
Tolkien, J. R. R. *The Return of the King: Being the Third Part of the Lord of the Rings*. London: HarperCollins, 2001.

Van Seters, John. *Abraham in History and Tradition*. New Haven: Yale University Press, 1975.
Vanhoozer, Kevin J. *Biblical Narrative in the Philosophy of Paul Ricoeur*. Cambridge: Cambridge University Press, 1990.
Vaux, Roland de. *La Genèse*. 2nd rev. ed. Paris: Éditions du Cerf, 1962.
Vawter, Bruce. *On Genesis: A New Reading*. London: Geoffrey Chapman, 1977.

Walfish, Barry. *Esther in Medieval Garb: Jewish Interpretation of the Book of Esther in the Middle Ages*. SSJ. Albany: State University of New York Press, 1993.
Wallace, Mark I. "Can God Be Named without Being Known? The Problem of Revelation in Thiemann, Ogden, and Ricoeur." *JAAR* 59.2 (1991): 281-308.
---. "From Phenomenology to Scripture? Paul Ricoeur's Hermeneutical Philosophy of Religion." *MTh* 16.3 (2000): 301-13.
Waltke, Bruce K., and Michael P. O'Connor. *An Introduction to Biblical Hebrew Syntax*. Winona Lake: Eisenbrauns, 1990.
Walton, Kendall L. *Mimesis as Make-Believe: On the Foundations of the Representational Arts*. Cambridge, Mass.: Harvard University Press, 1990.
Watts, John D. W. *Isaiah 34-66*. WBC. Edited by David A. Hubbard and Glenn W. Barker. Waco: Word Books, 1987.
Weber, Robertus, ed. *Genesis – Psalmi*. BSIVV 1. Stuttgart: Württembergische Bibelanstalt, 1969.
Weil, Gérard E. *Massorah Gedolah Iuxta Codicem Leningradensem B 19 A*. Vol. 1. Rome: Pontificium Institutum Biblicum, 1971.
Weingreen, J. *Introduction to the Critical Study of the Text of the Hebrew Bible*. Oxford: Clarendon Press, 1982.

Wenham, Gordon J. *Genesis 1-15*. WBC. Edited by David A. Hubbard and Glenn W. Barker. Waco: Word Books, 1987.

---. *Genesis 16-50*. WBC. Edited by David A. Hubbard and Glenn W. Barker. Waco: Word Books, 1994.

Westermann, Claus. *Genesis 12-36: A Continental Commentary*. Translated by John Scullion. Minneapolis: Fortress Press, 1995.

Wevers, John William. *Genesis*. SVTG 1. Göttingen: Vandenhoeck & Ruprecht, 1974.

White, Hugh C. "The Joseph Story: A Narrative Which 'Consumes' Its Content." *Semeia* 31 (1985): 49-69.

Whybray, R. N. *The Making of the Pentateuch: A Methodological Study*. JSOTSup 53. Edited by David J. A. Clines and Philip R. Davies. Sheffield: JSOT Press, 1987.

Wilch, John R. *Time and Event: An Exegetical Study of the Use of 'Eth in the Old Testament in Comparison to Other Temporal Expressions in Clarification of the Concept of Time*. Leiden: Brill, 1969.

Wink, Walter. *The Bible in Human Transformation: Toward a New Paradigm for Biblical Study*. Philadelphia: Fortress Press, 1973.

Wolff, Hans Walter. *Anthropology of the Old Testament*. Translated by Margaret Kohl. London: SCM, 1974.

Wonneberger, Reinhard, and Dwight R. Daniels. *Understanding BHS: A Manual for the Users of Biblia Hebraica Stuttgartensia*. SubBi 8. 2nd rev. ed. Roma: Pontificio Istituto Biblico, 1990.

Wood, David, ed. *On Paul Ricoeur: Narrative and Interpretation*. WSPL. London: Routledge, 1991.

Woods, Tim. *Beginning Postmodernism*. Manchester: Manchester University Press, 1999.

Woolf, Virginia. *Mrs. Dalloway*. London: The Hogarth Press, 1929.

Ziolkowski, Theodore. Foreword to *Magister Ludi (The Glass Bead Game)*, by Hermann Hesse. New York: Bantam Books, 1969.

Index of Authors

Abbott, H. P. 117, 150, 219, 222-23
Abrams, M. H. 132-33, 140, 256-61
Ackroyd, P. 24
Aichele, G. 126-27, 133-34
Albert the Great 112
Alter, R. 9, 12, 15, 34, 45, 62, 93-94,
    96-97, 105, 140, 153, 199, 201, 219,
    232
Anderson, J. C. 132
Anselm of Canterbury 245
Aquinas 112, 187, 233-34, 245
Aristotle 7-8, 78, 113, 139, 200-204,
    206-212, 224-25, 254, 259, 268
Auerbach, E. 15-16, 18-19, 96, 105, 232
Augustine 8-9, 84-85, 113, 189, 234,
    244-45
Austen, J. 215

Bacon, F. 5
Bal, M. 1, 89
Balthasar, H. U. von 167, 183-199, 232,
    255-56, 268
Bar-Efrat, S. 9, 138
Barnes, J. 203, 208, 211
Barnes, R. 12, 19, 117, 119
Barr, J. 10-12, 20, 29, 92, 119, 238-39
Barry, P. 126-27, 129, 139, 141, 144-45,
    202, 209
Barth, K. 183, 244-46, 248, 250-51
Barthes, R. 1, 139, 141, 215
Barton, J. 7-9, 29, 34-35, 74, 87-88,
    126-27, 129-30, 133-34, 137, 156,
    199, 215, 222, 257, 261-62
Bateson, F. W. 21
Baudrillard, J. 128-29
Baumgartner, W. 38
Bealer, G. 111
Berlin, A. 9-10, 12, 208

Berlinerblau, J. 34
Bernard, of Clairvaux 9
Bernays, J. 211
Bigelow, J. C. 111
Blackburn, S. 111-12
Bloom, H. 128
Bodine, W. R. 203
Boethius 245
Boland, V. 113, 121, 233
Bonaventure 112
Booth, W. C. 1, 73-84, 89, 93, 95,
    148-51, 154, 169-70, 173, 178, 201,
    209, 212, 215, 224-27, 266-67
Botterweck, G. J. 176
Boyle, N. 102, 109, 261
Bradley, F. H. 22
Bridges, R. 172
Brodie, T. L. 177
Brown, R. E. 35-36
Brueggemann, W. 44, 61
Budde, K. 66
Burrow, J. A. 7
Butchvarov, P. 113-14

Carritt, E. F. 172
Carroll, L. 131
Celan, P. 20
Chateaubriand, R. de 186
Chatman, S. B. 79, 139-40
Childs, B. S. 29, 69-71, 91-92
Chrysostom, John 43, 92
Clark, S. H. 244
Clements, R. E. 176
Clines, D. J. A. 28, 70-71, 127, 158,
    160-62, 174, 176
Coats, G. W. 45, 61-62, 64, 156
Collins, J. J. 119, 130, 135
Conrad, J. 139

Cotter, D. W. 60, 153, 163
Crane, R. S. 2
Cuddon, J. A. 7-8, 21, 57, 71, 80-81, 88, 128, 139-41, 168-69, 176, 207, 211
Culler, J. 117, 131, 141
Currie, G. 118-19, 121
Curtis, M. C. 74
Cyril of Alexandria 93

Dalman, G. 46
Dante 9, 23, 26
Darwin, C. 118
De Man, P. 128
Delitzsch, F. 153
Derrida, J. 126, 128-31, 214-15
Detweiler, R. 11, 13-14, 18, 165
Dickinson, E. 113
Donoghue, D. 236, 252
Dornisch, L. 164-65, 260-62
Dostoevsky, F. 77
Doyle, A. C. 33
Driver, S. R. 43-45, 61, 63-64, 67-68, 153
Duke, P. D. 153
Dumm, D. 16-17

Eagleton, T. 117
Eco, U. 88-90, 164, 203, 223
Eliot, T. S. 11, 21-30, 79, 81, 87, 103, 106, 109, 186, 200-01, 236, 252, 265
Exum, J. C. 28, 127

Fiddes, P. 19
Fish, S. 75, 214-15, 223
Fitzmyer, J. A. 3, 14, 84-85, 95, 155
Flaubert, G. 169
Flew, A. 112
Fowler, R. M. 27-28, 84, 154, 219
Freedman, D. N. 53
Frei, H. W. 244, 261
Freud, S. 132, 260
Frye, N. 37, 139
Fyfe, W. H. 208, 212

Gadamer, H.-G. 6-7, 104
Gall, A. F. von 36

Gamble, H. Y. 6
Gardner, H. L. 236
Gasset, J. O. y 169
Gaut, B. 172
Genette, G. 80, 139-46, 215, 267
Gesenius, W. 50
Gillingham, S. E. 262
Golden, L. 210-11
Goldmann, L. 170, 215
Goldthorpe, R. 247
Good, E. M. 153
Gracia, J. 112
Gray, C. G. 74
Gregory of Nazianzus 255-56
Greimas, A. J. 139, 215
Gressmann, H. 157
Gügler, A. 186
Gulley, N. 211
Gunkel, H. 45, 61, 64, 66, 157
Guyer, P. 169-70

Hamann, J. G. 186
Hamilton, V. P. 45, 61, 65, 67
Hardison, O. B. 211
Hartman, G. H. 128, 215
Heidegger, M. 100, 236
Herbert, G. 19, 81
Herder, J. G. 186
Herodotus 10
Hesse, H. 235, 263-64
Hiltunen, A. 201
Hirsch, E. D. Jr. 73, 86-88, 90, 93, 137-38, 154-55, 163-64
Holland, N. N. 75, 214-15, 223
Homer 16, 18, 20, 26, 82, 172, 175
Hospers, J. 166
Husserl, E. 100, 104
Hynes, S. 25

Ingarden, R. 198, 218
Iser, W. 75, 200, 212, 214-15, 218-225, 260, 262, 268-69

Jacobs, L. 84
James, H. 169
Janko, R. 210-11

Jasper, D. 85-86
Jauss, H.-R. 215
Jenni, E. 238
Jerome 258
Johnson, B. 128
Johnson, D. W. 35-36
Josipovici, G. 10, 18-20, 182-83
Joüon, P. 39

Kafka, F. 20
Kant, I. 167-171, 184, 268
Kautzsch, E. 50
Kelley, P. H. 36
Kermode, F. 12
Kerr, F. 183
Kintgen, E. R. 117
Kitto, H. D. F. 175
Köhler, L. 38
Kratz, R. G. 68
Kselman, J. S. 258
Kugel, J. 10

Labov, W. 57
Leftow, B. 121-22
Lessing, G. E. 211
Lévi-Strauss, C. 131, 139
Lewis, C. S. 12, 200
Lloyd, G. 245
Lodge, D. 141
Longacre, R. E. 203
Lopes, D. M. 172
Loretz, O. 239
Lubac, H. de 183
Lubbock, P. 179
Lucas, F. L. 211
Lyotard, J.-F. 126

MacDonald, S. 112
Magnus, B. 126
Mann, T. 247
Martyn, J. L. 59
Marx, K. 132, 260
McKnight, E. V. 127, 130-31, 215
Meredith, A. 256
Meynell, H. A. 167, 172-73, 175, 177-79, 197, 268

Milton, J. 223
Mlakuzhyil, G. 58-59
Moore, C. A. 6
Moore, S. D. 132
Mudge, L. S. 101, 116
Muecke, D. C. 153
Muraoka, T. 39
Murphy, F. A. 112-13
Murphy, R. E. 63
Murray, P. 252

Newsom, C. A. 52-53
Nichols, A. 183-86, 189-90, 192-94
Nicholson, E. 158, 161
Nietzsche, F. 131-32, 260
Nikaido, S. 160
Norton, G. J. 35
Noth, M. 64, 161

O'Connell, K. G. 35-36
O'Connor, M. P. 36, 38, 50-52, 219
Origen 44, 92, 258

Peters, M. K. H. 159
Plato 113
Plotinus 245
Polanus 245
Powell, M. A. 74, 213-15
Preuss, H. D. 237-38
Prickett, S. 1, 12, 19, 117, 119
Priest, G. 116, 120-21
Priest, S. 112
Prince, G. 139-40
Procksch, O. 66
Proust, M. 20, 142, 247
Propp, V. 139
Przywara, E. 183
Pseudo-Dionysius 113, 234

Quine, W. 121

Rad, G. von 16, 43, 60, 63, 153, 161
Rashi 17
Ricoeur, P. 6, 13-14, 19, 33, 73, 88, 97-103, 106-09, 116, 132, 137, 164-66, 211, 221, 229, 236, 241-44,

246-51, 260-62, 266, 269
Robbins, V. K. 11, 165
Rochelle, J. de la 112
Russell, B. 121

Sanders, J. A. 6
Sarna, N. M. 45, 61
Schaff, P. 256
Schaper, E. 168
Scheeben, M. 186
Scholes, R. 7
Shakespeare, W. 19, 26, 201
Sheppard, A. 167-68, 170-71
Sidney, P. 117
Ska, J. L. 28, 56-59, 76, 144, 152, 216, 218
Skinner, J. 45, 61, 64, 66
Socrates 172
Sophocles 20
Speiser, E. A. 43-44, 60, 63-66, 153
Sperber, A. 36
Speyr, A. von 183
Steiner, G. 27
Stendhal 144
Sternberg, M. 9, 216-17
Stróżewski, W. 198
Suárez, F. 112
Suelzer, A. 258
Suleiman, S. R. 75, 214-15, 222
Swift, J. 118

Taylor, M. C. 127
Thiessen, G. E. 172
Thiselton, A. C. 35, 213, 215, 218, 222, 230-31, 260, 262
Thomas, R. S. 230
Thomasson, A. L. 121
Thompson, J. B. 98-99

Todorov, T. 140-41, 143
Tolkien, J. R. R. 200
Tolstoy, L. N. 172

Van Seters, J. 67-68, 158, 162
Vanhoozer, K. J. 100, 107, 244, 246-49, 251, 260-61
Vaux, R. de 45, 61, 64
Vawter, B. 45, 64
Virgil 26

Wace, H. 256
Walfish, B. 17
Wallace, M. I. 100-03, 116, 165
Waltke, B. K. 36, 38, 50-52, 219
Walton, K. L. 115-21
Watts, J. D. W. 162
Weber, R. 36
Weil, G. E. 36
Weingreen, J. 35
Wenham, G. J. 45-46, 62-64
Westermann, C. 43-44, 46, 51, 58, 60-61, 65-68, 82, 90, 92, 115, 118-19, 153, 156-60, 213
Wevers, J. W. 36
White, H. C. 145
Whybray, R. N. 68
Wilch, J. R. 239
Willoughby, B. E. 53
Wilson, R. R. 156
Wink, W. 96
Wolff, H. W. 238
Wonneberger, R. 36
Wood, N. 141
Woods, T. 128-29
Woolf, V. 215, 247

Ziolkowski, T. 264

Index of Subjects

aesthetics 166-67; aesthetic distance 168-70; aesthetic judgment 168-72; aesthetic theories 167-68, 172, 199, 258; philosophical (= literary) approach 172-73, 196-99, in *Gen 21* 173-83; theological approach 183-87, 196-99, its main categories 187-90, in *Gen 21* 190-95

biblical criticism 29, 140, 265; conditions for 262-63; intuitive approach 22-23, 30, 65, 261, 265; synchronic versus diachronic 33-35, 69-71, 138, 197-98, 266; various approaches 256-62

canonical criticism 29, 69, 91-92, 161, 257
catharsis 7-8, 209-12, 226, 265, 268
critic 25-28, 30

deconstruction 28-29, 127-35, 214, 267

ethical criticism 24-26, 75, 227

fiction 7-8, 10-11, 74, 81-82, 97, 100, 102, 107, 116-21, 130, 137, 247, 250, 260, 267; and truth 8, 10-11; and reality 8, 117, 119; fictional truth 116, 120; fictional world 117, 120-21, 234, 267

gaps 212, 215-17, 219-23; and blanks 216; in *Gen 21* 216-18, 220, 223-24
genre 100-03, 119, 155-56, 250-51; of patriarchal narratives 59, 61-62, 82, 156-58

Hebrew narratives: features 13-20, 96, 183, 219, 248
historical-critical method 23, 29, 46, 63, 87-88, 94-96, 98, 130, 133-34, 137, 155-56, 208, 258-59, 261, 268; textual criticism of *Gen 21* 35-55; textual cruces in *Gen 21* 43-46, 52-53; source criticism of *Gen 21* 63-70, 158

intention 15, 85, 88-89, 98, 102, 108, 118-19, 179, 214, 239, 261; intentional fallacy 71, 88
interests of the reader 76-79, 81-83, 173, 209
irony 148-50; features of 150; in *Gen 21* 150-54

knowledge: immanent 103-04, 106, 108, 114-15, 125-26, 134, 229, 254-55, 266-67; narrative 103-06, 108, 125, 137, 229, 234, 259-60, 266-67; transcendental 104, 106-08, 134, 229, 233-34, 267, 269; levels of emergence 108, 229-36, 269

literature: definition of 6-9; and text 6-7; and the Bible 5, 9-12, 19-21, 235-36

meaning 85-96; and significance 86-88, 90-94, 96; aesthetic meaning 93-96, 166-67; aesthetic significance 167-95, in *Gen 21* 173-83, 190-95; cognitive meaning 154-62, in *Gen 21* 158-62; cognitive

significance 138-54, in *Gen 21* 146-48, 150-54; practical meaning 93-96, 200-01; practical significance 202-23, in *Gen 21* 203-09, 211, 216-18, 220, 222-23
metaphysical realism 111-14, 126, 233, 267, 269; conceptualism 111, 113, 198, 233; nominalism 111, 113, 121, 198, 233
modern reader 27-28

narrative theory 138-44, 152, 165, 201, 212, 246, 262; and narrative criticism 74-76, 201, 214, 224; and narratology 139-40, 142; its concepts 143-46; in *Gen 21* 146-48; narrative delimitation of *Gen 21* 56-63
New Criticism 21, 74-75

Pentateuch: theological themes 91-92, 160-62, 174-76, 179-83, 240, 242
Platonic triad 109-13, 229-34, 267, 269
plot 57, 71, 81, 105, 169, 172, 177, 182-83, 196, 202-03, 211, 221, 259, 266, 268-69; in *Gen 21* 57-58, 177-78, 203-09, 225
postmodernism 28, 126-35, 267

reader-response criticism 75-76, 133, 212-15, 222-23, 268-69
reality: actuality 103-04, 106-08, 123, 125, 137, 226, 229-30, 232, 234-36, 254-55, 266, 269-70, its ontological status 114-15, 267; quasi-reality 103-08, 114, 123, 137, 212, 234, 255-56, 266-67, its ontological status 113-21, 267; trans-reality 104, 106-08, 114, 123, 137, 226, 229-30, 232-36, 255-56, 262, 267, 269-70, its ontological status 114, 121-23, 267
refinement 231-32; of truth 166; of beauty 199-200; of goodness 226; of eternity 239
rhetorical criticism 73-75, 138, 165, 214-15, 260
Ricoeurian hermeneutics 97-103, 106-09; being-in-the-world 97, 100, 102, 107, 247, 260, 262; distanciation 97-100, 102, 163; limits of narrative 250-52, 269; monumental time 247-52, 269; reference 98-100, 102, 108; refiguration 248-52, 269; revelation 13, 101-03, 109, 266; suspicion versus retrieval 132, 260-61, 269-70; types of discourse 101-03; world of the text 102, 107-09, 266

structuralism 22-23, 139, 141-42, 214, 259

theological dimension 29, 70, 84-85, 93-94, 266
time: for original reader 237-44, 251-52; for modern reader 244-52; monumental time 247-52, 269; refiguration of 248-52, 269

universals 111-12; and particulars 111; and transcendentals 112-13